Joel M. Gora is a professor of law at Brooklyn Law School, where he teaches constitutional law. He is a graduate of Pomona College and Columbia Law School. Formerly a staff counsel and associate legal director of the American Civil Liberties Union, Professor Gora has served as a general counsel and on the board of directors of the New York Civil Liberties Union. His previous books include *The Rights of Reporters* (1974) and *Due Process of Law* (1976).

David Goldberger is a professor of law and director of clinical programs at Ohio State University College of Law. A graduate of the University of Chicago and its law school, Professor Goldberger was staff attorney and legal director of the Illinois Division, American Civil Liberties Union, for more than ten years. His most prominent First Amendment litigation involved the efforts of the American Nazi Party to speak in the predominantly Jewish suburb of Skokie. He currently serves as general counsel of the American Civil Liberties Union of Ohio.

Gary M. Stern is a research associate at the Center for National Security Studies, a joint project of the ACLU and the Fund for Peace. He also serves as legislative counsel on intelligence issues for the ACLU Washington Office and as a staff attorney for the ACLU National Security Litigation Project. He graduated from Yale Law School, where he was editor-in-chief of the *Yale Journal of International Law*, and from Vassar College, where he majored in ancient Greek.

Morton H. Halperin, the director of the Washington Office of the American Civil Liberties Union, is responsible for the ACLU's national legislative program. He graduated from Columbia College and holds a Ph.D. from Yale University. An expert on foreign policy and national security issues, Dr. Halperin held many academic and governmental positions prior to assuming his ACLU post. He is the author of numerous books and articles on foreign affairs, national security, and civil liberties.

Also in this series

AN AMERICAN CIVIL LIBERTIES UNION HANDBOOK

THE RIGHT TO PROTEST

THE BASIC ACLU GUIDE TO
FREE EXPRESSION

Joel M. Gora
David Goldberger
Gary M. Stern
Morton H. Halperin

General Editor of the Handbook Series:
Norman Dorsen, President, ACLU

SOUTHERN ILLINOIS UNIVERSITY PRESS
CARBONDALE AND EDWARDSVILLE

Copyright © 1991 by the American Civil Liberties Union
Printed in the United States of America
Edited by Sally Master
Production supervised by New Leaf Studio

94   93   92   91   4   3   2   1

Library of Congress Cataloging-in-Publication Data

The Right to protest: the basic ACLU guide to free expression / Joel
M. Gora . . . [et al.].
     p. cm. —(An American Civil Liberties Union handbook)
   1. Demonstrations—Law and legislation—United States.
2. Assembly, Right of—United States.   3. Freedom of speech—United
States.   4. Dissenters—Legal status, laws, etc.—United States.
I. Gora, Joel M.   II. American Civil Liberties Union.   III. Title:
Basic ACLU guide to free expression.   IV. Series.
KF4778.R54   1991
342.73'0854—dc20
[347.302854]   90-19977
ISBN 0-8093-1699-4 (pbk.)   CIP

The paper used in this publication meets the minimum requirements of
American Standard for Information Sciences—Permanence of Paper for
Printed Library Materials, ANSI Z39.48-1984. ⊛

Contents

Preface

This guide sets forth your rights under the present law and offers suggestions on how they can be protected. It is one of a continuing series of handbooks published in cooperation with the American Civil Liberties Union (ACLU).

Surrounding these publications is the hope that Americans, informed of their rights, will be encouraged to exercise them. Through their exercise, rights are given life. If they are rarely used, they may be forgotten and violations may become routine.

This guide offers no assurances that your rights will be respected. The laws may change, and in some of the subjects covered in these pages they change quite rapidly. An effort has been made to note those parts of the law where movement is taking place, but it is not always possible to predict accurately when the law *will* change.

Even if the laws remain the same, their interpretations by courts and administrative officials often vary. In a federal system such as ours, there is a built-in problem, since state and federal law differ, not to speak of the confusion between states. In addition, there are wide variations in the ways in which particular courts and administrative officials will interpret the same law at any given moment.

If you encounter what you consider to be a specific abuse of your rights, you should seek legal assistance. There are a number of agencies that may help you, among them ACLU affiliate offices, but bear in mind that the ACLU is a limited-purpose organization. In many communities, there are federally funded legal service offices that provide assistance to persons who cannot afford the costs of legal representation. In general, the rights that the ACLU defends are freedom of inquiry and expression; due process of law; equal protection of the laws; and privacy. The authors in this series have discussed other rights (even though they sometimes fall outside the ACLU's usual concern) in order to provide as much guidance as possible.

These books have been planned as guides for the people directly affected: thus the question-and-answer format. (In some areas there are more detailed works available for experts.) These guides seek to raise the major issues and inform the nonspecialist of the basic law on the subject. The authors of these books are themselves specialists who understand the need for information at "street level."

If you encounter a specific legal problem in an area discussed in one of these handbooks, show the book to your attorney. Of course, he or she will not be able to rely exclusively on the handbook to provide you with adequate representation. But if your attorney hasn't had a great deal of experience in the specific area, the handbook can provide helpful suggestions on how to proceed.

Norman Dorsen, President
American Civil Liberties Union

The principal purpose of this handbook, as well as others in this series, is to inform individuals of their legal rights. The authors from time to time suggest what the law should be, but their personal views are not necessarily those of the ACLU. For the ACLU's position on the issues discussed in this handbook, the reader should write to Public Education Department, ACLU, 132 West 43d Street, New York, N.Y. 10036.

Acknowledgments

I wish to express my appreciation to the Brooklyn Law School Summer Research Stipend Fund, which provided support for this book, and to Brooklyn Law School students David Garren, Class of 1989, and Rita Anne O'Keeffe and David Lee, Class of 1991, for their research assistance. I particularly want to express my love and appreciation for my wife, Ann Ray, and my daughter, Susannah, who saw a lot of movies by themselves so that I could work on this book.

J. M. G.

I want to thank Barbara O'Toole and my Ohio State University College of Law research assistants, Tracy Barbaree, Robin Green, Daphne Meimaridis, Jaimie Schwartz, and Jennifer Sosteric for their help. I also want to thank my wife, Abigail Harding, for her support. I dedicate my work on this book to my father, Melvin Goldberger, a profoundly committed civil libertarian.

D. G.

I thank Eric Nestor for his fine research and assistance, especially on chapters 15 and 16, and James X. Dempsey, Janlori Goldman, Doug Cassel, David Rudovsky, and Chip Berlet for their assistance in providing information and reviewing my section of the manuscript. And to Nancy Segal, whom I love.

G. M. S.

THE RIGHT TO PROTEST

I
General Principles

As Americans we have a great many legal rights that government must respect and courts will enforce. These include protection of our persons and property from harmful action by others, protection of our interests and opportunities from discrimination, and protection of our rights if government should attempt to deprive us of life, liberty, or property in civil or criminal proceedings.

This book is dedicated to the rights of those people who become involved in the vital issues of our time and seek to effect—or perhaps resist—political change by having an impact on matters of politics, government, and public concern. Our system of government has fashioned a number of critical rights and opportunities for political activists. Of central importance are the freedoms of speech, press, assembly, petition, and religion safeguarded by the First Amendment to the United States Constitution. Most of this book—parts 1 and 2—is devoted to describing these constitutional rights to free speech and explaining how they sharply limit the ability of government to suppress protest and dissent.

But political activists are concerned not only about freedom from direct official interference, but also about the right to speak and organize without the indirect intimidation of official scrutiny and surveillance. So part 3 of this book will discuss government surveillance of political activists and the remedies to prevent such surveillance. These include not only constitutional protections of privacy against unwarranted government surveillance, but also important protections afforded by statutes and even executive regulations that restrict undue government scrutiny or surveillance of political activities by the FBI, the CIA, and state and local law enforcement agencies.

Criticizing the status quo or otherwise seeking political change also requires knowledge of what the government is doing. There are important statutory protections of the right of citizens to learn about government, such as the freedom of information laws, which are important weapons in the arsenal of activists; this book will discuss those rights as well.

Finally, it is not only government that interferes with the right to protest; private organizations or corporations interfere as well, for example, by denying protestors the right to hand out leaflets at a privately owned shopping center or by penalizing employees for political speech or whistleblowing. Political activists have some rights in those circumstances as well, usually provided by state or local law.

HOW AND WHY SPEECH AND PROTEST ARE PROTECTED

How does the Constitution protect the right to protest?

The core protections of political freedom are found in the First Amendment to the Constitution, which provides as follows: "Congress shall make no law respecting an establishment of religion, or prohibiting the free exercise thereof; or abridging the freedom of speech, or of the press; or the right of the people peaceably to assemble, and to petition the Government for a redress of grievances." Although the First Amendment only mentions Congress, it has been interpreted as limiting the other branches of the federal government as well. The First Amendment restricts the power of government to restrain political speech and association, while the Fourth Amendment curtails the power of government to surveil or scrutinize political activists by protecting people against unreasonable searches and seizures or other invasions of political privacy by government. Finally, the Fourteenth Amendment to the Constitution, which stipulates that no state may "deprive any person of life, liberty or property, without due process of law," assures that state and local government agencies or officials are likewise bound to respect the rights of citizens and honor the restrictions on government contained in the First and Fourth Amendments.

Is it only the Constitution that protects political activists?

No. Often, the government itself will pass laws or regulations that enhance the rights of protestors in ways that go beyond the protections of the Constitution. For example, government may provide a public forum for speakers or organizations, even though the Constitution does not require such facilities: a university may provide a meeting room for student groups; a mayor or city council may host an open forum at which community representatives can state their views and grievances. Similarly, a state court may interpret state law generously to afford rights that even the United States Constitution has been interpreted not to safeguard. For example, some state courts have found in their state constitutions a right of protestors to distribute leaflets and speak at privately owned shopping malls and shopping centers, even though the First Amendment has not been construed to afford such rights. Likewise, the primary source of people's rights to learn about what government is doing comes not from the First Amendment, but from the various freedom of information and government-in-the-sunshine laws that legislatures have passed at the federal and state levels in the past two decades. Finally, government itself sometimes passes rules and regulations restricting its own scrutiny and investigation of activists, quite apart from First Amendment court decisions. Examples include internal FBI guidelines promulgated in the wake of revelations of government spying on peaceful dissenters and proposals for legislative charters to control the surveillance activities of intelligence agencies. See part 3 below.

The point is that while the Constitution—particularly the First Amendment—is the primary source of the rights of protestors and dissenters, it is by no means the sole source.

Why do we protect freedom of speech?

Since freedom of speech is not deemed "absolute," it is important to understand why it is protected in order to judge whether particular government restrictions on speech violate the Constitution.

The framers of the Constitution, steeped in the Enlightenment's emphasis on free and open inquiry and the search for truth, understood the importance of freedom of speech. Although the immediate concern was to guard against the kind of official licensing and censorship of speech and press associated with England, the First Amendment has been interpreted to embody a number of broad purposes drawn from history, philosophy, and the experiences of democracy.

First, freedom of speech facilitates the search for truth. This theme was powerfully stated by Justice Oliver Wendell Holmes:

> [W]hen men have realized that time has upset many fighting faiths, they may come to believe even more than they believe the very foundations of their own conduct that the ultimate good desired is better reached by free trade in ideas—that the best test of truth is the power of the thought to get itself accepted in the competition of the market, and that truth is the only ground upon which their wishes safely can be carried out.[1]

Second, and equally important, freedom of speech is indispensable to individual self-fulfillment through self-expression. Freedom of speech is vital, not just because it may lead to the truth, but because its very exercise is essential to the development of individual liberty and personality our Constitution safeguards. This notion was most clearly expressed by Justice Louis D. Brandeis: "Those who won our independence believed that the final end of the State was to make men free to develop their faculties. . . . They valued liberty both as an end and as a means. They believed liberty to be the secret of happiness and courage to be the secret of liberty."[2]

Third, and of particular relevance to political activists, the First Amendment reflects the concept of democratic self-government and, in the words of Justice William J. Brennan, "a profound national commitment to the principle that debate on public issues should be uninhibited, robust and wide open."[3] Similarly, the combined rights of free speech, free press, and free assembly can provide the people and the press with the "checking function" to monitor, condemn, and correct government wrongdoing and abuse of power.[4]

Taken together, these values reflect the idea that freedom of speech is the sparkplug of our system, "the matrix, the indispensable condition, of nearly every other form of freedom."[5] No matter what their circumstances or grievances, people who are armed with freedom of speech can talk freely, protest, criticize, advocate unpopular causes, and safeguard and expand their rights. Six decades ago, in holding that the First Amendment protected the right of radicals to march under the red flag of revolution, the Supreme Court declared, "The maintenance of the opportunity for free political discussion to the end that government may be responsive to the will of the people and that changes may be obtained by lawful means, an opportunity essential to the security of the Republic, is a fundamental principle of our constitutional system."[6]

To be sure, as a nation we have not consistently honored the values served by freedom of speech. Government still tries to restrict what Americans can see and hear at home and from abroad, and private groups seek to impose their ideas of what is moral and proper upon local communities.[7] And throughout, government has tried to justify interference with the speech of those seeking political change by claiming speech can be harmful, ideas can be dangerous, and government must intervene to protect the public good and the national interest. But despite historical blemishes, the vision of freedom of speech has grown. The core of that vision is the understanding that the preference is for freedom and for speech and that government suppression of bad or wrong or harmful ideas will, in the long run, be self-destructive and cause infinitely more harm than the ideas feared: "[T]he constitutional protection accorded to the freedom of speech and of the press is not based on the naive belief that speech can do no harm but on the confidence that the benefits society reaps from the free flow and exchange of ideas outweigh the costs society endures by receiving reprehensible or dangerous ideas."[8] As the Supreme Court put it, "Under the First Amendment, there is no such thing as a false idea."[9]

The result of this philosophy is the voicing of a great many ideas that the government or a majority of the people might find pernicious or hateful: "The ideas of the Klan may be propagated. . . . Communists may speak freely and run for office. . . . The Nazi Party may march through a city with a large Jewish population. . . . People may criticize the President by misrepresenting his positions. . . . People may teach religions that others despise. . . . People may seek to repeal laws guaranteeing equal opportunity in employment or to revoke the constitutional amendments granting the vote to blacks and women."[10] But the alternative would be to have government or the majority dictate what ideas are acceptable and what are not—in other words, what is the truth and what is false—the hallmark of censorship. That is why the Supreme Court has firmly declared, "[Above] all else, the First Amendment means that government has no power to restrict expression because

of its message, its ideas, its subject matter, or its content."[11]
The First Amendment assumes people are capable of thinking
for themselves and do not need government to think for them.

**Do the rights of protestors have special claim to constitu-
tional protection?**
Yes. While free speech rights are there for all who seek to
exercise them on almost any issue or subject, the Supreme
Court has shown a special solicitude for the political rights of
dissenters and protestors, particularly those who challenge the
status quo. Such groups have played an important role in gener-
ating the ideas—seemingly radical at the time—that years later
become recognized and assimilated into the mainstream of
our political culture: "History has amply proved the virtue of
political activity by minority, dissident groups, who innumera-
ble times have been in the vanguard of democratic thought and
whose programs were ultimately accepted. Mere unorthodoxy
or dissent from the prevailing mores is not to be condemned.
The absence of such voices would be a symptom of a grave
illness in our society."[12] Thus courts have been particularly
vigilant to ensure such groups are not hampered in their ability
to speak: "It is precisely those who are least well-known who
most desperately require access to means of attracting attention. Hitherto unaccepted or unfashionable views most demand
the blare of trumpets to draw the public's consideration. . . .
The American song is one best sung by a plurality of voices."[13]
The First Amendment affords special protection to the rights
of the provocative and challenging; those rights have "been
hammered out largely in behalf of the temperamentally
unforbearing who are fortunate enough to live in a society
that protects their right immediately to 'stand on their
rights.' "[14]

WHAT THE FIRST AMENDMENT PROTECTS

What is speech?
In the most basic sense, speech is written or spoken words.
But it is much more than that, and sometimes less as well. It
is the expression or communication of facts and information,
ideas and opinions, thoughts and feelings. The First Amend-

ment protects the freedom of speech, as well as the freedoms of press, assembly, and petition, from being "abridged" by government. Taken together, those concepts form a broader concept expressed as freedom of expression or freedom of communication. Yet freedom of speech is not synonymous with the right to say anything at any time under any circumstances. And not every government inhibition of speech is found to "abridge" that freedom. Much of modern constitutional law has been devoted to safeguarding and expanding freedom of expression, but also to identifying those exceptional situations where freedom of speech is not absolute but can be limited or restricted by government to serve important or compelling public purposes. Much of this book will explore the nature—and the limits—of freedom of speech.

Does the First Amendment protect more than just speaking and writing?

Yes. The First Amendment's separate protections of speech, press, petition, assembly, and religion, taken in the aggregate, protect more than just spoken or written words. Freedom of expression includes, for example, the handing out of leaflets or handbills on a street corner, as well as the words and ideas those leaflets convey.[15] It also extends to picketing, carrying a sign, marching, demonstrating, and gathering at the seat of government to protest its policies.[16] Similarly protected is the right to associate with others to advance ideas. "Effective advocacy of both public and private points of view, particularly controversial ones, is undeniably enhanced by group association."[17] In addition, soliciting and making contributions to a cause, as well as the expenditure of funds and resources to publicize one's political views and advocacy are a part of the freedom of speech.[18] The same is true of lobbying one's elected representatives at the Capitol or the state house.[19] Indeed the right to petition the government even includes the right of the publisher of Hustler magazine to give free subscriptions to members of Congress, though they may prefer not to receive them: "The right to petition the Government is part of our heritage from the earliest times and represents a cornerstone of our national liberty. . . . While Members of Congress may not share the views embodied in *Hustler,* the right to present unwelcome petitions is entitled to no less protection than the right to petition for causes long espoused by the majority. The First Amendment protects controversial as well as conventional dialogue."[20]

Does the First Amendment protect activities that communicate ideas?

Yes. Freedom of speech also includes the expression of ideas through activity. That activity may include demonstrating or picketing—where the very fact of group activity amplifies and adds dimension to the verbal message. First Amendment recognition may even extend to such expressive events as sleeping in the park to dramatize the plight of the homeless and erecting shanties on college campuses to protest apartheid in South Africa.[21]

The display of flags has long been recognized as symbolic speech that is constitutionally protected. As far back as 1931, the Court ruled that carrying the red flag of revolution was protected symbolic speech and overturned a California law that prohibited displaying a red flag "as a sign, symbol or emblem of opposition to organized government."[22] More recently, the Court held that wearing a black armband of mourning (by public school students as an antiwar protest during the Vietnam era) was also protected symbolic speech.[23]

Of course the most potent flag symbol is the American flag, which protestors have long used to convey messages, pro and con. During the 1988 presidential campaign, much attention was focused on a landmark Supreme Court ruling that public school students could not be compelled to salute the American flag if their religious scruples precluded honoring the symbolism inherent in the flag.[24] Similarly, the Court has upheld the right of protestors to tape a peace symbol on a flag in order to communicate their distress at public policy and events, to wear a small flag replica on the seat of their pants, to remove the flag emblem from a police uniform to protest racial discrimination in the department, and to direct verbal abuse at the flag.[25] Most recently the Court applied this reasoning to uphold the right of protestors to burn the American flag to express their political ideas and dissent. In this 1989 ruling, the Court explained that the act of flag burning was the expression of ideas through activity or expressive conduct and that the only interests the government pointed to as justifying punishment under a Texas law were based upon disapproval of those ideas—an impermissible reason.[26] This distinguished an earlier case which upheld punishment of antiwar protestors who publicly burned their draft cards in protest because there the Court found the symbolic expression outweighed by the government interest in requiring eligible young men to possess their draft cards for administrative processing.[27] Congress reacted immediately to the Court's 1989 decision by passing a new federal statute prohibiting flag burning or mutilation. But the Court swiftly ruled that this law also violated the First Amendment.[28] Bear in mind, however, that flag burning, though protected speech, may risk arrest and police harassment, even though prosecution would probably be unsuccessful.

Just as the First Amendment protects symbolic expression, so too does it protect art and music.[29] As one court observed: "Art stretches our understanding of feeling and ideas in ways which frequently cannot be put into words. Many of art's expressive benefits can be communicated only through art."[30] For similar reasons, the Supreme Court has upheld the otherwise unauthorized wearing of a military uniform as part of an antiwar protest play, and lower courts have upheld wearing masks to protest the former Shah of Iran, agreeing that the masks both protected the anonymity of the protestors and expressed their fear of being revealed and facing retaliation from the Shah's secret police.[31]

But symbolic speech has its limits. Failing to comply with the tax laws may be a tradition of civil disobedience dating back to the Boston Tea Party and Henry David Thoreau, but courts have not upheld it as protected symbolic expression from either the right or the left.[32] The same is true of the draft laws. Likewise, throwing eggs at a congressman is not symbolic speech but criminal assault. "Even if meant only to punctuate the communication of a protest, hurling missiles at a speaker is not under any circumstances worthy of inclusion under the protection afforded symbolic speech no matter how entangled with forms of protected speech."[33]

Does the First Amendment protect only individuals?

No. The protections of the First Amendment are not only for individuals. Corporations, unions, membership organizations, unincorporated associations, and ad hoc committees have all been afforded the rights of freedom of speech, either to enhance the speech rights of their individual members or, as in the case of corporations, to protect the right of the public to receive ideas and information regardless of the source. Among individuals, the freedom of speech extends to resident aliens as well as citizens and to young people as well as adults. Finally, free speech rights are available, albeit in less rigorous form, to groups such as public school students, government employees, military personnel, and even prisoners.

RULES AND DOCTRINES TO PROTECT FREE SPEECH

What rules does the Supreme Court use to protect free speech?

The basic theory of freedom of speech is that the government may not ban the expression of any idea. Otherwise the government could manipulate and control public information and thereby determine the outcome of public debate on all important issues. The First Amendment protects "the societal interest in the fullest possible dissemination of information."[34] "If there is any fixed star in our constitutional constellation, it is that no official, high or petty, can prescribe what shall be orthodox in politics, nationalism, religion, or other matters of opinion."[35] "Under the First Amendment the government must leave to the people the evaluation of ideas. . . . One of the things that separates our society . . . is our absolute right to propagate opinions that the government finds wrong or even hateful."[36] That means the government may not declare one point of view as correct and ban or disfavor political ideas or attitudes that it deems "false."

This does not mean that a person can say anything in any manner at any place or at any time. The Court has recognized certain exceptions to free speech and certain circumstances where its exercise can be curtailed. These restrictions take two basic forms: direct restrictions on the content of speech and less direct restrictions limiting the time, place, and manner of speech.

The basic approach to restrictions on content, i.e., what you can say, is that such limitations are presumed to be impermissible unless: (1) the speech comes within a few limited categories of less worthy speech that is given limited constitutional protection or (2) presents an imminent threat to certain vital governmental interests. Speech in the first category includes words inherently likely to cause a fight, defamatory statements that falsely assault a person's reputation, certain kinds of obscene speech, and deceitful commercial speech advertising goods or products. In the second category, the kinds of critical governmental interests cited as justifying the restriction of speech that poses a clear and present danger to them include the prevention of subversion or lawlessness and the protection of the integrity of the judicial system and the electoral process. Beginning in the next chapter, we will set forth in detail these limited kinds of allowable restrictions on the content of speech.

Often government will seek to restrict not what is said, but where, when, and how it is said. Such so-called time, place, and manner limitations, so long as they are neutral with respect to who is speaking and what is being said, will be allowed by the courts if the rules do not unreasonably inhibit the ability to get one's message across. But, in implementing these restrictions the Court has declared certain places, such as streets and parks, to be essential public forums for speech and has permitted only those restrictions which are needed to maintain public order and safety. These rules are spelled out in part 2 of this book.

The Right to Associate

Does the First Amendment protect the right to join with others in advancing a cause?

Yes. The Supreme Court has drawn on the constitutional protections of speech, assembly, and petition to fashion a distinct, separate right of freedom of association.[37] Courts recognize that individual speech and protest are inevitably and immeasurably enhanced when individuals join together to advance a common cause: "An individual's freedom to speak, to worship, and to petition the Government for the redress of grievances could not be vigorously protected from interference by the State unless a correlative freedom to engage in group effort towards those ends were not also guaranteed."[38]

The Court has developed a number of rules to protect the right to associate and limit the ability of government to interfere with or penalize the exercise of that right. Membership in or association with an organization can rarely be made a crime or the basis for a penalty, unless the group is actively engaged in lawless conduct or its imminent incitement and the individual is an active participant in such conduct.[39] Government efforts to control or dictate the structure, procedures, or membership in organizations is impermissible unless the government can establish that it has an overriding interest in mind.[40] Finally, the courts have vigorously protected the individual's right of anonymity, or "associational privacy," in choosing to associate with a group by restricting the government's ability to compel disclosure of membership or contributor lists or the identity of the supporters of a cause.[41]

Does the Constitution protect the right *not* to speak or associate?

Yes. The flipside of the right to speak and associate is the right not to be compelled to do so. From the time that it recognized the right of religious dissenters not to be compelled to salute the American flag,[42] the Supreme Court has protected the individual's right not to be forced to speak or associate. Applying this principle, the Court has recognized the right of newspaper publishers to refuse to run an adversary's editorial, of utility corporations to decline to include their opponents' criticisms in their monthly bills to consumers, and of workers in both private employment and government service to refuse to join or contribute to the political activities of unions that represent them in the work place.[43] The Court has even upheld the right of protestors to refuse to display a personally offensive state motto ("Live Free or Die") on their automobile license plates.[44]

The Doctrine Against Prior Restraints

Is there a difference between government's power to prevent a person from speaking or protesting in advance and the power to punish a person for that speech or protest after the fact?

Yes. One of the main reasons the framers of the Constitution wrote the First Amendment was to prevent prior approval, licensing, or censorship of speech, which had been a prevalent abuse in England, where books and pamphlets could not even be printed without official authorization. Such prior approval is particularly harmful to free speech values because it suppresses ideas before they are voiced and become part of public debate.

For that reason, the Supreme Court has created the doctrine against prior restraints. A prior restraint is an official order—administrative or judicial—decreeing that a particular person may not engage in certain kinds of speech. Such prior restraints might include an order prohibiting a newspaper from publishing a story containing "malicious, scandalous and defamatory" material or a civil rights group from holding a proposed march which might cause "disorder." The most well-known prior restraint in recent times was the Vietnam era attempt by the government to have courts prevent the *New York Times* and other newspapers from publishing the Pentagon Papers on grounds that their contents would harm the national security. In that case the Court ruled that any prior restraint bears "a heavy presumption against its constitutional validity" and that the government had not met its "heavy burden of showing justification for the enforcement of such a restraint."[45] Accordingly, even though a majority of justices could not agree on whether the press might subsequently be punished under national security laws for revealing the secret information, the prior restraint doctrine allowed the Court to rule that the press could not be prevented in advance from publishing such information. Thus although the government is not absolutely prevented from seeking a prior restraint on speech, it is rarely successful in its efforts. One cautionary note: where a lower court has entered a prior restraint order against an individual or a group, that order must generally be obeyed until appealed, not ignored and violated while the judicial process proceeds, unless the order is transparently invalid.[46]

The Rules Against Vagueness and Overbreadth

Even if a particular speech or protest is of a kind not protected by the First Amendment, can the law or regulation being applied still be challenged?

Sometimes. Because protecting free speech is so important, the Supreme Court has developed important doctrines to insure that government restrictions on speech are confined as narrowly as possible.

One such doctrine is "overbreadth." This rule requires that laws regulating speech and association be as narrow as possible, rather than so broad that as written on the books they seem to prohibit speech that is not punishable. The theory is that overly broad laws will exert a "chilling effect" on speakers who have a clear right to speak but whose speech seems to come within the prohibition of the statute or regulation at issue. Such speakers should not have to choose between silence and speech that might lead to prosecution—however unsuccessful. To prevent the chilling effect of such substantially overbroad laws, the courts will invalidate them as written even in a case where the particular speech or activity might be subject to punishment under a more narrowly drawn and proper regulation. The consequence is that the speaker who might have been punished under a narrower law goes free, and the existing law is invalidated until the government can write a better one.[47]

A classic example of this doctrine involved a group of religious activists, "Jews for Jesus," who handed out literature inside the Los Angeles International Airport. While overbearing solicitation inside a public facility might be subject to reasonable government restriction, the airport regulation banned "First Amendment activities" in the airport terminal. This would literally include talking, reading, or even thinking, so the Supreme Court held the ban to be substantially overbroad as written and invalidated the entire regulation, rather than wait for a case-by-case interpretation that might limit its reach, but would in the meantime have an intolerable chilling effect.[48] The same rule helped a Texas gay activist who was punished—for asking police officers why they were arresting a suspect—under an ordinance making it a crime to "oppose" or "interrupt" a police officer. Whether or not the activist's particular conduct was allowable, the ordinance was overly broad and unenforceable.[49]

Finally, a concept related to overbreadth is the "void for vagueness" doctrine, which holds that regulations on speech that are couched in vague and indefinite terms are impermissible because they chill political activity and confer impermissible discretion on police officers to arrest whom they please. Here, too, it does not matter that the particular speaker could be punished for what he did or said; if the law itself is too vague, the law and the punishment will be invalidated. Thus, for example, a Cincinnati ordinance that made it a crime for people to assemble on a sidewalk "and conduct themselves in a manner annoying to persons passing by" was thrown out as being too vague and uncertain a standard to serve as a basis for restricting the right of assembly.[50] Courts have also thrown out laws making it a crime to treat the American flag "contemptuously."[51] The same is true for statutes prohibiting speech that constitutes "harassment" or campus rules preventing students from engaging in demonstrations that are not "wholesome."[52]

GOVERNMENT SURVEILLANCE OF PROTESTORS

Can the government investigate or surveil political activists?

Not without some controls. Government monitoring, investigating, and surveilling of politically active groups can have almost as restrictive an impact on advocacy by such groups as direct government prohibition of such advocacy. In order to justify such actions, the government has often claimed the need to guard against subversion and disorder by learning the plans and programs of dissident groups. Until recent years, there were few if any judicial, legislative, or executive controls on such monitoring. Following revelations of FBI, CIA, and local police spying on civil rights activists, antiwar protestors, and other dissenters, steps were taken to impose significant control on such law enforcement overreaching. The executive branch has imposed various restrictions on FBI inquiry and investigation into political groups through promulgation of the attorney general's guidelines. Methods of surveillance such as wiretapping, electronic eavesdropping, and mail covers have been sharply limited by statute, regulation, and judicial decision. Infiltration and disruption of peaceful, though militant, activist groups has been curtailed by court order. At the state and local levels, judicial decisions and consent decrees have restricted the activities of so-called red squads, which had been operated by law enforcement agencies in many of our major states and urban areas. See chapter 16 below.

Surveillance and scrutiny of political activists can also take the form of disclosure and reporting of members and contributors. Here too the courts have restricted the ability of government to require such disclosure—in contexts such as campaign finance laws, disclosure of the identities of speakers and leafletters, listings of the organizations to which teachers and other public employees belong, and laws regulating charitable, membership, and lobbying organizations—by insisting that disclosure of political affiliation or membership support be justified by a compelling government interest and be narrowly drawn to cover only such concerns. See chapters 2 and 5 below.

In all of these instances, courts have been particularly concerned about the deterrent or chilling effect that disclosure or surveillance can have on the right of people to join and associate with controversial groups.

Can political activists investigate the government?

Yes. Not only does the law limit the ability of government to investigate political activists, but the law often provides positive means for activists to "investigate" or discover information about the government. Such information can be vital in providing the basis for criticizing government action and policy, and it enables political activists to know whether they are being investigated by the government.

First, the Constitution has been construed to afford citizens some limited right of access to government processes and proceedings, or at least those which historically have been open to the public, for example, criminal trials.[53] Beyond that, the most important source of learning about what government is doing is the Freedom of Information Act, which affords citizens presumptive access—subject to a number of limitations and exemptions—to any information in the possession of the executive branch of the federal government, whether or not that information relates to the person requesting it. Likewise, most states have freedom of information laws affording similar access to state and local government files. At the federal level, there is also the Privacy Act, which affords access to information the government maintains about individuals and the right to correct those files. The Privacy Act also contains a provision stating federal agencies shall "maintain no record describing how any individual exercises rights guaranteed by the First Amendment unless expressly authorized by statute or by the individual about whom the record is maintained or unless pertinent to and within the scope of an authorized law enforcement activity."[54] Also important are various federal and state open meeting laws which mandate that various kinds of governmental meetings and proceedings be open to the public.

PROTESTORS' REMEDIES AGAINST GOVERNMENT AND PRIVATE ENTITIES

What remedies are available when government seeks to deny or inhibit the rights of political activists?

A variety of remedies are available. Some remedies flow from the laws that create the rights being sought. For example, freedom of information and privacy statutes set out detailed administrative and judicial remedies to secure the rights afforded by those provisions. More generally, the law and the judicial system have traditionally provided a variety of remedies to those who claim their rights have been or are being infringed.

First, if an individual or group is inhibited or restricted from engaging in free speech or association by virtue of a law, regulation, or executive action, they can go to court and seek "affirmative relief." This usually takes the form of a court order declaring the challenged law or regulation unconstitutional or otherwise invalid and/or ordering the relevant officials not to enforce it against the individual or group. If the group or individual wins such a case, they may be awarded attorneys' fees and costs by the court as well.

Sometimes, however, protestors and dissenters engage in speech or conduct that seems to violate or come within a restrictive law or regulation *before* they file a court challenge to that law. In those circumstances, the government may bring a lawsuit against the protestor for violating the relevant law. It may be a civil lawsuit seeking an injunction or a fine, or it may be a criminal prosecution seeking conviction and confinement. In those circumstances, free speech and other constitutional objections can be raised as defenses, i.e., reasons why the government should not succeed in its case.

In recent years, a new remedy has become available to political activists: monetary damages for violation of constitutional rights. If the government has violated or is violating activists' free speech rights, not only can they try to stop the violation, but they may be able to seek monetary compensation for the harm that has been done to them. Dissenters who have been unlawfully targeted for government surveillance, infiltration, or disruption have been awarded damages for violation of their First Amendment rights, as have those illegally arrested for engaging in protected protest activities and demonstrations.[55] Public employees who have been fired or disciplined for engaging in protected speech have likewise received damage awards and reinstatement to their positions, as have individuals who have been wrongly denied government benefits in violation of the Constitution.[56] However, monetary damages can be sought against the federal or state governments only when Congress or state legislatures have authorized such suits. Damages can also be sought against executive branch officials or employees if it can be shown they knew or should have known they were clearly violating the activists' rights at the time; damages can be sought against local government entities even without such a showing.[57]

Are there any remedies against private individuals or organizations if they violate protestors' rights?

Yes and no. The First Amendment and the Constitution generally are limitations on government, not on private individuals or corporations. For that reason, only government—or those actively involved with government—can be charged with violating one's *constitutional* rights. Thus if a privately owned shopping center or mall prohibits protestors from peacefully handing out leaflets, that does not violate the First Amendment because the restriction comes from a private company, not from government.[58] Similarly, if union supporters interfere with the rights of anti-union individuals, the latter cannot sue the former for claimed violation of the Constitution.[59] That does not mean, however, that protestors are without recourse if their political activity is infringed by private entities or individuals.

First, while the First Amendment may not protect the right to protest at a shopping center, state law might. Sometimes state law, particularly provisions in state constitutions, provides protection against private interference with free speech. For example, in the shopping center situation, if state law provides that those who open their facilities to the general public may not exclude peaceful protestors, that right can be enforced against the shopping center.[60] Similarly, state law may provide a more generous protection for the content of speech than the

Supreme Court has afforded under its interpretation of the
First Amendment. In those situations you have rights other
than or in addition to those protected by the First Amendment.

State law may provide other protections as well. State civil
rights laws may make it an impermissible employment practice
to discriminate against employees because of their political
beliefs, thus giving you rights under those provisions. Similarly, many states have begun to restrict the power of private
employers to dismiss employees for irrational or arbitrary reasons, and that might include firing someone for their off-duty
political activities. Individuals who forcibly interfere with free
speech opportunities can sometimes be sued for claims under
the private law of torts, such as assault and battery or conspiracy. Civil rights groups have secured damages against Ku Klux
Klan groups on such grounds for interfering with marches and
demonstrations. The actress, Vanessa Redgrave, successfully
sued the private Boston Symphony Orchestra for breach of
contract, among other things, claiming a contract was cancelled
because of opposition to her political views and associations.[61]
(It should be noted that the BSO claimed that such a suit
violated its First Amendment rights to pursue artistic judgments without judicial interference.)

Likewise, the law permits individuals to sue for defamation
when their reputation has been falsely damaged. Although
the ACLU opposes allowing public officials, public figures,
or persons involved in a matter of public concern to sue for
defamation—on the ground that such suits punish speech and
violate the First Amendment—the Supreme Court does permit
such suits. Political activists who are defamed through negligent, reckless, or intentional false statements of fact can try to
sue for damages. A liberal lawyer in Chicago successfully sued
American Opinion, a right-wing magazine, for calling him "a
Communist-fronter."[62]

The point is that political activists whose rights are violated
by someone or some entity other than the government are not
totally without recourse or remedy.

NOTES

1. *Abrams v. United States,* 250 U.S. 616, 630 (1919) (dissenting
   opinion).

2. *Whitney v. California*, 274 U.S. 357, 375 (1927) (concurring opinion).

3. *New York Times Co. v. Sullivan*, 376 U.S. 254, 270 (1964).

4. *Richmond Newspapers, Inc. v. Virginia*, 448 U.S. 555, 593–97 (1980) (concurring opinion).

5. *Palko v. Connecticut*, 302 U.S. 319, 327 (1937).

6. *Stromberg v. California*, 283 U.S. 359, 369 (1931).

7. See Dorsen, *The Need for a New Enlightenment: Lessons in Liberty from the Eighteenth Century*, 38 Case W. Res. 479 (1988).

8. *Herceg v. Hustler Magazine, Inc.*, 814 F.2d 1017, 1019 (5th Cir. 1987).

9. *Gertz v. Robert Welch, Inc.*, 418 U.S. 323, 339 (1974).

10. *American Booksellers Association v. Hudnut*, 771 F.2d 323, 328 (7th Cir. 1985).

11. *Police Department of Chicago v. Mosely*, 408 U.S. 92, 95 (1972).

12. *Sweezy v. New Hampshire*, 354 U.S. 234, 251 (1957).

13. *Rhode Island Chapter of the National Women's Political Caucus, Inc. v. Rhode Island Lottery Commission*, 609 F. Supp. 1403, 1413 (D.C.R.I. 1985).

14. *Berger v. Battaglia*, 779 F.2d 992, 1001 (4th Cir. 1985).

15. *Lovell v. Griffin*, 303 U.S. 444 (1938); *Edward Bartolo Corp. v. Florida Gulf Coast Building & Construction Trade Council*, 485 U.S. 568 (1988).

16. *Edwards v. South Carolina*, 372 U.S. 229 (1963).

17. *NAACP v. Alabama*, 357 U.S. 449, 460 (1958).

18. *Buckley v. Valeo*, 424 U.S. 1 (1976) (political funding); *Riley v. National Federation of the Blind of North Carolina*, 488 U.S. 781 (1988) (charitable contributions).

19. *United States v. Rumely*, 345 U.S. 41 (1953); *United States v. Harriss*, 347 U.S. 612 (1954).

20. *United States Postal Service v. Hustler Magazine, Inc.*, 630 F. Supp. 867, 872, 875 (D.D.C. 1986).

21. *Clark v. Community for Creative Non-Violence*, 468 U.S. 288, 293 (1984); *Students against Apartheid Coalition v. O'Neill*, 838 F.2d 735 (4th Cir. 1988).

22. *Stromberg v. California*, 283 U.S. 359, 361 (1931).

23. *Tinker v. Des Moines Independent Community School District*, 393 U.S. 503 (1969).

24. *West Virginia State Board of Education v. Barnette*, 319 U.S. 624 (1943).

25. *Spence v. Washington*, 418 U.S. 405 (1974); *Smith v. Goguen*, 415 U.S. 566 (1974); *Leonard v. City of Columbus*, 705 F.2d 1299 (11th Cir. 1983); *Street v. New York*, 394 U.S. 357 (1969).

26. *Texas v. Johnson,* 109 S. Ct. 2533 (1989).

27. *United States v. O'Brien,* 391 U.S. 368 (1968).

28. *United States v. Eichman,* 110 S. Ct. 2404 (1990).

29. *Ward v. Rock against Racism,* 109 S. Ct. 2746 (1989); *Piarowski v. Illinois Community College District 515,* 759 F.2d 265 (7th Cir. 1985); *Mission Trace Investments, Ltd. v. Small Business Administration,* 622 F. Supp. 687 (D. Colo. 1985).

30. *Mission Trace, supra* note 29, at 700.

31. *Schacht v. United States,* 398 U.S. 58 (1970); *Aryan v. Mackey,* 462 F. Supp. 90 (N.D. Tex. 1978).

32. *See, e.g., Kahn v. United States,* 753 F.2d 1208 (3d Cir. 1985).

33. *Calderon v. United States,* 655 F.2d 1037, 1039 (10th Cir. 1981).

34. *Central Hudson, Gas & Electric Co. v. Public Service Commission,* 447 U.S. 557, 561–62 (1980).

35. *West Virginia State Board of Education v. Barnette,* 319 U.S. 624, 642 (1943).

36. *American Booksellers Association v. Hudnut,* 771 F.2d 323, 327–28 (7th Cir 1985).

37. *NAACP v. Alabama,* 357 U.S. 449 (1958); *NAACP v. Button,* 371 U.S. 415 (1963).

38. *Roberts v. United States Jaycees,* 468 U.S. 609, 622 (1984).

39. *United States v. Robel,* 389 U.S. 258 (1967); *Keyishian v. Board of Regents,* 385 U.S. 589 (1967).

40. *Cousins v. Wigoda,* 419 U.S. 477 (1975); *Democratic Party of United States v. Wisconsin ex. rel. La Follette,* 450 U.S. 107 (1981); *Tashjian v. Republican Party of Connecticut,* 479 U.S. 208 (1986).

41. *Talley v. California,* 362 U.S. 60 (1960); *Buckley v. Valeo,* 424 U.S. 1 (1976); *Brown v. Socialist Workers '74 Campaign Committee,* 459 U.S. 87 (1982).

42. *West Virginia State Board of Education v. Barnette,* 319 U.S. 624 (1943).

43. *Miami Herald Publishing Co. v. Tornillo,* 418 U.S. 241 (1974); *Pacific Gas & Electric Co. v. Public Utilities Commission of California,* 475 U.S. 1 (1986); *Abood v. Detroit Board of Education,* 431 U.S. 209 (1977); *Chicago Teachers Union v. Hudson,* 475 U.S. 292 (1986); *Communication Workers of America v. Beck,* 487 U.S. 735 (1988). The Supreme Court has also ruled that lawyers cannot be made to pay bar association dues that support political activities the individual might oppose. *Keller v. State Bar of California,* 110 S. Ct. 2228 (1990).

44. *Wooley v. Maynard,* 430 U.S. 705 (1977).

45. *New York Times Co. v. United States,* 403 U.S. 713, 714 (1971).

46. *Walker v. City of Birmingham,* 388 U.S. 307 (1967).

47. *Broadrick v. Oklahoma,* 413 U.S. 601, 613 (1973). But the doctrine is employed sparingly.
48. *Board of Airport Commissioners of Los Angeles v. Jews for Jesus, Inc.,* 482 U.S. 569 (1987).
49. *City of Houston v. Hill,* 482 U.S. 451 (1987).
50. *Coates v. City of Cincinnati,* 402 U.S. 611 (1971).
51. *Smith v. Goguen,* 415 U.S. 566 (1974).
52. *E.g., United States v. Sturgill,* 563 F.2d 307 (6th Cir 1977), *Shamloo v. Mississippi State Board of Trustees of Higher Learning,* 620 F.2d 516 (5th Cir. 1980).
53. *Richmond Newspapers, Inc. v. Virginia,* 448 U.S. 555 (1980).
54. 5 U.S.C. § 552a (e)(7).
55. *Hobson v. Wilson,* 737 F.2d 1 (D.C. Cir. 1984); *Alliance to End Repression v. Chicago,* 742 F.2d 1007 (7th Cir. 1984); *Socialist Workers Party v. Attorney General,* 642 F. Supp. 1357 (S.D.N.Y. 1986).
56. *Memphis Community School District v. Stachura,* 477 U.S. 299 (1986); *Mission Trace Investments, Ltd. v. Small Business Administration,* 622 F. Supp. 687 (D. Colo. 1985).
57. *Owen v. City of Independence,* 445 U.S. 622 (1980).
58. *Hudgens v. NLRB,* 424 U.S. 507 (1976).
59. *United Brotherhood of Carpenters and Joiners v. Scott,* 463 U.S. 825 (1983). But one might be able to sue a private entity if it actively worked with government officials to violate one's rights; then "state action" might be present, so that constitutional protections would apply. See *Adickes v. S. H. Kress & Co.,* 398 U.S. 144, 152 (1970).
60. *Pruneyard Shopping Center v. Robins,* 447 U.S. 74 (1980).
61. *Redgrave v. Boston Symphony Orchestra, Inc.,* 855 F.2d 888 (1st Cir. 1988).
62. *Gertz v. Robert Welch, Inc.,* 418 U.S. 323 (1974).

PART 1

The Sounds of Protest: Regulation of the Content of Political Speech

Relying on the absolute language of the First Amendment ("Congress shall make no law . . . abridging the freedom of speech, or of the press") or on the theory that free speech requires that the people, not the government, determine political truth, some of the most famous Supreme Court justices have taken an "absolute" First Amendment position: the content of public political speech should be completely protected against government restriction. Justice Louis D. Brandeis said:

> Those who won our independence by revolution were not cowards. They did not fear political change. They did not exalt order at the cost of liberty. To courageous, self-reliant men, with confidence in the power of free and fearless reasoning applied through the processes of popular government, no danger flowing from speech can be deemed clear and present, unless the incidence of the evil apprehended is so imminent that it may befall before there is opportunity for full discussion. If there be time to expose through discussion the falsehood and fallacies, to avert the evil by the processes of education, the remedy to be applied is more speech, not enforced silence.[1]

More recently, Justices Hugo L. Black and William O. Douglas have adhered to similar views.

But the Supreme Court has not rigorously applied this vision. Rather it has said that freedom of political speech is not "absolute" and that in certain circumstances and for certain purposes the government may suppress or punish such speech. The next several chapters will discuss the boundaries that demark protected political and protest speech and identify those situations where such speech can be prevented or punished.

NOTE

1. *Whitney v. California*, 274 U.S. 357, 377 (1927) (concurring opinion).

II
Challenging the State

In 1798, in order to quell dissent, Congress made it a federal crime to "write, print, utter, or publish . . . any false, scandalous and malicious writing . . . against the government . . . with intent to defame . . . or to excite the hatred of the good people of the United States."[1] In 1902, following the assassination of President McKinley, New York made it a crime to advocate "criminal anarchy," defined as "the doctrine that organized government should be overthrown by force or violence, or by assassination . . . or by any unlawful means."[2] In 1940, Congress passed the Smith Act, targeted primarily at the Communist party, making it a felony to "advocate, abet, advise or teach the duty, necessity, desirability, or propriety of overthrowing or destroying any government in the United States by force or violence" or to organize any group to advocate or teach such doctrines.[3] Thus, despite the First Amendment, government has long sought to proscribe the advocacy of the forceful or violent overthrow of government, on the claim that such advocacy is not entitled to constitutional protection. This chapter will discuss the extent to which such laws and others that restrict speech, association, and protest on the ground they are necessary to safeguard national and domestic security against subversion are consistent with First Amendment principles.

ADVOCATING VIOLENT RESISTANCE
TO GOVERNMENT

Can violent resistance to government be advocated?
Yes, but this is only recently the case. In 1969, following a half-century of dealing with this problem, the Supreme Court ruled that preaching or advocating the violent overthrow of the government or the use of force to accomplish political objectives could not, per se, be made a crime. The case was *Brandenburg v. Ohio*,[4] and it involved a Ku Klux Klan group that held a small rally on a farm in Ohio. Speakers engaged in predictably obnoxious comments about blacks and Jews, vaguely threat-

ened "revengeance" and hinted at violence to secure their objectives. A television station broadcast portions of the rally which led to convictions under Ohio laws making it a crime to advocate violence as a method of political change and to organize with others to teach such views and doctrines. The Court summarily overturned the convictions because the law prohibited advocating the use of violence even where such speech was not directed to inciting immediate unlawful actions; the law was thus overly broad and sweeping. Although such laws had been upheld in the 1920s, court rulings since that time "have fashioned the principle that the constitutional guarantees of free speech and free press do not permit a State to forbid or proscribe advocacy of the use of force or of law violation except where such advocacy is directed to inciting or producing imminent lawless action and is likely to incite or produce such action."[5] Because the statute could apply to "mere advocacy" of violence, as distinct from "incitement to imminent lawless action," the law itself was defective, and so were the convictions for violating it. The dividing line became clear: teaching or advocating the need for violence is protected; specifically urging and preparing a group for imminent and probable violent action is not.

Have the courts always protected advocacy of resistance, violent change, or revolution?

No. In the earliest encounters with speakers who advocated revolution, resistance, or violence, the Supreme Court took a much more restrictive view of robust public advocacy of fundamental change or resistance to governmental authority.

In three cases under the Espionage Act of 1917, passed during World War I to prevent interference with the military effort, the Court unanimously upheld convictions of antiwar dissenters—on both the right and the left—who had done nothing more than publicly urge resistance to the draft and wartime military authority in speeches and writings. The Court reasoned that freedom of speech was not absolute but depended "in every case . . . [on] whether the words used are used in such circumstances and are of such a nature as to create a clear and present danger that they will bring about the substantive evil that Congress has a right to prevent."[6] Finding that the circulation of antiwar pamphlets or the giving of such speeches might have a "tendency" to cause resistance to government authority, the Court upheld punishment of such dissent.[7]

Later that year, for similar reasons, the Court allowed the punishment of socialist radicals on the Lower East Side of New York for printing leaflets urging workers not to cooperate with the war effort by making weapons to be used against the fledgling Russian Revolution. Since the purpose of the leaflets was "to excite, at the supreme crisis of the war, disaffection, sedition, riots, and as they hoped, revolution, in the country," the Court reasoned, the fact that there probably wasn't the remotest possibility of these leaflets actually bringing about such dire evils was irrelevant; the mere possibility of such consequences was sufficient.[8] This prompted a landmark dissenting opinion, by Justice Oliver Wendell Holmes, developing the concept of a free market place of ideas: "when men have realized that time has upset many fighting faiths, they may come to believe . . . that the ultimate good desired is better reached by free trade in ideas—that the best test of truth is the power of the thought to get itself accepted in the competition of the market."[9] In his view the expression of loathful opinions could be suppressed only when they so "imminently threaten immediate interference with the lawful and pressing purposes of the law that an immediate check is required to save the country."[10]

Nonetheless in the 1920s the Supreme Court continued to allow punishment of revolutionary rhetoric and advocacy by leaders of small Communist and Socialist parties who were charged with using spoken and written words "advocating, advising or teaching the overthrow of organized government by unlawful means." The radicals had urged revolutionary mass political action to foment industrial disturbances and overthrow and destroy organized government. To the Court, this was not mere "philosophical abstraction" but was "the language of direct incitement," and its very utterance could be punished once the legislature had determined that such utterances were harmful to the social order.[11] Individuals who organized groups to advocate such ideas or doctrines "inimical to the public welfare, tending to incite to crime, disturb the public peace, or endanger the foundations of organized government and threaten its overthrow by unlawful means" could likewise be jailed.[12]

These rulings generated impassioned opposition by Justices

Holmes and Brandeis who insisted that the advocacy of any idea or doctrine was protected by the First Amendment, unless there was a clear and present danger of an attempt by the advocates to try to overthrow the government by force.[13] Justice Brandeis insisted that even the most reprehensible advocacy of force, violence, or law violation should be protected

> where the advocacy falls short of incitement and there is nothing to indicate that the advocacy would be immediately acted on. The wide difference between advocacy and incitement, between preparation and attempt, between assembling and conspiracy, must be borne in mind. In order to support a finding of clear and present danger it must be shown either that immediate serious violence was to be expected or was advocated, or that the past conduct furnished reason to believe that such advocacy was then contemplated.[14]

These bold visions of free speech would have to wait another generation before they effectively became the law of the land in the *Brandenburg* decision.

In the meantime, the Court at least softened the repressive effects of its rulings by making it clear that dissenters could not be punished for unlawful advocacy of violent revolution or resistance without some evidence that their speeches or writings contained words that could be fairly interpreted as teaching prohibited doctrine.[15] Likewise, a state could not convict a Communist party organizer of "attempting to incite insurrection" simply by proving that he had enlisted a few members in the cause and had party literature in his possession advocating a number of positions, some lawful some not.[16] Finally, the Court also made plain that a person attending a lawful public meeting to discuss police brutality could not be punished on the sole ground that the meeting was held under the auspices of the Communist party.[17]

Can an individual be punished for guilt by association?

No. It should be noted that this particular principle, that people cannot be punished for guilt by association, has been enforced by the courts ever since 1937. In other words, participation in lawful political association and activities cannot be punished because some people who share your platform, letterhead, or banner engage in illegal advocacy or violence. For example, a public employee cannot be penalized for joining groups or coalitions that have some illicit purposes when the individual does not share or subscribe to those purposes.[18] A local campus group of the militant Students for a Democratic Society (SDS) could not be denied campus recognition simply because of acts or advocacy of the national organization or of other SDS groups in other parts of the country.[19] Finally, leaders of a civil rights coalition organizing and implementing a boycott against discriminatory merchants could not be sanctioned on the ground that other members of the coalition had engaged in sporadic acts of violence and illegal behavior.[20]

Has the government enforced laws to prevent groups such as the Communist party from organizing to advocate the overthrow of the government?

Yes. As noted above, Congress in 1940 passed the Smith Act which made it a crime to "advocate" or "teach" the need to overthrow any government in the United States by force or violence, and to organize any "group of persons who teach, advocate, or encourage the overthrow or destruction of any government in the United States by force or violence."[21] In the somber atmosphere of the early cold war period, the federal government used that statute to prosecute the top echelon leadership of the Communist party. In 1951 the Court upheld those prosecutions.[22] Although no real harm had actually resulted from the teaching and advocacy of violent revolution, the possibility of grave danger from such advocacy, coupled with the highly organized and disciplined nature of the party and the unsettled conditions in the world, justified, according to the Court, nipping the problem in the bud.

> Overthrow of the Government by force and violence is certainly a substantial enough interest for the Government to limit speech. . . . Obviously [the clear and present danger test] can not mean that before the Government may act, it must wait until the *putsch* is about to be executed, the plans have been laid and the signal is awaited. If Government is aware that a group aiming at its overthrow is attempting to indoctrinate its members and to commit them to a course whereby they will strike when

the leaders feel the circumstances permit, action by the Government is required.[23]

The Court concluded that the invasion of free speech was justified: "[The Party leaders] intended to overthrow the Government of the United States as speedily as the circumstances would permit. Their conspiracy to organize the Communist Party and to teach and advocate the overthrow of the Government of the United States by force and violence created a 'clear and present danger' of an attempt to overthrow the Government by force and violence."[24]

For the dissenters, Justices Black and Douglas, the party's organizing and teaching of doctrine about the desirability and inevitability of violent revolution could not be punished, certainly not unless some immediate injury to society could be shown likely.

Are such laws still valid?

Probably not, unless they are substantially restricted. In later cases interpreting the meaning of the Smith Act, the Court substantially narrowed its scope and effect and made it clear that even Communist party officials cannot be convicted merely for advocating the violent overthrow of government.

In one case, the Supreme Court ruled that advocacy of forcible overthrow of government as an abstract doctrine had to be distinguished from advocacy of action to that end.[25] The Smith Act does not punish "mere doctrinal justification of forcible overthrow. . . . That sort of advocacy, even though uttered with the hope that it may ultimately lead to violent revolution, is too remote from concrete action to be regarded as the kind of indoctrination preparatory to action which was condemned in *Dennis*."[26] The law "reaches only advocacy of action for the overthrow of government by force and violence. The essential distinction is that those to whom the advocacy is addressed must be urged to *do* something, now or in the future, rather than merely to *believe* in something."[27] Only advocacy or teaching "directed to stirring people to action" can possibly be punished. Convictions cannot be based almost entirely on talk about the need for violent overthrow—advocacy of doctrine—

with only a few instances of urging specific illegal acts—advocacy of action.

Even though later cases allowed prosecution of "active" Communist party members who specifically intended to engage in illegal advocacy of illegal action, i.e., resort to violence, the Supreme Court stressed that convictions cannot be based solely on showing the party's organizational structure and Marxist-Leninist doctrines; only the systematic teaching and advocacy of illegal action, to be taken either immediately or in the future, can be punished.[28]

Although these cases involved interpretations of the Smith Act, not the First Amendment, they were important in setting the stage for the 1969 *Brandenburg* ruling which took these limitations and incorporated them into First Amendment doctrine. The result is that any law prohibiting the advocacy of revolution or lawlessness to accomplish political objectives may not punish "advocacy of the use of force or of law violation except where [1] such advocacy is directed to inciting or producing imminent lawless action and [2] is likely to produce such action."[29]

Are there any limits on the right to advocate forcible or violent overthrow of government authority?

Possibly. Bear in mind that the Court in *Brandenburg* stated the Smith Act had been upheld on the premise that it embodied such limiting principles and had been applied in *Dennis* and later cases in conformity with those limitations. Thus the *Brandenburg* ruling, though an important milestone for free speech, did not reject all government power to punish revolutionary or violence-oriented advocacy where the elements of the new formula could be proven. Nor did it remove the Smith Act from the federal statute books. Also, the *Brandenburg* ruling involved a small and inconsequential group. The government retains its potential power to try to prosecute certain kinds of advocacy of violence by tightly controlled and highly organized radical groups.

Indeed, in recent years, federal prosecutions of radical groups have sometimes included not only charges that the group members have planned and engaged in acts of violence or political terrorism, but charges of seditious conspiracy, i.e., plotting to overthrow the government by force, in settings and contexts that might arguably meet the tightened *Brandenburg* requirements, even though the government has largely been unsuccessful in making such charges stick.[30] Such prosecutions usually succeed by proving actual acts of violence, and the courts have not had much occasion to consider whether *advocacy* of violence, as distinct from clear illegal violent *actions*, can give rise to punishment in such settings.

The Supreme Court has not dealt directly with the validity of the Smith Act and other similar laws since *Brandenburg*. But lower courts have discussed these issues and have applied the *Brandenburg* principles in other contexts. The basic approach seems to be that, so long as radical advocacy remains mostly rhetoric and does not ripen into actual violence, the beliefs and advocacy will be protected under the First Amendment. "Marxist or Communist beliefs, like other political beliefs, are protected under the First and Fourteenth Amendments, and such beliefs, or one's association with others holding them is protected activity for which a State may not impose . . . disabilities."[31] Thus, Marxist-Leninist groups are entitled to espouse their views in the absence of any evidence of the use or advocacy of immediate or specific violence, regardless of whether such a group advocates violent revolution as an ultimate political goal, as distinct from an immediate or interim political weapon or tactic.[32] Another court ruled, "Government cannot constitutionally punish individual or group advocacy of any position, unless it amounts to incitement to lawless action."[33]

When Congress tried to prevent people who "publicly advocate the violent overthrow of the Federal Government" from receiving certain federal employment training subsidies, the courts declared the law unconstitutional because it penalized mere advocacy of revolutionary doctrine: "The first amendment clearly bars the government from penalizing mere advocacy of any idea, including violent revolution."[34] Under *Brandenburg*, government can restrict only advocacy directed to and likely to incite violence, i.e., reasonably calculated to incite persons to lawless action; "doctrinal" advocacy of violence is protected, only "inciteful" advocacy of violence is theoretically subject to punishment.[35]

MEMBERSHIP IN RADICAL ORGANIZATIONS

Can an individual be punished or penalized for merely being a member of a radical organization?

Not unless the organization engages in illegal incitement to violence and the individual is an "active and knowing" member who actively supports such advocacy.

The Smith Act contains a provision making it a crime to be a "knowing" member of groups advocating violent or revolutionary change. In order to uphold this provision, the Supreme Court construed it to require clear proof of "specific intent" to advance the illegal advocacy and active rather than merely passive or nominal membership.[36] The act does not criminalize all association with an organization that has engaged in illegal advocacy; there must be clear proof that the individual specifically intended to accomplish the aims of the organization by resort to violence.[37]

The Court has applied these principles to rule that later federal statutes, barring members of "Communist organizations" or "Communist-action organizations" from certain benefits like working at a defense facility or obtaining a passport, are facially defective because they fail to incorporate these careful distinctions.[38] At the very least penalties and restrictions must be focused on those who are *knowing* and *active* members of such organizations and limited to sensitive positions or locations.

These rulings sharply limit federal, state, and local laws that target on membership in "subversive" organizations or prohibit the making of "seditious" statements. A public employee, for example, cannot be penalized for membership in such an organization unless the person knows of the group's illegal objectives or methods, and specifically intends to help further those goals or actively assists in pursuing those goals.[39] In other words, organizations cannot be made illegal in the absence of a clear showing that they actively engage in lawless conduct or in such incitement to lawless action as would itself be punishable. And an individual cannot be punished for joining or associating with such an organization unless the association meets these criteria and the person affiliates with the group with knowledge of its illegality and with the specific intent of furthering its illegal aims.[40] Personal advocacy of protected doctrines of violent overthrow of government cannot be the basis for penalty either.[41] Nor can job opportunities be withheld on the basis of vague criteria such as whether the employee or applicant holds views that are "disloyal" or advocates "sedition."[42] Under these principles, for example, mere membership in the Communist party cannot justify denial of an opportunity to practice law, work in the merchant marine, receive a security clearance, travel abroad on a passport, be a union official, or work in a defense plant.[43]

Finally, political beliefs and associations cannot be used punitively in the criminal justice setting. Radicals convicted or charged with crimes such as possession of weapons and explosives or involvement in terrorist activities cannot be subjected to additional punishment because of their political beliefs. "A sentence based to any degree on activity or beliefs protected by the first amendment is constitutionally invalid."[44] Nor can such beliefs and activities be used to justify isolated conditions of penal confinement. "[T]he designation of prisoners solely for their 'subversive' statements and thoughts is the type of overreaction that the Supreme Court has repeatedly warned against."[45] Evidence about political beliefs and associations might be admissible in criminal cases, however, to attempt to prove the defendant had a motive for committing the crime or to undermine the credibility of a witness.[46]

Can an individual be asked about his or her membership in organizations that subscribe to the goals of violent overthrow?

The phrase, "Are you now, or have you ever been . . ." has become part of our political culture, suggesting the broad power that government was once believed to have to inquire into "subversive" beliefs, activities, and association. The question was typically linked in the public's mind with prominent legislative investigations into subversive activities, but the question appeared also on countless application forms for government licenses, benefits, and employment. As the courts dramatically restricted the kinds of advocacy of change that can be penalized, so too have they curtailed the kinds of inquiries that can be made about such advocacy or association with groups that engage in it.

But not all such inquiries into political association with radical groups are impermissible. In certain contexts, most notably admission to the legal profession, the courts have allowed authorities a limited power to ask applicants about Communist party and similar membership, not as an automatic disqualifying factor, but as the basis for further inquiry into whether the applicant is a knowing member of an organization engaged in prohibited illegal advocacy.[47] But a bar applicant cannot be denied admission to the legal profession because of a refusal to answer general questions about advocacy of revolution or association with groups that engage in such advocacy.[48] For certain sensitive federal positions, greater scrutiny of one's political involvement with militant groups may be allowed.[49] Indeed the federal government's Office of Personnel Management uses a questionnaire for sensitive positions—see Standard Form 86, Part II—that asks sweeping questions about membership in the Communist party or affiliation with groups that advocate the overthrow of government or the use of violence. The validity of these inquiries has not been addressed by the courts.

Can the government investigate a group or its members because of its political advocacy?

Not if it is engaged in clearly protected political advocacy. But where the advocacy begins to involve possible threats of serious illegal action, the government's power to investigate may increase. The history and proper scope, if any, of government investigation and surveillance of political dissenters is discussed in detail in part 3. But since it is often a group's political rhetoric or ideology that triggers such scrutiny, some points will be discussed now.

Until the mid-1970s federal and local law enforcement agencies targeted a wide variety of political groups for surveillance and sometimes worse. After many of these secret government activities came to light, steps were taken to circumscribe and control them. The attorney general's list of subversive organizations, which had been used for a variety of purposes such as screening for federal employment, was abolished in 1974.[50] Attorney General Levi's 1976 guidelines on FBI monitoring of political dissent sought to limit the basis and extent of such surveillance. Numerous lawsuits in federal and state courts resulted in judicial rulings or consent decrees whereby law enforcement was required to curtail sharply its surveillance of legitimate dissent.[51]

Two basic themes have emerged from these developments. Law enforcement efforts to use surveillance or investigation to deter and intimidate lawful, peaceful dissent and protest are basically illegitimate. But investigation and even infiltration of groups engaged in planning or carrying out specific acts of serious violence or terrorism are legitimate and even necessary. The problem that has divided courts and officials is whether groups that *advocate* violence or serious lawlessness, as part of their ideology or activism, can be targeted for investigation on the basis of such advocacy, even though the advocacy is protected in the sense that it cannot, by itself, be subject to criminal prosecution under the *Brandenburg* principles.

Many of the consent decrees and judicial decisions in antisurveillance cases stipulated that law enforcement cannot even investigate groups engaged in "advocacy protected by the First Amendment," i.e., advocacy that falls short of imminent and likely incitement to violence. But in 1983 the Reagan administration's Attorney General Smith made major revisions in the Justice Department guidelines that seem to broaden the premise for FBI investigation of militant groups by permitting focus on those who make statements advocating violence. As the revised guidelines state, "When, however, statements advocate criminal activity or indicate an apparent intent to engage in crime, particularly crimes of violence, an investigation under these Guidelines may be warranted unless it is apparent from the circumstances or the context in which the statements are made, that there is no prospect of harm."[52] FBI officials said the guidelines attempt to distinguish between "simple expressions of ideology" and "statements or conduct that pose a threat."[53]

The dispute was discussed in a Chicago antisurveillance lawsuit, where an appellate court ruled that, despite an earlier consent decree, the FBI can at least investigate groups threatening violence, even though such advocacy is theoretically protected from criminal punishment under *Brandenburg*. The court explained that while the FBI cannot investigate views or beliefs such as Puerto Rican independence, the government can monitor "any group that advocates the commission, even if not immediately, of terrorist acts in violation of federal law. It need not wait till the bombs begin to go off, or even till the bomb factory is found."[54] Thus, the FBI can investigate advocacy that it cannot prosecute; the possible, though indirect repression of free speech was deemed less important than monitoring, investigating, and discouraging groups with violent aims. A sharp dissent contended that the consent decree's ban on investigations of groups whose advocacy is "protected by the First Amendment" means precisely no surveillance of speech threatening *future* violence or illegal conduct, although this does not preclude investigation of groups once they go beyond advocacy and engage in actions, e.g., suspicious travel or buying supplies usable for criminal purposes.[55] Otherwise, investigatory excesses can be used as a powerful weapon against political dissent. The Supreme Court has not made an effort to resolve the dispute.

Can a person be penalized for involvement with far-right, racist, or "hate" groups?

That depends on the nature of the person's involvement and the activities of the group. As with membership in militant groups on the left, subscribing to racist and even violent views and associating with groups on the right that espouse such views cannot be the basis for criminal prosecution. But the law has focused particular attention on the two groups that for many symbolize the polar extremes of the right and left: the Ku Klux Klan and the Communist party. The Klan's violent racist activities during and after the Civil War prompted the enactment of the nation's first civil rights laws, explicitly entitled the Ku Klux Klan Act and designed to try to prevent the Klan's violent racist activities. Likewise, the subversive advocacy laws enacted at the turn of the century were used primarily against Marxist-Leninist parties, and the Smith Act and later federal statutes were focused almost entirely on the Communist party. Similarly, the two organizations whose membership the government has been accorded the greatest power to monitor are the Klan and the Party.[56] Ironically, the case that finally overturned the 1920s rulings that had allowed prosecution of socialist and communist organizations because of their advocacy involved not those groups, but a meager band of Klansmen.[57] Thus, the courts generally have treated right-wing, racist, or fascist advocacy as equally protected with Marxist advocacy on the left.

But the Klan and the Communist party seem almost antique when compared to some of the contemporary extremist groups that constantly preach and occasionally practice acts of serious violence. It is clear that active and knowing involvement in such groups and the violence that they adhere to cannot be characterized as protected speech. Indeed, First Amendment issues of advocacy of violence arise infrequently because the government is able to prove participation in actual or attempted acts of violence.[58]

Nonetheless, important First Amendment issues are sometimes raised by an individual's association with a far-right "hate group." Courts have held that membership in the Klan is protected by the First Amendment, even while describing the Klan as "a violence-prone group with a history of harassing, intimidating, and injuring blacks and members of other minority groups."[59] But a group publishing literature that overtly and virulently espouses racism and antisemitism and repeatedly calls for violence, could be denied tax advantages and subsidies available to "charitable or educational" organizations, even though such advocacy was protected against criminal prohibition.[60] Similarly, a police department clerk in a racially tense Southern city could be fired from his position when he publicly identified himself as a member of and recruiter for the Ku Klux Klan and handed out Klan literature while off-duty. Though individuals have a right to join the Klan and cannot be punished for mere membership without specific advocacy of any illegal conduct, "a law enforcement agency does not violate the First Amendment by discharging an employee whose active participation in an organization with a history of violent activity, which is antithetical to enforcement of the laws by state officers, has become known to the public and created an understandably adverse public reaction that seriously and dangerously threatens to cripple the ability of the law enforcement agency to perform effectively its public duty."[61] Finally, a student who was a member of the Nazi party could be excluded from participation in a college ROTC program, because the student's racist and antisemitic beliefs shed doubt on his ability to follow orders or accept leadership responsibilities. "This case falls within that very narrow class of cases where a citizen's admittedly protected beliefs are demonstrably incompatible with the important public office he seeks and inimical to the vital mission of the agency he would serve."[62]

SPEECH INVOLVING NATIONAL SECURITY CONCERNS

Can punishment result if speech involves classified or secret information or reveals information harmful to "national security"?

Possibly. Occasionally people who criticize national policy in the defense or foreign affairs areas rely on or disclose information the government claims is secret or compromises national defense or national security.

Obviously, acts of hardcore treason in the strict sense of actively aiding formal wartime enemies of the United States can be punished. So too can espionage in the sense of classic spying for secrets against the United States and on behalf of a foreign government. The problem is that treason and similar statutes are often so broadly worded that they can be used potentially against dissenters whose only crime is criticizing or condemning national policy. Remember that the first prosecutions of antiwar dissenters during World War I were brought under the Espionage Act, which, in addition to punishing spying, also punished speech advocating resistance to military or national authority.[63] The application of the *Brandenburg* formula would probably prevent such overly broad uses of the espionage laws to punish public criticism of national policy.

The problem today typically involves government efforts to restrict or punish the communication of secret or classified information in a number of contexts. Although Congress "has repeatedly refused to enact a statute which would make criminal the mere unauthorized disclosure of classified information,"[64] there are more specific statutes protecting secret or sensitive information that can be employed by the government to try to restrict or punish speech.[65] When the government tried to stop publication of the Pentagon Papers, it relied in part on a provision of the espionage laws making it a crime to communicate information "relating to the national defense," with reason to believe it could harm the United States, to "someone not entitled to receive it."[66] The Court ruled that the government had not met the extraordinary burden necessary to justify a prior restraint injunction against the press. But some justices suggested that subsequent prosecution of the newspapers under these espionage statutes is conceivable, and most justices agreed there could be penalties for revealing secret, highly sensitive information that "would surely result in direct, immediate, and irreparable damage to our Nation or its people."[67] Similarly an injunction prevented a magazine from publishing an article entitled "The H-Bomb Secret: How We Got It, Why We're Telling It." Though the article was based on publicly available sources, the government claimed that assembling information from public sources in such a way that it compromises sensitive secret information warrants an injunction. Relying on statutes protecting nuclear information, a lower court agreed.[68] This ruling was vacated by a higher court only when the same information began to appear in other publications.

Can the government prosecute people for "leaking" secret information to the press?

Yes. The government used the espionage statutes to convict a Defense Department employee who "leaked" secret defense information for an article in a British magazine specializing in military affairs. An appeals court rejected the argument that the statute only reached "classic spying" and should not be used against those who "leak" information to the press to inform the public and enhance the debate over national policy. Conceding that the espionage statute was not the best tool to separate the "leaker" from the "mole," the court still found nothing in the First Amendment to prohibit the prosecution or to allow the release of properly classified damaging information, at least where done by a government employee.[69]

Government employees with access to classified or secret information have been mostly unsuccessful in persuading courts to recognize any significant First Amendment protection from restrictions on their release of classified information. Courts have upheld so-called secrecy agreements whereby CIA employees and other sensitive officials agree, as part of their employment, not to publish classified information without approval or publish anything related to their employment without prior submission to the government agency for clearance. Although unclassified information cannot be censored, and courts may review the propriety of the classification of items of information,[70] courts have granted injunctions enforcing such agreements and have imposed monetary and other penalties on employees and former employees who failed to seek prior clearance, even where their writings disclosed no classified information.[71]

Indeed, the Supreme Court has stated that the government can restrict employees from releasing classified information even in the absence of a signed secrecy agreement. Similarly the Court allowed revocation of the passport of Philip Agee, a former CIA employee whose "whistleblowing" writings and speeches were claimed to have revealed secret information and endangered CIA operatives and agents. Agreeing with the government that such speech activity was likely to cause serious damage to the national security or foreign policy of the United States, the Court upheld the sanction and further held, speaking in harsh tones, that the First Amendment does not protect the disclosures of intelligence operations and names of intelligence personnel.[72]

Prompted by activities of Agee and others, and encouraged by the Supreme Court ruling, Congress passed a statute making it a serious felony to "name names," i.e., to divulge information that might reveal the identity of intelligence operatives. Although most of the statute covers present and former government employees who learn such information during their employment, the most controversial provision extends punishment to anyone who, "with reason to believe that such activities would impair or impede the foreign intelligence activities of the United States, discloses any information that identifies an individual as a covert agent," if such disclosure is part of a "pattern of activities intended to identify or expose covert action."[73] The legislative history of the statute makes it clear that this law does not apply to news reporting, but only to "naming names" for its own sake. To date, there have been no prosecutions under this statute, and many stories, articles, and speeches have included names of covert agents. The Reagan administration efforts to require the vast majority of federal civilian and military personnel to sign "nondisclosure agreements" pledging to submit all writings for prior review have been largely checked or restricted by Congress.[74]

IMPORTING OR EXPORTING PROTEST SPEECH

Can protest or speech activities be imported or exported?
Although most protestors are concerned with national or local issues, many activists are engaged in causes that have a foreign policy or international dimension to them: support for Israel (or the PLO); being for (or against) independence in Northern Ireland; condemning apartheid in South Africa; or human rights violations in Soviet bloc countries. Americans whose protest activities involve issues of foreign relations often have to contend with a myriad of government restrictions and regulations designed to control the import or export of people and/or their ideas. These legal barriers have been called a "nylon curtain" designed to keep provocative foreign ideas and speakers out and dissenting Americans within the borders of our country.[75] Most of these restrictions on the import or export of free speech are the product of the cold war and are directed against foreign countries, groups, or individuals who are subversive, communist, or Marxist; other restrictions are more neutral and have been applied against both ends of the political spectrum. Dealing with the First Amendment problems presented by such restrictions has been difficult for the courts because of the judiciary's traditional deference to the president and Congress in matters of foreign policy, national security, and international relations. Nonetheless, the courts have placed some limits on the ability of these branches to control the import or export of ideas.

Can the government require U.S. persons to register as foreign agents?
Probably yes. Domestic groups or individuals whose speech activities involve some sort of connection to foreign governments or institutions can be subject to certain kinds of regulation of their political activities that would be unacceptable if imposed on groups engaged strictly in domestic issues. For example, courts have traditionally upheld the requirement that Americans who act as propagandizers or "agents" for foreign entities must register with the government and be subject to punishment if they do not.[76] This law has been applied to a newspaper the government claimed was basically an agent for pro-IRA groups in Ireland.[77] The Supreme Court upheld a law

which required the American Communist party to register with the government, partly on the theory that the party was different from other socialist or Marxist groups because of the incidents of foreign domination and operation to advance the objectives of the world communist movement. The act was upheld because it applied "only to *foreign-dominated* organizations which work primarily to advance the objectives of a world movement controlled by the government of a *"foreign* country."[78]

By similar reasoning, the government ordered the closing of the Palestine Information Office in Washington, D.C., staffed mostly by American citizens, on the ground that the office was a foreign mission representing the PLO and thus came within the statutory power of the secretary of state to control the functioning of foreign missions. First Amendment objections were rejected by the courts on the ground that this was a proper exercise of foreign affairs which only incidentally burdened the free speech rights of those associated with the office and their supporters.[79] But an act of Congress that had the effect of ordering the closing of the PLO Mission to the United Nations in New York City was overturned by a federal judge because the law conflicted with American treaty obligations as host country to the United Nations headquarters.[80]

Can the government deny visas to foreign visitors on political grounds?

The answer is unclear. Among the most potent government restrictions on the importation of ideas is the power to deny visas to foreign nationals who wish to visit the United States to speak. American groups who wish to hear what such foreigners have to say are often frustrated by the government's denial of visas to such individuals. The McCarran-Walter Act, a cold-war era statute designed to permit government to deny visas to individuals affiliated with various communist movements at home or abroad, was used extensively by the State Department to bar the entry of foreigners.[81]

In 1972 the Supreme Court upheld the validity of excluding a Belgian Socialist on the ground that the government's sovereign power to control its borders and immigration outweighs the First Amendment rights of the speaker and his potential audience.[82] Since then, however, both Congress and the courts have put substantial restrictions on the ability of the State Department to exclude foreign visitors on ideological grounds.[83]

Indeed, a federal judge in California has ruled that provisions of the McCarran-Walter Act that allow deportation of aliens in the United States who merely advocate world communism or subversion violate the First Amendment. The court reasoned that this section of the act is substantially overbroad under *Brandenburg* because it penalizes advocacy that falls far short of imminent incitement to lawless behavior.[84] Moreover, at this writing, a bill to repeal permanently the act's ban on visits by people because of their ideology is about to pass in Congress; a temporary law to prohibit visa denials on ideological grounds is currently in effect.[85]

Can the government restrict importation of books and other informational materials?

To some degree. The government has not been wholly successful in restricting the importation of newspapers, magazines, and books containing "communist political propaganda."[86] In 1988 Congress amended the export control acts to prohibit restrictions on the import and export of informational materials.[87] But in 1987 the Supreme Court upheld a provision of the Foreign Agents Registration Act that requires that people who distribute political propaganda in the United States from a foreign source must file statements with the government and label the books or films as "political propaganda." The Court rejected the argument that this would discourage the presentation of such materials.[88]

Can the government restrict the right to travel abroad?

To some extent. Americans who wish to travel abroad to pursue free speech interests are often met with restrictions. In the past, government efforts to deny passports to members of the Communist party were invalidated as too broad and sweeping.[89] Nonetheless the government retains two powerful devices to control foreign travel by American activists. First, the Court upheld the power of the secretary of state to sharply restrict expenditure of funds in certain disfavored nations, such as Cuba, effectively frustrating travel to such countries.[90] Similarly, in a case involving an ex-CIA agent, the Court accorded the secretary broad power to control the passports of those Americans whose foreign speech activities abroad were deemed "likely" to cause "serious damage" to the nations's foreign policy or national security, even if the harm comes only from speech.[91]

But some courts have continued to show a willingness to apply strong traditional First Amendment principles to safeguard rights in the foreign policy arena. For example, a federal appellate court ruled against denying duty-free export certification, and thereby imposing less favorable export treatment, for American films found to lack "balance" or to "espouse a cause."[92] "[I]t is clear that there is no 'sliding scale' of First Amendment protection under which the degree of scrutiny fluctuates in accordance with the degree to which the regulation touches on foreign affairs. Rather the only permissible non-neutral inquiry into the content of the speech is whether the statements adversely affect foreign policy interests to such a degree that the speech is completely unprotected."[93] "We . . . reject . . . the suggestion that the First Amendment's protection is lessened when the expression is directed abroad. The cases cited by the government do not support its contention that otherwise protected free speech interests may be routinely subordinated to foreign policy concerns."[94]

NOTES

1. Sedition Act of 1798, 1 Stat. 596.
2. New York Penal Law §§ 160, 161; see *Gitlow v. New York*, 268 U.S. 652 (1925).
3. 18 U.S.C. § 2385; *see Dennis v. United States*, 341 U.S. 494 (1951).
4. 395 U.S. 444 (1969).
5. *Brandenburg v. Ohio*, 395 U.S. 444, 447 (1969).
6. *Schenck v. United States*, 249 U.S. 47, 52 (1919).
7. *See also Frohwerk v. United States*, 249 U.S. 204 (1919); *Debs v. United States*, 249 U.S. 211, 214 (1919).
8. *Abrams v. United States*, 250 U.S. 616 (1919).
9. *Id.* at 630 (dissenting opinion).
10. *Id.*
11. *Gitlow v. New York*, 268 U.S. 652, 665 (1925).
12. *Whitney v. California*, 274 U.S. 357, 371 (1927).

13. *Gitlow v. New York, supra* note 11, at 672–73.
14. *Whitney v. California, supra* note 12, at 376 (concurring opinion).
15. *Fiske v. Kansas,* 274 U.S. 380 (1927).
16. *Herndon v. Lowry,* 301 U.S. 242 (1937).
17. *De Jonge v. Oregon,* 299 U.S. 353 (1937).
18. *Elfbrandt v. Russell,* 384 U.S. 11 (1966).
19. *Healy v. James,* 408 U.S. 169 (1972).
20. *NAACP v. Claiborne Hardware Co.,* 458 U.S. 886 (1982).
21. 18 U.S.C. § 2385.
22. *Dennis v. United States,* 341 U.S. 494 (1951).
23. *Id.* at 509.
24. *Id.* at 516–17.
25. *Yates v. United States,* 354 U.S. 298 (1957).
26. *Id.* at 321, 322.
27. *Id.* at 324–25.
28. *Scales v. United States,* 367 U.S. 203 (1961).
29. *Brandenburg v. Ohio, supra* note 5, at 447.
30. The seditious conspiracy statute is 18 U.S.C. § 2384. *See also* New York Times, April 8, 1988, at A14; New York Times, January 12, 1989, at A24; New York Times, November 28, 1989, at A23.
31. *Ollman v. Toll,* 518 F. Supp. 1196, 1201–2; *aff'd,* 704 F.2d 139 (4th Cir. 1983).
32. *Clark v. Library of Congress,* 750 F.2d 89 (D.C. Cir. 1984); *Socialist Workers Party v. Attorney General,* 642 F. Supp. 1357 (S.D.N.Y. 1986).
33. *Hobson v. Wilson,* 737 F.2d 1, 28 (D.C. Cir. 1984).
34. *Blitz v. Donovan,* 538 F. Supp. 1119, 1125 (D.D.C. 1982), *vac. as moot,* 459 U.S. 1095 (1983). *See also Cooper v. Ross,* 472 F. Supp. 802 (E.D. Ark. 1979) (college professor's membership in Progressive Labor party protected under First Amendment).
35. *See Blitz v. Donovan, supra; see also Shapiro v. Roudebush,* 413 F. Supp. 1177 (D. Mass. 1976).
36. *Scales v. United States, supra* note 28, at 221–23.
37. *Id.* at 232.
38. *United States v. Robel,* 389 U.S. 258 (1967); *Aptheker v. Secretary of State,* 378 U.S. 500 (1964).
39. *Keyishian v. Board of Regents,* 385 U.S. 589 (1967).
40. *See* L. Tribe, *American Constitutional Law,* 1015 (2d ed. 1988); *see also Shapiro v. Roudebush, supra* note 35.
41. *Ozonoff v. Berzak,* 744 F.2d 224 (1st Cir. 1984).
42. *Hinton v. Devine,* 633 F. Supp. 1023 (E.D. Pa. 1986).
43. *See Schware v. Board of Bar Examiners,* 353 U.S. 232 (1957); *Schnei-*

der v. Smith, 390 U.S. 17 (1968); *Greene v. McElroy*, 360 U.S. 474 (1959); *Aptheker v. Secretary of State*, 378 U.S. 500 (1964); *United States v. Brown*, 381 U.S. 437 (1965); *United States v. Robel*, 389 U.S. 258 (1967). *See generally* Tribe, *supra* note 40, at 1017–18.

44. *United States v. Lemon*, 723 F.2d 922, 938 (D.C. Cir. 1983); *See also United States v. Rosenberg*, 806 F.2d 1169 (3d Cir. 1986); *but cf. United States v. Rosenberg*, 888 F.2d 1406 (D.C. Cir. 1989) (severe sentences for weapons possession and other similar charges imposed on political radicals).

45. *Baraldini v. Meese*, 691 F. Supp. 432, 443 (D.D.C. 1988).

46. *United States v. Abel*, 469 U.S. 45 (1984); *cf. United States v. Yarborough*, 852 F.2d 1522 (9th Cir. 1988).

47. *Baird v. State Bar of Arizona*, 401 U.S. 1 (1971); *In re Stolar*, 401 U.S. 23 (1971). *But cf. Law Students Civil Rights Research Council v. Wadmond*, 401 U.S. 154 (1971).

48. *Pushinsky v. West Virginia State Board of Law Examiners*, 266 S.E.2d 444 (W. Va. 1980).

49. *Clark v. Library of Congress*; 750 F.2d 89, 94–95 (D.C. Cir. 1984) (dictum); *Socialist Workers Party v. Attorney General*, 642 F. Supp. 1357 (S.D.N.Y. 1986); *See also Turner v. Air Transport Lodge*, 590 F.2d 409 (2d Cir. 1978) (protections of communist beliefs for union member under labor laws).

50. Exec. Order No. 11785, 39 Fed. Reg. 20053 (1974).

51. *See, e.g., Alliance to End Repression v. Chicago*, 742 F.2d 1007 (7th Cir. 1984); *Hobson v. Wilson*, 737 F.2d 1 (D.C. Cir. 1984); *Handschu v. Special Services Division*, 605 F. Supp. 1384 (S.D.N.Y. 1985), *aff'd*, 787 F.2d 828 (2d Cir. 1986); *See generally* Chevigny, *Politics and Law in the Control of Local Surveillance*, 69 Cornell L. Rev. 735 (1984).

52. Quoted in Elliff, *The Attorney General's Guidelines for FBI Investigations*, 69 Cornell L. Rev. 785, 808 (1984).

53. *Id.* at 809–10.

54. *Alliance to End Repression v. Chicago*, *supra* note 51, at 1015.

55. *Id.* at 1027–28.

56. *Bryant v. Zimmerman*, 278 U.S. 63 (1928); *Communist Party v. Subversive Activities Control Board*, 367 U.S. 1 (1961).

57. *Brandenburg v. Ohio*, *supra* note 5.

58. *E.g., United States v. Yarborough*, 852 F.2d 1522 (9th Cir. 1988).

59. *Marshall v. Bramer*, 110 F.R.D. 232, 235, *aff'd*, 828 F.2d 355 (6th Cir. 1987); *see also Courier-Journal v. Marshall*, 828 F.2d 361 (6th Cir. 1987) (denying press and public access to Klan membership lists).

60. *National Alliance v. United States*, 710 F.2d 868 (D.C. Cir. 1983).

61. *McMullan v. Carson*, 754 F.2d 936, 940 (11th Cir. 1985). *Contra Curle v. Ward*, 59 App. Div. 2d 286 (3d Dept. 1977), *modified*, 46 N.Y.2d 1048 (1979) (state corrections officer).

62. *Blameuser v. Andrews*, 630 F.2d 538, 544 (7th Cir. 1980). In 1986 the army promulgated guidelines barring service personnel from joining "hate groups." *See* New York Times, October 30, 1986, at A23.

63. *See Schenck v. United States*, *supra* note 6; *Abrams v. United States*, *supra* note 8. *See also Hartzel v. United States*, 322 U.S. 680 (1944) (World War II prosecution).

64. *United States v. Truong Dinh Hung*, 629 F.2d 908, 927, (4th Cir. 1981).

65. These statutes include 18 U.S.C. § 798 (criminal punishment for publishing certain types of classified information), 18 U.S.C. § 794 (communicating national defense information to a foreign government). *See Snepp v. United States*, 444 U.S. 507, 517, n. 3 (1980) (dissenting opinion).

66. 18 U.S.C. §§ 793, 794.

67. *New York Times Co. v. United States*, 403 U.S. 713, 730 (1971).

68. *United States v. Progressive, Inc.*, 467 F. Supp. 990 (W.D. Wisc. 1979).

69. *United States v. Morison*, 844 F.2d 1057 (4th Cir. 1988).

70. *E.g., McGehee v. Casey*, 718 F.2d 1137 (D.C. Cir. 1983).

71. *United States v. Marchetti*, 466 F.2d 1309 (4th Cir. 1972); *Snepp v. United States*, 444 U.S. 507 (1980).

72. *Haig v. Agee*, 453 U.S. 280 (1981).

73. Intelligence Identities Protection Act, 50 U.S.C. § 421.

74. *See American Foreign Service Association v. Garfinkel*, 109 S. Ct. 1307 (1989).

75. *See* Neuborne and Shapiro, *The Nylon Curtain: America's National Border and the Free Flow of Ideas*, 26 Wm. and Mary L. Rev. 719 (1985); *see also Free Trade in Ideas*, ACLU Public Policy Report (May 1984).

76. Foreign Agents Registration Act, 22 U.S.C. §§ 611–21; *see Viereck v. United States*, 318 U.S. 236 (1943).

77. *See Attorney General v. Irish People, Inc.*, 796 F.2d 520 (D.C. Cir. 1986).

78. *Communist Party v. Subversive Activities Control Board*, 367 U.S. 1, 104 (1961) (emphasis in original).

79. *Palestine Information Office v. Schultz*, 853 F.2d 932 (D.C. Cir., 1988).

80. *Mendelsohn v. Meese*, 686 F. Supp. 75 (S.D.N.Y. 1988).

81. *See* 8 U.S.C. §§ 1101, *et seq.*

82. *Kleindienst v. Mandel*, 408 U.S. 753 (1972).

83. *Abourezk v. Reagan,* 785 F.2d 1043 (D.C. Cir., 1986), *aff'd by an equally divided Court,* 484 U.S. 1 (1987).

84. *See American-Arab Anti-Discrimination Committee v. Meese,* 714 F. Supp. 1060, (C.D. Cal. 1989).

85. *See* New York Times, February 2, 1990, at A6. The temporary statute is § 901 of the Foreign Relations Authorization Act, Pub. L. No. 100-24, 101 Stat. 1331 (1987) (1988).

86. *Lamont v. Postmaster General,* 381 U.S. 301 (1965).

87. *See* Omnibus Trade and Competitiveness Act of 1988, Pub. L. No. 100-418, 102 Stat. 1107 (1988).

88. *Meese v. Keene,* 481 U.S. 465 (1987);

89. *Aptheker v. Secretary of State,* 378 U.S. 500 (1964). Earlier the Supreme Court held that the Secretary of State lacked statutory authority to deny passports on political grounds. *Kent v. Dulles,* 357 U.S. 116 (1958).

90. *Regan v. Wald,* 468 U.S. 222 (1984); *See also Walsh v. Brady,* 729 F. Supp. 118 (D.D.C. 1989).

91. *Haig v. Agee,* 453 U.S. 280 (1981).

92. *Bullfrog Films, Inc. v. Wick,* 847 F.2d 502 (9th Cir. 1988).

93. *Id.* at 512.

94. *Id.* at 511–12; *see also American-Arab Anti-Discrimination Committee v. Meese, supra* note 84.

III

Advocating Unlawful Action

The previous chapter discusses advocacy of the forceful overthrow of government, usually in the context of groups whose ideology insists upon the necessity of using force on a broad scale to spark fundamental, revolutionary change. But more commonly, protest leaders and groups have far less sweeping objectives in mind and are not ideologically committed to advocating the need for violence. Nonetheless even in the context of more traditional protest activities—and certainly in national political causes such as the civil rights, antiwar, and pro-life, and pro-choice movements—the question of urging violent or unlawful acts as a method of achieving a group's political objectives is a frequent issue. Can protestors or activists urge their followers to engage in acts of force, violence, or illegal behavior or conduct? Of course actual acts of violence or illegal behavior can be substantively punished. The free speech issue is whether advocating or urging such actions can be punished as well.

Here too the basic approach comes from *Brandenburg v. Ohio*,[1] which distinguishes between specific incitement to immediate illegal conduct versus more general or theoretical advocacy of such unlawful behavior. Indeed even John Stuart Mill, the patron saint of modern free speech, recognized, "An opinion that corn-dealers are starvers of the poor, or that private property is robbery, ought to be unmolested when simply circulated through the press, but may justly incur punishment when delivered orally to an excited mob assembled before the house of a corn-dealer, or when handed about the same mob in the form of a placard."[2] Advocating or seeking to persuade one's followers to engage in unlawful actions is generally viewed as protected expression, while instructing, instigating, preparing, or planning illegal behavior is generally viewed as impermissible "incitement" of illegality. This core free speech distinction between advocacy and incitement is the essence of the *Brandenburg* ruling that advocacy of force, violence, or law violation cannot be punished unless (1) the advocacy is directed to inciting or producing imminent lawless action and (2) is likely to incite or produce such action.

As one appellate court observed, "incitement" requires not only the specific urging of illegal or harmful behavior, but the high likelihood that the speech will imminently induce such action: "The crucial element to lowering the first amendment shield is the imminence of the threatened evil."[3] Planting a harmful or illegal idea in someone's mind, but one that would not germinate until sometime in the future, is generally immune from punishment under the First Amendment. But difficulties remain over where to draw the line between permissible advocacy and impermissible incitement to illegal behavior.

Two final introductory points should be made. First, the Supreme Court once stated in a labor case that speech that is "an integral part of unlawful conduct in violation of a valid criminal statute" is not protected.[4] In other words, where words themselves are part of a crime, the words are not protected by the First Amendment. As a common-sense proposition, this seems unobjectionable. Words used to help someone actually prepare a fraudulent tax return to protest government policy, for example, can be punished, as compared to words generally urging or advocating tax resistance by protestors. Help-wanted ads in a newspaper that have separate listings for men and women can be penalized as direct acts of employment discrimination.[5] Words that reveal the identity of a secret intelligence operative can be punished, assuming such revelations can validly be made a crime.[6] In all these instances, the speech is literally an integral part of the unlawful conduct or behavior, i.e., the speech is part of the crime. Unfortunately the labor case that articulated this understandable concept did not involve such a scenario. Instead, it concerned punishment for advocating an illegal strike, and the Court failed to distinguish carefully between words that constitute part of the commission of a crime and words that advocate or even incite the commission of a crime.

Secondly, a distinction should be drawn between speech that may cause, induce, or incite the speaker's followers, adherents, or supporters to engage in unlawful behavior—the subject of this chapter—as opposed to words that may anger or provoke the speaker's opponents or members of the general public—

which will be discussed in the next chapter. Different considerations might govern the validity of suppressing speech that
stirs one's followers as compared to speech that provokes one's
adversaries. Arguably, protestors should be more accountable
for causing illegal actions by their own supporters than for
sparking violent reactions by their opponents. Yet here, too,
courts have not always carefully differentiated the two situations but have often spoken without distinction of punishing
speech that threatens or causes a breach of the peace either by
one's followers or by one's opponents.[7]

ADVOCATING THE USE OF FORCE OR VIOLENCE

**Can speakers advocate the use of force or violence by their
supporters to accomplish their political objectives?**

Yes, unless the speech immediately generates acts of violence by the followers. But this was not always true.

Until the *Brandenburg* decision, rabble-rousing speakers
who exhorted their followers to engage in acts of violence
were often punished for incitement to riot, solicitation of illegal
behavior, or similar charges, regardless of whether their followers immediately took the cue and actual violence ensued. For
example, during the labor strife of the early part of the century,
radicals were prosecuted for publicly urging striking workers
to "break foreman's windows at their homes. Watch the scabs
when they come from work, lay for them, especially on payday.
Take them in a dark alley and hit them with a lead pipe. . . .
Don't forget to bump off a few now and then."[8] Another worker
was convicted for urging his fellow strikers to "go to the silk
mills, parade through the streets, and club them out of the
mills."[9] In the 1960s, a black militant speaker in Harlem, giving
a speech following several days of rioting touched off when an
off-duty police officer killed a black youth, condemned the
police and urged the crowd to "[d]eclare war on them and every
time they kill one of us damn it, we'll kill one of them . . . we
had better stop talking about violence as a dirty word. . . . [w]e
will not be fully free until we smash this state completely and
totally. . . . And in that process of making [our] state we're
going to have to kill a lot of these cops, a lot of these judges,
and we'll have to go up against their army."[10] The speaker was

convicted for advocating the overthrow of the government by
force and violence.

Can speakers engage in this kind of rough, strident, violence-advocating talk post-*Brandenburg*?

The *Brandenburg* formula clearly makes it much more difficult to punish such speech because it requires both incitement
to and likelihood of "imminent lawless action."

The Court has dealt with two relevant cases since *Brandenburg*. In one case students had been arrested for disorderly
conduct for blocking a street during a campus antiwar demonstration. As police moved the demonstrators onto the sidewalks, one of them shouted, "We'll take the fucking streets
later [or again]." The Court ruled that this remark does not
constitute incitement to imminent lawless action; "nothing
more than advocacy of illegal action at some indefinite future
time" was involved, with no evidence that the words were
intended or likely to produce imminent disorder.[11]

A decade later the Court held that civil rights leaders of a
long-running economic boycott against white merchants could
not be held civilly liable for sporadic and occasional acts of
violence to persons or property that occurred during the boycott where those actions were not directly traceable to the
activities or speeches of the leaders. Even though one of those
leaders had given a fiery speech stating that people who violated
the boycott would be "disciplined" and that there was a possibility "necks would be broken," the Court nonetheless found that
"mere *advocacy* of the use of force or violence does not remove
speech from the protection of the First Amendment."[12] But the
Court also observed, "If that language had been followed by
acts of violence, a substantial question would be presented
whether [the speaker] could be held liable for the consequences
of that unlawful conduct."[13] Since some of the sporadic violence
occurred weeks or months after the speech, however, the Court
found no incitement of imminent lawless action.

It should be noted that, in the wake of the urban riots and
disorders of the 1960s, Congress made it a federal crime to
travel interstate or use the facilities of interstate commerce to
"incite a riot." This so-called Rap Brown statute, aimed at the
perceived activities of "outside agitators" who supposedly came
into communities to foment violence, was part of the basis for

prosecuting the Chicago Seven for causing disorders at the Democratic National Convention in 1968. The statute was upheld, as written, by lower court rulings.[14]

Since advocating violence cannot be punished when violence does not directly or imminently result, the mere expression of a wish to have violence occur surely cannot serve as the basis for punishment. Thus a police department could not fire an employee who, upon hearing that President Reagan had been shot, told a coworker, "[I]f they go for him again, I hope they get him."[15] Nor can "planting" in someone's mind the idea of committing violence or engaging in harmful behavior be punished. Accordingly, news media have not been held accountable for the consequences of descriptions or depictions of violence that then supposedly caused a viewer or reader to commit similar acts.[16]

THREATS OF VIOLENCE

Can an individual be punished for making verbal threats to commit acts of violence against government officials?

It depends on whether they are true threats. Closely related to the issue of advocating violence is the question of more specific or focused threats to commit or solicit others to commit violence. Real threats of, or attempts at, actual violence are punishable under traditional criminal laws. But often such "threats" are made as part of a political expression or political speech.

It is a federal crime to make "any threat to take the life" of the president.[17] This is a reasonable prohibition to the extent it is designed to deter and punish serious plots of violence against the president. But political speakers, caught up in the heat of debate or public advocacy, will sometimes make apparently rhetorical threats to "get" the president. Statutes punishing such "threats" trace their origins to the Middle Ages when it was a capital offense, under the Statute of Treasons of 1352, to imagine, let alone publicly wish for, the death of the king. "The [S]tatute was interpreted to declare treasonous any intention, however manifested, which pointed at the death of the King, including mere words which showed such an intent."[18] Over the years, dozens of people have been prosecuted under the federal statute for making harsh but harmless statements such as "I wish [President] Wilson was in Hell, and if I had the power I would put him there" or displaying a poster that urged Roosevelt to be hanged.[19]

In a major case during the Vietnam War era, a speaker addressed a rally in Washington, D.C., and gave an impassioned speech against the war and the draft, during which he stated: "They always holler at us to get an education. And now I have already received my draft classification as I-A and I have got to report for my physical this Monday coming. I am not going. If they ever make me carry a rifle, the first man I want to get in my sights is L.B.J. They are not going to make me kill my black brothers." The Supreme Court upheld the statute as written but further ruled that since the law "makes criminal a form of pure speech," it should be interpreted to apply only to "true" threats and not to the kind of "political hyperbole" that the defendant had expressed. Given the national commitment to robust political debate and the recognition that "the language of the political arena . . . is often vituperative, abusive and inexact," the words did not constitute a "true threat."[20]

Despite this decision, there have been many questionable prosecutions under this statute. The lower courts are divided over whether a person can be convicted for simply making a threat of harm and intending it to be understood as a serious expression of intent to harm the president, regardless of whether the speaker actually has the serious intention or the capacity to try to carry out the threat.[21] Thus some courts have held that speakers can be prosecuted if they knew what they were saying, regardless of whether they intended to carry out the threat. Context and detail separate true threats from political rhetoric, hyperbole, or anti-Establishment speech. But the fact that the threat is uttered within the context of a political diatribe will not necessarily render the remarks protected. In other words, expression of political opposition is protected; a true threat, even though motivated by political opposition, is not. Thus, for example, a statement by a disturbed drifter to the police that he was planning to "eliminate all the pigs from the President on down," was viewed as a crude, though protected, method of expressing anti-Establishment antagonism; but more specific threats to kill the president made during the same conversation with police were held punishable.[22]

Not only are threats of physical harm against the president punished, but Congress has also made it a crime to threaten to harm a former president or vice-president or his family or even a "major candidate" for such offices or their spouses.[23] Presumably, that law would also be interpreted not to reach political rhetoric or hyperbole as distinct from statements that really are meant as or understood as actual threats.

What about making threats of harm against people other than high-level officials?

It is also a federal crime to use any facility of interstate commerce—e.g., mail, telephone, television—to communicate a threat of physical harm. Such laws are primarily directed at actual extortion and blackmail, but they have sometimes been employed in a political setting.

For example, a Jewish Defense League official was convicted for stating, at a public televised press conference, that Yasser Arafat, head of the PLO, would be "assassinated." The court ruled that whether the statements were "mere political hyperbole" or really showed an express intent to make a threat and carry it out was for the jury to resolve. As to free speech concerns, the court said: "So long as the threat on its face and in the circumstances in which it is made is so unequivocal, unconditional, immediate and specific as to the person threatened, as to convey a gravity of purpose and imminent prospect of execution, the statute may be properly applied. . . . '[C]ommunication has become so interlocked with violent conduct as to constitute for all practical purposes part of the [proscribed] action itself.' "[24] Another JDL activist was punished for proclaiming that the JDL was offering a $500 reward for anyone who killed or injured a member of the American Nazi Party in defense of the Jewish community. A California appellate court ruled that this was not mere political hyperbole. "[T]here was sufficient likelihood of his solicitation being interpreted as a call to arms, as a preparation of his group to violent action."[25]

Under similar reasoning, a court upheld possible liability of the paramilitary magazine, *Soldier of Fortune,* for carrying what were alleged to be thinly veiled "murder for hire" classified ads, where they arguably lead to illegal agreements to kill or harm victims; but a different appellate court rejected liability as too attenuated.[26] Likewise, a threat of bodily harm to a person in the Federal Witness Protection Program is not the kind of rhetorical or political threat that is part of the market place of ideas. "The statute's limited scope takes it out of the realm of social or political conflict where threats to engage in behavior that may be unlawful may nevertheless be part of the marketplace of ideas, broadly conceived to embrace the rough competition that is so much a staple of political discourse."[27] But statements that are "worded in the rowdy argot of the streets," such as an angry threatening letter from a client to a criminal lawyer appointed to represent him, yet do not "clearly convey a threat of injury" cannot be punished as threats.[28]

LAWS AGAINST HARASSMENT OR INTIMIDATION

To what extent can laws that make it unlawful to "harass," "coerce," or "intimidate" individuals or to "interfere with" public officials be validly applied to political speech and protest?

The answer is unclear and depends on how precisely the terms are defined and applied.

The purpose of the presidential and similar threats statute is clear: protecting top officials and others from serious threats of violence. The task for courts has been to confine the reach of such laws to that purpose and exclude their application to political rhetoric. Many state laws that more broadly make it a crime to "threaten," "harass," "coerce," or "intimidate" other individuals or "interfere with" public officials raise the same problems.

For example, a Houston, Texas, ordinance made it a crime to "oppose, molest, abuse or interrupt" a police officer making an arrest. A gay rights activist was prosecuted for questioning police who were arresting a friend of his. The Supreme Court found the ordinance defectively written because it broadly made punishable any interference with a police officer, including valid "verbal criticism and challenge directed at police officers" with no proof of actual disorderly conduct or direct interference with law enforcement functions.[29] Because the First Amendment protects a significant amount of verbal criticism and challenge against the police, the ordinance was too broadly written.

Another good example of overly broad statutes involves a man convicted of "intimidation" for making vulgar remarks to a woman on the street; the remarks were construed as a threat of sexual assault. Though the man's particular words could be punished, the statute was defective because it allowed punishment for even harmless words that might conceivably be viewed as a threat of illegal conduct, regardless of intent or likelihood. This would be too sweeping a chill on advocacy of political and social change. "[T]hreats of sit-ins, marches in the street, mass picketing and other such activities are frequently threats to commit acts prohibited by law. . . . The State, of course, may punish minor infractions when they actually occur. But to punish as a felony the mere communication of a threat to commit such a minor infraction where the purpose is to induce action—*any* action—by someone is to chill the kind of 'uninhibited, robust and wide-open' debate on public issues that lies at the core of the first amendment."[30] In throwing out a similar "threats" statute challenged by civil rights activists, a lower court ruled that making it a crime to "threaten" to commit any crime, no matter how minor, is an unacceptable limitation on political protest speech which often seeks to threaten consequences or "coerce" action.[31] In another case, the Supreme Court said, "The claim that the expressions were intended to exercise a coercive impact on [a realtor] does not remove them from the reach of the First Amendment."[32] But a person opposed to racial integration who wrote letters threatening officials of an organization that placed minority children for adoption could be convicted of unlawful intimidation under federal fair housing laws.[33]

Courts have also tried to keep laws against harassment within First Amendment boundaries. For example, a bankruptcy rule against harassing of debtors could not prevent a creditor from parking a truck outside a debtor's premises with a sign saying that the debtor "does *not* pay suppliers."[34]

Courts have upheld federal and state statutes banning "obscene, harassing, or abusive" telephone calls, ruling that such laws only punished calls made solely or intentionally to harass, even if the abusive calls have an arguably political content. But since the distinction between permissible communication and punishable harassment is not a clear one, the courts have been sharply divided over the proper application of such laws to callers who use the phone to press legitimate complaints to officials, albeit in an obnoxious, vituperative, or persistent fashion. In one case, for example, a university student was convicted for repeatedly complaining to university officials about his academic standing in phone calls laced with references to the employees as "pigs," "racist pigs," and "the head pig."[35]

There are limits to protecting people against harassment. An unusual Connecticut statute, the Hunter Harassment Act, was written to protect hunters against interference and harassment by animal rights activists who would approach hunters and try to persuade them of the immorality of their behavior. A federal appeals court ruled that the law was a thinly disguised form of censorship of the ideas of those opposed to hunting, with no compelling interest served by protecting hunters against ideas they might find offensive.[36]

To what extent can protestors be punished for threats or harassment in the context of demonstrations or rallies?

The answer depends on the definition in the law and the setting of the demonstration. In cases involving labor protestors, statutes often prohibit "threatening language" directed at strikebreaking workers to "intimidate" or influence them not to go to work. One law also outlawed "persisting in talking to or communicating in any manner with such person . . . against his . . . will." Noting that public speech is often provocative and challenging, one appellate court held that the "threatening language" provision was valid only if limited to a communicated intent to inflict physical or other harm on any person or property.[37] That would be a limited and proper ban on "fighting words," i.e., words likely to create an immediate breach of the peace. The "persistent talking" clause, however, was invalid because it "could be applied to peaceful requests to honor a picket line, to attempts to inform strikebreakers of the union's grievances, and to general calls for worker solidarity." Another appellate court questioned a Texas statute that had been used against organizing efforts by the Farm Workers Union because it outlawed "insulting, threatening or obscene language . . . to . . . intimidate" workers. The court upheld the statute on the stipulation that it only covered systematic use of intimidating or coercive speech that could be construed as "fighting words."[38]

Can foreign diplomats be protected against "harassment" by demonstrators?

Yes, to some degree. A federal statute designed to protect foreign embassy or consulate officials makes it a crime to "intimidate, coerce, threaten or harass" foreign officials.[39] An appellate court upheld this statute against a challenge by demonstrators protesting at the Honduran consulate in New Orleans since the law permits peaceful picketing or expression near such facilities and "merely proscribes actions of a threatening or intimidating nature." Moreover, words like "harass" were not vague in this setting since they were addressed to "such activities as may seriously alarm or persecute foreign officials" and only when done "wilfully." The court also noted that similar terms, prohibiting actions that coerce, obstruct, intimidate, or harass, were included in various voting rights and civil rights statutes without objection.[40] The Supreme Court seemed to put its stamp of approval on that reading of the law in a case involving a similar, but much more restrictive, District of Columbia statute that limited protest speech targeted at embassies and consulates. In striking down a portion of the law that made it a crime to display signs critical of the foreign government, the Court pointed to the ban on attempts to "intimidate, coerce, threaten or harass" foreign officials as a less restrictive—and presumably valid—way to protect the safety and security, but not the feelings or sensibilities, of foreign dignitaries and officials.[41]

Can abortion-providing clinics be protected against harassment or intimidation by demonstrators?

The problem of the extent to which government can restrict harassing or threatening speech has proven particularly difficult in the controversy over the protest activities of anti-abortion groups, such as "Operation Rescue," that demonstrate at medical facilities where abortions are performed and try to deter or prevent women, often forcibly, from having abortions. In such a highly charged setting, the line between persuasion and intimidation is a difficult one to draw. Courts have tried to strike a delicate balance between the free speech rights of the demonstrators and the free choice rights of women: clinics and their patients can be protected from physical obstruction, threats, intimidation, assault, and excessive noise that substantially interferes with the provision of medical services, but not from the content of anti-abortion messages or the tense, agitated, and intimidating "atmosphere" that the mere fact of a demonstration may create.[42]

Similarly difficult issues are raised by civil suits filed against anti-abortion demonstrators by clinics, charging that the repeated acts of the demonstrators constitute a racketeering or criminal enterprise under federal laws designed to allow those victimized by organized crime a civil remedy. The ACLU has generally criticized the broad use of these anti-racketeering laws, particularly where the activities that are the target of such suits have such a large free speech component. For example, do sit-ins at abortion centers—which can validly be punished as trespasses—turn into "attempted extortion" if designed to intimidate the employees and patients of the center? One court has described these problems as follows:

> Attempts to persuade another to action are clearly within the scope of the First Amendment. . . . The fact that the defendants' speech was intended to persuade patients to forgo their abortions or employees to leave their employment at an abortion-providing clinic does not, in itself, corrupt the speech nor diminish its protection under the Constitution. . . . Such pure speech activities cannot support a claim of extortion. Similarly, peaceful picketing, leafletting, and demonstrating enjoy the same freedom of expression. . . . That this expression was designed to have an "offensive" or "coercive" effect is of little significance provided that the means of expression retained its peaceful nature.
>
> The First Amendment will not, however, offer sanctuary for violence. . . .[43]

The court concluded that unauthorized entries that placed patients and employees in fear could constitute extortion, and a pattern of such activity would provide the basis for a racketeering claim and monetary damages against the anti-abortion demonstrators.

ECONOMIC BOYCOTTS FOR POLITICAL PURPOSES

Can economic pressure or boycotts be threatened or organized to achieve political objectives?

Basically, yes. The abortion clinic cases also raise the question of whether protestors can organize and apply economic pressures and boycotts to achieve political or social objectives. For example, in the clinic case, anti-abortion protestors could not be sued for an economic conspiracy to restrain trade, business, or competition because the objective of the group was not to reduce or monopolize economic competition, but to put a particular clinic out of business for essentially political, not economic, reasons.

Can protestors engage in labor boycotts or economic pressure?

To some degree, but the area is heavily regulated by federal labor law. Long ago the Court recognized that peaceful union and labor picketing and demonstrations are protected by the First Amendment, even though the consequence is to bring economic and consumer pressure to bear upon business.[44] Since then, however, the Court has afforded government broad authority to regulate the labor-management relationship through the enactment of comprehensive labor laws that control the permissibility of strikes and boycotts used to achieve economic objectives, so long as such restrictions do not exceed First Amendment boundaries. Thus, for example, secondary boycotts (where a union with a dispute against an employer pickets or boycotts an uninvolved third party such as a market that handles the employer's products) and refusals to honor labor contracts even for political motives (such as where longshoremen, to protest the 1980 Russian invasion of Afghanistan, refused to unload cargoes shipped from the Soviet Union) are not protected by the First Amendment.

> We have consistently rejected the claim that secondary picketing by labor unions in violation of [the labor laws] is a protected activity under the First Amendment. . . . It would seem even clearer that conduct designed not to communicate but to coerce merits still less consideration under the First Amendment. . . . The labor laws reflect a careful balancing of interests. . . . There are many ways in which a union and its individual members may express their opposition to Russian foreign policy without infringing upon the rights of others.[45]

But peaceful handbilling to make consumers aware of a labor dispute, without attempting to coerce workers or customers through the use of a picket line, is protected by the First Amendment. "The loss of customers because they read a hand-bill urging them not to patronize a business, and not because they are intimidated by a line of picketers, is the result of mere persuasion, and the neutral who reacts is doing no more than what its customers honestly want it to do."[46]

Are consumer or political boycotts allowed?

Yes. Outside the labor relations context courts recognize broader First Amendment protection for consumer boycotts organized for political and social purposes, not to restrain trade for economic objectives. The most significant case upheld the right of the NAACP and other civil rights groups to bring economic pressure to bear against discriminatory merchants. The protestors were not motivated by a desire to lessen competition or to reap economic benefits, but by the aim of vindicating rights of equality and freedom lying at the heart of the Constitution. Absent actual or threatened violence or physical coercion, a long economic boycott that uses economic pressures to bring about social and political change is permissible, and the NAACP could not be sued for damages by local merchants who lost business because of the boycott.[47] For similar reasons an appeals court rejected a suit by Missouri against the National Organization of Women for having organized a boycott of businesses in states that had refused to ratify the Equal Rights Amendment. Such a politically motivated boycott could not, consistently with the First Amendment, be a violation of the antitrust laws prohibiting conspiracies to restrain trade and business.[48] But in an important 1990 case, where District of Columbia criminal defense lawyers had agreed to refuse to accept court appointments in criminal cases until the fees for court-appointed work were increased, the Supreme Court ruled that such politically motivated economic pressure was not protected by the First Amendment because the goal of the action was to gain economic advantage.[49]

But not all politically motivated actions with harmful economic consequences can be justified as protected free speech. When the Boston Symphony Orchestra cancelled a contract with Vanessa Redgrave, the politically active actress, because of fears that her prominent pro-PLO views would cause third parties to disrupt the performance, an appeals court ruled the BSO was liable for damages for breach of contract, though not for violating her civil rights.[50] Indeed, the appeals court suggested the BSO itself had a First Amendment right of artistic expression to decline to put on the show if it feared protests against Redgrave would undermine and distract from the artistic integrity of the performance, without being punished under government antidiscrimination laws for making that choice.

Finally, free speech rights also protect organized efforts to form groups and use lawful and peaceful means, such as holding meetings, filing lawsuits, and petitioning government, to oppose the plans and actions of other groups and individuals.[51] But the Supreme Court has said that "baseless litigation" is not protected as a form of speech or petition.[52]

ADVOCATING NONVIOLENT VIOLATION OF LAW

Can peaceful, nonviolent violations of the law be advocated?
It depends. Courts have had a surprisingly difficult time deciding to what extent speakers can urge their followers to violate or disobey valid laws in a peaceful or nonviolent manner. Such advocacy can reflect various points on a spectrum. At one end is speech only mildly critical of public policy but that might somehow indirectly and ultimately persuade people to disobey the law. At the other is speech that directly facilitates or participates in the violation of law.

Courts have struggled to find an acceptable point between suppressing all speech that might remotely inspire illegal action and tolerating the unrestrained advocacy of immediate and specific law violation. Sometimes courts ask whether the speaker urged or intended specific acts of illegal behavior or merely engaged in more general condemnation of existing law and policy. Others draw a distinction between simply advocating resistance or disobedience to law, as opposed to advising, preparing, and assisting people to violate the law. Efforts to fit the issues into the *Brandenburg* mold of "imminent incitement of lawless action" become a bit cramped, because *Brandenburg* dealt with advocacy of violent or revolutionary change, not just peaceful disobedience or resistance.[53] Of course the line between peaceful and forceful action is so often indistinct. Nonviolent action can have radical consequences, as the mass movements of this century have shown. A single unarmed student stopping a tank in Tianemin Square can be a revolutionary event.

The issue has prominently arisen in four notable contexts: draft resistance, tax protest, advocacy of drug use, and advocacy of unconventional sexual behavior.

Draft Resistance

Can peaceful resistance to the draft or the military be advocated?

Yes, unless the advocacy directly and specifically incites particular unlawful acts of resistance.

In connection with World War I, courts said that the First Amendment did not protect speakers who urged resistance to the war—even in the mildest way. Both well-known and unknown speakers alike were punished for directly, or even indirectly, suggesting violation of the draft or military preparedness laws. The unstated judicial premise was that such remarks would have the tendency to cause the listeners to act illegally. Similar prosecutions were upheld during World War II.[54] And later, even during formal peacetime, the First Amendment did not protect a religiously motivated college dean who told male students, "Do not let them coerce you into registering," or a pacifist doctor who counseled his stepson not to register for the draft and offered him financial assistance to leave the country—even though the youth ignored the advice and registered.[55] On the other hand, even during World War II the Court tossed out convictions of Jehovah's Witnesses who simply said it was "wrong for the President to send our boys [to war] for no purpose at all."[56]

This was the precedent the courts would try to work with in dealing with the turbulent antiwar protests and antidraft advocacy of the Vietnam era.

In the first case to reach the Supreme Court, it was ruled that Julian Bond, a young civil rights and antiwar activist, could not be denied his seat in a state legislature because he criticized the war and expressed his admiration for draft resisters. Such statements of opinion did not come close to counseling illegal conduct and could not "be interpreted as a call to unlawful refusal to be drafted" or an incitement to violation of law.[57] Nor could an offensive sign, stating "Fuck the Draft," be punished as an incitement to draft resistance: "At least so long as there is no showing of an intent to incite disobedience to or disruption of the draft, Cohen [cannot] consistently with the First and Fourteenth Amendments be punished for asserting the evident position on the inutility or immorality of the draft his jacket reflected."[58] In addition, actions by draft boards to punitively reclassify men with a valid statutory deferment, as punishment for antiwar protest and burning of their draft cards, were found to be "lawless."[59]

None of these cases involved a direct call for illegal draft resistance. In the one well-known case that did, Dr. Benjamin Spock and other prominent dissenters had organized and publicized a "Call to Resist Illegitimate Authority." The organizers also held a press conference to announce their activities, and some of the leaders later arranged and participated in ceremonies where draft cards were burned or turned in. Prosecuted for conspiring to counsel draft evasion, the defendants claimed their activities were protected by the First Amendment.

An appellate court partly agreed. Where a protest group's activities aim at legal goals—opposing the war and the draft—but involve methods that are both legal (holding rallies to oppose the war and the draft) and illegal (counseling refusal to obey draft laws and facilitating disobedience), a participant who specifically manifests an intent to adhere to, advocate or participate in the illegal components can be punished. But those who merely organize and sign "The Call," without specific intent to adhere to or further the illegal acts suggested in it, cannot be punished. Thus Dr. Spock was acquitted. "[H]is speech was limited to condemnation of the war and the draft, and lacked any words or content of counseling. The jury could not find proscribed advocacy from the mere fact . . . that he hoped that his frequent stating of his views might give young men 'courage to take active steps in draft resistance.' This is a natural consequence of vigorous speech."[60] General antiwar and antidraft remarks could not be the basis for punishment; nor could vigorous criticism of the government's program, even though the natural consequences might be interference with the program or unlawful action. The court thus accepted the distinction between the statement of an idea which may prompt those who hear it to take unlawful action and advocacy that such action be taken.

Although the issue remains unsettled, it would seem that a direct public call for peaceful violation of the draft or military laws, without advocating, identifying, or taking more specific steps to assist such violations, cannot be punished under the First Amendment.

Does the First Amendment provide the right to violate valid draft laws?

No. The Court upheld the convictions of draft resisters who publicly burned their draft cards. The Court explained that the law that punished the knowing destruction of draft registration documents was a valid governmental effort to further the effective functioning of the draft and not an impermissible attempt to silence antiwar criticism. In reaching that conclusion, the Court formulated an important general principle to measure government regulation of expressive or symbolic conduct or behavior:

> [W]hen "speech" and "nonspeech" elements are combined in the same course of conduct, a sufficiently important governmental interest in regulating the nonspeech element can justify incidental limitations on First Amendment freedoms. . . . [A] government regulation is sufficiently justified if it is within the constitutional power of the Government; if it furthers an important or substantial governmental interest; if the governmental interest is unrelated to the suppression of free expression; and if the incidental restriction on alleged First Amendment freedoms is no greater than is essential to the furtherance of that interest.[61]

During the draft registration of the early 1980s, this principle was applied to uphold the policy of selectively prosecuting those nonregistrants who had written the government and stated that they were protesting the draft registration by not complying. The Court ruled that these individuals were not being singled out because of their antiwar statements, but because they had called the government's attention to illegal refusals and had declined the government's offer to register rather than be prosecuted. The fact that the government's enforcement policy mostly targeted vocal dissenters was merely an incidental and justifiable consequence and was not intended to punish dissent, especially since no one was investigated for criticizing the draft registration, but only for refusing to comply with it.[62]

Tax Protest

Can violation of the tax laws be advocated?

It depends on whether the advocacy offers specific assistance on how to violate the laws.

Protesting taxes, like protesting war, is a noble part of America's tradition of dissent. The famed Boston Tea Party was a tax protest, and "no taxation without representation" was one of the rallying cries of American independence. Henry David Thoreau was a famous nineteenth century tax protestor and spent time in jail for his refusal to pay taxes to support the Mexican-American War.

Today tax protest occurs on both sides of the political aisle. Liberals often protest the payment of taxes to support military and defense programs. Conservatives often claim that federal taxes are unconstitutional examples of "Big Government." In cases involving both types of groups courts have drawn distinctions between general condemnation of taxes and specific advice on how to claim improper exemption and also between legitimate protest organizations and "seminars" which are simply a sham for conscious tax fraud.

For example, antiwar protestors have claimed a "war tax deduction" from their income taxes for the percentage of their tax dollar that supports military activities. Congress responded by adding a separate $500 frivolousness penalty for those people improperly claiming deductions that have no justifiable basis in law. Protestors have challenged this penalty as a restriction on their ability to protest on their tax returns, but the courts have rejected this argument.

> [T]axpayers were not penalized for expressing their political moral or religious beliefs on their returns, or for attaching letters to their returns stating their opposition to military spending. Instead . . . [the] penalty was assessed against them simply because they filed returns containing

substantially incorrect self-assessments based on clearly unallowable credits for "war taxes." . . .

Plaintiffs' attempt to transform a sincere belief in the moral rectitude of their vision of what the polity should be into absolution for flouting the laws of the polity that exists is not shielded by the First Amendment.[63]

Similar reasoning has sustained the application of penalties to conservative protestors who reduced their taxes 13 percent because of inflation.[64]

Right-wing tax resisters who hold seminars and advise people how to claim or manufacture unfounded exemptions or deductions based on clearly rejected economic or constitutional theories have been punished as well. Courts have upheld convictions for aiding and abetting tax evasion where tax protestors at public meetings asserted the unconstitutionality of the graduated income tax—which would be protected speech—but also recommended that members of the audience file false and fraudulent income tax returns and withholding certificates:

Although the speeches here do not invite the type of imminent lawless activity referred to in criminal syndicalism cases, the defendants did go beyond mere advocacy of tax reform. They explained how to avoid withholding, and their speeches and explanations incited several individuals to activity that violated federal law and had the potential of substantially hindering the administration of the revenue.[65]

Thus, giving speeches advocating violation of the tax laws is one thing; showing people how to prepare fraudulent returns is quite another.[66]

Supreme Court Justice Anthony M. Kennedy, while an appeals court judge, drew similar distinctions in a tax protest case.

Words alone may constitute a criminal offense, even if they spring from the anterior motive to effect political or social change. Where an indictment is for counseling, the circumstances of the case determine whether the First Amendment is applicable either as a matter of law or as a defense to be considered by the jury; and there will be some instances where speech is so close in time and substance to ultimate criminal conduct that no free speech defense is appropriate.[67]

Applying this principle to a tax protestor who organized seminars both to condemn taxes and to advise people how to claim false deductions and exemptions, Judge Kennedy suggested that advocacy of tax noncompliance as an abstract idea or general attacks on the fairness of the tax laws might be protected. But approving or helping prepare a false return would not. The test turns on how proximate or imminent the words and the ensuing illegal behavior are, an approach very reminiscent of the World War I *Schenck* case. As another court summed it up: "Arguing for or advocating changes in the existing tax law is certainly protected activity; even advocating the violation of the tax laws is constitutionally sanctioned. These defendants, however, have gone beyond that permissible stage. They are actually breaking the law themselves and instructing others on how they, too, can break it."[68]

Courts have also upheld surveillance, monitoring, and special record-keeping by the IRS against the activities of tax protestors.[69]

Courts have even upheld extraordinary prior restraint injunctions against tax seminars and literature that went beyond preaching tax resistance and showed participants how to prepare fraudulent returns. Again the court drew a distinction between protected advocacy of unlawful activity—nonpayment of taxes in general—and punishable speech that leads to imminent and lawless actions. A tax protest leader could *not* be banned from associating with a tax protest group or engaging in its protected advocacy but could be enjoined from inciting people to understate their tax liability or avoid paying taxes by means of false and frivolous theories if he "actually persuaded others, directly or indirectly, to violate the tax laws, or if . . . [his] words and actions were directed toward such persuasion in a situation where the unlawful conduct was imminently likely to occur."[70]

Advocating Other Kinds of Illegal or Unconventional Behavior

Can illegal drug use be advocated?
Courts have differed on the issue. Government prohibits the

sale of illegal drugs and may punish advertising or soliciting of such illegal acts. But can government ban advocating the use of illegal drugs? The issue came up when many cities passed laws to regulate so-called head shops which sold drug paraphernalia and literature "related to or advocating" drug use. Some courts have held that mere advocacy of illegal drug use at some future time is not a call to imminent illegal action.[71] But other courts have insisted that advocacy in the form of advertising of drug paraphernalia is not protected since it relates to, solicits and advises illegal drug use.[72]

Can unconventional sexual or lifestyle behavior be advocated?

Probably yes. Sexual mores have eased enormously in recent years, with greater community acceptance of sexual choice and diversity. Free speech principles and protections have generally followed suit. Indeed the Supreme Court long ago ruled that movies and books that seem to advocate "immoral" behavior such as adultery, but that are not technically obscene, cannot be banned simply because of the "immoral" ideas advocated.[73] Advocacy of "swinging" is protected speech as well.[74] Gay student groups cannot be denied campus recognition on the ground that they advocate sexual behavior claimed to be immoral or even illegal.[75] Even "advocacy" of potentially dangerous behavior—such as autoerotic asphyxiation—has been held protected against a damage suit seeking to hold a magazine responsible for an article that planted the fatal idea in a young man's mind.[76] Similarly, fundamentalist church leaders who, in response to the permissive society at large, actively preach home education for children cannot be punished for inciting or inducing truancy, unless they actually cause the truancy. The First Amendment protects "statements to parents that the education of their children is a religious duty and that the state should have no role in regulating the education of Christian children."[77]

What if you are a public employee?

The right to advocate illegal or immoral behavior is less clear when the speaker is a public employee, especially a teacher or a police officer. The Court narrowly ruled, five to four, that a civilian police department employee could not be fired for privately expressing her hope, after learning of the assassination attempt on President Reagan, that "If they go for him again, I hope they get him."[78] Similarly, the Court was evenly split in approving a lower court ruling that invalidated an Oklahoma statute prohibiting teachers from "advocating, soliciting, imposing, encouraging or promoting public or private homosexual activities." The lower court had ruled that a speaker could not be punished for advocating such illegal conduct at some indefinite time in the future.[79] But teachers or military personnel who disclose their homosexual or bisexual preferences have been disciplined on the ground that their statements were not protected advocacy, but merely an "admission" of improper behavior.[80] As one federal appeals court recently stated in a decision upholding the dismissal of a soldier who was an "avowed" lesbian: "[The sergeant's] First Amendment argument fails because it is not speech per se that the regulation against homosexuality prohibits. [She] is free under the regulation to say anything she pleases *about* homosexuality and about the Army's policy toward homosexuality. She is free to advocate that the Army change its stance; she is free to know and talk to homosexuals if she wishes. What [she] cannot do, and remain in the Army is declare herself to *be* a homosexual. Although that is, in some sense speech, it is also an act of identification. And it is the identity that makes her ineligible for military service, not the speaking of it aloud. Thus, if the Army's regulation affects speech, it does so only incidentally in the course of pursuing other legitimate goals."[81]

NOTES

1. 395 U.S. 444 (1969).
2. J. S. Mill, *On Liberty* 55 (Castell ed. 1947).
3. *Herceg v. Hustler Magazine, Inc.*, 814 F.2d 1017, 1022 (5th Cir. 1987) (no liability for magazine article that allegedly prompted teenage boy to engage in suicidal acts); *see also Watters v. TSR, Inc.*, 715 F. Supp. 819 (W.D. Ky. 1989) (no liability for maker of "Dungeons & Dragons" game which allegedly caused teenage suicide).
4. *Giboney v. Empire Storage & Ice Co.*, 336 U.S. 490, 498 (1949).
5. *Pittsburgh Press Co. v. Pittsburgh Commission on Human Relations*, 413 U.S. 376 (1973).

6. *Haig v. Agee,* 453 U.S. 280 (1981).

7. *See Cantwell v. Connecticut,* 310 U.S. 296 (1940); *see generally* F. Haiman, *Speech and Law in a Free Society* 245–60 (1981).

8. *State v. Schleifer,* 121 A. 805, 99 Conn. 432 (1923).

9. *State v. Quinlan,* 91 A. 111, 112, 86 N.J.L. 120 (1914); *see* F. Haiman *Speech and Law in a Free Society, supra* note 7, at 248–49.

10. *People v. Epton,* 19 N.Y.2d 496, 502, 227 N.E.2d 829, 832 (1967).

11. *Hess v. Indiana,* 414 U.S. 105, 107 (1973).

12. *NAACP v. Claiborne Hardware, Inc.,* 458 U.S. 886, 927 (1982).

13. *Id.* at 928. *See also Howard Gault Co. v. Texas Rural Legal Aid, Inc.,* 615 F. Supp. 916, 947–49 (N.D. Tex. 1985), *aff'd, in part, rev'd, in part,* 848 F.2d 544 (5th Cir. 1988).

14. *See, e.g., United States v. Dellinger,* 472 F.2d 340 (7th Cir. 1972).

15. *Rankin v. McPherson,* 483 U.S. 378, 381 (1987).

16. *See Herceg v. Hustler Magazine, Inc., supra* note 3; *Zamora v. Columbia Broadcasting System,* 480 F. Supp. 199 (S.D. Fla. 1979); *but compare Niemi v. National Broadcasting Company,* 74 Cal. App. 3d 383, *cert. denied,* 435 U.S. 1000 (1978).

17. 18 U.S.C. § 871.

18. *United States v. Carrier,* 672 F.2d 300, 304 (2d Cir. 1982).

19. *See Watts v. United States,* 394 U.S. 705, 711 (1969) (concurring opinion).

20. *Watts v. United States,* 394 U.S. 705, 708 (1969).

21. *See United States v. Callahan,* 702 F.2d 964 (11th Cir. 1983); *compare United States v. Hoffman,* 806 F.2d 703 (7th Cir. 1986) (dissenting opinion) *and United States v. Crews,* 781 F.2d 826, 836 (10th Cir. 1986) (dissenting in part).

22. *United States v. Frederickson,* 601 F.2d 1358, 1363–64 (8th Cir. 1979).

23. 18 U.S.C. § 879.

24. *United States v. Kelner,* 534 F.2d 1020, 1027 (2d Cir. 1976).

25. *People v. Rubin,* 158 Cal. Rptr. 488, 494 (1979).

26. *Compare Norwood v. Soldier of Fortune Magazine Inc.,* 651 F. Supp. 1397 (W.D. Ark. 1987) (liability possible) *with Eimann v. Soldier of Fortune Magazine Inc.,* 880 F.2d 830 (5th Cir. 1989) (no liability).

27. *United States v. Velasquez,* 772 F.2d 1348, 1357 (7th Cir. 1985).

28. *United States v. Barcley,* 452 F.2d 930 (8th Cir. 1971); *compare United States v. Lincoln,* 589 F.2d 379 (8th Cir. 1971) (upholding a conviction for making written death threats to all the judges on a federal appeals court).

29. *City of Houston v. Hill,* 482 U.S. 451 (1987).

30. *Wurtz v. Risley,* 719 F.2d 1438, 1442 (9th Cir. 1983).

31. *Landry v. Daley,* 280 F. Supp. 938 (N.D. Ill. 1968), *rev'd on other*

grounds, 401 U.S. 77 (1971); *see also State v. Robertson*, 649 P.2d 569, 588–89 (Ore. 1982).

32. *Organization for a Better Austin v. Keefe*, 402 U.S. 415, 419 (1971).

33. *United States v. Gilbert*, 813 F.2d 1523 (9th Cir. 1987).

34. *In re Stonegate Security Services, Ltd.*, 56 Bankr. 1014, 1018–20 (N.D. Ill. 1986); *see also Matter of National Service*, 742 F.2d 859 (5th Cir. 1984).

35. *Thorne v. Bailey*, 846 F.2d 241 (4th Cir. 1988); *see also Gormley v. Connecticut State Department of Probation*, 632 F.2d 938 (2d Cir. 1980).

36. *Dorman v. Satti*, 862 F.2d 432 (2d Cir. 1988).

37. *United Food and Commercial Workers International Union v. IBP, Inc.*, 857 F.2d 422 (8th Cir. 1988).

38. *Howard Gault Co. v. Texas Rural Legal Aid, Inc.*, 848 F.2d 544, 561–63 (5th Cir. 1988).

39. 18 U.S.C. § 112.

40. *See CISPES v. FBI*, 770 F.2d 468, 476 (5th Cir. 1985).

41. *Boos v. Barry*, 485 U.S. 312 (1988).

42. *Compare Portland Feminist Women's Health Center v. Advocates for Life, Inc.*, 859 F.2d 681 (9th Cir. 1988); (upholding carefully limited injunction) *with Mississippi Women's Medical Center v. McMillan*, 866 F.2d 788 (5th Cir. 1989) (denying injunction). *See also Medlin v. Palmer*, 874 F.2d 1085 (5th Cir. 1989) (upholding ban on sound amplifying equipment within 150 feet of abortion clinic); *Mahoney v. District of Columbia*, _____ F. Supp. _____, 58 Law Week 2454 (D.D.C. 1990) (invalidating ordinance that banned intimidating or harassing picketing within 100 feet of clinic).

43. *Northeast Women's Center, Inc., v. McMonagle*, 670 F. Supp. 1300, 1308 (E.D. Pa. 1987), *aff'd*, 868 F.2d 1342 (3d Cir. 1989). *See also National Organization for Women v. Terry*, 886 F.2d 1339 (2d Cir. 1989) (upholding civil rights violation suit against Operation Rescue, an anti-abortion organization).

44. *Thornhill v. Alabama*, 310 U.S. 88 (1940).

45. *International Longshoremen's Association v. Allied International, Inc.*, 456 U.S. 212, 226–27 (1982).

46. *Edward Bartolo Corp. v. Florida Gulf Coast Building & Construction Trade Council*, 108 S. Ct. 1392, 1400 (1988).

47. *NAACP v. Claiborne Hardware Co.*, 458 U.S. 886, 914 (1982). *Compare Allied Tube and Conduit Corp. v. Indian Head, Inc.*, 486 U.S. 492 (1988) (economic boycott for economic purposes not within *Claiborne* principle).

48. *Missouri v. National Organization for Women*, 620 F.2d 1301 (8th Cir. 1980).

49. *Federal Trade Commission v. Superior Court Trial Lawyers Association,* 110 S. Ct. 768 (1990).

50. *Redgrave v. Boston Symphony Orchestra, Inc.,* 855 F.2d 888 (1st Cir. 1988).

51. *See, e.g., Eastern R. R. Presidents' Conference v. Noerr Motor Freight, Inc.,* 365 U.S. 127 (1961); *Weiss v. Willow Tree Civil Association,* 467 F. Supp. 803 (S.D.N.Y. 1979); *cf. United Brotherhood of Carpenters and Joiners of America v. Scott,* 463 U.S. 825 (1983).

52. *Bill Johnson's Restaurants, Inc., v. NLRB,* 461 U.S. 731 (1983) (NLRB can seek to prevent groundless retaliatory litigation by employer against union).

53. *Brandenburg v. Ohio,* 395 U.S. 444 (1969).

54. *See Dunne v. United States,* 138 F.2d 137 (8th Cir. 1943).

55. *Gara v. United States,* 178 F.2d 38, 39 (6th Cir. 1949); *Warren v. United States,* 177 F.2d 596 (10th Cir. 1949).

56. *Taylor v. Mississippi,* 319 U.S. 583, 586 (1943).

57. *Bond v. Floyd,* 385 U.S. 116, 133 (1966).

58. *Cohen v. California,* 403 U.S. 15, 18 (1971).

59. *Oestereich v. Selective Service System Board,* 393 U.S. 233 (1968).

60. *United States v. Spock,* 416 F.2d 165, 178–79 (1st Cir. 1969).

61. *United States v. O'Brien,* 391 U.S. 367, 376–77 (1968).

62. *Wayte v. United States,* 470 U.S. 598 (1985).

63. *Welch v. United States,* 750 F.2d 1101, 1108 (1st Cir. 1985); *Accord Kahn v. United States,* 753 F.2d 1208 (3d Cir. 1985).

64. *Stelly v. Commissioner of Internal Revenue,* 804 F.2d 868 (5th Cir. 1986).

65. *United States v. Moss,* 604 F.2d 569, 571 (8th Cir. 1979); *see also United States v. Damon,* 676 F.2d 1060 (5th Cir. 1982).

66. *United States v. Holecek,* 739 F.2d 331 (8th Cir. 1984).

67. *United States v. Freeman,* 761 F.2d 549, 551 (9th Cir. 1985).

68. *United States v. Shugarman,* 596 F. Supp. 186, 190 (E.D. Va. 1984).

69. *McPherson v. Internal Revenue Service,* 803 F.2d 479 (9th Cir. 1986); *England v. Commissioner of Internal Revenue,* 798 F.2d 350 (9th Cir. 1986).

70. *United States v. Kaun,* 827 F.2d 1144, 1151–52 (7th Cir. 1987). The Supreme Court has agreed to decide if a tax protestor may defend against tax evasion charges on the ground of a belief that taxes are unconstitutional. *See Cheek v. United States,* O.T. 89–658 (February 20, 1990), *cert. granted,* 58 U.S.L.W. 3526 (February 21, 1990).

71. *High Ol' Times v. Busbee,* 456 F. Supp. 1035 (N.D. Ga. 1978), *aff'd,* 621 F.2d 141 (5th Cir. 1980).

72. *See Gasser v. Morgan,* 498 F. Supp. 1154 (N.D. Ala. 1980); *Cf. Village*

   of Hoffman Estates v. The Flipside Hoffman Estates, Inc., 455 U.S. 489 (1982).

73. *Kingsley International Pictures Corp. v. Regents*, 360 U.S. 684 (1959).

74. *Kraus v. Village of Barrington Hills*, 571 F. Supp. 538 (N.D. Ill. 1982).

75. *See Gay and Lesbian Student Association v. Gohn*, 850 F.2d 361 (8th Cir. 1988).

76. *Herceg v. Hustler Magazine, Inc.*, 814 F.2d 1017 (5th Cir. 1987).

77. *Bangor Baptist Church v. Maine, Department of Public Education*, 576 F. Supp. 1299, 1335 (D. Me. 1983).

78. *Rankin v. McPherson*, 483 U.S. 318 (1987).

79. *National Gay Task Force v. Board of Education of Oklahoma*, 729 F.2d 1270, (10th Cir. 1984), *aff'd by an equally divided Court*, 470 U.S. 903 (1985).

80. *Johnson v. Orr*, 617 F. Supp. 170 (E.D. Cal. 1985), *aff'd* 787 F.2d 597 (9th Cir. 1986) (per curiam); *Rowland v. Mad River Local School District*, 730 F.2d 444 (6th Cir. 1984); *Rich v. Secretary of Army*, 735 F.2d 1220 (10th Cir. 1984); *but cf. Watkins v. United States Army*, 875 F.2d 699 (9th Cir. 1989) (en banc).

81. *Ben-Shalom v. Marsh*, 881 F.2d 454, 462 (7th Cir. 1989).

IV

Provoking Adversaries or Offending the Public

Can an individual say provocative or offensive things in public?
Yes. On April 26, 1938, Jesse Cantwell, a Jehovah's Witness, set up a table on a public sidewalk in New Haven, Connecticut. He began handing out literature and playing a phonograph record attacking all organized religions as instruments of Satan; the Catholic church was a particular target of his diatribe. A small crowd of onlookers gathered, and, though Cantwell did not resort to epithets or personal abuse, many of the passersby became highly incensed at Cantwell's message. One bystander felt like hitting Cantwell; another warned him to leave before something happened to him. Although Cantwell packed up his things and moved up the street before any violence erupted, he was arrested for inciting a breach of the peace. In reversing his conviction, the Supreme Court identified the horns of the dilemma.

> When clear and present danger of riot, disorder, inter-ference with traffic upon the public streets, or other immediate threat to public safety, peace, or order, appears, the power of the State to prevent or punish is obvious. Equally obvious is it that a State may not unduly suppress free communication of views . . . under the guise of conserving desirable conditions. . . .
> . . . One may . . . be guilty of [breach of the peace] if he commits acts or makes statements likely to provoke violence and disturbance of good order, even though no such eventuality be intended . . . [B]ut [usually] the provocative language . . . consist[s] of profane, indecent, or abusive remarks directed to the person of the hearer. . . .
> . . . Although the contents of the record not unnaturally aroused animosity . . . [Cantwell's] communication . . . raised no such clear and present menace to public peace and order as to render him liable to conviction. . . .[1]

In 1940 Walter Chaplinsky, another Jehovah's Witness, was distributing literature on the streets of Rochester, New Hampshire, in front of city hall on a busy Saturday. He kept denouncing religion as "a racket." The onlooking crowd that had gathered became restless, some complained to the city marshal, and a few moments later a small disturbance occurred. At that point a police officer asked Chaplinsky to accompany him to the police station. On the way they encountered City Marshal Bowering, who was rushing back to the scene of "the riot." The marshal and Chaplinsky exchanged words at which point Chaplinsky stated, "You are a God damned racketeer and a damned Fascist, and the whole government of Rochester are Fascists or agents of Fascists." Chaplinsky was convicted under a law which made it a crime to address any "offensive, derisive or annoying word to any other person" in a public place.

Despite the political content of the remarks, the Supreme Court upheld the conviction. The remarks were found to be unprotected " '[f]ighting words'—those which by their very utterance inflict injury or tend to incite an immediate breach of the peace. . . . [S]uch utterances are no essential part of any exposition of ideas, and are of such slight social value as a step to truth that any benefit that may be derived from them is clearly outweighed by the social interest in order and morality."[2] The Court thus broadly suggested that highly provocative words that might cause a breach of the peace or highly offensive words that figuratively would assault the listener were not protected free speech. For the next five decades the courts have grappled with the proper application and limitation of these principles.

Can the American flag be burned publicly as an act of protest?

Yes. In the summer of 1984 in Dallas, Texas, Gregory Johnson burned an American flag to protest the Reagan administration. That act led to the Court's most important modern restatement of the law on provocative speech. In connection with the 1984 Republican National Convention, Johnson and a small group of followers handed out literature, gave speeches condemning the Republican party and corporate interests, and marched through the streets shouting anti-Reagan slogans. Some acts of vandalism were committed, and at one point

Johnson, who had been given a purloined American flag, proceeded to douse it with lighter fluid and set it on fire, while the other protesters chanted, "America, the red, white and blue, we spit on you." There was no outbreak of violence, though many onlookers were highly outraged and offended by the actions. Johnson was charged with desecrating the American flag.

In a landmark ruling written by Justice William J. Brennan, the Supreme Court said that the symbolic act could not be punished as unacceptably provocative or offensive. The state's claim that public flag burning could be banned as inherently likely to provoke violence by outraged onlookers was rejected.

> Our precedents do not countenance such a presumption. On the contrary, they recognize that a principal "function of free speech under our system of government is to invite dispute. It may indeed best serve its high purpose when it induces a condition of unrest, creates dissatisfaction with conditions as they are, or even stirs people to anger."
>
> Thus we have not permitted the Government to assume that every expression of a provocative idea will incite a riot, but have instead required a careful consideration of the actual circumstances surrounding such expression, asking whether the expression "is directed to inciting or producing imminent lawless action and is likely to incite and produce such action."
>
> Nor does Johnson's expressive conduct fall within that small class of "fighting words" that are "likely to provoke the average person to retaliation, and thereby cause a breach of the peace." No reasonable onlooker would have regarded Johnson's generalized expression of dissatisfaction with the policies of the Federal Government as a direct personal insult or an invitation to exchange fisticuffs. We thus conclude that the State's interest in maintaining order is not implicated on these facts.[3]

To the similar claim that flag burning was too inherently offensive to the flag as a symbol of nationhood and national unity, the Court's response was even more direct: "If there is a bedrock principle underlying the First Amendment, it is that the Government may not prohibit the expression of an idea simply because society finds the idea itself offensive or disagreeable."[4] And even mistreating the flag is no exception to this free speech principle: "We do not consecrate the flag by punishing its desecration, for in doing so we dilute the freedom that this cherished emblem represents."[5]

This decision sparked an outpouring of protest, from President Bush down. As a result, Congress was stampeded into passing a new federal statute to outlaw flag burning; the Supreme Court swiftly invalidated this law as well.[6] Likewise the ill-conceived attempt to amend the Constitution itself to allow government to outlaw flag desecration was defeated in the United States Congress. Thus, flag burning remains a protected form of political speech.

HOSTILE AUDIENCES

Can a hostile audience prevent a provocative speaker or group from speaking or demonstrating?

No. The flag burning case shows how far the law has come in recognizing the rights of the provocative speaker. But it also reflects the tensions between protecting such rights and meeting the valid concerns of order and security.

In a few early cases the Court seemed uncertain about how much leeway to give the provocative speaker. In a 1949 case, a racist right-wing speaker addressing a large audience of his followers in a Chicago auditorium referred to a large group of counterdemonstrators who had gathered outside to protest the rally as "snakes" and "slimy scums." The crowd outside grew angry and turbulent, and several disturbances broke out. Nonetheless the Court dismissed breach of the peace charges against the speaker: "speech that stirs the public to anger, invites public dispute, brings about a condition of unrest, . . . creates a disturbance, ... [c]reates dissatisfaction with conditions as they are, or even stirs people to anger [cannot be punished]. . . . Speech is often provocative and challenging."[7] Just two years later, however, the Court upheld the disorderly conduct conviction of a left-wing speaker in Syracuse, New York, who harangued a small crowd of onlookers by urging civil rights and attacking President Truman ("a bum") and the American Legion ("a Nazi Gestapo"). There was angry muttering and some pushing and shoving in the crowd; one man told the police that if they didn't stop the speaker, he would. They did, and the Court ruled against the speaker.

> [O]rdinary murmurings and objections of a hostile audience cannot be allowed to silence a speaker. . . . [But i]t is one thing to say that the police cannot be used as an instrument for the suppression of unpopular views, and another to say that, when as here the speaker passes the bounds of argument or persuasion and undertakes incitement to riot, they are powerless to prevent a breach of the peace.[8]

The dissenting justices thought the first obligation of the police was to protect the lawful speaker by arresting the violent members of the crowd. "The police of course have power to prevent breaches of the peace. But if in the name of preserving order they ever can interfere with a lawful public speaker, they must first make all reasonable efforts to protect him."[9]

Fortunately when the mass civil rights and antiwar demonstrations of the 1960s reached the Court, the dissenters' views tended to prevail. The mere possibility that hostile crowds and counterdemonstrations adverse to the marchers' message would gather could no longer automatically justify preventing the speech or punishing the speakers since the breach of the peace was threatened not by the protestors, but by the hostile and lawless reaction to their point of view.[10] Thus the "muttering," "grumblings," and "rumblings" in a hostile crowd of white onlookers could not justify arresting the leaders of a civil rights demonstration.[11] Such a "heckler's veto" is unacceptable.

Do these principles protect extremist groups?

Yes. Even the most provocative speakers and demonstrators have the right to speak and march, so long as disorder is not imminent and uncontrollable. In the famous Skokie cases, a small group of Nazis was accorded the right—which was never actually exercised—to march and speak in the downtown area of a largely Jewish suburb of Chicago, and even to display the swastika, no matter how provocative, offensive, and hurtful that symbol might be. The Illinois court stated:

> The display of the swastika, as offensive to the principles of a free nation as the memories it recalls may be, is

symbolic political speech intended to convey to the public the belief of those who display it. It does not . . . fall within the definition of fighting words. . . .

Nor can we find that the swastika, while not representing fighting words, is nevertheless so offensive and peace threatening to the public that its display can be enjoined. We do not doubt that the sight of this symbol is abhorrent to the Jewish citizens of Skokie, and that the survivors of the Nazi persecutions, tormented by their recollections, may have strong feelings regarding its display. Yet it is entirely clear that this factor does not justify enjoining defendants' speech. [12]

The same principles have also protected the rights of other hate groups, such as the Ku Klux Klan, to march and speak and use public facilities for protest, despite the severe hostile reaction their speech might cause. [13]

Of course these principles continue to protect civil rights protestors on whose behalf they were fashioned. Even past violence by hostile bystanders or the threat of future violence by such lawless elements cannot prevent the right to speak. "Thus, our laws bespeak what should be; for were it otherwise, enjoyment of constitutional rights by the peaceable and law-abiding would depend on the dictates of those willing to resort to violence." [14] Courts have also protected the provocative speech of militant left-wing activists whose right to speak or demonstrate is sought to be denied because of feared violence against them. [15] Even where protestors are abrasive in communicating their message, they are entitled to the fullest constitutional protection, and mere shoving, shouting, and cursing by hostile onlookers does not constitute the kind of threatened imminent violence that might justify punishing a provocative speaker. [16] Instead, we look to responsible law enforcement officials to "safeguard the precious First Amendment values of this country while maintaining order and civility." [17]

Are there limits to the right of provocative speech or protest?

Yes, but only where violence is imminent and cannot be prevented by reasonable police precautions and protections. When a civil rights march through a mostly white neighborhood

drew large and unruly hostile crowds of bystanders, who heck-
led, shouted racial epithets, and threatened violence, the Court
ruled that the marchers' peaceful and orderly demonstration
could not be punished as disorderly conduct. But even Justices
Black and Douglas, the Court's most vigorous free speech
champions, noted that the problems were not easy ones.[18]
Nonetheless the answer still must be police protection of provocative speakers so that the presence and threatened violence
of hostile bystanders cannot veto speech.

> The existence of a hostile audience, standing alone, has
> never been sufficient to sustain a denial of or punishment
> for the exercise of First Amendment rights. . . .
>   The state is not powerless to prevent imminent violence
> or lawlessness resulting from a clash between the marchers
> or onlookers. If this situation arises, the police must try
> first to disperse and control the crowd, and if that becomes
> impossible, the marchers may be arrested. Likewise, if
> the marchers exceed the bounds of persuasion and argu-
> ment and enter the realm of incitement to imminent law-
> less action, they can be punished. Such punishment or
> curtailment of First Amendment rights must be based on
> a present abuse of rights, not a pre-nascent fear of future
> misconduct.[19]

But the prospect of imminent violence prompted by provocative speakers may sometimes, in an exceptional case, justify
punishing the protestors.[20]
To sum up: the law gives a great deal of leeway to the
provocative speaker. Official distaste for the speaker or the
message can never justify official interference; nor can unfounded fear of hostile crowd reaction. Where such reaction
actually materializes, it cannot provide a basis for restricting
the provocative speaker, and the police generally are required
to protect the speaker from the heckler's veto. Should the
unruly crowd degenerate into violence directed at the speaker
or supporters, the police should try to control the crowd, not
the speaker. Otherwise the heckler's veto will triumph. "It is
true that if members of a mob have vowed beforehand to act
violently when a certain person speaks, that person will incite
a riot by saying anything at all. In such a case, however, it is
the obligation of the government to chastise the violent, not

the verbal. To do otherwise would put the right of free speech at the mercy of those who threaten disruption."[21]

Do hecklers or members of the hostile audience have free speech rights also?

Yes. Though threats of violence by members of an angry crowd or audience hostile to the speaker cannot prevent the speech, the fact that hecklers cannot veto speech they dislike does not mean that hecklers or hostile bystanders must remain silent. Within limits, they too have rights to voice their opposition to the speaker.

Hecklers may not totally disrupt or prevent an event by shouting down or drowning out the speaker. Thus farmers who protested farm foreclosures by "shouting down" the auctioneer were not engaging in protected speech, but were doing the equivalent of making an unbearable din with airhorns or throwing a stink bomb into the crowd.[22] On the other hand, an anti-Olympics protestor who unfurled a critical banner at an event on the steps of the Capitol commemorating the Olympics was engaged in free speech, and anyone who did not like his countermessage could ignore it.[23] Indeed heckling or chanting at rallies and meetings held in entirely public places such as the streets is protected unless it reaches the point of actual disruption of the event.

Courts have had more difficulty with the question of heckling at events held in places like stadiums, arenas, or indoor auditoriums. The more private the event, the more likely the heckler or counterdemonstrator can be kept away.[24] Where events are open to the public, some courts have vigorously protected the right to engage in nondisruptive, but noticeable heckling and carrying of signs and banners; but other courts have upheld disorderly conduct convictions for those who did so.[25] The rights of a speaker or group to force themselves onto the podium or into the parade of another group have been rejected.[26]

"FIGHTING WORDS"

Can a speaker be punished for uttering "fighting words" in public?

Yes. The Court still recognizes that sometimes speech may

be so provocative that, when targeted on particular listeners, the words in that context are found inherently likely to provoke a violent reaction. But there are important limitations on the power of government to place highly provocative speech into the punishable "fighting words" category.

First, the definition of fighting words has been narrowed sharply. As Justice Brennan ruled in the flag-burning case, fighting words are only those which can be characterized as "a direct personal insult or an invitation to exchange fisticuffs." Thus a generally provocative or offensive message does not inherently come within that category, nor do indecent words not directed at any individual, nor does burning the American flag.

Second, even a speaker who uses punishable or vulgar fighting words—for example, swearing at police officers—cannot be punished if the language of the relevant statute itself is impermissibly vague and overbroad. Convictions have been thrown out where statutes made it a crime to use language that is "abusive," "indecent or offensive," or "obscene or inappropriate" or to act in a manner "annoying to persons passing by."[27] In an important 1989 case, the New York Court of Appeals applied both of these limitations to invalidate a law against use of "abusive" language. The court ruled that a woman could not be punished for yelling obscenities and epithets at a neighbor walking down the street. The words were not "violence-provoking or substantial injury-inflicting," and the law was not limited only to punishing such utterances.[28]

Finally, cases have suggested that words that might be punishable fighting words if uttered to an average person might not be if said to police officers, who deal with truculent people routinely, who are trained to exercise a high degree of restraint, and who can more properly be verbally challenged by citizens questioning police conduct.[29]

Are there any other limits on the use of provocative language in public places?

Yes. Provocative or offensive speech may also be restricted where it constitutes an intolerable invasion of the privacy of a captive audience. In public places, unwilling listeners may be required to "avert their eyes" or ears and simply avoid speech they do not wish to hear or see. In other contexts or settings, however, provocative or offensive speech may be restricted if it is forced upon unwilling, captive listeners or viewers. For example, interpreting this principle broadly, a city was permitted to ban political ads from the inside of public buses in order to protect the peace and quiet of commuters.[30] Offensive language at a school board meeting might be punishable even though uttering those same words in more open and public places might be protected. The reason is that "the willful use of scurrilous language calculated to offend the sensibilities of an unwilling audience . . . a verbal assault on an unwilling audience may be so grossly offensive and emotionally disturbing as to be the proper subject of criminal proscription."[31] It might be different, however, when the audience has had effective notice of what was to come, as when such language was used in the course of a political meeting where the speaker had been invited to present a radical point of view from a group such as the Black Panther party.[32]

Similarly the home is a sanctuary from invasion by certain forms of provocative or offensive speech. Thus anti-abortion demonstrators can be banned from engaging in focused, targeted, and repeated picketing in front of the residence of a doctor who performs abortions. "There is simply no right to force speech into the home of an unwilling listener. . . . The First Amendment permits the government to prohibit offensive speech as intrusive when the 'captive' audience cannot avoid the objectionable speech."[33]

OFFENSIVE SPEECH

Can a speaker be punished for offensive or outrageous speech?

Basically, no. Government has long tried to restrict the public use of offensive speech, claiming that such speech may provoke violence and breach of the peace, hurt or inflict injury on the audience even if it is not prompted to violence, and generally demean or pollute the community atmosphere. The Court has basically rejected these contentions, holding instead that government may not automatically or even routinely punish "offensive" speech. As the Court said in the flag-burning case, "If there is a bedrock principle underlying the First Amendment, it is that the Government may not prohibit the expression of an idea simply because society finds that idea itself offensive or disagreeable."[34]

What is true of ideas is no less true of offensive words and symbols through which ideas are expressed. In upholding the right of a young man to display a sign that read, "Fuck the Draft," the Court stated: "For while the particular four-letter word being litigated here is perhaps more distasteful than most others of its genre, it is nevertheless often true that one man's vulgarity is another's lyric. . . . [W]e cannot indulge the facile assumption that one can forbid particular words without also running a substantial risk of suppressing ideas in the process. Indeed, governments might soon seize upon the censorship of particular words as a convenient guise for banning the expression of unpopular views."[35]

But, as noted above, the Court has recognized the possibility of certain narrow, contextual bases for limiting the right to use highly offensive speech: (1) face-to-face personal insults or epithets directed at another person that might constitute fighting words; (2) certain forms of offensive speech that intrude on the privacy of the home or are directed at a captive audience unable to avoid the message by averting their eyes and ears; and (3) offensive speech in certain more controlled settings such as public schools.

Can a speaker be punished for politically or patriotically offensive speech?

No. As the flag-burning case made clear, even the most obnoxious and offensive public expressions of contempt for the flag and the country are protected from general suppression. Under the First Amendment, there is no such thing as a politically offensive idea or point of view. Even the home is no sanctuary from politically disagreeable ideas or messages. When New York banned utility companies from discussing "controversial" public issues in their monthly billing statements to customers, the Court threw out the restriction.

> Even if a short exposure to Consolidated Edison's views may offend the sensibilities of some consumers, the ability of government "to shut off discourse solely to protect others from hearing it [is] dependent upon a showing that substantial privacy interests are being invaded in an essentially in-

tolerable manner.". . . [Where] a single speaker communicates to many listeners, the First Amendment does not
permit the government to prohibit speech as intrusive unless the "captive" audience cannot avoid objectionable
speech. Passengers on public transportation . . . or residents of a neighborhood disturbed by the raucous broad-
casts from a passing sound truck may well be unable to es-
cape an unwanted message. But customers who encounter
an objectionable billing insert may "effectively avoid further
bombardment of their sensibilities by simply averting their
eyes. . . ." The customer of Consolidated Edison may es-
cape exposure to objectionable material simply by transferring the bill insert from envelope to wastebasket.[36]

But homeowners can request the post office no longer deliver
mail from a sender whose previous mailing the homeowner
claims is sexually oriented.[37] The difference is that it is the
homeowner, not the government, doing the censoring. Similarly the Court upheld a ban on targeted, stationary picketing
in front of a private residential home because the "devastating
effect" of the targeted picketing intruded on residential privacy
in an essentially disturbing and offensive manner.[38] The result
might be different if demonstrators targeted the home of a
prominent public official or public figure.

**Can a speaker say outrageously offensive things to lampoon
or ridicule public officials or public figures?**
Yes, so long as the outrageous comments cannot be reasonably understood as assertions of actual fact.

When *Hustler* magazine ran an obnoxious and outrageous
"ad parody" about Reverend Jerry Falwell, head of the Moral
Majority, suggesting that his first sexual experience was a
drunken encounter in an outhouse with his mother, the Court
ruled the magazine could not be forced to pay monetary damages for outrageous or intentional infliction of emotional distress. Otherwise the biting political commentary, caricature,
and satire historically associated with political cartoonists who
have lambasted political figures from George Washington
through Boss Tweed to George Bush would have been threatened. Moreover, allowing any punishment for "outrageous"
or "distressing" speech provides too subjective a standard of

suppression and allows too easily government punishment of speech. "We conclude that public figures and public officials may not recover for the tort of intentional infliction of emotional distress by reason of publications such as the one here at issue without showing in addition that the publication contains a false statement of fact" made intentionally or recklessly.[39] Similarly outrageous and outlandish offensive lampoons by *Hustler* magazine of prominent antipornography feminist activists have been held protected for the same reason; even a local antipornography activist with no national stature on these questions could not recover damages for having been characterized as a "crackpot," "tight-assed housewife," and "Asshole of the Month."[40]

For similar reasons the use of politically offensive though rhetorical charges, epithets, and slurs against one's opponents—e.g., "communist," "Nazi," "Fascist," "racist," "sexist," "scab"—is protected and cannot be treated as punishable offensive speech.[41] As one court put it, "Such name-calling ["Nazi," "Commie"], in the context of public debate, is protected speech."[42]

Can a speaker use foul and vulgar language in public?

Basically yes, depending on the situation. In a landmark 1971 ruling, the Court said that a young protestor could not be punished for having a sign on his jacket that said, "Fuck the Draft" and wearing it in a courthouse corridor.[43] The words were not a real incitement to draft law violation, were not directed toward a specific person as a direct personal insult, were not intended to provoke a given group to a hostile and violent reaction, and did not intolerably intrude on the minimal privacy interests that one has out in public. Nor could such words be banned on a theory that their use in public would be inherently inflammatory to a "hypothetical coterie of the violent and lawless," nor were they so obnoxious and "offensive" as to be banned from public discourse. The Court rejected giving government power to define and punish "offensive" words.

Based on this principle, courts have upheld the right to use words such as "fuck" and "motherfucker" in a general way in most public places and contexts, especially when spoken to police officers who are required to exercise greater restraint than the average person.[44] In public, offensive words must do more than "offend, cause indignation or anger the audience" to lose First Amendment protection.[45] Nor can a political group be denied a parade permit on the ground that their speech may include "profanity."[46] And a woman could not be punished for calling a neighbor a "bitch" and a "dog."[47]

But the right to use vulgar language is not without limits. First, the courts have upheld restrictions on the time when such "indecent" language can be used on radio and television, at least where the words are used repeatedly and for apparent shock value. Thus a sharply divided Court upheld FCC sanctions against a free-wheeling radio station for broadcasting, during normal listening hours, a monologue by comedian George Carlin, satirizing the "seven dirty words" you can't say on the air. Emphasizing its concern with the captive audience and the impact on children, the Court concluded that the right to use such words depends on context.[48] A lower court reaffirmed FCC power to restrict the timing of indecent speech on radio and television in order to protect children.[49] The government may also have greater power to regulate vulgar words used on the telephone to an unwilling listener, at least under a narrowly drawn regulation.[50]

In the public school context, officials may discipline student speakers for making vulgar and lewd remarks during an official school assembly or perhaps in classroom discussions as well; and the same would probably be true of school-sponsored newspapers and other publications.[51] Similarly a college teacher was validly dismissed for repeatedly using words such as "bullshit" and "sucks" to harangue his students in class.[52] But "private" student speech and off-campus student speech of an indecent or vulgar nature is far less subject to school control and punishment, if at all. A student who "gave the finger" to a teacher he encountered off campus could not be punished by the school. "The First Amendment protection of freedom of expression may not be made a casualty of the effort to force-feed good manners to the ruffians among us."[53]

Finally, use of loudspeakers or sound trucks to broadcast profanity can be restricted, as can the use of loud and vulgar language by a visitor denied entrance to a government office. In such cases, the amplification of the offensive words is found to be objectionable on a theory similar to the restrictive regulation of the broadcast of profanity.[54]

Can an individual speak on subjects such as abortion, contraception, and sexuality that people might find offensive or indelicate?

Yes. In recent years, as a result of the major changes in public mores and attitudes toward sexuality—as well as public health crises such as AIDS—speech that was formerly restricted as too indelicate or offensive for public expression is now entitled to broad First Amendment protection.

For example, twenty years ago it was hard to imagine that speech and advertising about contraception, abortion, sexual diversity, drug abuse, and safe sex would become part of our everyday world. Now, however, sanctioned by Supreme Court First Amendment rulings and significant societal changes, advertisements and discussions of contraceptives, abortion, and all these other topics are commonplace.[55] Even mailing unsolicited advertisements for contraceptives and condoms is protected free speech; and the Court has rejected the argument that a ban on such mailings is necessary to protect the sensibilities of the audience or children. "[The] level of discourse reaching a mailbox cannot be limited to that which would be suitable for a sandbox."[56] Planned Parenthood family-planning advertisements could not be banned from subways and buses on the ground that they were in bad taste or would cause distress or discomfort to riders.[57]

Sexually provocative speech—so long as it is not legally obscene—is also entitled to extensive First Amendment protection, outside of special contexts like schools or the work place (where it may sometimes constitute impermissible sexual harassment of employees). For example, New York City officials could not deny transit advertising space to a *Penthouse* magazine pictorial cover that rather lewdly suggested that Vice President Walter Mondale was pandering to women supporters in his quest for the presidential nomination. The fact that the poster was in bad taste or might offend the sensibilities of most people was an insufficient basis for banning it. "Even speech that is arguably in bad taste, so long as it does not cross the border into obscenity, enjoys the same Constitutional protection as the most enlightened political discourse."[58] Gay rights advertisements have been protected on similar grounds.[59] *Hustler* magazine could not be prohibited from mailing free copies to all members of Congress: "While Members of Congress may not share the views embodied in *Hustler,* the right to present unwelcome petitions is entitled to no less protection than is the right to petition for causes long espoused by the majority. The First Amendment protects controversial as well as conventional dialogue."[60]

Art is also entitled to considerable constitutional protection even though people find certain themes provocative, offensive, or tasteless. Government does not usually try to ban offensive art directly. Indeed, even during the Congressional protest over the homoerotic photograph exhibit by Robert Mapplethorpe, which had been scheduled for display at the publicly funded Corcoran Gallery in Washington, D.C., most politicians who condemned the display did so on the ground that it was publicly subsidized, while grudgingly recognizing the right to create or display such art under private auspices without government prohibition. But since many artists or institutes are publicly subsidized or sponsored, government has used the power of the purse to try to achieve suppression indirectly that could not be done directly. A few cases have reached the courts, which are divided on the subject. Some courts have forbidden censorship where government imposes financial and funding sanctions on art it disapproves, while other judges have given broad discretion to government as art patron to dictate the content of art that it sponsors.[61]

Finally, speech or protest activities cannot be banned as offensive because they involve gay rights themes, causes, or advocacy. Gay rights groups can march or demonstrate, even though some might find their message of gay rights and sexual diversity offensive or embarrassing.[62] Student groups have generally secured the right to official campus recognition and status and equal treatment with other student groups.[63] Two young gay males were allowed to take each other to their high school senior prom, as a statement of gay pride, despite the emotional distress or hostile reactions of the other students. "The First Amendment does not tolerate mob rule by unruly school children."[64] And gay rights advocates were granted the right to use a municipal theater to hold a "Miss Gay America Pageant" in which men dressed as women to satirize the real Miss America contest. "The First Amendment values free and open expression, even if distasteful to the majority."[65] But the Supreme

Court ruled that holding a "Gay Olympic games" could be prohibited because it violated special statutory trademark protections given by Congress to the regular Olympic games.[66]

BIGOTED SPEECH

Does the law protect speech that is racist, sexist, antisemitic, or antigay?

Yes. In general, even the most bigoted, hateful, and hurtful speech, attacking groups on the basis of race, gender, religion, sexual orientation, or ethnic origin, is protected against government suppression or prohibition. With exceptions for special contexts such as the workplace or special circumstances like fighting words, the general venting of bigoted speech must be tolerated. This is the basic teaching of a host of Supreme Court cases and the basic lesson of the Skokie events. The rationale is twofold: (1) all ideas are entitled to be expressed and heard—no matter how obnoxious and hateful and (2) this is a lesser evil than the alternative—which is giving government the power to determine which ideas and words are acceptable and which are too offensive and must be suppressed.

For example, the flawed efforts to outlaw pornography that portrays women in a sexually "subordinate" manner, while permitting depictions of sexual encounters and activity "premised on equality," were condemned by courts as impermissible government preference for a "correct" point of view on these issues of sexuality.

> The state may not ordain preferred viewpoints in this way. The Constitution forbids the state to declare one perspective right and silence opponents. . . .
> Under the First Amendment the government must leave to the people the evaluation of ideas. . . .
> The ideas of the Klan may be propagated. . . . Communists may speak freely and run for office . . . the Nazi Party may march through a city with a large Jewish population. . . . People may teach religions that others despise. People may seek to repeal laws guaranteeing equal opportunity in employment or to revoke the Constitutional amendments granting the vote to blacks and women. They may do so

because "above all else, the First Amendment means that government has no power to restrict expression because of its message [or] its ideas."[67]

What is true of hateful ideas is no less true of the words and epithets through which they are sometimes expressed, words such as "kike," "nigger," and "faggot." Except perhaps in special situations such as direct face-to-face insults in personal encounters or repeated slurs that harshly affect the workplace environment, such words are protected because, despite the hurt they inflict, under the First Amendment words cannot be punished simply because they "may have an adverse emotional impact on the audience."[68] Thus, for example, anti-abortion demonstrators were protected in shouting words like "murderer" and "killers" at patients and staff of abortion centers, in the absence of young children to whom the words might be particularly traumatic.[69]

The same is true of racist speech. Such speech, of course, is highly offensive and hurtful. But, with certain possible exceptions, the courts have held that it cannot be regulated consistent with the First Amendment.

Thus, for example, groups like the Ku Klux Klan cannot be denied the right to speak or march just because their racist messages and symbols are highly offensive or even frightening. In ordering a parade permit for the Klan, one judge pointed out:

> It is no answer to state that the message of these plaintiffs is so offensive that justice is served by permitting it to be drowned out by a more responsible majority. However distasteful this judge finds plaintiffs' message to be, it is the duty of this court to reaffirm that speech may not be banned simply because some, or all, in a community find the ideas expressed to be offensive. . . .
>
> It is only necessary to look back a score of years in our history to find a situation in which speakers who advocated racial equality were denied their freedom of expression because of the angry response of a segment of the community to the message.[70]

When a white police officer who performed an off-duty nightclub act in blackface was disciplined by the police department because the performances angered members of the black community, the court held that an angry minority is no more entitled to exercise a veto over racist speech than is an offended majority to prevent speech it disapproves.

> Government's instinctive and understandable impulse to buy its peace—to avoid all risks of public disorder by chilling speech assertedly or demonstrably offensive to some elements of the public—is a recurring theme in first amendment litigation. . . . Though this "veto" has probably been most frequently exercised through legislation responsive to majority sensibilities, the same assault on first amendment values of course occurs where, as here, it is exercised by executive action responsible to the sensibilities of a minority.[71]

Efforts to make a restaurant chain called "Sambo's" change its name have been similarly unsuccessful, even though the name connotes pernicious racial stereotypes and is viewed by blacks as akin to fighting words.[72] In the *Brandenburg* ruling, the Supreme Court upheld the giving of a racist and antisemitic speech, laced with racist epithets such as "nigger," at a Ku Klux Klan rally.[73]

But despite these rules, a more troubling and difficult question is posed by the use of racial or other hateful epithets in face-to-face encounters or other immediate contexts. Are such epithets prohibitable by analogy to the fighting words concept? A debate has been raging on college and university campuses as university officials have responded to incidents of racial or similar epithets and harassment, symbols, and abusive speech by proposing rules and regulations to curtail such offensive speech. That in turn has prompted suits by ACLU affiliates against such rules and regulations to declare them violative of the First Amendment rights for even hateful speech.[74] Courts have sometimes upheld restrictions on the use of racist and similar slurs in situations where violence is imminent or in more regulated settings such as the workplace to enforce anti-discrimination laws, where the use of racial or similar epithets is so severe and pervasive as to create a hostile or abusive work environment and, in effect, undermine the employment relationship.[75] And some older cases have upheld emotional distress suits by the targets of slurs and epithets, again usually

in a workplace setting.[76] But it is questionable whether, outside
the workplace, such emotional distress rulings survive the Supreme Court's reasoning in both the *Hustler* magazine and flag-
burning cases, which strongly suggest that the emotional harm
and assault visited by speech that mortifies or shocks the audience provides no valid basis for punishment.

The same is probably true of criminal laws against group libel
or defamation—i.e., words that convey "depravity, criminality,
unchastity or lack of virtue" of racial, ethnic, or religious groups.
In the 1952 *Beauharnais* case, the Supreme Court upheld
punishment of a white racist for publishing leaflets attacking
blacks as being criminals and decrying the danger to "the white
race from being mongrelized by the negro." In a setting of racial
tension, the Court concluded that the state could punish "false
or malicious defamation of racial and religious groups, made
in public places and by means calculated to have a powerful
emotional impact on those to whom it was presented." Since
the government could penalize such false and inflammatory
speech directed at a particular person, it could likewise punish
such speech when directed at the group of which the individual
was a member.[77] But the dramatic strengthening of free speech
protection in the decades since then has cast considerable doubt
on whether such laws against defaming groups of people would
be upheld today. Given tightened free speech protection for
defamatory, offensive, and provocative speech, lower courts
have suggested that, for example, antipornography laws that
punish sexual speech "demeaning" women and ordinances to
try to ban groups such as the Nazis or the Klan that espouse
racial and religious hatred and contempt from speaking and
marching are invalid because *Beauharnais* is no longer good
law. As the Court stated in upholding flag burning and the
contempt for the nation that it displayed, "The First Amendment does not guarantee that other concepts virtually sacred to
our Nation as a whole—such as the principle that discrimination
based on race is odious and destructive—will go unchallenged
in the marketplace of ideas."[78]

NOTES

1. *Cantwell v. Connecticut*, 310 U.S. 296, 308–11 (1940).

2. *Chaplinsky v. New Hampshire,* 315 U.S. 568, 572 (1942).

3. *Texas v. Johnson,* 109 S. Ct. 2533, 2541–42 (1989).

4. *Id.* at 2544.

5. *Id.* at 2547–48.

6. *United States v. Eichman,* 110 S. Ct. 2404 (1990) (invalidating the Flag Protection Act of 1989, Pub. L. No. 101–131, 103 Stat. 777; 18 U.S.C. § 700).

7. *Terminiello v. Chicago,* 337 U.S. 1, 4 (1949).

8. *Feiner v. New York,* 340 U.S. 315, 320–21 (1951).

9. *Id.* at 326.

10. *Edwards v. South Carolina,* 372 U.S. 229 (1963).

11. *Cox v. Louisiana,* 379 U.S. 536 (1965).

12. *Village of Skokie v. National Socialist Party,* 69 Ill. 2d 605, 373 N.E.2d 21, 24 (1978); *see also Collin v. Smith,* 578 F.2d 1197 (7th Cir. 1978) (invalidating three Skokie ordinances designed to bar the Nazis from marching).

13. *Ku Klux Klan v. East Baton Rouge Parish School Board,* 578 F.2d 1122 (5th Cir. 1978); *Invisible Empire of the Knights of the Ku Klux Klan v. City of West Haven,* 600 F. Supp. 1427 (D. Conn. 1985); *Invisible Empire of the Knights of the Ku Klux Klan v. Mayor, Town of Thurmont,* 700 F. Supp. 281 (D. Md. 1988).

14. *Dr. Martin Luther King, Jr. Movement, Inc. v. City of Chicago,* 419 F. Supp. 667, 675 (N.D. Ill. 1976).

15. *Beckerman v. City of Tupelo,* 664 F.2d 502 (5th Cir. 1981).

16. *Sabel v. Stynchcombe,* 746 F.2d 728 (11th Cir. 1984); *Waller v. Butkovich,* 584 F. Supp. 909 (M.D.N.C. 1984).

17. *Olivieri v. Ward,* 637 F. Supp. 851, 873 (S.D.N.Y. 1986), *aff'd in part, rev'd in part,* 801 F.2d 602 (2d Cir. 1986).

18. *Gregory v. Chicago,* 394 U.S. 111, 117 (1970) (concurring opinion).

19. *Beckerman v. City of Tupelo,* 664 F.2d 502, 510 (5th Cir. 1981).

20. *Resident Advisory Board v. Rizzo,* 503 F. Supp. 383, 404 (E.D. Pa. 1980).

21. *Kelly v. United States Postal Service,* 492 F. Supp. 121, 130–31 (S.D. Ohio 1980) (postal worker entitled to wear "Death to the Shah" button despite threats of violence from coworkers).

22. *Carson v. Block,* 790 F.2d 562 (7th Cir. 1986).

23. *Kroll v. United States Capitol Police,* 590 F. Supp. 1282 (D.D.C. 1983), 683 F. Supp. 824 (D.D.C. 1987), *rev'd on other grounds,* 847 F.2d 899 (D.C. Cir. 1988).

24. *McIntosh v. Arkansas Republican Party-Frank White Election Committee,* 766 F.2d 337 (8th Cir. 1985).

25. *Compare In re Kay,* 1 Cal. 3d 930, 464 P.2d 142 (Cal. 1970) *and Bishop v. Reagan-Bush '84 Committee,* 635 F. Supp. 1020 (S.D.

Ohio 1986), *rev'd without opinion*, 819 F.2d 289 (6th Cir. 1987) *with Reynolds v. Tennessee*, 414 U.S. 1163 (1974) (Douglas, J. dissenting from the denial of certiorari); *see also Redgrave v. Boston Symphony Orchestra*, 831 F.2d 339 (1st Cir. 1987), *vacated and withdrawn*, en banc, 855 F.2d 888 (1988).

26. *Kay v. Bruno*, 605 F. Supp. 767 (D.N.H. 1985), *aff'd, Kay v. New Hampshire Democratic Party*, 821 F.2d 31 (1st Cir. 1987); *Gay Veterans Association v. American Legion-New York County Organization*, 621 F. Supp. 1510 (S.D.N.Y. 1985).

27. *Gooding v. Wilson*, 405 U.S. 518 (1972); *Lewis v. New Orleans*, 415 U.S. 130 (1974); *Rosenfeld v. New Jersey*, 408 U.S. 901 (1972); *Coates v. Cincinnati*, 402 U.S. 611 (1971).

28. *People v. Dietze*, 75 N.Y.2d 47 (1989).

29. *Lewis v. New Orleans*, 415 U.S. 130 (1974); *City of Houston v. Hill*, 482 U.S. 451 (1987); *Bovey v. City of Lafayette*, 586 F. Supp. 1460 (N.D. Ind. 1984); *aff'd per curiam*, 774 F.2d 1166 (7th Cir. 1985); *Lusk v. Roberts*, 611 F. Supp. 564 (D. La. 1985).

30. *Lehman v. City of Shaker Heights*, 418 U.S. 298 (1974).

31. *Rosenfeld v. New Jersey*, 408 U.S. 901, 905–6 (1972) (concurring opinion).

32. *Brown v. Oklahoma*, 408 U.S. 914 (1972).

33. *Frisby v. Schultz*, 108 S. Ct. 2495, 2502, 2503 (1988).

34. *Texas v. Johnson*, 109 S. Ct. 2533, 2544 (1989).

35. *Cohen v. California*, 403 U.S. 15, 25, 26 (1971).

36. *Consolidated Edison v. Public Service Commission*, 447 U.S. 530, 541–42 (1980).

37. *Rowan v. United States Post Office*, 397 U.S. 728 (1970).

38. *Frisby v. Schultz*, 108 S. Ct. 2495 (1988).

39. *Hustler Magazine v. Falwell*, 108 S. Ct. 876, 882 (1988). *See also L. L. Bean Inc. v. Drake Publishers, Inc.*, 811 F.2d 26 (1st Cir. 1987) (sexual parody of famous outdoor products catalogue protected); *Cliffs Notes, Inc. v. Bantam Doubleday Dell Publishing Group*, 886 F.2d 490 (2d Cir. 1989). *See generally* H. Dorsen, *Satiric Appropriation and the Law of Libel, Trademark, and Copyright: Remedies without Wrongs*, 65 B.U.L. Rev. 923 (1985).

40. *Dworkin v. Hustler Magazine, Inc.*, 867 F.2d 1188 (9th Cir. 1989); *Ault v. Hustler Magazine, Inc.*, 860 F.2d 877 (9th Cir. 1988).

41. *Koch v. Goldway*, 817 F.2d 507 (9th Cir. 1987); *Stevens v. Tollman*, 661 F. Supp. 702 (N.D. Ill. 1986).

42. *Lasky v. American Broadcasting Companies, Inc.*, 606 F. Supp. 934, 940 (S.D.N.Y. 1985).

43. *Cohen v. California*, 403 U.S. 15 (1971).

44. *Hess v. Indiana*, 414 U.S. 105 (1973); *Papish v. Curators of the*

University of Missouri, 410 U.S. 667 (1973); *Pringle v. Court of Common Pleas,* 778 F.2d 998 (3d Cir. 1985); *State v. Meyers,* 462 So. 2d 227 (La. App. 4th Cir. 1984) ("Fuck Charles Foti, Jr. [the local sheriff]" on bumper sticker held protected).

45. *Hammond v. Adkisson,* 536 F.2d 237 (8th Cir. 1976).
46. *Beckerman v. City of Tupelo,* 664 F.2d 502 (5th Cir. 1981).
47. *People v. Dietze,* 75 N.Y.2d 47 (1989).
48. *Federal Communications Commission v. Pacifica Foundation,* 438 U.S. 726, 747 (1978).
49. *Action for Children's Television v. Federal Communications Commission,* 852 F.2d 1332 (D.C. Cir. 1988).
50. See *Ghormley v. Director, Connecticut State Department of Probation,* 632 F.2d 938 (2d Cir. 1980); *Thorne v. Bailey,* 846 F.2d 241 (4th Cir. 1988).
51. *Bethel School District No. 403 v. Fraser,* 478 U.S. 675 (1986); *Hazelwood School District v. Kuhlmeier,* 484 U.S. 260 (1988).
52. *Martin v. Parrish,* 805 F.2d 583 (5th Cir. 1986).
53. *Klein v. Smith,* 635 F. Supp. 1440, 1442 (D. Me. 1986). See also *Ketchens v. Reiner,* 194 Cal. App. 3d 470, 239 Cal. Rptr. 549 (1987) (invalidating statute that made it a crime to insult school teacher in front of students or school personnel); *Commonwealth v. Ashcraft,* 691 S.W.2d 229 (Ct. App. Ky. 1985) (same).
54. *Reeves v. McConn,* 631 F.2d 377 (5th Cir. 1980); *pet. for reh'g,* 638 F.2d 762 (5th Cir. 1981); *United States v. Occhino,* 629 F.2d 561 (8th Cir. 1980).
55. *Bigelow v. Virginia,* 421 U.S. 809 (1975); *Carey v. Population Services International,* 431 U.S. 678 (1977).
56. *Bolger v. Youngs Drug Products Corp.,* 463 U.S. 60, 74 (1983).
57. *Planned Parenthood Association/Chicago v. Chicago Transit Authority,* 767 F.2d 1225 (7th Cir. 1985).
58. *Penthouse International Ltd. v. Koch,* 599 F. Supp. 1338, 1350 (S.D.N.Y. 1984).
59. *Alaska Gay Coalition v. Sullivan,* 578 P.2d 951 (S. Ct. Alaska 1978).
60. *United States Postal Service v. Hustler Magazine, Inc.,* 630 F. Supp. 867, 875 (D.D.C. 1986).
61. See *Piarowski v. Illinois Community College District 515,* 759 F.2d 625 (7th Cir. 1985); *Serra v. General Services Administrator,* 847 F.2d 1045 (2d Cir. 1988); *Advocates for Arts v. Thomson,* 532 F.2d 792 (1st Cir. 1976); *but see Sefick v. City of Chicago,* 485 F. Supp. 644 (N.D. Ill. 1979).
62. *Olivieri v. Ward,* 801 F.2d 602 (2d Cir. 1986).
63. *Gay and Lesbian Student Association v. Gohn,* 850 F.2d 361 (8th Cir. 1988); *Gay Student Services v. Texas A & M University,* 737 F.2d

1317 (5th Cir. 1984); *Gay Lib v. University of Missouri,* 558 F.2d 848 (8th Cir. 1977).

64. *Fricke v. Lynch,* 491 F. Supp. 381, 387 (D.R.I. 1980).

65. *Norma Kristie, Inc. v. City of Oklahoma City,* 572 F. Supp. 88, 92 (W.D. Okla. 1983).

66. *San Francisco Arts and Athletics, Inc. v. United States Olympic Committee,* 483 U.S. 522 (1987).

67. *American Booksellers Association v. Hudnut,* 771 F.2d 323, 325, 327, 328 (7th Cir. 1985). *See generally* Strossen, *Book Review: The Convergence of Feminist and Civil Liberties Principles in the Pornography Debate,* 62 N.Y.U. L. Rev. 201 (1987).

68. *Hustler Magazine v. Falwell,* 108 S. Ct. 876, 882 (1988).

69. *Bering v. SHARE,* 721 P.2d 918, 937 (Wash. 1986).

70. *Invisible Empire of the Knights of the Ku Klux Klan v. City of West Haven,* 600 F. Supp. 1427, 1434–35 (D. Conn. 1985); *cf. Kirksey v. City of Jackson,* 663 F.2d 659 (5th Cir. 1981) (right to hold, and vote on the basis of, racist views).

71. *Berger v. Battaglia,* 779 F.2d 992, 1001 (4th Cir. 1985); *see also Curle v. Ward,* 59 App. Div. 2d 286 (3d Dept.), *modified,* 46 N.Y.2d 1048 (1979); (state correctional officer cannot be dismissed for Klan membership); *but see McMullen v. Carson,* 754 F.2d 936 (11th Cir. 1985) (upholding dismissal of Klan officer from police department job and cited with approval in *Rankin v. McPherson,* 107 S. Ct. 2891, 2900 n. 18 [1987]).

72. *Sambo's Restaurants, Inc. v. City of Ann Arbor,* 663 F.2d 686 (6th Cir. 1981).

73. *Brandenburg v. Ohio,* 395 U.S. 444 (1969); *but cf. National Alliance v. United States,* 710 F.2d 868 (D.C. Cir. 1983) (denial of "educational" tax exemption to white supremacist organization).

74. *See, e.g., Doe v. University of Michigan,* 721 F. Supp. 852 (E.D. Mich. 1989).

75. *See Meritor Savings Bank v. Vinson,* 477 U.S. 57 (1986); *Davis v. Monsanto Chemical Co.,* 858 F.2d 345 (6th Cir. 1988).

76. *Contreras v. Crown Zellerbach Corp.,* 88 Wash. 2d 735, 565 P.2d 1173 (1977); *Alcorn v. Anbro Engineering, Inc.,* 2 Cal. 3d 493, 468 P.2d 216 (1970); *Agarwal v. Johnson,* 25 Cal. 3d 932, 603 P.2d 58, 160 Cal. Rptr. 141 (1979).

77. *Beauharnais v. Illinois,* 343 U.S. 250, 261 (1952).

78. *Texas v. Johnson,* 109 S. Ct. 2533, 2546 (1989).

V

Criticizing the Powerful

"If any person shall write, print, utter, or publish . . . any false, scandalous and malicious writing or writings against the government . . . with intent to defame . . . or to bring . . . into contempt or disrepute; or to excite the hatred of the good people of the United States . . . then such person . . . shall be punished by a fine not exceeding five thousand dollars, and by imprisonment not less than six months and exceeding five years."[1]

So reads the Sedition Act of 1798, passed by Congress to quell mounting criticism and dissent against the young American Republic in the first decade of its existence. The act basically made it a crime to harshly criticize the federal government. It is hard to believe this law was passed when the ink on the First Amendment was barely dry. After Thomas Jefferson became president two years later, he pardoned all those who had been sentenced under this law, and Congress repaid their fines. Although the constitutionality of the Sedition Act was never tested in the Supreme Court, "the attack upon its validity has carried the day in the court of history, [with] a broad consensus that the Act, because of the restraint it imposed upon criticism of government and public officials, was inconsistent with the First Amendment."[2] As a result, the modern Supreme Court has been on guard against laws, procedures, or practices that resemble the Sedition Act's effort to suppress criticism of government and its officials. The reason was made clear in a landmark 1964 decision restricting the ability of public officials to sue their critics for libel. The Supreme Court pointed to "a profound national commitment to the principle that debate on public issues should be uninhibited, robust and wide open, and that it may well include vehement, caustic and sometimes unpleasantly sharp attacks on government and public officials."[3] In that case the Court made it much more difficult—but not impermissible—for public officials to sue their critics for defamation and recover damages. Some justices would have gone further and absolutely disallowed any libel suit based on public discussion of public affairs and public officials.

Thus the law allows vigorous, but not totally unrestrained, criticism of the conduct of government officials. This chapter will discuss four kinds of issues that protestors should be aware of in criticizing government and its officials: (1) efforts to restrict "false" or unfounded criticism; (2) rules dealing with defamation or similar lawsuits brought against critics by public officials or public figures; (3) special problems when courts themselves become the target of protest and criticism; and (4) government efforts to control and regulate campaign speech and electoral protest.

CRITICIZING THE GOVERNMENT AND ITS OFFICIALS

Can an individual be penalized for criticizing, condemning, or defaming the government?

No. The lesson of history's condemnation of the Sedition Act, and the teaching of the landmark case of *New York Times Co. v. Sullivan* are that a protestor cannot be punished for criticizing or libelling government or its agencies. "[N]o court of last resort in this country has ever held, or even suggested, that prosecutions for libel on government have any place in the American system of jurisprudence."[4] For example, when the city of Philadelphia tried to sue a newspaper for libel, for publishing an unflattering article about the city, the claim was rejected on the ground that you can't libel government; otherwise we would have "the spectre of prosecutions for libel on government, which the Constitution does not tolerate in any form."[5] Thus, there is an absolute right to attack government and its policies. Moreover, impersonal criticism of government policy or practices cannot be automatically treated as if it were a focused and personal attack on the particular officials in charge of that policy.[6] The same is true for criticism of a private group.

Can an individual engage in vigorous or even false or wrongful criticism of government officials and their motives and behavior?

Yes, subject to the very narrow possibilities of a libel or defamation suit by that official, which will be discussed shortly. Of course truthful criticism of public officials is absolutely protected and cannot be the subject of punishment.[7] But even false or misleading criticism of government officials is protected speech as well. A political candidate cannot be penalized for making false and deceptive statements or promises to the voters.[8] A law that makes it a crime for picketing protestors to engage in any "slander or libel or the public display or publication of oral or written misrepresentation" was invalidated because "the State cannot criminalize the mere utterance of a falsehood."[9] When federal transit officials in Washington, D.C., asserted the right to prevent a photo montage poster from being displayed, on the ground that it contained a "deceptive and distorted" view of the Reagan administration, the courts were swift to overturn the censors. "[P]rior administrative restraint of distinctly political messages on the basis of their alleged deceptiveness is unheard of—and deservedly so."[10] By the same token, criticizing or impugning the motives of government officials for taking controversial actions is almost absolutely protected from punishment as well.[11] In one libel case, where the question was whether a former government advisor to Latin American police forces had been accused of condoning political torture, the court stated: "The article . . . was a piece of political and social criticism. We do not know whose side truth is on, but the First Amendment is on the side of the critic of government."[12] Similarly a city council member could not be suspended for "impugning the motives" of another member during a legislative debate.[13]

Do citizens have a right to complain to government about the conduct of its officials?

Yes, but false complaints sometimes can be punished. Citizens have a right to file complaints with government agencies or superiors about the conduct of government officials. This is protected both as a matter of free speech and as part of the explicit First Amendment right "to petition the Government for a redress of grievances."[14] Moreover, protest organizations who complain, for example, about police brutality or coverups by grand juries or police officials cannot be subject to harassing inquiries into the nature, membership, and policies of the group as a punishment for having made such charges. "It would be a sorry day were we to allow a grand jury to delve into the membership, meetings, minutes, organizational structure, funding and political activities of unpopular organizations on the pretext that their members might have some information relevant to a crime."[15]   But the fact of exercising one's right to petition government does not give absolute immunity against making false claims or statements. For example, a political figure who wrote a damning letter to the president and attorney general to torpedo (successfully) the appointment of another person to a high federal post could not avoid a libel suit by arguing that he had an absolute privilege to petition the government and not be sued for defamatory statements in the letter. As one justice put it, "There is no persuasive reason for according greater or lesser protection to expression on matters of public importance depending on whether the expression consists of speaking to neighbors across the backyard fence, publishing an editorial in the local newspaper, or sending a letter to the President of the United States."[16] Similarly the filing of knowingly or recklessly false reports or charges of police brutality or misconduct could conceivably be punished under false report or perjury laws.[17] A professor who made patently false and inaccurate statements about university officials could be dropped from the faculty.[18] But a police officer who wrote and posted a humorous poem lampooning the mayor's candidacy for reelection could not be subject to any official penalty.[19]

DEFAMATION SUITS

What is defamation?
Defamation is any false factual statement about a person which tends to harm the reputation of that person by lowering the community's estimation of him or her or deterring third persons from wanting to associate or deal with that person. The most common examples of defamatory statements are assertions of criminal, illegal, or corrupt acts, charges of fundamental incompetence or unfitness for one's profession, and charges of mental illness or immoral behavior. Libel is defamation by written word or other relatively permanent communication; slander is defamation by spoken word.

There is no federal law of defamation, but each state is free to define defamation and provide the target of a defamatory statement the right to sue and recover damages. The First Amendment comes into play because the courts have used it to impose substantial limitations on the states' power to permit defamation lawsuits. The theory is that the more difficult it is to bring and win a defamation suit, the more protection there will be for robust free speech and press, especially discussion and criticism of public officials, because speakers, writers, and protestors won't have to fear that any misstatement that harms reputation will lead to the possibility of a damage suit.

But the Court has refused to say that defamation suits are always barred by the First Amendment. Instead, the Court has struck a balance—permitting some defamation suits in order to protect the individual's important interest in reputation and personal integrity, while imposing restrictions on such lawsuits to protect free speech rights.

The essence of a defamation suit is that false and derogatory statements of a factual nature were made, either knowingly, deliberately, or recklessly (which is extremely hard for the plaintiff to prove), or carelessly (which is somewhat easier to substantiate). The plaintiff complaining of a defamatory statement must prove one of these different levels of fault, depending on whether the statement was about a public official, a public figure, or a public issue, on one hand, or an ordinary person and a private matter, on the other.

Can protestors, activists, or public interest groups be sued for defamation?

Yes. As a practical matter, the vast majority of defamation suits are brought against news media because they do so much reporting about factual matters and public affairs and because they often have the financial resources to pay damages if a judgment is awarded to a defamation plaintiff. But there is no legal barrier to bringing a defamation suit against individual protestors or groups and organizations. Indeed, the landmark *New York Times* case was brought against both a newspaper and a group of civil rights leaders and advocates responsible for a political advertisement published in the newspaper that contained claimed defamatory factual inaccuracies about public officials in the South. The leaders were sued because they wrote and sponsored the ad, and the newspaper was sued for publishing it.

Other political and public interest groups have been sued for defamation as well. For example, environmental groups have been sued over factual charges against claimed polluters, civil rights groups for alleging police misconduct, community groups for claiming corruption by local politicians, antiracist activists over charges that a well-known conservative was linked to right-wing hate groups, and advocates for the retarded for comments about welfare officials.[20] As one court said, "representation of a lofty cause—the rights of retarded citizens—does not entitle [an advocacy group] to any greater protection than any other person or group accused of libel or defamation."[21]

In addition to civil damage actions, there is also the remote possibility that protest leaders or organizations might be criminally prosecuted for criminal libel or group libel. But since the Court has cast extreme doubt on the validity of such a criminal prosecution, that threat is very unlikely.[22]

Can protestors or activist groups sue for defamation?

Yes, although protestors or public interest groups active in the public arena would probably be viewed as "public figures" who have a number of hurdles to overcome to win a defamation suit. In addition, if the defamatory statements about a protest group or individual are made by a government agency or official, there may be additional problems in overcoming various legal immunities that such officials or agencies may have.[23] Otherwise there is no reason why protestors and activists cannot sue for defamation. The ACLU, however, basically does not believe in allowing anyone to bring a libel suit over public issues and discussion, reasoning that the remedy for false statements should be in the market place of ideas, not in a courtroom hearing a defamation suit.

Are public officials allowed to sue protestors or organizations for defamation?

Yes, but winning such a suit is extremely difficult. In the *New York Times* case, the Supreme Court was extremely concerned about public officials using a defamation suit to silence their critics, through both the chilling effect of the possibility of such suits and the actual effect of having to pay damages for innocent factual errors. This possibility looked too much like the reviled Sedition Act, this time deterring and punishing criticism of government by allowing its criticized officials to sue personally for defamation when their official conduct was questioned. This would put a damper on vigorous criticism of public officials.

So the Court fashioned the "actual malice" doctrine—a federal constitutional rule "that prohibits a public official from recovering damages for a defamatory falsehood relating to his official conduct unless he proves that the statement was made with 'actual malice'—that is, with knowledge that it was false or with reckless disregard of whether it was false or not."[24] Moreover, such a plaintiff must establish all elements of the case—defamatory falsehood about the plaintiff, made with actual malice—with "convincing clarity." It is not clear whether any governmental employee is automatically a "public official," but where high-level public officials or political candidates are concerned, almost anything is relevant to their conduct or fitness for office. The effect of the *New York Times* rule is that false and defamatory statements may go uncompensated because the plaintiff cannot prove the case.

It is important to emphasize that the actual malice rule does not mean malice in the every day sense of that term, i.e., spite, ill-will, bad motives, or even hatred. Truthful statements or criticism can be made with the worst motives; so long as they are true, they are absolutely protected against defamation suits, civil or criminal.[25] "Actual malice" refers to the speaker's attitude toward the truth, not toward the target of the remarks. Similarly, outrageous and outlandish ridicule and satire—if not reasonably understood as having or representing factual assertions—is likewise absolutely protected, regardless of how malicious or mean-spirited the speaker's motive. As the Court said in the Reverend Jerry Falwell's case: "[I]n the world of debate about public affairs, many things done with motives that are less than admirable are protected by the First Amendment. . . . [W]e [have] held that even when a speaker or writer is motivated by hatred or ill-will, his expression was protected by the First Amendment."[26] And actual malice is refuted by having taken reasonable steps to verify the accuracy of the defamatory statement.

Can a public figure sue for defamation?

Yes, but to win, a public figure must prove the same elements of the case as a public official. The Court has defined "public figures" as persons "who, by reason of the notoriety of their achievements or the vigor and success with which they seek the public's attention, are properly classed as public figures. . . . For the most part those who attain this status have assumed roles of especial prominence in the affairs of society. Some occupy positions of such pervasive power and influence that they are deemed public figures for all purposes. More commonly, those classified as public figures have thrust themselves to the forefront of particular public controversies in order to influence the resolution of the issues involved. In either event, they invite attention and comment."[27]

Examples of public figures are people like Jackie Kennedy Onassis, Pete Rose, and the Reverend Jerry Falwell. But the Court has been restrictive in its interpretation of this concept and the following people have been held *not* to be public figures: a prominent Florida socialite, a lawyer active in liberal causes and organizations, an academic researcher, a person convicted of contempt of court, and a local contracting firm.[28]

Can a private person sue for defamation?

The Court has ruled that the actual malice requirement and other stringent barriers to a defamation suit apply only in suits brought by "public people"—i.e., public officials or public figures—since the First Amendment is designed to protect vigorous commentary and criticism about such prominent or powerful people.

Where the subject of a defamatory statement is a private person or entity, there is more of an even balance between free speech concerns and individual reputation interests; such an individual can win a defamation suit by proving the false statement was made negligently or carelessly, which is a lesser standard of fault than actual malice.[29] Moreover, if a private person is defamed over a matter that is not of general or public concern, it is even easier for that plaintiff to recover damages.[30] But since most statements by protestors criticizing private people probably relate to matters of public interest, protestors probably need not worry about this possibility.

Can corporations or other organizations sue for defamation?

Yes, many defamation suits are brought by corporations, organizations, or other group entities. Such suits are subjected to the same set of rules and distinctions as suits brought by people, i.e., much will depend on whether the entity is prominent or well-known. An electronics manufacturer of well-known stereo speakers was deemed a public figure when it sued *Consumer Reports* for criticizing its sound system; but a local contracting firm was treated like a private person when it sued Dun and Bradstreet over a false and damaging credit rating report.[31]

Can a speaker be sued for expressing a defamatory opinion about someone?

No, unless the opinion contains a provably false factual connotation. As the Supreme Court has ruled: "Under the First Amendment, there is no such thing as a false idea. However pernicious an opinion may seem, we depend for its correction not on the conscience of judges and juries but on the competition of other ideas. But there is no constitutional value in false statements of fact. Neither the intentional lie nor the careless error materially advances society's interest in 'uninhibited, robust and wide open' debate on public issues."[32]

What is the difference between a statement of fact and an expression of opinion?

The answer is not clear. In the most basic sense, "[w]hile an opinion can be right or wrong, it cannot be true or false."[33] If an expression of opinion contains no false factual defamatory statements or connotations it cannot be the basis of a successful defamation suit. If it is deemed a factual assertion and a defamatory one, however, then the speaker may be held responsible, but only if it was knowingly, recklessly, or negligently false—depending on who the target of the statement is and the context in which it was made. One court has summarized the law as follows:

> Expressions of "one's opinion of another, however unreasonable or vituperative, since they cannot be subjected to the test of truth or falsity, cannot be held libelous and thus are entitled to absolute immunity from liability under the First Amendment." Opinion may be expressed through "rhetorical hyperbole" and "vigorous epithets," even in the most pejorative terms, but when the criticism takes the form of accusations of criminal or unethical conduct, or derogation of professional integrity in terms sub-

ject to factual verification, the border line between fact and opinion has been crossed.[34]

Another court has suggested that "[s]tatements not themselves factual, and which do not suggest that a conclusion is being drawn from facts not disclosed in the statement are commonly statements of opinion, not fact."[35]

Certain key points should be kept in mind. First, opinion that takes the form of fantastical satire, parody, or ridicule that could not reasonably be taken as making factual assertions is absolutely protected. This is the message of decisions that rejected suits against *Hustler* magazine by Jerry Falwell, as well as by Andrea Dworkin and other prominent feminist anti-pornography activists, all of whom were brutally lampooned. "Ludicrous statements are much less insidious and debilitating than falsities that bear the ring of truth. We have little doubt that the outrageous and the outlandish will be recognized for what they are."[36] Second, statements a court concludes are "rhetorical hyperbole" or "vigorous epithet" will usually be viewed as expressions of opinion as well. Such terms encompass many types of statements, including what in other contexts would be a charge of illegal or criminal conduct or extremist or derogatory political behavior or beliefs.

Can a speaker use words like "blackmail" or "extortion" in political debate?

It depends. For example, calling the actions or proposals of political figures "blackmail" or "extortion," or calling someone a "traitor," or labeling a proposal a "scam" are usually protected as hyperbole or rhetoric.[37] The same is true of terms like "slimy sleazebag."[38] Most people understand that this is the kind of extreme hyperbole common in heated political disputes and debates. But if the specific context suggests the terms are used in a more strictly legal sense, they may be treated as defamatory factual assertion. When a community group referred to three local city councilmen as "the combine" and claimed the three had "extorted by blackmail" money from a development company—without also disclosing that the money was to be paid by the developer to the city, not the politicians personally, to settle a lawsuit against the city and receive permission to build a housing project—a divided California Supreme Court ruled that the charges could not automatically be labeled as opinion.[39] Stating that a politician "raped the city" is clearly rhetoric; suggesting that he once raped a woman is a factual statement, and it is not rendered otherwise by prefacing the assertion with the disclaimer "in my opinion"; such an opinion is more than a general derogatory remark and is laden with factual content charging the commission of a serious crime.[40] But when a law enforcement consultant claimed that an article in effect called him a "torturer" of political prisoners, a court found no clear factual meaning. "The defamatory claims of government officials, arising from a text which criticizes governmental conduct, must be based on statements which make an explicit charge, not on insinuation of defamatory meaning from possible implications in the text."[41] As one court summarized the law: (1) a pejorative statement of opinion concerning a public figure is constitutionally protected no matter how vituperative or vigorously expressed; (2) this principle applies even when the statement includes a term which could refer to criminal conduct if the term could not reasonably be so understood in context, but (3) the principle "does not cover a charge which could reasonably be understood as imputing specific criminal or other wrongful acts."[42] Applying this principle in an important 1990 ruling, the Supreme Court decided that implying that a sports coach had lied under oath at a hearing was a factual assertion that could be subject to a defamation suit.[43]

Can a speaker use political epithets such as "communist" or "fascist" to describe political figures?

Again, it depends on context. Defamation suits sometimes arise over politically derogatory words and epithets such as "communist," "Nazi," "fascist," "scab," "racist," or "bigot." Using such terms to capsulize and characterize one's attitude of an opponent's beliefs, views, policies or actions is generally given absolute protection against defamation suits. For example, stating that the well-known, right-wing journalist William F. Buckley, Jr., is a "fellow traveller" of fascism is protected opinion; but claiming he engaged in libelous journalism is a factually false statement.[44] Similarly, a charge of "racial and religious bigotry" when made in a dispute between two public figures is protected opinion. A Santa Monica, California, landlord, Ilsa Koch, complained on television that city council members who supported rent control laws were "communists"; the mayor responded at a political meeting by asking rhetorically whether Ms. Koch could be the same person as an infamous Nazi war criminal. When Ms. Koch sued for defamation over the suggestion that she was a notorious Nazi, the court said that, given the context, this was simply "a slur against a political opponent," "a vicious slur," but still an expression of opinion and not a factual statement. "In this case, if the mayor chose to get in the gutter, the law simply leaves her there. . . . This is the precise sort of contest that society can endure without redress from the courts. Base and malignant speech is not necessarily actionable."[45] Another court, in similarly rejecting a libel suit over charges and countercharges like "communist" and "Nazi" in television interviews, observed: "It is precisely this type of exchange which has been characterized in the law of libel as the expression of opinion, or more specifically, epithets which express a speaker's emotions rather than assertions of fact. Such name calling, in the context of public debate, is protected speech."[46]

On the other hand, where such charges are framed in terms of more specific allegations of membership in, affiliation with, or support for despised extremist groups, courts have permitted defamation suits to proceed. This has been true of a liberal lawyer accused of being "a Leninist," a "Communist-fronter," and an officer or member of specified, allegedly Marxist or communist organizations, or organizations that planned civil disturbances.[47] Similarly, charges that Liberty Lobby, a right-wing organization, was "neo-Nazi, anti-Semitic, racist and fascist" were the basis of a defamation suit, dismissed only for lack of sufficient evidence; the same was true of charges that the organization published racial supremacy material supplied by a Nazi organization. These charges, like accusing someone of being a member of the Ku Klux Klan, could be defamatory, but the target would have to show they were false.[48] Also problematic were charges by an antiracist group whose slide show, "Unmasking the KKK," suggested that the Joseph Coors beer family was "identified with the Klan and the John Birch Society."[49]

Obviously, much depends on exactly what is said and the setting in which it is said. For example, older cases held that epithets such as "bigot" were not automatically defamatory, but saying that about a white merchant in a black neighborhood might present a different situation.[50] In some cases, both protected opinion and unprotected factual statement have been at issue. For example, in one case, a county highway official called a subordinate a "gutless bastard," a "black son-of-a-bitch," a "liar," and an incompetent; a court found the first two terms, though offensive and abusive, to be protected as opinion; but the latter comments, however, were viewed as libelous assertions of fact.[51] In another case, black parents who succeeded in ousting a white school principal could not be charged with defamation for calling the principal "a very racist woman" who ran a "dictatorship" and "destroyed our children's minds"—that is protected opinion. Nor could they be penalized for seeking her ouster—that is protected expression and petition of the government for redress of grievances. But stating that the principal had called the parents "a bunch of welfare mothers" and that she "was under doctor's care"—if untrue—could bring a penalty.[52]

Finally, in a case involving a newspaper columnist whose article suggested that a wrestling coach lied under oath at a hearing, the Supreme Court said, "The dispositive question . . . [is] whether or not a reasonable factfinder could conclude that the statements in the . . . column imply an assertion that [the coach] perjured himself in a judicial proceeding. We think this question must be answered in the affirmative. This is not the sort of loose, figurative or hyperbolic language which would negate the impression that the writer was seriously maintaining petitioner committed the crime of perjury. Nor does the general tenor of the article negate this impression."[53]

Apart from defamation, are there other similar kinds of civil damage suits or other possible legal actions that protestors should be aware of?

Possibly. As we have seen, after the Jerry Falwell case public figures cannot sue for emotional distress based on even the most vicious ridicule or satire of them where the content of the attack could not reasonably be taken as making factual assertions: "[P]ublic figures and public officials may not recover for the tort of intentional infliction of emotional distress . . . without showing in addition that the publication contains a false statement of fact which was made with 'actual malice', i.e.

with knowledge that the statement was false or with reckless disregard as to whether or not it was true."[54] Some lower courts have extended the absolute protection to outlandish nonfactual ridicule of private people as well.[55] But it is unlikely that protestors would normally be targeting private people for such ridicule.

Another possible concern is that disclosing true, but highly damaging or embarrassing information about a person (for example, that someone was a rape victim or that someone once committed a crime) could be the basis of an invasion of privacy suit. But if the subject is a public figure or public official, almost any true information about such a person is relevant to the public debate, and you cannot be punished for revealing it— especially if the facts came from public records or documents. Moreover, since the essence of this claimed invasion of privacy is the emotional distress caused by the revelation, the *Falwell* case seems to reject such a harm under the First Amendment.

Where private people are concerned, however, the courts have not resolved whether disclosing true but disparaging information can lead to damages. If the information comes from official and publicly available documents—such as police reports—or was otherwise lawfully obtained and concerns a matter of public significance, there can be no liability. But the Court has not said whether the same is always true for truthful information, no matter how obtained or revealed.[56] Concerns with privacy have not been rejected out-of-hand. Indeed, in a nonconstitutional case, the Court ruled that the Freedom of Information Act did not require the Department of Justice to turn over arrest records or "rap sheet" information because of privacy concerns.[57]

Finally, even the most prominent public figures or organizations may have certain proprietary interests in their writings and activities that are afforded some protection against misappropriation under copyright and trade mark laws. For example, *The Nation* magazine was found to have violated copyright laws when it got an advance copy of former President Gerald Ford's memoirs and went beyond fair use of those materials by publishing extensive excerpts discussing his motivations for pardoning former President Richard Nixon. The Court ruled that the copyright laws had properly balanced the public's right to know with the author's interests in what he wrote.[58] Similarly, the

United States Olympic Committee, which by law has a trademark for the name and symbols of the Olympics, was able to block the "Gay Olympic Games" even though the promoters of that alternative event claimed that the restriction would interfere with their conveying "a political statement about the status of homosexuals in society."[59]

But where Jerry Falwell wanted to use the copies of the *Hustler* parody of him to raise money for his own cause, the courts held that *Hustler* had no right under the copyright laws to prevent that. "Although the first amendment does not provide a defense to copyright infringement, when an act of copying occurs in the course of a political, social, or moral debate, the public interest in free expression is one factor favoring a fair use."[60] More importantly, unauthorized use of a political figure's name or picture, short of active or fraudulent misrepresentation, cannot be prevented by that politician. Senator Phil Gramm's campaign committee sued a fundraising group called, "Americans for Phil Gramm," for unauthorized use of his name. The court ruled that, apart from fraud or election law restrictions, people cannot be prevented from using a politician's name to support or oppose him or her. "The right of individuals and organizations publicly to support or oppose a candidate for public office is indispensable to democratic decision-making. . . . This fundamental First Amendment right to advocate the defeat or election of a candidate necessarily carries with it a right to use a candidate's name. If courts were to allow a political candidate to obtain civil damages from, or injunctive relief against, those who use his name without authorization, the right to advocate the defeat or election of particular candidates would lack efficacy."[61]

PROTESTING AGAINST COURTS AND JUDGES

Can judges and courts be vigorously criticized?

Yes, but this was not always true. For many years, the courts followed the doctrine of "contempt by publication," which allowed judicial punishment for negative out-of-court comments or criticism—usually by the news media—about judges and their decisions. But the Supreme Court soon began to afford

First Amendment protection to out-of-court criticism and threw out a number of "contempt by publication" convictions. Now citizens or the press are entitled to criticize the courts freely, robustly, even maliciously.[62] Punishment can be imposed, if ever, only when "there is no doubt that the utterances in question are a serious and imminent threat to the administration of justice. Conceivably, a plan of reporting on a case could be so designed and executed as to poison the public mind, to cause a march on the courthouse, or otherwise so to disturb the delicate balance in a highly wrought situation as to imperil the fair and orderly functioning of the judicial process."[63]

Applying these rules, the Court held that a county sheriff, held in contempt for claiming that judges had empaneled a grand jury inquiry into election fraud just to intimidate black voters, could not be penalized because the criticism did not pose a clear and present danger to the administration of justice.[64] Nor could a prominent district attorney be punished for criminal libel for charging that all of the judges of the criminal court were inefficient, lazy, and possibly subject to "racketeer influences."[65] Finally, a newspaper could not be punished for revealing truthfully the contents of a confidential judicial misconduct report and identifying the judge being investigated, especially since these were matters of great public concern and interest.[66]

But three important limits on the right to criticize courts should be kept in mind. First, judges, like other public officials, can try to recover for libel if they can prove that false and defamatory factual statements have been made about them with actual malice.[67] Second, during the civil rights demonstrations of the 1960s, the Court showed special concern about mass demonstrations at courthouses or other kinds of "mob rule" pressures on courts, and particularly on jury trials, even though civil rights advocates were doing the demonstrating.[68] But more recently, the Court has considerably relaxed some of its concerns about larger demonstrations in front of courthouses, especially the Supreme Court itself.[69] Finally, courts and judges have extremely broad power to maintain order and decorum within the courtroom itself and to punish protestors or spectators, parties or attorneys who seriously breach that decorum and create disorder.[70]

Do members of the public have a right to attend criminal trials and other judicial proceedings?

Yes. Courtrooms can be very important places for political and public issues. In addition to the occasional "political trial," many court cases involve profound public issues: crime and punishment, civil rights, environmental concerns, consumer fraud, white collar crime. As a result the Court has held that there is a strong First Amendment right of the public and press to attend and observe criminal trials. Court orders closing portions of a trial or pretrial proceeding to the general public, in order to protect witnesses or parties against embarrassment or unfairness, are justified only if closing the courtroom is clearly the only way to protect compelling and overriding interests.[71]

Can participants in a court case be ordered not to discuss all or some aspects of a case?

The answer depends on who the participant is and what is being discussed. Courts sometimes impose so-called gag orders, directing lawyers, parties, or even the press not to report or disclose certain information about a case in order to preserve the right to a fair trial untainted by prejudicial pretrial publicity. Of course anything that occurs in open court or any matters learned from official public court documents can be discussed freely and without restraint. But in highly publicized cases, judges will sometimes order the participants not to reveal or discuss critical evidence or information, or even the entire case, until after the trial. Is this permissible?

Gag orders imposed against the press or public are an unconstitutional prior restraint unless there are basically no less drastic alternatives available to protect the defendant's right to a fair trial.[72] One such alternative is the possibility of restraining discussion or statements by the attorneys, the parties, law enforcement personnel, or other participants in the case. Gag orders on the participants might be more acceptable than gag orders on the press.[73]

Lower courts have wrestled with trying to decide whether attorneys (particularly defense lawyers) and parties (especially criminal defendants) can likewise be restrained. Prosecutors and other government attorneys can more arguably be controlled as government employees bound to honor and afford due process and fair trials; but are defense lawyers similarly subject to controls, especially where they need to publicize their side of the case to counter the adverse publicity surrounding the very filing of criminal charges?

Some courts have insisted that defense lawyers can only be restrained if their comments pose a serious and imminent threat to a fair trial; but other courts have applied a looser test of "reasonably likely to interfere" with a fair trial.[74] One federal appeals court, applying a strict standard of review to a gag order in an espionage case against a former FBI agent, held that the defendant and defense counsel might be barred from discussing certain specified categories of information and evidence; but an order barring all discussion of "the merits" of the case was too broad.[75] But some judges thought the entire question of the chilling effect of gag orders on lawyers called upon to represent unpopular defendants in high-visibility cases deserved more examination.

> When, as in this case, the indictment is the subject of great public interest, the damage to the accused's reputation and the accompanying emotional distress can be greatly magnified. . . . The range of options available to the lawyer must include speaking out publicly to mitigate the damage to the client in the eyes of the community at large. Marshalled against an accused is not only the awesome resources and prestige of the United States Government, but also the power of the media to disseminate the government's charges. . . . Suppose, for example, the accused wishes to charge that the indictment was politically or religiously motivated. The freedom to make such a charge against the state is surely paramount among the freedoms protected by the First Amendment. To deprive an accused of his most valuable resource in criticizing the government—his lawyer—is to restrict, and restrict severely his First Amendment rights.[76]

Another appeals court ruled that a broad gag order on government lawyers in a civil case was a violation of the First Amendment.[77] Nor could a reporter, called to testify before a grand jury about political corruption he had reported on, be banned from discussing, disclosing, or writing about his own testimony.[78]

Finally, is it proper to gag the defendant himself from speaking out against the charges? One appeals court answered with a resounding no in a case involving a black congressman indicted for mail and bank fraud, who was ordered by the trial court not to engage publicly in any "discussion of the case." The court said, "broadly based restrictions on speech in connection with litigation are seldom, if ever, justified. . . . The courts and public institutions funded with public resources for the purpose of resolving public disputes, and the right of publicity concerning their operations, goes to the heart of the function under our system of civil liberty. The courts have available other less restrictive approaches for insuring a fair trial. . . . To the extent that publicity is a disadvantage for the government, the government must tolerate it. The government is our servant, not our master."[79]

REGULATION OF POLITICAL CAMPAIGN AND ELECTORAL ACTIVISM

Can the government regulate political campaign and election activity?

Yes, but the First Amendment requires very strict scrutiny of most government restrictions on political campaign and electoral activity. Government regulation has taken a number of forms: requirements for getting on the election ballot, regulation of political parties, control of campaign funding, disclosure of campaign funding, restrictions on initiative and referendum campaigns, and bans on "deceptive" campaign speech. Since these are all restrictions on political and electoral activities—which are at the core of political speech—the Court gives such controls strict scrutiny and has invalidated many restrictions on campaign and electoral activity where no compelling interest for the restrictions can be shown. (These principles are discussed at greater length in the ACLU handbook, B. Neuborne and A. Eisenberg, *The Rights of Voters and Candidates* [rev. ed. 1980].)

Can the government regulate the affairs and activities of political parties?

Yes, but only to a limited degree. Government's conceded

power to regulate the manner and methods of elections in order to safeguard the integrity of the electoral process does not include blanket authority over the political parties who run candidates for elective office. States can regulate who may vote in elections and how long voters have to be registered and how they affiliate with a party for election and voting purposes. And government can regulate political parties directly, for example, by requiring major parties to choose their candidates by election rather than convention or not to engage in racial or similar discrimination in decreeing who may vote in its primary elections.[80]

Beyond these restrictions—which directly involve the conduct of elections—blanket government intrusions on political party structure, strategy, policies, membership, or personnel violate the First Amendment. The right of speech and association of political parties means that government cannot tell them who can vote in their primaries, who will be party members, how party candidates will be selected, or how party leaders will be chosen.

Recently, in applying these various principles, the Supreme Court overturned California laws that prevented party officials, committees, and groups from endorsing candidates in party primaries: "California's ban on primary endorsements . . . prevents party governing bodies from stating whether a candidate adheres to the tenets of the party or whether party officials believe that the candidate is qualified for the position sought. This prohibition directly hampers the ability of a party to spread its message and hamstrings voters seeking to inform themselves about the candidates and the campaign issues. . . . [It] also infringes upon their freedom of association."[81] The Court also threw out state regulation of the methods of selecting party officials. "A State cannot substitute its judgment for that of the party as to the desirability of a particular internal party structure, any more than it can tell a party that its proposed communication to party members is unwise. . . . In sum, a State cannot justify regulating a party's internal affairs without showing that such regulation is necessary to insure an election that is orderly and fair."[82]

Can the state regulate which candidates and parties can have access to and appear on the election ballot?

Yes, but here too the restrictions will be closely scrutinized to insure that the government is not trying impermissibly to disadvantage minor, dissident, or independent political parties, candidates, or groups.

The government has considerable power to control access to the election ballot to guard against voter confusion and political factionalism and instability from having an excessive number of frivolous candidates and splinter parties on the ballot. But the government may not achieve these objectives by placing undue burdens and obstacles on access to the ballot. While the government can insist on a "showing of a significant modicum of support before printing the name of a political organization and its candidates on the ballot,"—for example, nominating petitions signed by 5 percent of the eligible voters, burdensome signature requirements beyond that, or requirements that signatures be obtained throughout the state, are generally impermissible.[83] Filing deadlines cannot be set so far in advance of the election as to make it practically impossible for independent or minor parties or candidates to meet the requirements.[84] The same is true of filing fees and costs to secure a place on the ballot; they cannot be prohibitively costly if the consequence is effectively to exclude viable candidacies from the ballot.[85] Beyond these general principles and guidelines, there is no rule of thumb or litmus test to determine whether a particular requirement will be upheld or struck down.

Can government restrict the funding of election campaigns by political candidates and their supporters?

Yes, but only to serve the compelling interest in preventing political corruption.

In the wake of the Watergate scandals, Congress passed legislation sharply limiting contributions and expenditures for federal election campaigns. Many states followed suit. The ACLU and other political activists challenged these restrictions as unacceptable financial limitations on political speech and association, arguing that limitations on political funding are limitations on political speech. In the landmark case of *Buckley v. Valeo*,[86] the Court mostly agreed. Government cannot limit the amount of personal funds a candidate spends on his or her election campaign to promote his or her candidacy and ideas. Nor can government limit the overall expenditures of any campaign. On the other hand, because of the concern with corruption, individual contributions to a candidate or campaign committee can be limited to $1,000 per campaign; contributions by an established political committee (a PAC) can be limited to $5,000 to each candidate. Also the Court suggested government can provide public funding for political campaigns and impose the condition that candidates who accept such subsidies agree to limit the amount of expenditures they will make or contributions they will accept.[87] Such an arrangement is available in presidential campaigns, and many states have provided for similar conditioned subsidy schemes for state or local campaigns.

Disclosure of campaign contributions is another control measure on political financing. In *Buckley* the Court upheld a sweeping requirement that political candidates and political committees disclose the identity of any contributor who gave more than $100 to a campaign, in order to help deter corruption and give the public a better sense of a candidate's supporters. But in a subsequent case the Court recognized that such a wholesale disclosure requirement could prove extremely problematic for small and controversial political parties—such as the Socialist Workers party and the Communist party—whose members and supporters would be extremely reluctant to have their identities disclosed for fear of the possible harassment to which they might be exposed. Accordingly, the Court ruled that where such a party can show "a reasonable probability that disclosing the names of contributors and recipients [will lead to] threats, harassment, or reprisals" against people identified as its supporters or members, the Constitution requires exempting such groups from having to identify and report their contributions or their disbursements as well.[88]

At the federal level, the contribution limitations, reporting, and disclosure requirements and presidential subsidies are enforced by the Federal Election Commission.

Can political activity and expenditures by independent groups and individuals be restricted?

Basically no, except for limits on direct contributions to candidates.

The post-Watergate reform laws, in addition to controlling candidates and their political committees, also severely restricted the amount of money that individuals and groups totally independent of campaigns could spend to communicate their messages to the voters. This effectively meant that such individuals and groups that wanted to use their funds to support the election of candidate X or oppose the election of candidate Y were barred from doing so. The Court found that, unlike contributions to a candidate, independent political expenditures contained no potential for corruption and, on the other hand, represented citizen speech in its most classic and basic form. "While the independent expenditure ceiling thus fails to serve any substantial governmental interest in stemming the reality or appearance of corruption in the electoral process, it heavily burdens core First Amendment expression."[89] For that reason, there can be *no* financial restrictions on the ability of independent campaign groups and individuals to use their resources to engage in campaign advocacy. But such individual and group contributions and expenditures can be subject to reporting and disclosure requirements, although presumably there would be an exemption for controversial groups that would suffer real harassment as a result of such disclosure.

In 1985 the Court applied these principles to hold that independent campaign expenditures made in support of—but not in coordination with—a publicly subsidized presidential candidate could not be restricted either. Independent citizen speech about presidential candidates, no matter how extensively the group is funded, cannot be restricted in the interests of electoral purity. The Court observed that many such groups are made up of a large number of modest contributors, and pooling their resources enables them to amplify their political voice.[90]

Finally, even independent political groups that happen to be incorporated but are basically more like voluntary political associations than like business firms can use their resources to engage in independent election campaign speech, despite their corporate form. For many years, corporations and unions have been barred from using their treasury funds to make contributions directly to federal candidates or public expenditures on behalf of the campaigns of such candidates. But a local, incorporated pro-life group was held constitutionally exempt from such prohibitions on the ground that (1) it was formed for political and ideological advocacy, not business activity, (2) it had no capital or shareholders and (3) it was not under the control of a business corporation or union. Thus the group could publish a right-to-life newsletter urging the election or defeat of political candidates without restriction.[91] But the Court refused to extend this protection to business organizations, such as the Chamber of Commerce, which are incorporated and comprised mostly of corporations.[92] In any event, disclosure and reporting requirements may have to be complied with if funds are expended for express advocacy of the election or defeat of specified candidates.[93]

Can nonpartisan, issue-oriented organizations be regulated like partisan political organizations?

No. One particularly objectionable feature of the post-Watergate campaign finance laws was the attempt to include within their reach public advocacy by cause organizations that related to public officials who were also candidates for election. The law declared that public discussion and criticism of campaign issues, voting records, public policies, and official performance could influence the outcome of an election by shaping public opinion and attitudes and therefore had to be regulated under the campaign laws. But the courts unanimously rejected such regulation because it would permit government monitoring and control of all issue-oriented speech during the campaign season, a clear First Amendment violation.

There must be a sharp dividing line between the funding of partisan, candidate advocacy—which can be regulated to some degree—and nonpartisan issue-oriented speech—which cannot. The dividing line is based on "explicit words of advocacy" of the election or defeat of particular political candidates. Issue-oriented speech that mentions and discusses candidates but that stops short of "express advocacy" of the candidate is immune from campaign finance regulations.[94] As a result, the courts have generally held that nonpartisan groups like the ACLU cannot be subject to campaign finance regulations and have thrown out laws that would impose such regulation.[95]

The Federal Election Commission has persisted, however, in bringing complaints against antiwar, environmental, pro-choice, and other issue organizations for engaging in sharp criticism of politicians during an election year. Just recently, however, one federal court ruled that the National Organization for Women could not be deemed a partisan organization merely because of its sharp opposition to politicians like Ronald Reagan, Jesse Helms, and others. "NOW's use of corporate funds to finance letters criticizing certain politicians who do not share NOW's political opinions does not fall within the prohibitions of the federal election campaign laws. The Court holds that NOW did not violate [campaign laws] when it used its corporate treasury to engage in issue advocacy, rather than express advocacy of the election of specific candidates. NOW was exercising its constitutional right of advocating and defending points of view. It was not spending its money to influence an election or to call for the election or defeat of particular persons seeking political office."[96]

Can the government restrict the funding of political activity involving state or local referendum campaigns?

No. Initiative and referendum mechanisms are forms of direct democracy whereby citizens vote on new laws for their state or locality. Most states permit such ballot questions to be voted on at elections, and they can be extremely important to protest groups who can use the process to propose or enact laws or provisions of concern to them.

States have tried to limit this process by restricting the amount of funds that can be expended to influence the outcome of a ballot question, but the Court has invalidated most such restrictions. For example, the Court has held that corporations cannot be banned from making corporate expenditures of funds to lobby the public on ballot questions. Since the expenditure of funds presented no possibility of corrupting public officials, because none was being elected, there was no compelling justification for preventing corporations from expressing their views to the public on these questions. Although corporate advertising might influence the outcome of the election, "the fact that advocacy may persuade the electorate is hardly a reason to suppress it."[97]

Limitations on the amount of contributions to a referendum campaign committee are unconstitutional as well. Thus where the City of Berkeley said that no one could contribute more than $250 to a group trying to oppose a referendum that would establish municipal rent control, the Court held: "The restraint imposed by the Berkeley Ordinance on rights of association and in turn on individual and collective rights of expression plainly contravenes both the right of association and the speech guarantees of the First Amendment."[98]

Finally, in 1988 the Court unanimously threw out a Colorado law that prohibited hiring people to collect petition signatures in order to put a voter initiative on the ballot. Such a ban limits the ability of the group to communicate with voters and get their question on the ballot and thus violates the fundamental principle that people and groups are entitled to use their funds and resources to advance their political advocacy and communicate their views to the public.[99] This decision calls into question earlier lower court rulings that reasoned that since the state did not have to allow ballot questions at all, it had greater leeway to impose serious obstacles to putting questions on the ballot.[100] Thus the Colorado ruling is extremely important for protestors who want to put controversial questions to the voters.

Although there can be no direct restrictions on expenditures or contributions of funds to support or defeat a ballot question, disclosure of the funding of such efforts can probably to some extent be required. On the one hand, since there is no corruption concern with a ballot question, the major justification for requiring disclosure of contributions to political candidates and committees is not present. Indeed, one court ruled that the NYCLU did not have to disclose its contributors to a statewide ERA effort.[101] On the other hand, the Court in the corporate referendum spending case suggested that, since it could not ban corporate spending in referendum campaigns, states might at least be able to require disclosure of the sources of such funding to help inform the electorate of the interests supporting or opposing a ballot question.[102]

In lobbying the legislature, can a group be required to report its expenditures and disclose its members, contributors, and funding sources?

The answer is unclear. The right to lobby is protected under the First Amendment.[103] The Court has broadly recognized and protected the right of political association and the corresponding right of associational privacy. In the political campaign setting, the Court permits enforced disclosure of contributors as an antidote to official corruption but holds that small and controversial parties have to be given a constitutional exemption from such disclosure. In terms of influencing the legislature, the Court long ago upheld required registration and disclosure by hardcore lobbying groups that actively buttonhole legislators or engage in other acts of direct, face-to-face lobbying but questioned whether such rules could be applied more broadly to those engaged in grass roots lobbying or general efforts to influence public opinion or legislative questions.[104] It is unclear whether the distinctions drawn in the area of campaign reporting and disclosure would apply to lobbying disclosure as well.[105]

If leaflets or literature on public issues are distributed, does the material have to identify its sponsors?

Probably not. In 1960 the Supreme Court struck down a Los Angeles ordinance that prohibited the distribution of leaflets that failed to identify the author or sponsor. Observing that the Federalist Papers, written in favor of the adoption of the Constitution, were published under fictitious names, the Court ruled that the First Amendment protected a right of political anonymity in speech.[106] In *Buckley v. Valeo*, the Court upheld a reporting requirement for any group or person independently spending more than $100 for express candidate-oriented advocacy, suggesting that the flaw in the Los Angeles ordinance was that it applied to all leaflets and literature and was not focused on election campaign activity and the concerns with false or deceptive campaign charges. Nevertheless, where political campaign leaflets are concerned, most courts continue to invalidate bans on anonymous campaign material.[107]

Can a speaker be punished for a false or deceptive political campaign speech?

Probably not. One of the arguments against anonymous campaign literature is that such anonymity may serve as a cover for false, fraudulent, or defamatory campaign speech or charges. But as with defamation of public officials, the problem is how to define intentionally false or deceptive campaign speech in such a precise and careful way that vigorous and good faith political advocacy is not broadly chilled or deterred. For if it is a crime to engage in false campaign speech, then government will be deciding what is true and false in the political arena, a chilling prospect for free speech. "The very purpose of the First Amendment is to foreclose public authority from assuming a guardianship of the public mind. . . . In this field every person must be his own watchman for the truth, because the forefathers did not trust any government to separate the true and the false for us."[108]

Thus, for example, the Supreme Court threw out a penalty against a local political candidate who made an "illegal" campaign promise to lower his salary if elected. Under the law, it didn't matter if the promise was made in good faith or later withdrawn. "The chilling effect of such absolute accountability for factual misstatements in the course of political debate is incompatible with the atmosphere of free discussion contemplated by the First Amendment in the context of political campaigns."[109] A New York statute that banned "deliberate misrepresentations" in campaign literature was overturned for similar reasons.[110] But courts have recognized, at least potentially, some power to control calculated, willful, false, factual statements—the knowing lie—even in a political setting.[111] The problem is how to prohibit only such lies without subjecting sharp criticism of government and politicians to undue official control.

NOTES

1. 1 Stat. 596.
2. *New York Times Co. v. Sullivan,* 376 U.S. 254, 276 (1964).
3. *Id.* at 270.
4. *Id.* at 291.
5. *City of Philadelphia v. Washington Post Co.* 482 F. Supp. 897, 899 (E.D. Pa. 1979).
6. *Rosenblatt v. Baer,* 383 U.S. 75 (1966).
7. *Henry v. Collins,* 380 U.S. 356 (1965).
8. *Brown v. Hartlage,* 456 U.S. 45 (1982); *Vanasco v. Schwartz,* 401 F. Supp. 87 (E.D.N.Y. 1975), *aff'd,* 423 U.S. 1041 (1976); *Loza v. Panish,* 102 Cal. App. 3d 821, 162 Cal Rptr. 596 (1980); *but see DeWine v. Ohio Elections Commission,* 61 Ohio App. 2d 25, 399 N.E.2d 99 (1978) (upholding statute that prohibited making knowingly false statements about any political candidate).
9. *Howard Gault Co. v. Texas Rural Legal Aid, Inc.,* 848 F.2d 544, 564 (5th Cir. 1988).
10. *LeBron v. Washington Metropolitan Area Transit Authority,* 749 F.2d 893, 898, (D.C. Cir. 1984).
11. *Janklow v. Newsweek,* 788 F.2d 1300, 1305 (8th Cir. 1986).

12. *Saenz v. Playboy Enterprises, Inc.*, 653 F. Supp. 552, 555 (N.D. Ill. 1987), *aff'd*, 841 F.2d 1309 (7th Cir. 1988).

13. *Kucinich v. Forbes*, 432 F. Supp. 1101 (N.D. Ohio 1977).

14. See *Bodenmiller v. Stanchfield*, 557 F. Supp. 857 (E.D.N.Y. 1983); *Stevens v. Tillman*, 661 F. Supp. 702 (N.D. Ill. 1986).

15. *Ealy v. Littlejohn*, 569 F.2d 219, 229 (5th Cir. 1978).

16. *McDonald v. Smith*, 472 U.S. 479, 489–90 (1985) (Brennan, J., concurring).

17. *Gates v. City of Dallas*, 729 F.2d 343 (5th Cir. 1984).

18. *Megill v. Board of Regents*, 541 F.2d 1073 (5th Cir. 1976).

19. *Eiland v. City of Montgomery*, 797 F.2d 953 (11th Cir. 1986); *see also Leonard v. City of Columbus*, 705 F.2d 1299 (11th Cir. 1983).

20. *Edwards v. National Audubon Society, Inc.*, 556 F.2d 113 (2d Cir. 1977); *Gates v. City of Dallas*, 729 F.2d 343 (5th Cir. 1984); *Good Government Group of Seal Beach, Inc. v. Superior Court*, 22 Cal. 3d 672, 586 P.2d 572 (Cal. 1978); *Adolph Coors Co. v. Movement against Racism and the Klan*, 777 F.2d 1538 (11th Cir. 1985).

21. *Ray v. Edwards*, 725 F.2d 655, 660–61 (11th Cir. 1984).

22. See *Garrison v. Louisiana*, 379 U.S. 64 (1964).

23. *Barr v. Matteo*, 360 U.S. 564 (1959); *Paul v. Davis*, 424 U.S. 693 (1976).

24. *New York Times Co. v. Sullivan*, 376 U.S. 254, 280 (1964).

25. *Garrison v. Louisiana*, 379 U.S. 64 (1964).

26. *Hustler Magazine v. Falwell*, 108 S. Ct. 876, 880 (1988).

27. *Gertz v. Robert Welch, Inc.*, 418 U.S. 323, 342–45 (1974).

28. *Time, Inc. v. Firestone*, 424 U.S. 448 (1976); *Gertz v. Robert Welch, Inc.*, 418 U.S. 323 (1974); *Hutchinson v. Proxmire*, 443 U.S. 111 (1979); *Wolston v. Reader's Digest Association, Inc.*, 443 U.S. 157 (1979); *Dun and Bradstreet, Inc. v. Greenmoss Builders, Inc.*, 472 U.S. 749 (1985).

29. *Gertz v. Robert Welch, Inc.*, 418 U.S. 323 (1974).

30. *Dun and Bradstreet, Inc. v. Greenmoss Builders, Inc.*, 472 U.S. 749 (1985).

31. Compare *Bose Corporation v. Consumers Union of United States, Inc.*, 466 U.S. 485 (1984) *with Dun and Bradstreet, Inc. v. Greenmoss Builders, Inc.*, 472 U.S. 749 (1985).

32. *Gertz v. Robert Welch, Inc.*, 418 U.S. 323, 339–41 (1974). In *Milkovich v. Lorain Journal Co.*, 110 S. Ct. 2695 (1990), the Court ruled there is no separate, "absolute" protection for "opinions" that contain false factual connotations, such as that someone lies under oath.

33. *Brown and Williamson Tobacco Co. v. Jacobson*, 827 F.2d 1119, 1131 (7th Cir. 1987).

34. *Trump v. Chicago Tribune Co.*, 616 F. Supp. 1434, 1435 (S.D.N.Y.

1985) (citations omitted); *see also McManus v. Doubleday and Co., Inc.*, 513 F. Supp. 1383, 1385 (S.D.N.Y. 1981).

35. *Koch v. Goldway*, 817 F.2d 507, 509 (9th Cir. 1987).

36. *Dworkin v. Hustler Magazine, Inc.*, 867 F.2d 1188, 1194 (9th Cir. 1989); *see generally* H. Dorsen, *Satiric Appropriation and the Law of Libel, Trademark, and Copyright: Remedies without Wrongs*, 65 B.U.L. Rev. 923 (1985).

37. *Greenbelt Cooperative Publishing Association v. Bresler*, 398 U.S. 6 (1970); *Old Dominion Branch No. 496, National Association of Letter Carriers v. Austin*, 418 U.S. 264 (1974); *McCabe v. Rattiner*, 814 F.2d 839 (1st Cir. 1987).

38. *Henderson v. Times Mirror Co.*, 669 F. Supp. 356 (D. Colo. 1987), *aff'd*, 876 F.2d 108 (10th Cir. 1989).

39. *Good Government Group of Seal Beach, Inc. v. Superior Court*, 22 Cal. 3d 672, 586 P.2d 572 (1978).

40. *See Cianci v. New Times Publishing Co.*, 639 F.2d 54 (2d Cir. 1980). The Supreme Court agreed with this reasoning in its 1990 decision in *Milkovich v. Lorain Journal Co.*, 110 S. Ct. 2695 (1990).

41. *Saenz v. Playboy Enterprises, Inc.*, 653 F. Supp. 552, 562) (N.D. Ill., 1987).

42. *Cianci v. New Times Publishing Co.*, 639 F.2d 54, 64 (2d Cir. 1980).

43. *Milkovich v. Lorain Journal Co.*, 110 S. Ct. 2695 (1990).

44. *Buckley v. Littell*, 539 F.2d 882, 893 (2d Cir. 1976). *See also Cafeteria Employees Union v. Angelos*, 320 U.S. 293 (1943) ("fascist" epithet protected in labor dispute).

45. *Koch v. Goldway*, 817 F.2d 507, 510 (9th Cir. 1987).

46. *Lasky v. American Broadcasting Companies, Inc.*, 606 F. Supp. 934, 940 (S.D.N.Y. 1985); *see also Holy Spirit Association for Unification of World Christianity v. Sequoia Elsevier Publishing Co., Inc.*, 75 A.D. 2d 523, 426 N.Y.S. 2d 759 (1st Dept. 1980).

47. *Gertz v. Robert Welch, Inc.*, 418 U.S. 323, 326 (1974). Under more recent decisions the first two charges might be viewed as protected epithet or hyperbole.

48. *Anderson v. Liberty Lobby, Inc.*, 447 U.S. 242 (1986); *Liberty Lobby v. Dow Jones & Co., Inc.*, 838 F.2d 1287 (D.C. Cir. 1988).

49. *Adolph Coors Co. v. Movement against Racism and the Klan*, 777 F.2d 1538 (11th Cir. 1985).

50. *Compare Raible v. Newsweek, Inc.*, 341 F. Supp. 804 (W.D. Pa. 1972) *with Afro-American Publishing Co. v. Jaffe*, 366 F.2d 649 (D.C. Cir. 1966).

51. *Fleming v. Kane County*, 636 F. Supp. 742 (N.D. Ill. 1986).

52. *Stevens v. Tillman*, 661 F. Supp. 702, 709–11 (N.D. Ill. 1986).

53. *Milkovich v. Lorain Journal Co.*, 110 S. Ct. 2695, 2707 (1990).

54. *Hustler Magazine v. Falwell*, 108 S. Ct. 876, 882 (1988).

55. *Ault v. Hustler Magazine, Inc.*, 860 F.2d 877 (9th Cir. 1988).

56. *See Cox Broadcasting Corp. v. Cohn*, 420 U.S. 469 (1975); *The Florida Star v. B.J.F.*, 109 S. Ct. 2603 (1989).

57. *United States Department of Justice v. Reporters Committee for Freedom of the Press*, 109 S. Ct. 1468 (1989).

58. *Harper & Row Publishers, Inc. v. Nation Enterprises*, 471 U.S. 539 (1985).

59. *San Francisco Arts and Athletics, Inc. v. United States Olympic Committee*, 483 U.S. 522, 535 (1987).

60. *Hustler Magazine, Inc. v. Moral Majority*, 606 F. Supp. 1526, 1536 (C.D. Cal. 1986).

61. *Friends of Phil Gramm v. Americans for Phil Gramm*, 587 F. Supp. 769, 774 (E.D. Va. 1984); *see also Riddell v. National Democratic Party*, 508 F.2d 770 (5th Cir. 1975); *but cf. Tomei v. Finley*, 512 F. Supp. 695 (N.D. Ill. 1981) (deliberate and fraudulent use of the abbreviation "Rep." by Democrats in a local election to deceive voters can be enjoined).

62. *Bridges v. California*, 314 U.S. 252 (1941).

63. *Craig v. Harney*, 331 U.S. 367, 373–75 (1947); *See also Pennekamp v. Florida*, 328 U.S. 331 (1946).

64. *Wood v. Georgia*, 370 U.S. 375 (1962).

65. *Garrison v. Louisiana*, 379 U.S. 64, 66 (1964).

66. *Landmark Communications, Inc. v. Virginia*, 435 U.S. 829 (1978).

67. *E.g., Rinaldi v. Holt, Rinehart & Winston, Inc.*, 42 N.Y.2d 369, 366 N.E.2d 1299 (1977) (decision against judge).

68. *Cox v. Louisiana*, 379 U.S. 559 (1965).

69. *See Grace v. United States*, 461 U.S. 171 (1983).

70. *See Illinois v. Allen*, 397 U.S. 337 (1970); *but cf. In re Snyder*, 472 U.S. 634 (1985) (cannot disbar attorney for writing rude letter to court). *See generally* N. Dorsen and L. Friedman, *Disorder in the Court* (1973).

71. *See e.g. Richmond Newspapers, Inc. v. Virginia*, 448 U.S. 555 (1980); *Globe Newspaper Co. v. Superior Court*, 457 U.S. 596 (1982); *Press-Enterprise Co. v. Superior Court*, 464 U.S. 501 (1984); *Press-Enterprise Co. v. Superior Court*, 478 U.S. 1 (1986); *but cf. Norris v. Risley*, 878 F.2d 1178 (9th Cir. 1989) (presence of spectators wearing "Women Against Rape" buttons could deprive rape defendant of fair trial).

72. *Nebraska Press Association v. Stuart*, 427 U.S. 539 (1976).

73. *See Journal Publishing Co. v. Mechem*, 801 F.2d 1233 (10th Cir. 1986).

74. *Compare Chicago Council of Lawyers v. Bauer*, 522 F.2d 242 (7th

Cir. 1975) *with Hirschkop v. Snead*, 594 F.2d 356 (4th Cir. 1979) *and United States v. Simon*, 664 F. Supp. 780 (S.D.N.Y. 1987), *aff'd* 842 F.2d 603 (2d Cir. 1988).

75. *Levine v. United States District Court*, 764 F.2d 590 (9th Cir. 1985); *Radio Television News Association v. United States District Court*, 781 F.2d 1443 (9th Cir. 1986).

76. *Levine v. United States District Court*, 775 F.2d 1054, 1055 (9th Cir. 1985) (petition for rehearing en banc rejected).

77. *Bailey v. Systems Innovation, Inc.*, 852 F.2d 93 (3d Cir. 1988).

78. *Butterworth v. Smith*, 110 S. Ct. 1376 (1990).

79. *United States v. Ford*, 830 F.2d 596, 599–600 (6th Cir. 1987).

80. *American Party of Texas v. White*, 415 U.S. 767, 779–80 (1974); *Smith v. Allwright*, 321 U.S. 649 (1944).

81. *Eu v. San Francisco County Democratic Central Committee*, 109 S. Ct. 1013, 1020 (1989); *see also Geary v. Renne*, 911 F.2d 280 (9th Cir. 1990) (en banc) (cannot ban parties from endorsing candidates in nonpartisan elections).

82. *Id.* at 1025; see also *Tashjian v. Republican Party of Connecticut*, 479 U.S. 208 (1986).

83. *Compare Williams v. Rhodes*, 393 U.S. 23 (1968), *Illinois Election Board v. Socialist Workers Party*, 440 U.S. 173 (1979), *and Anderson v. Celebreeze*, 460 U.S. 780 (1983) *with Jenness v. Fortson*, 403 U.S. 431 (1970) *and Munro v. Socialist Workers Party*, 479 U.S. 189 (1986).

84. *See Anderson v. Celebreeze*, 460 U.S. 780 (1983); *but see American Party of Texas v. White*, 415 U.S. 767, 787, n. 18 (1974).

85. *Bullock v. Carter*, 405 U.S. 134 (1972); *Lubin v. Panish*, 415 U.S. 709 (1974).

86. 424 U.S. 1 (1976).

87. *See Republican National Committee v. Federal Election Commission*, 487 F. Supp. 280 (S.D.N.Y. 1980), 616 F.2d 1 (2d Cir. 1980), *aff'd*, 445 U.S. 955 (1980) (upholding conditional expenditure limitations on presidential campaigns that accept subsidies).

88. *Brown v. Socialist Workers '74 Campaign Committee*, 459 U.S. 87, 100 (1982); *Federal Election Commission v. Hall-Tyner Election Campaign Committee*, 678 F.2d 416 (2d Cir. 1981).

89. *Buckley v. Valeo*, 424 U.S. 1, 48 (1976).

90. *Federal Election Commission v. National Conservative Political Action Committee*, 470 U.S. 480 (1985).

91. *Federal Election Commission v. Massachusetts Citizens for Life, Inc.*, 479 U.S. 238 (1986).

92. *Austin v. Michigan State Chamber of Commerce*, 110 S. Ct. 1391 (1990).

93. *See Federal Election Commission v. Furgatch,* 807 F.2d 857 (9th Cir. 1987); *Goland v. United States,* 903 F.2d 1247 (9th Cir. 1990).
94. *Buckley v. Valeo,* 424 U.S. 1, 74–82 (1976).
95. *United States v. National Committee for Impeachment,* 469 F.2d 1135 (2d Cir. 1972); *American Civil Liberties Union, Inc. v. Jennings,* 366 F. Supp. 1041 (D.D.C. 1973), *vacated as moot,* 422 U.S. 1030 (1975); *Federal Election Commission v. Central Long Island Tax Reform Immediately Committee,* 616 F.2d 45 (2d Cir. 1980) (en banc).
96. *Federal Election Commission v. National Organization for Women,* 713 F. Supp. 428 (D.D.C. 1989).
97. *First National Bank of Boston v. Bellotti,* 435 U.S. 765 (1978).
98. *Citizens against Rent Control Coalition for Fair Housing v. City of Berkeley,* 454 U.S. 290, 300 (1981).
99. *Meyer v. Grant,* 486 U.S. 414 (1988).
100. *E.g., Gerges v. Carney,* 691 F.2d 297 (7th Cir. 1982) (upholding severe petition signature requirements to put nuclear freeze on ballot).
101. *See New York Civil Liberties Union, Inc. v. Acito,* 459 F. Supp. 75 (S.D.N.Y. 1978).
102. *First National Bank of Boston v. Bellotti,* 435 U.S. 765, 792, n. 32 (1978); *Michigan State Chamber of Commerce v. Austin,* 637 F. Supp. 1192 (E.D. Mich. 1986), *aff'd,* 832 F.2d 947 (6th Cir. 1987).
103. *E.g., Citizens Energy Coalition of Indiana, Inc. v. Sendak,* 459 F. Supp. 248 (S.D. Ind. 1978), *aff'd,* 594 F.2d 1158 (7th Cir. 1979); *cf. Regan v. Taxation with Representation of Washington,* 461 U.S. 540 1983).
104. *Compare United States v. Harriss,* 347 U.S. 612 (1954) *with United States v. Rumely,* 345 U.S. 41 (1953).
105. *See Minnesota State Ethical Practices v. National Rifle Association of America,* 761 F.2d 509 (8th Cir. 1985); *American Civil Liberties Union, Inc. v. New Jersey Election Law Enforcement Commission,* 509 F. Supp. 1123 (D.N.J. 1981); *cf. Federal Election Commission v. Machinists Non-Partisan League,* 655 F.2d 380 (D.C. Cir. 1981).
106. *Talley v. California,* 362 U.S. 60 (1960).
107. *Wilson v. Stocker,* 819 F.2d 943 (10th Cir. 1987); *Rosen v. Port of Portland,* 641 F.2d 1243 (9th Cir. 1981); *People v. White,* 116 Ill. 2d 171, 506 N.E. 2d 1284 (1987) *but see KVUE, Inc. v. Moore,* 709 F.2d 922 (5th Cir. 1983), *aff'd,* 465 U.S. 1092 (1984) (disclosure of TV ad sponsors permissible).
108. *Thomas v. Collins,* 323 U.S. 516, 545 (1945) (Jackson, J., concurring); *accord Meyer v. Grant,* 486 U.S. 414 (1988).

109. *Brown v. Hartlage*, 456 U.S. 45, 61 (1982).
110. *Vanasco v. Schwartz*, 401 F. Supp. 87 (E.D.N.Y. 1975), *aff'd*, 423 U.S. 1041 (1976); *see also Galliano v. United States Postal Service*, 836 F.2d 1362 (D.C. Cir. 1988); *Friends of Phil Gramm v. Americans for Phil Gramm*, 587 F. Supp. 769 (E.D. Va. 1984); *Tomei v. Finley*, 512 F. Supp. 695 (N.D. Ill. 1981) *cf. Commonwealth of Pennsylvania v. Wadzinski*, 492 Pa. 35, 422 A.2d 124 (1980).
111. *See Pestak v. Ohio Elections Commission*, 670 F. Supp. 1368, *clarified* 677 F. Supp. 534 (S.D. Ohio 1987); *Dewine v. Ohio Election Commission*, 61 Ohio App. 2d 25, 399 N.E. 2d 99 (1978); *Treasurer of Committee to Elect Lostracco v. Fox*, 150 Mich. App. 617, 389 N.W. 2d 446 (1986).

VI
The Funding of Protest

A leading California politician, Jesse Unruh, once observed that "money is the mother's milk of politics." The Supreme Court recognized the same thing in the campaign finance case: "[a] restriction on the amount of money a person or group can spend on political communication during a campaign necessarily reduces the quantity of expression by restricting the number of issues discussed, the depth of their exploration and the size of the audience reached. This is because virtually every means of communicating ideas in today's mass society requires the expenditure of money."[1] Printing leaflets and handbills, holding speeches and rallies, using the print or electronic media—all these methods of political communication are indispensable, yet may be costly. And what is true of partisan politics is no less true of protest speech and activities generally.

Of course almost all individuals and groups generate money to support and facilitate their speech and protest "the old-fashioned way": they raise it. The costs of protest are underwritten by people's own resources and support from contributions to and membership in groups and organizations. People often respond to significant events and issues by increasing (or decreasing) their support for the groups and organizations involved in those issues.

For the most part, such funding matters are wholly removed from legal or constitutional questions. There are two important areas, however, where the funding of protest does raise significant constitutional questions: (1) where government tries to restrict or discourage the funding of protest and (2) where government provides financial and other subsidies, but tries to withhold them from groups or individuals espousing particular, disfavored causes or points of view.

RESTRICTIONS ON PRIVATE FUNDING OF PROTEST

Can the government restrict the use of personal or organizational funds for political protest activities?

No. Where persons or groups wish to use their own funds or resources for political activities, the government may not impose direct restraints on their right to do so. The campaign finance cases show that, except for the limited power to restrict campaign contributions to and by political candidates and committees, government may not control the amount or nature of expenditures for partisan political activities or, certainly, for nonpartisan issue speech and protest. The Court has repeated that the First Amendment prevents government from restricting the funding of political advocacy and protest.[2]

Can government compel disclosure of membership in or contributors to protest groups?

No. Except for explicitly partisan campaign activities, government cannot even require reporting and disclosure of funding by protest groups or individuals. (And even in the partisan context, it cannot require financial information from controversial groups and parties.)

During the 1950s and 1960s, many Southern states tried to compel groups like the NAACP to disclose their members and contributors in order to harass and deter civil rights activities under the guise of regulating business or charitable groups. It was clear that such disclosure would have exposed members to economic reprisal, loss of employment, threat of physical assault, and other manifestations of public hostility. The Supreme Court ruled that such efforts interfered with freedom of speech and association with no compelling justification: "[c]ompelled disclosure of affiliation with groups engaged in advocacy may constitute [an effective] restraint on freedom of association."[3] These principles have also protected the ACLU and other nonpartisan advocacy groups from having to disclose their members and contributors.[4] The Court departed somewhat from these principles where disclosure was targeted on groups such as the Communist party that were deemed to pose national security concerns.[5]

Can government regulate the methods of fundraising that protest and advocacy groups use?

Generally not. Solicitation of funds for protest, advocacy, or charitable groups is protected speech under the First Amendment: "charitable appeals for funds, on the street or door to door, involve a variety of speech interests—communication of information, the dissemination and propagating of views and ideas, and the advocacy of causes—that are within the protection of the First Amendment. Soliciting financial support is undoubtedly subject to reasonable regulation but the latter must be undertaken with due regard for the reality that solicitation is characteristically intertwined with informative and perhaps persuasive speech seeking support for particular causes or for particular views on economic, political, or social issues and for the reality that without solicitation the flow of such information and advocacy would likely cease."[6]

In one case, the Supreme Court rejected a local ordinance that barred door-to-door or street solicitations by any charitable organization—there an environmental group—that did not use at least 75 percent of its receipts for "charitable purposes." The Court ruled that such a restriction improperly intruded on the group's choice to advance its cause by employing professional staff to generate position papers and advocacy statements. While government has a legitimate interest in protecting the public from fraud, crime, and undue annoyance by solicitors for charitable or other causes, the 75-percent rule did not directly achieve that purpose. The Court also threw out a similar rule that restricted the fundraising and advocacy work of a police benevolent organization and its ability to hire a professional fundraiser.[7] Finally, the Court has invalidated regulations of the fees that professional fundraisers can charge and the information they must disclose to potential contributors; the state could more narrowly achieve its concerns with regulating fraud and financial irregularities by direct prohibition of such practices and by requiring that information reports be filed with the state.[8] But government can neutrally and narrowly regulate the time, place, and manner of fund solicitation that takes the form of door-to-door canvassing or occurs in a crowded setting like a state fair or airport.[9] See part 2 below.

Can the government restrict public advertising and solicitation of funds by protest or public interest organizations?

No. Advancing and soliciting support for a cause through advertisements, direct-mail campaigns, and other forms of public solicitation are just as protected as the views the funds and support would advance. Indeed, in the landmark defamation case of *New York Times Co. v. Sullivan*,[10] the Court ruled that the alleged libelous statements did not lose their First Amendment protection just because they were contained in a paid advertisement that solicited funds for civil rights causes. Advertisements for services with a public interest dimension—such as ads for abortion clinics and legal services—are protected speech as well and cannot be banned by government.[11] Indeed, even soliciting clients for ACLU or NAACP cases has been held protected by the First Amendment, despite the fact that the organizations may benefit financially through court-awarded attorneys' fees if such cases are won.[12]

GOVERNMENT REFUSALS TO ALLOW PUBLIC FUNDS TO SUBSIDIZE SPEECH AND PROTEST

Is government required to subsidize political advocacy and protest?

No. The First Amendment, which is designed to serve as a negative check against government restrictions on speech, does not mean that government has an affirmative obligation to support or subsidize protest activities. Of course government does facilitate speech to the extent it must allow the streets, parks, and public forums to be used for speech and protest and usually picks up the incidental costs of doing so (police protection, sanitation, traffic control). But government generally is not required to pay for protest either directly through financial grants or subsidies or indirectly through tax credits and deductions.

That does not mean, however, that government can use the financial clout of its taxing and spending powers to deter or penalize political protest and advocacy. Even the power of the purse is subject to considerable First Amendment limitations. But it is often difficult to draw a line between government's merely withholding a financial subsidy from views and activities it disapproves, which it may do, and imposing a financial penalty on groups and views it disapproves, which it may not. The issue generally comes up in two contexts: indirect subsidies through tax deductions and credits and direct subsidies through government-provided funds and forums.

Does government have to give a tax deduction or advantage to political advocacy?

Basically, no. For example, government can decline to subsidize lobbying activities—clearly protected by the First Amendment—by refusing to allow a business or other deduction for such expenses.[13] Likewise, charitable organizations that get tax exemptions for their income and tax deductibility for contributions to them can be told that they may not substantially engage in lobbying if they want to keep the tax advantages. In a case involving a tax protest group, the Court said that such a condition does not violate the First Amendment since government has no obligation to underwrite or subsidize lobbying through tax preferences or subsidies. "Congress has not infringed any First Amendment rights or regulated any First Amendment activity. Congress has simply chosen not to pay for . . . lobbying. We again reject the notion that 'First Amendment rights are somehow not fully realized unless they are subsidized by the State.' "[14] Some justices saw more of a problem because the group literally was losing a benefit—tax-exemption—because it exercised a First Amendment right—lobbying. But since the group could solve the problem easily—by setting up a separate fund for its lobbying work—without jeopardizing its charitable status, the problem was eased. The Court also ruled that the tax law was not discriminatory even though it exempted veterans' organizations and allowed them to keep their charitable status and also engage in lobbying.

Can government discriminate among the kinds of advocacy or protest groups or viewpoints that can receive preferential tax treatment?

Probably not. Although it upheld a special lobbying exemption for veterans' organizations, the Court clearly stated that tax breaks or other government subsidies could not be allocated "in such a way as to aim at the suppression of dangerous ideas." Similarly, the Court has adamantly resisted the imposition of special sales or business taxes targeted on newspapers and has overturned tax advantages which discriminate among different members of the press based on the content of their medium. Thus, for example, an Arkansas sales tax that exempted newspapers and religious, professional, trade, and sports journals but taxed other periodicals including political journals was impermissible content discrimination.[15] And a law that taxed all periodicals except religious ones was likewise thrown out, although as an impermissible and focused support for religion.[16] Conversely, a general sales tax on the sale of all books, including religious books, is allowable.[17]

The point that the First Amendment does not allow government a free hand where tax advantages are concerned was made in a recent case involving preferential export license fees for films approved as "educational" by the United States Information Agency. The government claimed the power to deny the preferential treatment to films that contained "propaganda," or "misrepresentation" or "espoused a cause." An appellate court ruled: "The challenged regulations require that in order to be certified, a film must be balanced and truthful; must neither criticize nor advocate any political, religious, or economic views, and must not, by 'special pleading,' seek to influence opinion or policy. Each of these requirements draws content-based lines forbidden by the First Amendment."[18]

How much leeway does government have to decide which groups or activities qualify for "charitable" or "educational" status?

The answer is unclear. As indicated in the movie export license case, the First Amendment does impose considerable limits on the government's power to label certain groups or speech activities as not "charitable" or "educational." But the issues are difficult.

For example, the Court upheld the power of the federal government to exclude advocacy groups from the federal workplace charity drive, so long as the exclusion was not intended "solely to suppress the point of view" of the excluded groups.[19]

Two cases in the federal appeals court in Washington, D.C., illustrate the difficulties of determining when the government can properly deny favorable tax or other similar treatment to groups it claims are not "educational" or "charitable." In one case, the IRS claimed that a feminist organization that published a monthly magazine, *Big Mama Rag*, and promoted women's rights was not educational because of political and legislative commentary and because of "the articles, lectures, editorials, etc., promoting lesbianism." The IRS reasoned that although an organization could be educational even though it advocates a position or viewpoint so long as it permits a "full and fair exposition" of the facts, the feminist group had "adopted a stance so doctrinaire" that it could not satisfy this requirement. The court disagreed, ruling that the tax laws could not be used to penalize dissenting speech and that the IRS guidelines were so vague that they invited impermissible government censorship through the administration of charitable and educational tax benefits.[20]

Three years later, however, under a revised set of IRS guidelines, the same court rejected ACLU arguments and upheld an IRS decision to deny "educational" status to a white supremacy, antisemitic organization. This time the court found the group was not educational: "In sum, National Alliance repetitively appeals for action, including violence, to put to disadvantage or to injure persons who are members of named racial, religious or ethnic groups. It both asserts and implies that members of these groups have common characteristics which make them sufficiently dangerous to others to justify violent expulsion and separation. Even under the most minimum requirement of a rational development of a point of view, National Alliance's material falls short. . . . The material may express the emotions felt by a number of people, but it cannot reasonably be considered intellectual exposition." Distinguishing the feminist case, the court reasoned that "in the present case we see no possibility that the National Alliance publications can be found educational within any reasonable interpretation of that term." And the court concluded: "We have no doubt that publication of the National Alliance material is protected by the First Amendment from abridgement by law. . . . But it does not follow that the First Amendment requires a construction of the term 'educational' which embraces every continuing dissemination of views."[21]

Can government deny tax advantages to people or groups because government disapproves of their political views or activities?

No. In a 1958 case the Court ruled that California could not withhold a property tax exemption for veterans who were otherwise qualified taxpayers but who refused to sign a loyalty oath or prove their loyalty. Even though government did not have to provide a tax exemption in the first place, once it did so, it could not withhold the benefit because of people's political views. That would be using the tax laws to impose a penalty for things and speech unrelated to taxation and would permit government to achieve indirectly a result it could not command directly.[22] That is still the law; the exercise of free speech cannot cause the loss of an otherwise available benefit unrelated to that free speech activity. Whether or not a person has a "right" to a government benefit, it cannot be taken away because that person exercises free speech rights; that would be an improper penalty on the exercise of such rights.

When government makes subsidies and benefits available to facilitate political activities, can it withhold those benefits from certain groups on a political basis?

It depends. On one hand, the Court upheld public funding of presidential campaigns even though small and minor parties were ineligible for the funds because of poor past showing at the polls.[23] But postal rate subsidies cannot be given to major political parties, but withheld from minor or independent parties.[24] Similarly, where a state that generally banned lotteries allowed political committees to hold lotteries for fundraising, it could not exclude dissident or minor party groups from that benefit; nor could an ACLU affiliate be barred from the right, given to other charities, to hold a raffle on the basis of an official's claim that the event would be held at the home of "a communist or something."[25]

Finally, militant 1960s student groups, such as the SDS, cannot be denied the campus benefits of official recognition because of their beliefs and protest activities.[26] The same principle was applied in an important recent case establishing that a recognized campus university gay rights organization could not be denied campus activity funds available to all student groups: "a public body that chooses to fund speech or expression must do so evenhandedly, without discrimination among recipients. . . . The University need not supply funds to student organizations; but once having decided to do so, it is bound by the First Amendment to act without regard to the content of the ideas being expressed."[27]

Can the government stipulate that recipients of public funds refrain from engaging in First Amendment activity unrelated to the purpose of the grant and paid for by the recipient's own resources?

No. The government cannot grant funds to otherwise eligible recipients on the condition that they refrain from engaging in otherwise protected speech or protest where that expression is not paid for out of public funds and is otherwise unrelated to the grant. The Court would characterize that as a penalty exacted as a condition of obtaining the subsidy. Just as the government cannot withhold a tax deduction to those who will not sign a loyalty oath, neither can the receipt of direct financial grants be conditioned on refraining from unrelated or privately subsidized speech. For example, a Congressional statute prohibited "editorializing" by any public television station that received grants from the federal Corporation for Public Broadcasting, even though the grants made up only a small portion of the station's budget and the "editorializing" was basically paid for out of privately contributed funds. The Supreme Court held this an unacceptable regulation of the content of the speech of a recipient of public funds.[28] The same rule has been used to strike down as penalties requirements that recipients of family planning grants not use even their own privately raised funds to counsel or advocate abortion.[29] For the same reason, a federal statute that denied employment training funds to any person "who publicly advocates the violent overthrow of the Federal Government" was held an unconstitutional penalty on protected speech.[30] And an environmental group could not be denied grants to assist energy consumers because that group also lobbied the legislature on environmental issues.[31]

Can the government condition a grant of benefits on giving up protected protest where there is some relationship between the two?

Arguably yes. In 1981 Congress limited eligibility for food stamps where a family's need resulted from the fact that a member of the household had gone on strike. In other words Congress did not want food stamps to help subsidize striking workers. The Court held that this condition did not violate a union member's rights of speech or association. "[Strikers] and their union would be much better off if food stamps were available, but the strikers' right of association does not require the government to furnish funds to maximize the exercise of that right."[32] The restriction was viewed as the withholding of a subsidy for protest, not the imposition of a penalty on protest.

Can government withhold or withdraw funding from specific speech or protest activities that the government does not want to subsidize?

This is the most troublesome issue and the answer is unclear. It is plain that government can decline to fund or subsidize an entire category of protected speech, e.g., denying tax breaks for lobbying. Does that mean government can decline to subsidize specific kinds and contents of speech? Government can also refuse to fund other constitutionally protected activities, such as the choice of an abortion, by withholding public funds for indigent women who wish to have an abortion.[33] Does this mean the same is true of advocacy or counseling of abortion, i.e., can family planning groups be given government funds, but only on the condition that they not use *those funds* to advocate abortion, whatever they do with privately raised funds?[34] The same problem has been raised with respect to government funding of controversial works of art.

In the few cases involving art, the courts have tended to treat government much like any other art patron, largely free to pick and choose what art and artists to fund, without serious First Amendment scrutiny. In one case, a governor was permitted to withdraw a small arts grant made to a magazine because he thought a poem it published was obscene.[35] In another case, a court ruled that the government could remove a sculpture entitled *Tilted Arc* from in front of the federal building in Manhattan. Since the government had bought the sculpture when it commissioned the work, the government could remove it over the artist's objection, so long as the decision was based on aesthetic considerations and not on political censorship grounds. "Government can be a significant patron of the arts. Its incentive to fulfill that role must not be dampened by an unwarranted restriction on its freedom to decide what to do with art it has purchased."[36]

In a related context, another court held that a university could cease funding all litigation by a student legal services office on behalf of students; this was not preventing the students from filing lawsuits, but only refusing to fund such suits. The case probably would have been different if the university had stopped funding only lawsuits advocating liberal (or conservative) causes.[37] But other courts have taken a different position, holding that government may not decline to make otherwise appropriate grants simply because they would be used for artistic expression or other kinds of protected advocacy that government disfavors or disapproves.[38] Indeed, one court even held that it was unconstitutional for the Library of Congress, yielding to pressure, to withdraw its collection of Braille versions of Playboy magazine. "Although individuals have no right to a government subsidy or benefit, once one is conferred, as it is here through the allocation of funds for the program, the government cannot deny it on a basis that impinges on freedom of speech."[39]

Finally, courts have divided with respect to conditioning family planning grants on not using any of the funds to counsel or advocate abortion. One appeals court held that federal regulations prohibiting use of such funds to counsel or advocate abortion are unconstitutional as imposing undue burdens on a woman's right to choose and impermissible, viewpoint-based restrictions on the First Amendment right to publicly advocate abortion, even with the aid of public funds.[40] But another federal appeals court upheld the limitations.[41] The Supreme Court has agreed to rule on these questions.[42]

NOTES

1. *Buckley v. Valeo*, 424 U.S. 1, 19 (1976).
2. *Buckley v. Valeo*, 424 U.S. 1 (1976); *Meyer v. Grant*, 486 U.S. 414 (1988).
3. *NAACP v. Alabama*, 357 U.S. 449, 462 (1958); *Bates v. City of Little Rock*, 361 U.S. 516 (1960); *Gibson v. Florida Legislative Investigating Committee*, 372 U.S. 539 (1963).
4. *Buckley v. Valeo*, 519 F.2d 821, 869–78 (D.C. Cir. 1975); *Federal Election Commission v. Central Long Island Tax Reform Immediately Committee*, 616 F.2d 45 (2d Cir. 1980).
5. *Compare Communist Party v. Subversive Activities Control Board*, 367 U.S. 1 (1961) *with Gibson v. Florida Legislative Investigating Committee, supra* note 3.
6. *Village of Schaumberg v. Citizens for a Better Environment*, 444 U.S. 620, 632 (1980).
7. *Secretary of State v. Joseph H. Munson Co., Inc.*, 467 U.S. 947 (1984).
8. *Riley v. National Federation of the Blind of North Carolina*, 487 U.S. 781 (1988).

9. *Hynes v. Mayor and Council of Oradell*, 425 U.S. 610 (1976); *Heffron v. International Society for Krishna Consciousness, Inc.*, 452 U.S. 640 (1981); *cf. Board of Airport Commissioners v. Jews for Jesus, Inc.*, 482 U.S. 569 (1987).

10. 376 U.S. 254 (1964).

11. *Bigelow v. Virginia*, 421 U.S. 809 (1975); *Bates v. State Bar of Arizona*, 433 U.S. 350 (1977).

12. *In re Primus*, 436 U.S. 412 (1978); *NAACP v. Button*, 371 U.S. 415 (1963).

13. *Cammarano v. United States*, 358 U.S. 498 (1959).

14. *Regan v. Taxation with Representation of Washington*, 461 U.S. 540, 546 (1983).

15. *Arkansas Writers Project, Inc.. v. Ragland*, 481 U.S. 221 (1987); *see also Minneapolis Star & Tribune Co. v. Minnesota Commissioner of Revenue*, 460 U.S. 575 (1983); *Grosjean v. American Press Co., Inc..*, 297 U.S. 233 (1936).

16. *Texas Monthly, Inc. v. Bullock*, 109 S. Ct. 890 (1989).

17. *Jimmy Swaggert Ministries v. Board of Equalization of California*, 110 S. Ct. 688 (1990).

18. *Bullfrog Films, Inc. v. Wick*, 847 F.2d 502, 510 (9th Cir. 1988); *but cf. Meese v. Keene*, 481 U.S. 465 (1987) (upholding the requirement of a "political propaganda" label on films and books imported from abroad, based on their content).

19. *Cornelius v. NAACP Legal Defense and Education Fund*, 473 U.S. 788, 806 (1985).

20. *Big Mama Rag, Inc., v. United States*, 631 F.2d 1030, 1037 (D.C. Cir. 1980).

21. *National Alliance v. United States*, 710 F.2d 868, 873, 875 (D.C. Cir. 1983).

22. *Speiser v. Randall*, 357 U.S. 513 (1958).

23. *Buckley v. Valeo*, 424 U.S. 1, 93–108 (1976); *cf. Regan v. Taxation with Representation of Washington, supra* note 14.

24. *Greenberg v. Bolger*, 497 F. Supp. 756 (E.D.N.Y. 1980); *Spencer v. Hardesty*, 571 F. Supp. 444 (S.D. Ohio, 1983); *but see Common Cause v. Bolger*, 574 F. Supp. 672 (D.D.C. 1982) (upholding the use of the frank by members of Congress to send free mail to their constituents).

25. *Rhode Island Chapter of the National Women's Political Caucus v. Rhode Island Lottery Commission*, 609 F. Supp. 1403 (D.R.I. 1985); *Rhode Island ACLU v. Rhode Island Lottery Commission*, 553 F. Supp. 752 (D.R.I. 1982).

26. *Healy v. James*, 408 U.S. 169 (1972).

27. *Gay and Lesbian Students Association v. Gohn*, 850 F.2d 361, 362

(8th Cir. 1988). *Cf. Department of Education v. Lewis*, 416 So. 2d 455 (Fla. 1982) (overturns funding ban on college facilities used by gay rights groups).

28. *Federal Communications Commission v. League of Women Voters*, 468 U.S. 364 (1984).

29. *E.g., Planned Parenthood v. Arizona*, 789 F.2d 1348 (9th Cir. 1986), *aff'd*, 479 U.S. 925 (1986). *But see DKT Memorial Fund, Ltd. v. Agency for International Development*, 887 F.2d 275 (D.C. Cir. 1989).

30. *Blitz v. Donovan*, 538 F. Supp. 1119 (D.D.C. 1982), *vacated as moot*, 459 U.S. 1095 (1983).

31. *Citizens Energy Coalition of Indiana v. Sendak*, 459 F. Supp. 248 (S.D. Ind. 1978), *aff'd*, 594 F. 2d 1158 (7th Cir. 1979); *but cf. Regan v. Taxation with Representation of Washington*, *supra* note 14.

32. *Lyng v. International Union, UAW*, 485 U.S. 360, 368 (1988).

33. *Harris v. McRae*, 448 U.S. 297 (1980).

34. *Cf. Planned Parenthood Federation of America, Inc., v. Agency for International Development*, 838 F.2d 649 (2d Cir. 1988); *Alan Guttmacher Institute v. McPherson*, 616 F. Supp. 195, 205 (S.D.N.Y. 1985), *modified*, 805 F.2d 1088 (2d Cir. 1986).

35. *Advocates for the Arts v. Thomson*, 532 F.2d 792 (1st Cir. 1976).

36. *Serra v. General Services Administration*, 847 F.2d 1045, 1051 (2d Cir. 1988); see also *Piarowski v. Illinois Community College District 515*, 759 F.2d 625 (7th Cir. 1985). *But see Sefick v. City of Chicago*, 485 F. Supp. 644 (N.D. Ill. 1979).

37. *Student Government Association v. Board of Trustees of University of Massachusetts*, 868 F. 2d 473 (1st Cir. 1989); *but see Westchester Legal Services, Inc. v. County of Westchester*, 607 F. Supp. 1379 (S.D.N.Y. 1985) (government may not refuse to renew legal services contracts with private organization solely because those organizations file lawsuits against government).

38. *E.g., Gay and Lesbian Students Association v. Gohn*, 850 F.2d 321 (8th Cir. 1988); *Mission Trace Investments, Ltd. v. Small Business Administration*, 622 F. Supp. 687 (D. Colo. 1985) (invalidating an SBA rule barring financial assistance to all applicants engaging in the creation and dissemination of ideas and values); *see also Gay Men's Health Crisis v. Sullivan*, 733 F. Supp. 619 (S.D.N.Y. 1989) (pending challenge to ban on use of AIDS education funds "to promote or encourage, directly, homosexual sexual activities"); *New School for Social Research v. Frohnmeyer*, No. 90 Civ. 3510 (S.D.N.Y., filed May 23, 1990) (challenge to new nonobscenity certification procedures imposed on NEA grant recipients); *Bela Levitsky Dance Foundation v. Frohnmeyer*, 90 Civ. 3616 (C.D. Cal., filed July 12, 1990) (same).

39. *American Council of the Blind v. Boorstin*, 644 F. Supp. 811, 815 (D.D.C. 1986).
40. *See Commonwealth of Massachusetts v. Secretary of Health and Human Services*, 899 F.2d 53 (1st Cir. 1990) (en banc).
41. *New York v. Sullivan*, 889 F.2d 401 (2d Cir. 1989); *cert. granted, sub nom. Rust v. Sullivan*, 110 S. Ct. 2559 (1990).
42. *See Rust v. Sullivan, supra* note 41; *see also DKT Memorial Fund, Ltd. v. Agency for International Development*, 887 F.2d 275 (D.C. Cir. 1989); *Planned Parenthood v. Agency for International Development*, 915 F.2d 59 (2d Cir. 1990).

VII

Protesting by Public Employees

Nearly a century ago, in totally rejecting a public employee's free speech claim, the great Judge (later Justice) Oliver Wendell Holmes wrote, "[A policeman] may have a constitutional right to talk politics, but he has no constitutional right to be a policeman."[1] On this issue, Justice Holmes was not prophetic, for the law now holds that whether or not public or governmental employees have a right to their jobs, they most assuredly have a right not to be dismissed, disciplined, or demoted for reasons that violate the First Amendment. Today government may not condition public employment on any basis that infringes an employee's constitutionally protected interest in freedom of expression; the employee's rights of free speech and protest as a citizen cannot be defeated unless, on balance, the speech unacceptably damages the government's interest as an employer.[2]

This chapter will focus on these First Amendment rights of public employees. But it is important to remember that employees today—in the public and private sectors—have a wide range of protections available to them in addition to the First Amendment to protect their right to protest and to safeguard their employee status. At the federal level, civil service employees have elaborate protections against arbitrary and wrongful actions under a number of statutes, especially the Civil Service Reform Act of 1978, that established the Merit Systems Protection Board and also provided new protection for "whistleblowers."[3] Judicial review in the courts is available as well. Many state and local governments provide similar civil service systems and protections for most employees of those governmental entities. There are also statutory protections of membership in various federal employee unions.[4] Of course, comparable protections have long been available to union members and employees in most areas of private industry and commerce as well.

In addition, most governmental employees are guaranteed the constitutional rights of due process of law, meaning that public agencies and employers cannot deprive their employees of liberty or property without fair procedures. Public employees who have "tenure" or can otherwise not be fired except "for cause" have a court-recognized "property" interest in continued employment that cannot be "deprived" without some fair procedures.[5] Similarly, government as employer may not deny equal protection of the laws and thus cannot discriminate against applicants or employees on the basis of race, gender, national origin, religious belief, or other arbitrary criteria. These constitutional protections are augmented by the federal laws barring race, gender, national origin, or religious discrimination in employment and covering most federal, state, and local government employees as well as employees in the private sector. Private employees may also have the job protections secured by unions through collective bargaining agreements with employers, and management-level employees or others not covered and protected by union contracts may have contractual protections found in company guidelines or regulations. Finally, many state courts, rejecting the old-fashioned concept that private employees serve "at the will" of their employer, have ruled that such employees may not be dismissed on arbitrary and capricious grounds or for reasons that violate public policy.[6]

These various protections are set forth in greater detail in the ACLU handbooks, *The Rights of Government Employees* (1978) and *The Rights of Employees* (1984). The discussion here focuses on the First Amendment rights of public employees.

PARTISAN POLITICAL ACTIVITY

Can public employees be politically active?

Yes. So long as they do not "take an active part in political management or in political campaigns," federal employees are free to express their opinions on political subjects and be politically active. For almost fifty years, the Hatch Act has restricted federal civil service employees from taking an active part in political campaigns or electioneering.[7] The act is designed to prevent improper partisan political pressures and practices in the federal workplace and to insure the impartial execution of the laws. All fifty states have local versions, called "little Hatch Acts," that impose the same kinds of restrictions on state and local governmental employees. The Supreme Court has upheld the constitutionality of the act, even though it concededly limits the right of public employees to engage in otherwise protected partisan political activities.[8]

In upholding the law the Court relied heavily on federal regulations that spell out which activities are allowed and which are prohibited. Disallowed activities include serving on party or partisan campaign committees or organizations, active campaigning in partisan election campaigns, political fundraising, publicly endorsing partisan candidates, and running for partisan office. Permitted activities include wearing campaign buttons, displaying bumper stickers, working with nonpartisan groups, contributing to political parties, attending political functions, and even extensive campaigning in nonpartisan candidate or referendum election campaigns.[9]

Despite this elaborate list of partisan do's and don't's, the courts have made sure that restrictions on First Amendment activity by government workers are kept as narrow as possible, consistent with the core purposes of the Hatch Act. In important recent cases, for example, appellate courts have ruled that articles by union leaders in federal employee union newspapers, endorsing one presidential candidate over the other and urging members to make political contributions to the unions' political action committees, were not prohibited by the Hatch Act.[10] In one of these cases, involving leaders of postal workers unions, the court ruled that finding a "partisan activity" implicitly requires a nexus between the government employee and the effort to promote the political party or elect its candidate. It is not enough that the federal employee and the partisan candidate pursue the same political goals independently; the two must work in tandem or be linked for there to be a violation of the Hatch Act. "[T]here was no nexus between [the union leaders] and the Mondale campaign or the Democratic Party. The nexus required to establish the activities as partisan under the Act is therefore lacking." Thus petitioners' actions were the individual expression of permitted personal opinion on political subjects and candidates. The Court concluded, "absent a showing of concerted action with a partisan campaign or organization, petitioners' rights of freedom of political expression outweigh the asserted risk of inefficient or corrupt government administration."[11]

Can public employees be required to be politically active in partisan campaign work?

No. Requiring political patronage or loyalty to the winning party as a condition of obtaining or retaining one's job is basically violative of the First Amendment. If the winning party can throw out employees who do not support it or are not loyal to it, those employees are being punished for their political convictions. Thus, with the exception of high-level, confidential, policy-making positions—where political loyalty to the new administration can be required—middle-level and other employees who are not protected by civil service are protected by the First Amendment. The Court has applied this rule to protect ministerial employees of a sheriff's office and assistant district attorneys in a prosecutor's office.[12] Thus, unless the hiring authority can demonstrate that party affiliation is an appropriate requirement for the effective performance of the office involved, the employee may not be dismissed.

In an important 1990 ruling the Supreme Court extended this principle from firing to hiring. The Court held that several related patronage practices, such as promotion, transfer, recall, and hiring decisions involving low-level public employees, may not constitutionally be based on party affiliation and support.[13]

PUBLIC ISSUES

Can public employees be involved in speech or protest activities on any public issue?

Yes. People who happen to be public employees do not lose their basic right to become involved in public issues or causes, such as the pro-choice movement, antiwar activities, environmental matters, or civil rights protests. When public employees engage in expression unrelated to their employment and while away from the workplace, their First Amendment rights are no different from any other member of the public. There are only three exceptions to this general principle: (1) active political party or campaign involvement prohibited by the Hatch Act, (2) political loyalty on policy matters that high level appointees can be required to demonstrate, and (3) speech or protest activities that have a direct and negative impact on the interest of the government as employer in promoting the efficiency of the public services it performs through its employees, therefore requiring a balance between the employee's free speech and the government's efficiency and performance.

Do public employees have the right to strike?
Basically not. Courts have consistently upheld laws banning strikes by public employees. The rationale is that the public at large should not be denied the vital services of public employees.[14]

Do probationary or "at will" government employees have First Amendment rights?
Yes. As the Court said in overturning the dismissal of a probationary clerical employee of the Dallas Police Department:

> It is clearly established that a State may not discharge an employee on a basis that infringes that employee's constitutionally-protected interest in freedom of speech. Even though [the employee] was merely a probationary employee, and even if she could have been discharged for any reason or for no reason at all, she may nonetheless be entitled to reinstatement if she was discharged for exercising her constitutional right to freedom of expression.[15]

How do the courts arrive at the balance between an employee's free speech rights and the government's interest in effective performance of government service?
Where an employee's speech or protest has a direct relationship or impact on the employee's job performance or obligations, the courts have developed a four-part formula to balance the interests and resolve the matter: (1) was the employee speaking or protesting on a matter of public concern; (2) what was the direct and negative impact on the government's interest as an employer; (3) was the speech a substantial or motivating factor in the decision to dismiss or discipline the employee, and (4) would the government employer have reached the same adverse decision absent the speech or protest? The employee has the burden of proof on issues (1) and (3), while the agency must establish points (2) and (4).[16]

In applying these rules, the Court has given protection to

the following kinds of employee speech: a teacher who wrote a letter to a newspaper attacking the school board's handling of financial matters could not be disciplined where the letter contained no knowingly or recklessly made false statements; the same was true for a teacher who complained privately to the school principal about what she felt were the school's racially discriminatory policies and practices; a nonunion teacher who spoke out at a school board meeting to criticize pending labor negotiations was protected; and the Court even protected a clerical police department employee, who, upon learning of the 1981 attempted assassination of President Reagan, remarked to a coworker, "[I]f they go for him again I hope they get him."[17] On the other hand, the Court upheld the dismissal of an assistant district attorney who complained to her boss about office morale, discipline, and work assignments and attempted to circulate an intraoffice questionnaire on these matters; these were held to be basically internal employee grievances and dissatisfactions of interest to the employee and not matters of public concern.[18] In addition to these Supreme Court rulings, there have been hundreds of lower court decisions applying the balancing formula in a wide variety of circumstances.

What are matters or issues of public concern?

The key prerequisite for protecting protest speech despite an impact on the public employer's workplace needs is that the speech involves a matter of public concern. Comments on matters of private concern—typically wholly internal employee grievances that do not involve matters concerning the agency that the public has an interest in learning—do not receive protection if they have a negative impact. One court has described the dividing line as follows: "Speech by public employees may be characterized as not of 'public concern' when it is clear that such speech deals with individual personnel disputes and grievances and that the information would be of no relevance to the public's evaluation of the performance of governmental agencies. . . . On the other hand, speech that concerns 'issues about which information is needed or appropriate to enable members of society' to make informed decisions about the operation of their government merits the highest degree of first amendment protection."[19]

Claims of racial discrimination within a government

agency—whether in its treatment of employees or its handling of public business—are always matters of public concern.[20] And this is true whether the protest is expressed privately to agency superiors or publicly to the community at large. Similarly, employee speech that discloses evidence of corruption, impropriety, or other malfeasance on the part of public officials is always of public concern as well. Indeed, such a "whistleblower" is entitled to even greater protection in striking the balance: "Speech that seeks to expose improper operations of the government or questions the integrity of governmental officials clearly concerns vital public interests."[21] And federal employee whistleblowers are protected by statute from retaliation where their disclosures are intended to inform the public of problems or irregularities.[22]

On the other hand, abrasive conduct and carping criticism of superiors to coworkers, especially in a small unit that requires a higher degree of harmony and close working relations, has been held unprotected.[23] But lampooning the mayor by posting a humorous poem belittling his need for three bodyguards is protected public and political criticism.[24] With respect to police officers and other law enforcement personnel, some courts have treated them no differently than any other government employees in terms of affording free speech protection, while other courts have shown greater deference to the claimed needs of discipline in a "quasi-military organization."[25]

What kinds of public employer interests can outweigh an employee's free speech rights?

The Court has identified the pertinent considerations as follows: "whether the statement impairs discipline by superiors or harmony among co-workers, has a detrimental impact on close working relationships for which personal loyalty and confidence are necessary, or impedes the performance of the speaker's duties or interferes with the regular operation of the enterprise"; the ultimate concern is "the effective functioning of the public employer's enterprise."[26] Assessment of these different factors will vary depending on the nature of the particular unit (for example, a building inspection department verses a police department), whether or not the employee is in higher echelons where more loyalty can be required, and also the manner, time, and place of the expression.[27] But most courts have insisted the government must show actual, not presumed or potential, disruption in the work place.[28]

Can teachers join together with parents to protest or criticize school policies and actions?

Yes. A teacher's rights of speech and association protect the ability to join with parents to protest school policies generally as well as disciplinary actions against a particular teacher.[29]

Do gay or lesbian employees have the right to discuss gay issues and concerns publicly without fear of discipline?

It depends. Courts have generally afforded substantial protection of the rights of gay employees to discuss and be active on gay rights issues. For example, a controversial Oklahoma law outlawing homosexual advocacy by school employees was invalidated by a federal appeals court; however, a Supreme Court majority could not be mustered to support the result on the merits, and the lower court ruling was affirmed by a tie vote.[30] And some courts have held that employees could not be dismissed for public statements about their homosexuality.[31]

But the situation is much more problematic where a public employee's gay rights speech is used by government as an indication or "admission" of gay or lesbian behavior which then is used as the predicate for employment discrimination, especially by schools, police departments, and the military.[32] In 1989 an appeals court used this theory to uphold the dismissal of a lesbian soldier who had discussed her homosexuality. The court ruled that she was not being punished for free speech, but for being gay.[33] The situation is eased somewhat by the fact that many states and cities now include sexual orientation in their antidiscrimination employment laws as a prohibited ground of discrimination. When employment sanctions cannot be imposed because of sexual orientation, protest and advocacy on such issues will be made easier for gay and lesbian public employees.

Can public employees be denied or dismissed from public employment because of affiliation with extremist political groups?

Not usually. As the discussions in chapters 1 and 2 above show, in a reversal of the situation during the McCarthy era, court decisions have given extensive protection to public employee membership in socialist or communist organizations, such as the Socialist Workers party, the Communist Workers party and the Progressive Labor party. The only organizations in which membership has recently been held to be a valid disqualification for certain public positions are the Nazis and the Ku Klux Klan.

NOTES

1. *McAuliffe v. Mayor of New Bedford*, 155 Mass. 216, 220, 29 N.E. 517, 518 (1892).
2. *See, e.g., Pickering v. Board of Education*, 391 U.S. 563 (1968); *Connick v. Myers*, 461 U.S. 138 (1983); *Rankin v. McPherson*, 483 U.S. 378 (1987); *Zamboni v. Stamler*, 847 F.2d 73 (3d Cir. 1988).
3. 92 Stat. 1134, 5 U.S.C. §§ 7501 *et seq.*; 92 Stat. 1217, 5 U.S.C. §§ 7211 *et seq. See also* Whistleblower Protection Act of 1989, Pub. L. No. 101–12, 103 Stat. 16, 5 U.S.C. §§ 1201, *et seq.*
4. *See* Federal Service Labor-Management Relations Act, 5 U.S.C. §§ 7101–35; *see, e.g., Immigration and Naturalization Service v. Federal Labor Relations Authority*, 855 F.2d 1454 (9th Cir. 1988).
5. *Cleveland Board of Education v. Loudermill*, 470 U.S. 532 (1985).
6. *See, e.g., Monge v. Beebe Rubber Co.*, 114 N.H. 130, 316 A.2d 549 (1974).
7. *See* Hatch Political Activities Act, 5 U.S.C. §§ 7321–27.
8. *United States Civil Service Commission v. National Association of Letter Carriers*, 413 U.S. 548 (1973).
9. The list of permissible and prohibited activities is contained at 5 C.F.R. §§ 733.111 and 733.121 and is set forth in *Biller v. United States Merit System Protection Board*, 863 F.2d 1079 (2d Cir. 1988).
10. *See Blaylock v. United States Merit System Protection Board*, 851 F.2d 1348 (11th Cir. 1988); *Biller v. United States Merit System Protection Board*, 863 F.2d 1079 (2d Cir. 1988).
11. 863 F.2d at 1090, 1091.
12. *Elrod v. Burns*, 427 U.S. 347 (1976); *Branti v. Finkel*, 445 U.S. 507 (1980); *cf. Hall v. Ford*, 856 F.2d 255, 261–62 (D.C. Cir. 1988).
13. *Rutan v. Republican Party of Illinois*, 110 S. Ct. 2729 (1990).
14. *See PATCO v. Federal Labor Relations Authority*, 685 F.2d 547 (D.C. Cir. 1981) (air traffic controllers); *Brown v. Department of Transportation*, 735 F.2d 543 (C.A.F.C. 1984) (same).
15. *Rankin v. McPherson*, 483 U.S. 378, 383–84 (1987)(citations omitted).

16. *See, e.g., Hall v. Ford*, 856 F.2d 255 (D.C. Cir. 1988); *Zamboni v. Stamler*, 847 F.2d 73 (3d Cir. 1988); *Price v. Brittain*, 874 F.2d 252 (5th Cir. 1989); *Conner v. Reinhard*, 847 F.2d 384 (7th Cir. 1988); *Conaway v. Smith*, 853 F.2d 789 (10th Cir. 1988).

17. *Pickering v. Board of Education*, 391 U.S. 563 (1968); *Givhan v. Western Line Consolidated School District*, 439 U.S. 410 (1979); *City of Madison Joint School District No. 8 v. Wisconsin Employment Relations Commissions*, 429 U.S. 167 (1976); *Rankin v. McPherson*, 483 U.S. 378 (1987).

18. *Connick v. Myers*, 461 U.S. 138 (1983).

19. *McKinley v. Eloy*, 705 F.2d 1110, 1114 (9th Cir. 1983)(citations omitted); *Hall v. Ford*, 856 F.2d 255, 259 (D.C. Cir. 1988); *but cf. Zamboni v. Stamler*, 847 F.2d 73, 77 (3d Cir. 1988) ("This court has repeatedly found that public employees' criticism of the internal operations of their places of public employment is a matter of public concern.")

20. *Leonard v. City of Columbus*, 705 F.2d 1299 (11th Cir. 1983); *Zamboni v. Stamler*, 847 F.2d 73 (3d Cir. 1988); *cf. Givhan v. Western Line Consolidated School District*, 439 U.S. 410 (1979).

21. *Conaway v. Smith*, 853 F.2d 789, 797 (10th Cir. 1988); *see also Jackson v. Bair*, 851 F.2d 714 (4th Cir. 1988) (prison guard's warning of explosive conditions); *Allen v. Scribner*, 812 F.2d 426 (9th Cir. 1987).

22. *See* 5 U.S.C. § 2302 (b) (8); *Fiorillo v. United States Department of Justice, Bureau of Prisons*, 795 F.2d 1544 (C.A.F.C., 1986).

23. *Marshall v. City of Atlanta*, 614 F. Supp. 581 (N.D. Ga. 1984), *aff'd without opinion*, 770 F.2d 174 (11th Cir. 1985).

24. *Eiland v. City of Montgomery*, 797 F.2d 953 (11th Cir. 1986).

25. *Compare Egger v. Phillips*, 710 F.2d 292 (7th Cir. 1983 (FBI agent) *and Leonard v. City of Columbus*, 705 F.2d 1299 (11th Cir. 1983) (police officers) *with Hughes v. Whitmer*, 714 F.2d 1407 (8th Cir. 1983) (en banc) (state police); *cf. Kelley v. Johnson*, 425 U.S. 238 (1976) (hair length rules upheld for police); *Goldman v. Weinberger*, 475 U.S. 503 (1986) (religious headgear not allowed in military); *Reeder v. Kansas City Board of Police Commissioners*, 733 F.2d 543 (8th Cir. 1984) (upholding ban on police officers making political contributions).

26. *Rankin v. McPherson*, 483 U.S. 378, 388 (1987) (citations omitted).

27. *See Conaway v. Smith*, 853 F.2d 789, 798 (10th Cir. 1988).

28. *Zamboni v. Stamler*, 847 F.2d 73, 78–79 (3d Cir. 1988).

29. *Hatcher v. Board of Public Education*, 809 F.2d 1546 (11th Cir. 1987); *see also Wichert v. Walter*, 606 F. Supp. 1516 (D.N.J. 1985).

30. *National Gay Task Force v. Board of Education*, 729 F.2d 1270 (10th Cir. 1984), *aff'd by an equally divided Court*, 470 U.S. 903 (1985).

31. *Aumiller v. University of Delaware*, 434 F. Supp. 1273 (D.C. Del. 1977).

32. *See, e.g., Gaylord v. Tacoma School District,* 88 Wash. 2d 286, 559 P.2d 1340 (1977) (high school teacher); *Childers v. Dallas Police Department,* 513 F. Supp. 134 (D. Texas 1981); *Johnson v. Orr,* 617 F. Supp,. 170 (E.D. Cal. 1985), *aff'd per curiam,* 787 F. 2d 597 (9th Cir. 1986) (military); *Rowland v. Mad River Local School District,* 730 F.2d 444 (6th Cir. 1984) (school); *High Tech Gays v. Defense Industrial Security Clearance Office,* 895 F.2d 563 (9th Cir. 1990) (gay applicants for top-secret industrial security clearances may be subjected to more expanded investigations than are other applicants); *Rich v. Secretary of Army,* 735 F.2d 1220 (10th Cir. 1984); *but cf. Watkins v. United States Army,* 875 F.2d 699 (9th Cir. 1989) (en banc).

33. *Ben-Shalom v. Marsh,* 881 F.2d 454, 462 (7th Cir. 1989).

PART 2
Protest Activities in Public Places

VIII

Access to Traditional Public Forums, Reasonable Regulations, and Permit Requirements

What can protestors do before engaging in speech activities in public places in order to minimize the chances of arrest?

Before engaging in speech activities in a place open to the public, it is wise to learn about any statutes, ordinances, regulations, and customs that might be enforced at the site. For example, public sidewalks near court buildings might seem like appropriate places for protest activities; yet sometimes protest activities are prohibited there,[1] and sometimes they are permissible because constitutionally protected.[2] Similarly, in most states, private property is usually out of bounds for speech activities unless the owner consents. However in some states, the state constitution may protect speech activities on certain private property that is open to the public without regard to the owner's permission.[3] When there is uncertainty about the law governing speech activities, consult with a local lawyer who is familiar with relevant laws and governmental practices applicable to a site that has been selected for speech activities. It is also a good idea to talk to officials in charge of the site or a representative of the local police department. These officials can apprise you of permit requirements, their approaches to crowd or traffic control, and other information.

TRADITIONAL PUBLIC FORUMS: STREETS, SIDEWALKS, AND PARKS

What is a public forum?

A public forum is public property traditionally used for public speech activities. As a general rule, it is property owned by the government and open to the general public. The most traditional public forums are public streets, sidewalks, and parks. According to the United States Supreme Court:

[W]herever the title of streets and parks may rest, they have immemorially been used for purposes of assembly, communicating thought between citizens, and discussing public questions. Such use of the streets and public places has, from ancient times, been a part of the privileges, immunities, rights, and liberties of citizens. The privilege of a citizen of the United States to use the streets and parks for communication of views on national questions may be regulated in the interest of all; it is not absolute, but relative, and must be exercised in subordination to the general order; but it must not, in the guise of regulation, be abridged or denied.[4]

The reason the Supreme Court has been so protective of speech activities on traditional public forums like streets, sidewalks, and parks is twofold. First, freedom of speech in public places is a highly prized constitutional value that the courts have assumed responsibility to safeguard. Second, all citizens are entitled to use streets, sidewalks, and public parks so long as they do not interfere with the rights and activities of others. Thus, when a member of the public who is using a street, sidewalk, or park engages in orderly communication, he or she merely combines the right to such use with the right to communicate. The right to use traditional public forums guarantees that any speaker, even one without money, can find an audience for his or her views.

What kind of speech activities are allowed on traditional public forums?

As a theoretical matter, any kind of speech activity is allowed on a public forum so long as it does not unreasonably interfere with the rights and activities of others. This includes the communication of political views[5] as well as speech activity having religious content.[6] Typical kinds of speech activities on public forums that the courts have found to be constitutionally protected include spontaneous speechmaking, leafletting,[7] picketing,[8] holding public assemblies,[9] and holding parades.[10] Other constitutionally protected speech activities do occur on traditional public forums,[11] but these are by far the most frequent.

Does the fact that streets are regarded as traditional public forums mean that all streets can be used for speech activities?

The fact that streets are "historically associated with the free exercise of expressive activities"[12] means they can be used freely for speech activities, such as parades, so long as the expressive activities do not interfere unreasonably with competing activities. For example, officials can prohibit using streets to solicit political or other contributions from occupants of passing cars.[13] Similarly, street performances and solicitations at busy intersections may be banned for their capacity to disrupt traffic.[14]

Does the fact that sidewalks are regarded as traditional public forums mean that all sidewalks can be used for speech activities?

While sidewalks can be used freely for speech activities, those activities are subject to reasonable regulations. Municipal authorities can restrict the use of sidewalks adjacent to courthouses[15] and of school buildings[16] when school is in session to protect activities in these buildings from being disturbed.

Does the fact that public parks are regarded as traditional public forums mean that all park premises can be used for speech activities?

No. In spite of the fact that parks are also traditional public forums, they can be used for speech activities pursuant to reasonable regulations. Therefore, as a practical matter, only those parts of any park that are suitable for speech activities are actually usable as public forums. Portions of a park that have special functions and are intrinsically unsuitable for speech activities do not have to be opened by park officials to speech activities. These portions include flower beds, swimming pools, and bathroom facilities. Their use for speech activities can be restricted because the activities may result in damage to the forum or accidental harm to participants.

REGULATIONS OF TIME, PLACE, AND MANNER

Can government officials regulate speech activities that take place on public forums?

Yes. Government officials can regulate speech activities that take place on public forums so long as the officials are not trying to censor the content of speakers' ideas. In order to guide this regulatory process, the Supreme Court has formulated a doctrine frequently referred to as the "time, place, and manner doctrine." This doctrine authorizes government officials in charge of public forums to impose "reasonable" regulations of time, place, and manner of speech activities. Thus, officials may enforce regulations and restrictions designed to prevent speech activities from unreasonably interfering with nearby activities and individuals. In addition, the doctrine precludes enforcement of regulations designed to censor particular ideas. In other words, the government can regulate the timing, the location, and the manner of conducting speech activities, so long as the regulation is "content neutral," seeking to serve a state interest unrelated to the content of the message communicated.[17]

When is the regulation of the time, place, and manner of speech activities on a public forum "reasonable"?

Although public officials can impose reasonable regulations of the time, place, and manner of speech activities on public forums, it is often difficult to say with certainty whether a particular regulation is "reasonable." One of the best guides is common sense. If the regulation is designed to censor the speech, it is unreasonable because the First Amendment forbids censorship. Similarly, if it is excessively broad or so obviously unnecessary that the speaker will have difficulty reaching his or her audience, it may also be unreasonable. If the purpose of the regulation is maintenance of public order or safety, it may well be reasonable. Put differently, the time, place, and manner doctrine has been characterized as a sort of *Roberts Rules of Order* for ensuring the orderly use of traditional public forums.[18] The Supreme Court has summarized the time, place, and manner doctrine in the following terms:

> In [public places historically associated with the free exercise of expressive activities] the government's ability to permissibly restrict expressive conduct is very limited: the government may enforce reasonable time, place, and manner regulations as long as the restrictions "are content-neutral, are narrowly tailored to serve a significant govern-

ment interest, and leave open ample alternative channels of communication."[19]

In what form do regulations of time, place, and manner usually appear?

Regulations governing the time, place, and manner of use of traditional public forums can be enforced at any time and in a wide variety of ways. One of the most common ways these regulations are imposed is through statutes and ordinances requiring the obtaining of a permit as a prerequisite to the use of a public forum. Other forms include police instructions during the course of speech activities, statutes and ordinances explicitly regulating speech activities, and rules and regulations promulgated by government administrators.

PERMIT REQUIREMENTS

Can a speaker be required to obtain a permit as a prerequisite for the use of a public forum?

Yes. A permit can be required as a prerequisite to engaging in many of the speech activities that ordinarily occur on public forums. However the requirement is only enforceable if a valid permit statute, ordinance, or administrative regulation is actually on the books. The courts routinely uphold permit requirements that contain specific standards defining when a permit must be granted. In order to be constitutional, these standards must be limited to considerations of time, place, and manner and cannot authorize denial of a permit based on the content of the speaker's intended communication.[20] The courts generally sustain properly drafted permit requirements because the requirements allow public officials to obtain advance notice of speech activities that may create crowd control, traffic control, or other related regulatory problems. The advance filing of a permit application provides officials with preparation time during which regulatory problems can be addressed. On the other hand, if the permit requirement lacks specific standards stating when a permit must be granted, the law is invalid and cannot be enforced. This type of permit requirement grants too much discretion and may too easily result in censorship.

There are, of course, speech activities on public forums for which permits are not usually required. They are discussed in the next chapter.

What if a speaker ignores an applicable permit law because he or she believes the permit law is unconstitutional?

A speaker can ignore an applicable permit law if it is unconstitutionally drafted. However, if the permit law is ignored on the mistaken belief it is unconstitutional, and it turns out to be valid, the speaker can be prosecuted for failing to obtain a permit. This is because most permit laws contain provisions that incorporate criminal penalties in the event they are violated.[21]

What kind of information does a permit applicant have to supply to obtain a permit?

The answer to this question varies a great deal from place to place. Typically, the questions on a permit application seek information about the time, place, and manner of the activity for which a permit is sought. Thus an applicant may be asked to supply the name, address, and phone number of the individual or group sponsoring and organizing the activity. In addition the applicant may be asked general information including the nature of the event, the number of expected participants, the time, and the proposed location.

The purpose for asking for such information is to enable officials in charge of the forum to make appropriate preparations. Therefore, to the extent that the information requested is responsive to this purpose, the inquiry is legitimate. However, if the information requested on the permit application is unrelated to this purpose or is sought to facilitate the regulation of the content of the communication on the public forum, the inquiry may well be unlawful. Thus, if the application form asks personal questions about such items as income or prior convictions, the inquiry may well be improper.[22]

If a permit application is arbitrarily or discriminatorily denied, but the ordinance is valid, can a protestor ignore the denial and use the public forum anyway?

Not usually. A protestor cannot ignore an arbitrary or discriminatory permit denial and use the public forum anyway. The courts have developed a rule peculiar to public forums to deal with arbitrary permit denials. Under this rule, protestors faced with an arbitrary permit denial are obliged to abide by the denial until they can get it overturned by administrative appeal or a court of law. Therefore, ignoring an arbitrary or discriminatory permit denial by using the public forum may result in a speaker being arrested and prosecuted.

Moreover, if criminal proceedings are initiated for ignoring a permit denial, the courts usually will not allow demonstrators to raise the defense that the denial was arbitrary or discriminatory.[23] The Supreme Court has determined that the use of public forums for speech activities often involves a large number of people and therefore brings with it a potential for disruption of competing activities or a potential for disorder. In order to be sure that public officials can prepare for such problems, the Supreme Court prefers to require that would-be protestors seek a legal remedy for a wrongful permit denial rather than resorting to the self-help activity of ignoring the wrongful denial.

How far in advance of an event must a permit application be filed?

The timing of the filing of a permit application usually depends on the specific provisions of the relevant permit law. Most permit laws specify the time periods during which an application giving advance notice of the speech activity on a public forum must be filed. The purpose of an advance filing requirement is to give officials time to process the application and to notify appropriate law enforcement officials. A twenty-day advance filing requirement is not unusual.[24] However, if protestors cannot comply with the advance filing requirement because of a need to respond to a fast-breaking political situation, the courts have often compelled officials to waive the usual requirement and issue the permit more quickly.[25] Similarly, if an advance filing requirement is unreasonably long, a court may find it to be unconstitutional.[26]

How long can officials take to decide whether to grant or deny a permit application?

As a general rule, officials have a constitutional obligation to act on a permit request promptly because where speech is involved, time is often of the essence.[27] Moreover, when time is of the essence, some courts have required that the permit be granted or denied within a matter of days. And where officials are unduly slow in processing a permit request or the permit law does not provide for prompt processing, the courts have found the permit procedure to be constitutionally defective.[28]

What can be done if a permit application is denied?

If a permit application is turned down, the applicant has three alternatives. First, the denial can be accepted and the plans for speech activities on a public forum can be canceled. Second, if the permit law provides for an administrative review procedure, that procedure can be initiated. Finally, the applicant can go to court and file a civil rights suit to challenge the denial.

Any decision to file an administrative appeal or to initiate a civil rights suit must be prompt. The courts have ruled that properly drafted permit laws must provide for prompt administrative and judicial review of permit denials.[29] In some cases the applicant whose permit has been denied may choose to forgo an appeal and initiate suit in federal court. This is because permit denials are unlikely to be overturned by another official who works in the same agency. In addition, if, as a part of the review process, the officials who have denied a permit initiate a state court action calling for judicial consideration of their denial, they may well bring their case before local judges who have a bias favoring the officials.

Can a permit fee be charged as a prerequisite for obtaining a permit?

A permit fee can be charged to cover the costs of processing a permit application, so long as it does not constitute a significant burden on speech.[30] The courts have not yet explained exactly what is included in the costs of processing, but they have made clear that a permit fee that is not tailored to cover out-of-pocket administrative costs is invalid.[31] Similarly, the courts have rejected fees designed as a general tax for the purpose of replenishing the municipal treasury.[32] In addition, some courts have invalidated permit fees simply because the amount of money to be paid was unreasonably burdensome. A burdensome fee discourages First Amendment activities by making them too costly.[33]

Among the fees of questionable validity are those that impose a daily charge for an activity scheduled to occur on two or more consecutive days.[34] As a practical matter, a single permit for an activity is sufficient notice of a speaker's plan whether the activity is to occur on one day or on successive days. Moreover, the aggregation of fees for activities happening on successive days could become so burdensome that speakers may be forced to cut back on their activities.[35]

Can the issuance of a permit for use of a public forum be conditioned on payment for police assigned to maintain order at the event?

There is no definitive answer to this question. The Supreme Court has not addressed the question directly, and other courts do not agree on what to do about it. Some decisions conclude that police have a duty to protect people using public forums, and this duty includes a requirement that the government undertake the protection without charging for it.[36] Such charges are likely to be heavy enough to deter would-be speakers.[37] Other courts have stated that such charges are reasonable time, place, and manner regulations.[38]

Can speakers be charged for the costs of police protection generated by the presence of a hostile audience?

Charging speakers for the costs of police present to protect them from members of a hostile audience has been held to be a violation of the First Amendment. The First Amendment violation occurs because the charges are based on the reaction of the audience to the content of the speaker's ideas. The charges increase in proportion to the controversial nature of the speaker's message. The burden of the charges therefore becomes a form of censorship. This was explained in *Central Florida Nuclear Freeze Campaign v. Walsh*, where the court said:

> The possibility of hostile counter-demonstrators, as a reaction to the [demonstration and rally], was considered by the deputy chief of police in assessing the amount of costs [the city] would charge . . . for the additional police protection in conducting their activities. Such an inquiry into the content of the speakers' views in determining how much police protection is needed and as a consequence,

how much the speakers would have to pay to voice their views, constitutes an impermissible price tag on the exercise of free speech based on the content of speech.[39]

Can speakers be required to obtain insurance as a prerequisite for using public property to communicate their views?

Although the Supreme Court has never addressed the constitutionality of requiring protestors to obtain insurance as a prerequisite to using a public forum, lower courts have generally invalidated such a requirement.[40] The reasons vary from case to case. One court said it was unconstitutional to require insurance because the ordinance which created the requirement lacked sufficiently clear standards defining precisely what kind of insurance had to be obtained.[41] Another court invalidated the requirement because municipal officials had presented no evidence of a need for insurance.[42] Yet another case invalidated an insurance requirement because municipal officials enforced it even though they knew that an extremely controversial group could not obtain it in the marketplace.[43] Moreover, to the extent that insurance requirements are imposed because city officials want to be protected against all liability claims arising during speech activities, they are requiring the speaker to insure against the negligent and intentional torts of persons over whom the speakers usually exercise no control.

What if a fee, police service charge, or insurance requirement is imposed on a user of a public forum who cannot afford to pay for it?

While this question has rarely been addressed in public forum cases, there are cases addressing similar questions in parallel areas of the law indicating that "[f]reedom of speech, freedom of press, freedom of religion are available to all, not merely to those who can pay their own way."[44] For example, where indigent candidates for public office have been denied a place on the ballot because they could not afford to pay the state filing fee, the Supreme Court has ruled that "the process of qualifying candidates [may] not constitutionally be measured solely in dollars."[45] Similarly an ordinance requiring demonstrators to pay for police services has been invalidated because, among other things, the court concluded that "[i]ndigent persons who wish to exercise their First Amendment rights of speech and assembly and as a consequence of the added costs of police protection, are unable to pay such costs, are denied an equal opportunity to be heard."[46]

NOTES

1. *Cox v. Louisiana*, 379 U.S. 559 (1965).
2. *Grace v. United States*, 461 U.S. 171 (1983).
3. *Pruneyard Shopping Center v. Robins*, 447 U.S. 74 (1980).
4. *Hague v. CIO*, 307 U.S. 496, 515–16 (1939).
5. *Grace v. United States, supra* note 2.
6. *Widmar v. Vincent*, 454 U.S. 263 (1981).
7. *Schneider v. State*, 308 U.S. 147 (1939); *Pledge of Resistance v. We the People 200*, 665 F. Supp. 414 (E.D. Pa. 1987).
8. *Grace v. United States, supra* note 2; *Mosely v. Chicago Police Department*, 408 U.S. 92 (1972).
9. *Collin v. Chicago Park District*, 460 F.2d 746 (7th Cir. 1972).
10. *Cox v. New Hampshire*, 312 U.S. 569 (1941); *Dr. Martin Luther King, Jr. Movement Coalition, Inc. v. City of Chicago*, 419 F. Supp. 667 (N.D. Ill. 1976).
11. *Lakewood v. Plain Dealer Publishing*, 486 U.S. 750 (1988) (selling newspapers); *Village of Schaumberg v. Citizens for a Better Environment*, 444 U.S. 620 (1980).
12. *Grace v. United States*, 461 U.S. 171, 177 (1983).
13. *International Society for Krishna Consciousness of New Orleans, Inc. v. Baton Rouge*, 876 F.2d. 494 (5th Cir. 1989).
14. *Friedrich v. City of Chicago*, 619 F. Supp. 1129 (N.D. Ill. 1985).
15. *Cox v. Louisiana*, 379 U.S. 559 (1965).
16. *Grayned v. Rockford*, 408 U.S. 104 (1972).
17. *Cox v. New Hampshire*, 312 U.S. 569 (1941).
18. Kalven, *The Concept of the Public Forum: Cox v. Louisiana*, 1965 Sup. Ct. Rev. 1 (1965).
19. *Grace v. United States*, 461 U.S. 171, 177 (1983).
20. *Cox v. New Hampshire, supra* note 17.
21. *Id.*
22. *Fernandes v. Limmer*, 663 F.2d 619 (5th Cir. 1981).
23. *Poulos v. New Hampshire*, 345 U.S. 395 (1953).
24. *NAACP Western Region v. City of Richmond*, 743 F.2d 1346 (9th Cir. 1984).
25. *Id.*

26. *See Freedman v. Maryland,* 380 U.S. 51 (1965), *Robinson v. Coopwood,* 292 F. Supp. 926 (N.D. Miss. 1968).

27. *Collin v. Chicago Park District, supra* note 9.

28. *Freedman v. Maryland,* 380 U.S. 51 (1965); *Teitel Film Corp. v. Cusack,* 390 U.S. 139 (1968); *Collin v. Chicago Park District, supra* note 9.

29. *Freedman v. Maryland,* 380 U.S. 51 (1965); *Collin v. Chicago Park District, supra* note 9.

30. *Murdock v. Pennsylvania,* 319 U.S. 105, 113–14 (1943); *United States Labor Party v. Codd,* 527 F.2d 118 (2d Cir. 1975).

31. *NAACP v. City of Chester,* 253 F. Supp. 707 (E.D. Pa. 1966) (overturned $25 per day fee for a permit to operate a sound truck because the city offered no evidence showing a relation between the fee and the costs of regulating sound trucks).

32. *Fernandes v. Limmer,* 663 F.2d 619 (5th Cir. 1981) (invalidated a $6 per day fee for permit to distribute religious literature and solicit donations in a municipal airport because of airport authority's failure to restrict use of fee receipts to payment for expenses of licensing process).

33. *See Central Florida Nuclear Freeze Campaign v. Walsh,* 774 F.2d 1515 (10th Cir. 1985); *see also Bayside Enterprises, Inc. v. Carson,* 450 F. Supp. 696, 705 (M.D. Fla. 1978) (struck down municipal ordinance requiring that adult bookstores pay a $1,200 license fee on the ground that the city had failed to demonstrate that the fee was necessary to cover the reasonable costs of operating the licensing system); *compare Bayside Enterprises, Inc. v. Carson,* 470 F. Supp. 1140, 1149 (M.D. Fla. 1979) (upheld $400 fee, imposed after the invalidation of the previous ordinance on ground that the city had met its burden of proving that the fee was reasonable and was designed to further valid nonspeech interests of the city.)

34. *Fernandes v. Limmer, supra,* note 22.

35. *Id.; Murdock v. Pennsylvania,* 319 U.S. 105, 115 (1943).

36. *O'Hair v. Andrus,* 613 F.2d 931 (D.C. Cir. 1979).

37. In *O'Hair v. Andrus* police costs connected to a mass said by the Pope in a Washington, D.C., park exceeded $100,000 and were held to be properly borne by the city; *see also Central Florida Nuclear Freeze Campaign v. Walsh, supra* note 33.

38. *Stonewall Union v. City of Columbus,* No. C–2–85–849, order upholding charges for police entered June 28, 1990, U.S. District Court, Southern District of Ohio.

39. *Central Florida Nuclear Freeze Campaign v. Walsh,* 774 F.2d 1515, 1524 (10th Cir. 1985).

40. *Collin v. Smith,* 447 F. Supp. 676 (N.D. Ill. 1978).

41. *Houston Peace Coalition v. Houston City Council*, 310 F. Supp. 457 (S.D. Tex. 1970).
42. *Collin v. Smith, supra* note 40, at 685.
43. *Collin v. O'Malley*, No. 76 C 2024, Conclusion of Law, para. 3 (N.D. Ill. modified order September 22, 1978).
44. *Murdock v. Pennsylvania*, 319 U.S. 105, 111 (1942).
45. *Lubin v. Panish*, 415 U.S. 709, 716 (1974).
46. *Central Florida Nuclear Freeze Campaign v. Walsh*, 774 F.2d 1515, 1523 (10th Cir. 1985).

IX

Government Regulation of Specific Speech Activities: Demonstrations and Parades

PUBLIC ASSEMBLIES AND DEMONSTRATIONS

What is a public assembly or demonstration?

There are two ways to define a public assembly or demonstration. First, common usage tells us that a public assembly or demonstration is a gathering of a large number of people at a traditional public forum or other public place to demonstrate their support for a particular viewpoint or belief. Second, relevant statutes, ordinances, regulations, and judicial decisions contain specific definitions. Both types of definitions are important: the first triggers constitutional protections for public speech activities; the second identifies important nonconstitutional sources of law where regulations of public speech activities are often found.

To what extent are public assemblies and demonstrations protected by the First Amendment?

So long as a public assembly or demonstration is held on a traditional public forum in compliance with applicable laws, it receives broad protections from the First Amendment. Occasional judicial comments suggest that large gatherings of people seeking to communicate particular viewpoints present such difficult problems of law enforcement that First Amendment protections may not be as extensive as for other speech activities.[1] Nonetheless, there has never been a judicial decision that specifically dilutes the degree of First Amendment protections applicable to public assemblies and demonstrations.

Is it necessary to obtain a permit in order to hold a public assembly or demonstration?

Yes, if there is a law requiring a permit. In some jurisdictions, the law requires that a permit be obtained prior to holding assemblies or demonstrations that have more than a minimum number of participants. However, in other jurisdictions, no permit is required for any assembly or demonstration. It is important to check the applicable law of each jurisdiction in advance because a failure to comply with a valid permit requirement may lead to the arrest and prosecution of participants. Moreover, it is important to keep in mind that if for one reason or another the assembly or demonstration will occur on adjacent sites under the control of more than one government agency, permits may have to be obtained from each agency. For example, if a large public assembly is planned to occur in a public park and will probably spill over onto part of a nearby local street, it may be necessary to obtain two permits, one for the park and one for the street.

Does the time, place, and manner doctrine apply to public assemblies and demonstrations?

Yes. Government officials routinely impose regulations of time, place, and manner on public assemblies and demonstrations. This is because the presence of large gatherings of people who wish to communicate their views often create regulatory problems. Government officials are obligated to respond to these problems by assuring that the gathering is orderly, that there is no property damage, and that nearby activities are not unduly disrupted. In order to accomplish these purposes, the courts have ruled that officials can impose reasonable, content-neutral regulations of time, place, and manner.[2] However, the regulations of time, place, and manner cannot be imposed in a way that regulates the content of the ideas expressed at the demonstration. This is usually accomplished through the permit procedure. Thus, at the time the permit is issued, the police or the official responsible for the site usually communicates the time, place, and manner regulations that will be imposed on the demonstration. The permit is issued subject to compliance with those regulations and can be revoked in the event that the regulations are violated.

Reasonable Regulation of the Time of Assemblies and Demonstrations

Can public officials prohibit a demonstration planned on a public forum because it is scheduled at a time when a previously scheduled public assembly is expected to occur?

Usually, but not always. An obvious rule of thumb for the timing of public assemblies is that there cannot be two public assemblies at the same time and at the same place. Both will be disrupted, and neither will be able to communicate its desired message. In order to avoid such problems, the courts routinely allow officials to grant permits on a first-come-first-served basis. Public officials often will require the organizers of the assembly that filed their application second to be moved to a different site or to be rescheduled for a different time.

On the other hand, if there is enough room on the public forum for two peaceful demonstrations at the same time, the need to invoke the first-come-first-served approach is not automatic. Under such circumstances, spontaneous counter-demonstrations and other speech activities may legitimately be held at the forum.[3] So long as there is no reason to anticipate problems of crowd control or maintaining order, there is no justification for changing the time or place of either demonstration. If officials insist on doing so anyway, a court challenge may be appropriate.

Can public officials prohibit a demonstration planned on a public forum because it is scheduled in conflict with a previously scheduled nonspeech activity?

Yes. The courts generally defer to nondiscriminatory official decisions as to how to allocate use of public forums. This deference extends to reconciling the scheduling of demonstrations with previously scheduled nonspeech events. That usually means that so long as all competing uses for a public forum are scheduled on a first-come-first-served basis, such scheduling is lawful. If, on the other hand, the forum is large enough to accommodate both activities or the competing nonspeech event permanently monopolizes the forum, the first-come-first-served approach may not be applicable. For example, if park officials refuse to allow any public assemblies on a large park site because they claim that the site has been permanently reserved by an athletic league for its practices or games, the courts may rule that the refusal is unreasonable. The officials can postpone the athletic activities for a period long enough to allow the demonstration. If the forum is large enough, it may also be possible to allow both to occur. Permanent refusal of access to a suitable site is often evidence that officials are engaging in censorship.[4]

Can public officials limit the duration of an extremely long public demonstration?

Although this question is rarely litigated, it can be answered by resort to the time, place, and manner doctrine. According to the terms of the doctrine, reasonable limitations can be imposed on demonstrations as long as they are not forms of content regulation. Thus, if officials issue a permit for a demonstration that imposes a restriction on the duration of an extremely long demonstration, the restriction is probably valid if it is designed to ensure that the forum is not unduly monopolized or seriously damaged. For example, in *Clark v. Community for Creative Non-Violence,*[5] the Supreme Court upheld a National Park Service regulation prohibiting demonstrators from sleeping overnight in Lafayette Park, even though the demonstrators contended that sleeping overnight was an integral part of an around-the-clock "sleep-in" designed to protest the plight of the homeless.

> It is . . . apparent to us that the regulation narrowly focuses on the Government's substantial interest in maintaining the parks in the heart of our capital in an attractive and intact condition, readily available to the millions of people who wish to [enjoy them]. To permit camping [would] be totally inimical to these purposes, as would be readily understood by those who have frequented the National Parks across the country and observed the unfortunate consequences of the activities of those who refuse to confine their camping to designated areas.[6]

Can public officials require that a demonstration initially planned to be several hours long be held for a shorter period?

Not unless they have a sufficient justification for doing so. On one hand, if an official decision to curtail the duration of a demonstration is made in order to accommodate identifiable, competing activities at the same site or to accommodate legitimate law enforcement needs, the curtailment is probably valid. Similarly, if officials seek to curtail the duration of a demonstration because the requested termination time is after the forum is usually closed to the public, or is late at night, the curtailment may also be valid. On the other hand, if the curtailment creates an unnecessary barrier to communication of the intended message of the demonstrators, it may well be unreasonable. For example, if police try to limit a demonstration to one hour, though the demonstration is planned for two hours, the limitation is unlikely to be lawful unless the police can point to a competing activity that will be disrupted. In almost all situations occurring on public forums in which the time or duration of a demonstration is at issue, the applicable standard remains the time, place, and manner doctrine.

Reasonable Regulation of the Place of an Assembly or Demonstration

Are officials obligated to permit assemblies and demonstrations on any government property that is open to the public?

No. The Supreme Court has held that streets, sidewalks, and parks are traditional public forums available to demonstrators for speech activities so long as the activities do not unduly interfere with the nonspeech activities of others. However, the Court has also indicated that areas such as state fairgrounds that are open to the public, are not public forums that demonstrators are constitutionally entitled to use.[7] In the Supreme Court's view, locations other than traditional public forums are considered to be designated forums if public officials voluntarily choose to open them to speech activities. Once designated, they become the rough equivalent of traditional public forums until the designation is rescinded. However, if places that are not traditional public forums have not been opened to speech activities, they are regarded as nonpublic forums and demonstrators do not have a broad constitutional entitlement to use them.[8] The problem of speech activities on nontraditional forums is explored in more detail in chapter 10.

Can public officials refuse to permit a public assembly on a forum because of potential harm to grass, flower beds, or shrubs?

The time, place, and manner doctrine allows public officials to impose reasonable regulations on demonstrations that are designed to protect against significant damage to a public forum. This would include a restriction on a public assembly to prevent damage to vegetation. However, the power to protect against such damage does not justify completely closing down the forum, nor does it justify unnecessary restrictions that interfere with the communication of the demonstration's message. In other words, a restriction that tries to protect against normal wear and tear on a forum is not likely to be viewed as reasonable, while a restriction that tries to prevent significant damage in excess of normal wear and tear is more likely to be upheld by the courts.

Because it is sometimes difficult to distinguish between reasonable and unreasonable regulations claimed to be necessary to protect against property damage, the courts often look for evidence related to the motivation behind a regulation. If there is evidence that a regulation said to protect vegetation is actually a product of official distaste for the demonstration or its message, then it is unlikely to meet with a favorable judicial reception.[9] If, on the other hand, the regulation is a genuine effort to protect vulnerable parts of the forum, it is much more likely to be found to be a reasonable regulation of time, place, and manner.

Can a public park be declared off-limits to demonstrations because the demonstrations will interfere with the routine, competing, unscheduled recreational uses of the park such as picnicking, strolling, and sightseeing?

No. If the park is physically suitable for speech activities like demonstrations, park officials cannot rely on the presence of competing recreational uses to justify the claim that the park is inappropriate for speech activities. This was explained in *A Quaker Action Group v. Morton.* "The use of parks for public assembly and airing of opinions is historic in our democratic society, and one of its cardinal values. Public assembly for First Amendment purposes is as surely a 'park use' as any tourist or recreational activity."[10] Any effort of public officials to argue that recreational activities take priority over speech activities at the site ignores the high priority given to official protection of speech activities by the First Amendment.

Can officials in charge of a traditional public forum permanently designate a portion of the forum for demonstrations and declare the rest of the forum to be out-of-bounds?

If officials wished to make a permanent designation of a portion of a traditional public forum for demonstrations, they would have to establish two things. First, they would have to prove that the designated portion of the forum permits demonstrators to reach their intended audience approximately as effectively as the out-of-bounds portion would. Second, they would have to establish identifiable characteristics of the out-of-bounds portion of the forum that make it unsuitable for demonstrations and that make the designated area more suitable. The designation of portions of traditional public forums for speech activities was rejected by the courts in *Collin v. Chicago Park District*.[11] There park officials designated four forum areas out of a citywide park system for which no permits would be required. The rest of the system was limited to use for picnicking and other recreational activities. Chicago Park District officials contended they could prohibit controversial demonstrations in nondesignated portions of the park system because they were inconsistent with the recreational uses of these same portions. This arrangement was held to be a violation of the First Amendment because it had the effect of denying controversial speakers meaningful access to their intended audience.

Are officials in charge of a public forum obliged to make nearby public facilities like fieldhouses, park shelters, and toilets available to participants in a demonstration?
The general rule that opens public forums to speech activities does not necessarily extend to nearby facilities. Therefore officials ordinarily need not open nearby facilities to demonstrators unless those same facilities are usually open to the public or are an inseparable part of the forum. And if such facilities are usually open to the public, they cannot be arbitrarily closed to demonstrators. Thus, public bathrooms near a forum for a demonstration should be left open during the demonstration. But a nearby fieldhouse for which no permit has been sought can be closed down until the demonstration is over.

Can public officials impose a limit on a demonstration at a public forum because the forum is too small?
The answer to this question depends on the nature of the demonstration and the particular characteristics of the public

forum. The time, place, and manner doctrine allows public officials to impose restrictions on the size of a demonstration if reasonably necessary to avoid crowd control, safety, and other similar problems.[12] However, an unnecessary restriction is invalid. An ordinance that flatly prohibits picketing by more than two people at a time on all public streets and sidewalks in front of businesses and public buildings is invalid.[13] Similarly, a limit of one hundred demonstrators on the sidewalk next to the White House was found to be unconstitutional because the sidewalk could accommodate between four thousand and six thousand demonstrators comfortably without blocking pedestrian traffic and because large demonstrations had been permitted previously at the same site without creating problems.[14]

The circumstances under which a limitation on the size of a demonstration may be upheld are not limited to the size of the forum in light of the proposed size of the demonstration. "The . . . location of the park, traffic conditions, the location and size of other parks and places available for public assembly and the relative increase in the possibility of danger to the public and property as the size of the crowd increases are but a few of the many factors which would enter into such a determination."[15]

Can officials require organizers of a public assembly to move the assembly to a location that is likely to reduce the size of the audience or the impact of the message?

Not usually. If demonstrators seek to use a traditional public forum and their activities are not in conflict with previously scheduled activities, an official decision to move the demonstration to another location raises serious First Amendment questions. If moving the demonstration does not serve a significant governmental interest, it probably violates the First Amendment. Also, if moving the demonstration unnecessarily interferes with the intended audience, it may be unconstitutional.[16] "[O]ne is not to have his liberty of expression in appropriate places abridged on the plea that it may be exercised in some other place."[17] On the other hand, there may be circumstances, such as the prevention of conflict between competing demonstrations, that can justify a decision by public officials to move the site of a demonstration.[18]

Can officials require a change in the location of a controversial demonstration because its message will offend nonparticipants who would normally be in the vicinity?

No. The power to impose reasonable regulations on the place of the demonstration does not include the encouragement or discouragement of the communication of particular viewpoints, even if those viewpoints are potentially upsetting to members of the audience. To impose a change in location of a demonstration merely because the message is controversial or upsetting is a form of censorship. "[I]t is settled law that hostile demonstrators or bystanders do not justify the restraint of otherwise legal First Amendment activities."[19] In fact before police can stop speech activities that are provoking disorderly hecklers, they are obliged to make a reasonable effort to protect speakers by dealing first with the hecklers.[20] On the other hand, if a counterdemonstration is controversial and officials can establish that the only way they can maintain order is by keeping the main demonstration and the counterdemonstration apart, a change in the location of one of the demonstrations may be lawful.[21]

Do counterdemonstrators have a First Amendment right to hold their counterdemonstration in proximity to the demonstration they wish to protest?

Yes. Counterdemonstrators have the same First Amendment right to communicate their views as everyone else. Moreover, the systematic application of the time, place, and manner doctrine would require that peaceful, nondisruptive counterdemonstrations be accorded the full protection of the First Amendment, including selection of an appropriate public forum. However, it should be kept in mind that counterdemonstrations present special law enforcement problems. There is always the risk that if the counterdemonstration occurs in close proximity to the main demonstration, tempers may flare and trouble may occur. As a consequence, there have been times when the judiciary has been unsympathetic to the right to participate in peaceable counterdemonstrations. For example, counterdemonstrators who sought to hold their parade near the Philadelphia bicentennial celebration were required to hold the parade at a great distance from the celebration to avoid potential trouble.[22] On the other hand, where police prohibited demonstrations by gay persons on the sidewalk in front of St. Patrick's Cathedral along the route of a gay rights parade because of the presence of counterdemonstrators, both groups of demonstrators were held to be entitled to use the forum at different intervals during the main parade.[23]

Reasonable Regulation of the Manner of an Assembly or Demonstration

Can public officials impose limits on the size of a demonstration?

Public officials cannot impose size limitations unless there is a reason to do so related to the time, place, or manner of the demonstration. If the forum is comparatively small, then public officials can limit the size of the demonstration accordingly.[24] Similarly, if a large demonstration creates special law enforcement problems, limitation on its size may be lawful.[25] But a uniform limitation on size that is not related to the specific circumstances of each demonstration on a case by case basis has been held to be unconstitutional.[26]

What authority over the demonstration do police have after it is underway?

Police have ongoing authority to maintain order and to try to make sure the demonstration does not unduly interfere with others. Thus, the police may give orders to demonstrators during the course of a demonstration that are reasonably related to the time, place, and manner of the event. For example, during a demonstration, police often give instructions to participants that are designed to prevent the demonstration from spilling onto the street and blocking traffic or from expanding into areas of a public forum where property damage may inadvertently occur. On the other hand, police directives ordering demonstrators in a public park to stop distributing leaflets or "passing the hat" to raise money are a form of content regulation and are probably not legally enforceable.

Unfortunately, demonstrators confronted with a police directive that they suspect is illegal face a difficult dilemma. If they decline to obey it, they run the risk of arrest whether or not the directive is legitimate. The wisest course is to obey the directive until a police officer with command duties can be located and asked to countermand the directive.

Can public officials refuse to allow demonstrations because the content of the signs carried or the clothing worn by participants is offensive to onlookers?

No. According to the time, place, and manner doctrine, regulations of the manner of a demonstration must be unrelated to the content of the ideas expressed. An official refusal to allow an assembly because of offensive signs, costumes, or uniforms is a regulation based on content and is therefore a form of censorship. Thus, in *Village of Skokie v. National Socialist Party of America*[27] an injunction against a demonstration based on the offensive nature of the demonstrators' neo-Nazi uniforms and emblems was held to violate the First Amendment.

Is there a First Amendment right to use sound amplification equipment at a demonstration?

There is a right to use sound amplification equipment at a demonstration subject to reasonable regulation of time, place, and manner.[28] One of the most frequent regulations of sound equipment is a requirement that a special permit be obtained as a prerequisite to use of the equipment. The justification for such a requirement is that amplified sound may be so loud as to be distracting or irritating to people who are not involved in the demonstration. A permit requirement gives officials some opportunity to assure that the volume is not so great as to create an unanticipated disturbance. Thus, a prohibition against sound amplification that is at a "loud and raucous volume" has been upheld.[29] It is also likely that prohibition on the use of sound amplification equipment would be sustained on a public forum near a facility, such as a hospital, where the sound would carry off of the forum and interfere with the operation of the facility.[30] However a flat ban on the use of sound amplification equipment at any time on traditional public forums has been held to be unconstitutional.[31]

Can officials in charge of a public forum require that demonstrators use a sound system supplied and operated by the officials?

The answer to this question is unclear. The Supreme Court

has ruled that public officials can require that a rock band using the New York Central Park band shell must use a sound system that is officially supplied and controlled.[32] The requirement was found to be a legitimate means of protecting nonparticipants in an antiracism rock concert from having to endure the inconvenience of excessively loud open-air sound amplification. The Court stated that sponsors of the concert would have to show that the requirement had a "substantial deleterious effect"[33] before the Court would find a First Amendment violation.

Whether the requirement that a government supplied and controlled sound system be used at a band shell extends to more traditional political speech activities is unclear, although it seems unlikely that amplification of public speeches would create the same degree of disturbance of outsiders that is created by electric musical instruments.

Is it legal to raise money at demonstrations by selling T-shirts or printed materials or by soliciting donations?

Yes. Selling things or soliciting donations during the course of a demonstration in order to raise money to pay for related speech or other political activities is constitutionally protected.[34] Money that is paid or received in support of First Amendment activities is itself protected by the First Amendment.[35] The government has the power to regulate and tax sales and solicitations that are incidental to political speech so long as the regulation applies to similar activities in similar settings. However, because fundraising activities to support the goals of the demonstration are constitutionally protected, the government may not ban them on the theory that fundraising activities are inappropriate for public forums.

A note of caution must be added here. Some public officials may refuse to allow any fundraising during the course of a public assembly. Because the officials have the power to revoke permits or to authorize arrest, the wisest course is to consult with an attorney before ignoring the refusal and proceeding with the fundraising.

Can officials responsible for administering a public forum require sponsors of a demonstration to clean it up after it is over?

This question has not been addressed by the courts. The

closest the courts have ever come to discussing it is *Schneider v. State*,[36] where the Supreme Court held that leafletting could not be flatly prohibited merely because it resulted in littering. In light of the *Schneider* decision, it is doubtful that organizers of a public assembly can be required to cleanup litter that is a normal part of the use of the forum for speech purposes. It is also doubtful that organizers of a demonstration could be required to do any more cleanup than is required of other users of the public forum. However, if there is something about the assembly that can be expected to create unusual cleanup burdens, officials may be able to require forum users to assume some cleanup responsibility.

PARADES

What is a parade?

The dictionary defines a parade in common-sense terms as "any organized procession or march."[37] However, in many jurisdictions, applicable statutes and ordinances also contain important definitions. In the event that they do, the legal definition rather than the common sense definition is the operative one. Thus, by local law, a procession or march may only be a parade if it is on the street and not if it is on the sidewalk. It is therefore important to be familiar with applicable local laws during the planning stages of any parade.

Are parades held on traditional public forums protected by the First Amendment?

Yes. Parades held on traditional public forums—particularly those held on public streets and sidewalks—have been found by the judiciary to be protected by the First Amendment. In the words of Professor Harry Kalven, "[t]he parade, the picket, the leaflet, the sound truck, have been the media of communication exploited by those with little access to the more genteel means of communication."[38]

The scope of First Amendment protections for parades is limited by the fact that parades often present regulatory problems to public officials. The source of the limitation is the large numbers of participants in a parade who are moving from place to place, on public sidewalks or streets, via an agreed route.

Through use of reasonable regulations of time, place, and manner, officials can attempt to accomodate the need to keep automobile and pedestrian traffic moving as smoothly as possible without unnecessarily interfering with the parade's progress.

Is a permit required to hold a parade?

Permits are usually required for parades on public streets. The nature of parade permit requirements vary from place to place. The few jurisdictions that do not require permits for street parades are usually those that have paid little attention to regulating them. In contrast, many of the jurisdictions that require permits for street parades do not require permits for sidewalk parades. It is necessary to consult statutes, ordinances, and regulations applicable to each forum to find out when parade permits must be obtained.

Reasonable Regulation of the Time of a Parade

Can public officials prohibit a parade planned for a sidewalk, street, or park because it is scheduled at a time when a previously scheduled parade is to occur?

It depends on the circumstances. As is often true for demonstrations, it is physically impossible to have two parades at the same time and the same place. Moreover, because parades are moving groups of people, police are often reluctant to try to accommodate more than one at a time when they are in close proximity to one another. This is especially true if one of the two parades is really a counterdemonstration aimed at the other. However, in some instances officials may be willing to accommodate two parades scheduled for the same time so long as they do not interfere with one another and so long as their respective routes do not create insurmountable crowd control or traffic problems.[39]

Can public officials prohibit a parade because it is scheduled during the rush-hour period?

As a general rule, the courts have recognized that the First Amendment right to have a parade does not automatically override a municipality's interest in keeping traffic moving during heavy rush-hour periods.[40] However, to the extent that a rush-hour prohibition applies to a street that is not heavily traveled or has been the site of previous rush-hour parades, it is vulnerable to attack on the ground that it is unreasonable and discriminates based on a dislike of the parade's message.

Can public officials prohibit all street parades in a business district during business hours?

Probably not. An absolute prohibition of street parades during business hours in downtown Denver was found to be unconstitutional in *Sixteenth of September Planning Committee, Inc. v. The City and County of Denver.*[41] The court in that case explained that downtown streets are traditional public forums and are therefore appropriate sites for parades. It rejected Denver's argument that the restriction on street parades was a legitimate traffic regulation. It concluded that the prohibition was tantamount to a flat ban effective during times when parades would create no serious traffic problems.

In order for a restriction on the time of a parade to be valid, it must be designed to respond to a significant regulatory problem and not be unnecessarily burdensome on speech activities. Moreover, if officials claim that they have a legitimate reason to restrict the time of a parade but do not offer a reasonable alternative time or route, they may be imposing an illegitimate restriction based on distaste for the message to be communicated by the parade.

Can officials prohibit parades after dark?

The courts have been generally sympathetic to official prohibitions on parades after dark. They have given several justifications for this attitude. Among the most persuasive is that because of reduced visibility at night the difficult law enforcement problems ordinarily created by parades are aggravated. "One who would consider violating the law during a parade might also find psychological comfort in the knowledge that he could more easily evade the authorities after a lawless act committed at night."[42] Another explanation is that there is a significant community interest in peace and quiet after dark.[43]

On the other hand, some municipalities allow nighttime parades when there are ample street lights along the parade route. Other municipalities may sponsor such parades for causes they support. It is therefore important to learn about local practice. In addition, the claim for a nighttime parade may be taken more seriously by public officials and by the courts if the organizers can show that the hours selected are related to the message communicated by the parade. For example, a parade held at night to protest the fact that the streets are not safe for women who are out during nighttime hours would relate the time of the parade to its subject. Such parades have been held in many cities during recent years.

Reasonable Regulation of the Place of a Parade

Are there any officially preferred locations for parades?

As a general rule, the most common locations for parades are streets and sidewalks. Official preferences are likely to vary from community to community and from situation to situation. However, officials often try to steer parades away from locations where there is likely to be a substantial amount of automobile or pedestrian traffic. In the event that officials object to a request for a particular parade route and offer an alternate one that is unacceptable to organizers, it is important to show that the initial route allows the parade to communicate its message in a way that the proposed alternate does not. This occurred in *Dr. Martin Luther King, Jr. Coalition, Inc. v. City of Chicago*,[44] where city officials tried to compel demonstrators to use an alternative route that avoided a hostile audience. The city officials in that case were ordered to grant a permit for the requested route.

Is there a difference in the degree of First Amendment protection accorded to parades on public streets as opposed to those held on public sidewalks?

No. The First Amendment protections for street parades are equally applicable to sidewalk parades. However, because the regulatory problems posed by street parades are different from those posed by sidewalk parades, the actual time, place, and manner regulations may be quite different. As noted previously, one of the most frequently encountered differences is that permits that may be required for a street parade may not be required for a sidewalk parade that travels over the same route. The presence or absence of such differences can only be determined by reference to the relevant statutes and ordinances in each jurisdiction.

Can public officials issue a parade permit that changes the route of a parade from that which was requested by the parade's organizers?

Sometimes. The right to use any particular parade route is subject to the presence of competing activities. Public officials often alter proposed parade routes to minimize traffic problems and interference with other previously scheduled activities. Similarly, changes may be made to avoid a portion of the route that is under repair. To the extent that the alteration does not unreasonably interfere with access to the targeted audience, the alteration is likely to meet with judicial approval. However, if officials make a change in the parade route because of the identity of the participants or the content of the message communicated by the parade, the change probably violates the First Amendment.[45]

Can police order changes in the parade route after the parade is under way?

Not usually. If a permit to hold a parade has been obtained, the officials who issued the permit are legally obliged to allow the parade to follow the approved route. However, occasionally, police accompanying a parade will become aware of an unforeseen circumstance that requires an immediate change of route. If, for example, there is a fire or automobile accident along the route of a parade, an impromptu change of route might be the only reasonable way to avoid interfering with official efforts to deal with the emergency.

Can officials reroute a parade because its route will take it past hostile onlookers who officials believe may try to disrupt it?

Not as a general rule. A parade on a public forum is a constitutionally protected activity. As a result, police have a responsibility to protect it from interference just as they have a responsibility to protect any other lawful activities against interference.[46] On the other hand, the obligation to protect a demonstration from outside disruption is not an absolute one. If officials can establish that they have made every effort and still cannot protect the parade against harm by outsiders, they may be able to reroute it.[47]

What can parade organizers do if they are being required to reroute their parade, and they think that the rerouting is unjustified?

In the event that there is a rerouting to which organizers legitimately object, they have several options. If they learn of rerouting in sufficient time before the parade, they can try to initiate negotiations to obtain a more satisfactory route. If that does not work, they can initiate a court challenge. If a court challenge cannot be initiated or is unlikely to succeed, the organizers can decide whether to call off the parade or to accept the rerouting and proceed.

If the rerouting occurs at the time of the parade, organizers have only two options. They can accept the rerouting or terminate the parade. If demonstrators elect to ignore the rerouting and to proceed on the original route, they risk subjecting every participant in the parade to arrest. Moreover, police may stop the parade once they determine that the rerouting order is being ignored. As a consequence, a police order rerouting a parade should not be ignored, even if it seems arbitrary or unlawful.

Reasonable Regulation of the Manner of a Parade

Can limitations be placed on the size of a parade?

There are no published decisions specifically addressing the question of the government's power to limit the size of a parade. However, the cases addressing the power of the government to regulate the size and location of demonstrations provide some guidance.[48] They suggest there might be some circumstances in which a size limitation imposed as a reasonable regulation of time, place, and manner would be sustained if it were needed to enable police to maintain order or to prevent disruption of competing activities. Thus, a size limitation imposed on parades to be held on sidewalks or other locations too small to accommodate a large number of demonstrators would probably be treated by the courts as a reasonable regulation.

It should be noted, however, that size limitations are rarely imposed on privately sponsored street parades. Officials are reluctant to impose them because the judiciary is not likely to approve of them without proof that the limitations are really necessary. Moreover, extremely popular parades are often quite large. Once such large parades have been allowed in a particular place, officials are obliged to provide similar treatment to all other parades in the same place.

If floats and vehicles are part of a parade, are they subject to regulations?

Floats and vehicles that are part of a privately sponsored parade are subject to reasonable regulations of time, place, and manner. The most likely regulations pertain to safety and traffic control. Thus police may require that floats or vehicles not be so big that they extend into lanes of traffic not reserved for the parade. They can also require that floats be soundly constructed and operated so as to protect observers and participants from potential injury.

Can officials confine the parade route to a single lane of traffic or other portion of the street or sidewalk?

While such limitations are rarely discussed in reported cases, they are frequently imposed. They are usually characterized by a restriction that limits a parade to specified traffic lanes so that traffic can continue to move in other lanes. Similarly, some municipalities limit sidewalk parades to one half of the sidewalk so that pedestrians can continue to use the remaining portion.

A frequent objection to confining a parade to a portion of the street is that the restriction makes the parade longer and narrower than sponsors want it to be. Sponsors object that a longer parade consumes much more time from start to finish and is therefore harder to manage. Disputes over limitations to a portion of streets and sidewalks are best handled by direct negotiations with officials in charge of the parade route, rather than litigation, because the courts are likely to sustain all but the most burdensome of such restrictions.

Do participants in a parade have to obey traffic control signals and signs along the parade route?

As a general rule, protestors are required by law to obey traffic signals on the same basis as everyone else. "One would not be justified in ignoring the familiar red traffic light because he thought it his religious duty to disobey the municipal command or sought by that means to direct public attention to an announcement of his opinions."[49] Moreover, as a practical matter, police sometimes seek to have parade participants obey traffic control signals so that traffic on streets perpendicular to the parade can cross the parade route safely. On the other hand, there are often parades in which police want traffic control signals ignored so that the parade will proceed to its destination quickly. The problem posed by stopping for traffic signals is that each stop tends to spread the parade out over a longer distance and slow down its progress. Therefore, this is a matter that is often worked out with police before the parade begins.

Do protestors who organize a parade have an obligation to allow persons of all viewpoints participate in the parade?

No. Parades are held for the purpose of expressing the views of the organizers and their supporters. Therefore, there is no right to participate in a parade that is organized and sponsored by private persons or a private group if the organizers object. The procurement of a permit assures the route will be set aside for the parade and its message at a particular time and date so that the views can be communicated to interested spectators and the media. Participation in the parade by uninvited persons whose viewpoints differ significantly from the purpose of the parade would have the effect of interfering with or diluting the parade's message and would interfere with the organizers' freedom to associate with like-minded persons.[50] The uninvited participants remain free to sponsor their own parade.

If a parade is sponsored by the government, can anyone who wishes to participate be excluded?

As a general rule, the government cannot pick and choose among privately held viewpoints when it holds a parade that is open to public participation. Therefore, some courts have ordered government sponsors of a parade to let people participate without regard to their particular viewpoint. For example, in one case, sponsors of a Memorial Day parade were found to be holding the parade as an agent of a town's government and were therefore obliged to let an anti-abortion group participate.[51] Other courts have held that to the extent that there is a right to participate in a government-sponsored parade, it is not unlimited. If the government can establish that its limits on participation are based on time, place, and manner considerations such as avoiding an excessively long parade, a decision to exclude may be sustainable in court.[52]

Can permission to hold a parade be denied because participants have engaged in disorderly conduct during prior parades?

Permission to hold a parade cannot be denied solely on the basis of prior misconduct. For example in *Kunz v. New York*,[53] the Supreme Court overturned a conviction for holding a religious meeting following the city's revocation of the group's permit after learning that some of defendants' past meetings had resulted in disorder. Whether or not there has been disorder at sometime in the past, law enforcement officials always remain free to make appropriate arrests anytime the disorder recurs. However, in order to impose an advance prohibition of a parade based on violence occurring at past parades, "such past violence, if relevant at all, must be extremely closely related in time and character" to the current parade.[54]

NOTES

1. *Cox v. Louisiana*, 379 U.S. 536, 577 (1965) (Black, J., concurring).
2. *Cox v. New Hampshire*, 312 U.S. 569 (1941).
3. *Olivieri v. Ward*, 801 F.2d 602 (2d Cir. 1986).
4. *Collin v. Chicago Park District*, 460 F.2d 746 (7th Cir. 1972).
5. 468 U.S. 288 (1983).
6. *Id.* at 296.
7. *Heffron v. International Society for Krishna Consciousness*, 452 U.S. 640 (1981).
8. *Perry Education Association v. Perry Local Educators' Association*, 460 U.S. 37 (1983).
9. *See A Quaker Action Group v. Morton*, 516 F.2d 717, 725 (D.C. Cir. 1975).
10. 516 F.2d 717, 724 (D.C. Cir. 1975).
11. 460 F.2d 746 (7th Cir. 1972).
12. *Blasecki v. Durham*, 456 F.2d 87 (4th Cir. 1972).
13. *Davis v. Francois*, 395 F.2d 730 (5th Cir. 1968).
14. *A Quaker Action Group v. Hickel*, 421 F.2d 1111 (D.C. Cir. 1969).
15. *Blasecki v. Durham*, 456 F.2d at 92.
16. *Collin v. Chicago Park District, supra* note 4.

17. *Schneider v. Town of Irvington*, 308 U.S. 147, 163 (1939).
18. *We've Carried the Rich v. City of Philadelphia*, 414 F. Supp. 611 (E.D. Pa.), *aff'd mem.*, 538 F.2d 322 (3d Cir. 1976).
19. *Dr. Martin Luther King, Jr. Movement Coalition, Inc. v. City of Chicago*, 419 F. Supp. 667, 674 (N.D. Ill. 1976).
20. *Gregory v. City of Chicago*, 39 Ill. 2d 47, 233 N.E.2d 422 (1968), *rev'd on other grounds*, 394 U.S. 111 (1969).
21. *We've Carried the Rich v. City of Philadelphia, supra* note 18.
22. *Id.*
23. *Olivieri v. Ward, supra* note 3.
24. *Blasecki v. Durham, supra* note 12.
25. *Olivieri v. Ward, supra* note 3.
26. *Davis v. Francois, supra* note 13.
27. 69 Ill. 2d 605 (1978).
28. *Beckerman v. City of Tupelo, Miss.*, 664 F.2d 502 (1981).
29. *Kovacs v. Cooper*, 336 U.S. 77 (1949).
30. *Medlin v. Palmer*, 874 F.2d 1085 (5th Cir. 1989). *See also Concerned Jewish Youth v. McGuire*, 621 F.2d 471 (2d Cir. 1980).
31. *Saia v. New York*, 334 U.S. 558 (1948).
32. *Ward v. Rock against Racism*, 109 S. Ct. 2746 (1989).
33. 109 S. Ct. at 2759.
34. *City of Blue Island v. Kozul*, 379 Ill. 511, 41 N.E.2d 515 (1942); *Milwaukee Mobilization for Survival v. Milwaukee County Park Commission*, 474 F. Supp. 881 (E.D. Wis. 1979).
35. *Buckley v. Valeo*, 424 U.S. 1 (1976).
36. 308 U.S. 147 (1939).
37. *New World Dictionary* 1029 (2d ed. 1976).
38. Kalven, *The Concept of the Public Forum, Cox v. Louisiana*, Sup. Ct. Rev. 1, 30 (1965).
39. *See Olivieri v. Ward, supra* note 3.
40. *Cox v. Louisiana*, 379 U.S. 536, 554 (1965).
41. 474 F. Supp. 1333 (D. Colo. 1979).
42. *Abernathy v. Conroy*, 429 F.2d 1170, 1174 (4th Cir. 1970). *See also Beckerman v. City of Tupelo, Miss.*, 664 F.2d 502, 512 (5th Cir. 1981).
43. *Abernathy v. Conroy*, 429 F.2d at 1174.
44. 419 F. Supp. 667 (N.D. Ill. 1967).
45. *Dr. Martin Luther King, Jr. Movement, Inc. v. City of Chicago, supra* note 19.
46. *Id.*
47. *Feiner v. New York*, 340 U.S. 315 (1951); *We've Carried the Rich v. City of Philadelphia*, 414 F. Supp. 611 (E.D. Pa. 1976).
48. *See Blasecki v. Durham, supra* note 12.
49. *Cox v. New Hampshire*, 312 U.S. 569, 574 (1941).

50. *Invisible Empire KKK v. Thurmont*, 700 F. Supp. 281 (D. Md. 1988).
51. *North Shore Right to Life Committee v. Manhasset American Legion Post No. 304*, 452 F. Supp. 834 (E.D.N.Y. 1978).
52. *Tacynes v. City of Philadelphia*, 687 F.2d 793 (3d Cir. 1982).
53. 340 U.S. 290 (1941).
54. *Collin v. Chicago Park District*, 460 F.2d at 754.

X

Government Regulation of Specific Speech Activities: Individual Speakers, Leafletting, Picketing, and Display of Signs and Posters

INDIVIDUAL SPEAKERS

Can government regulate individual speakers who walk around public forums stating their views to anyone who will listen?

Most jurisdictions allow individual speakers to move about freely on sidewalks and other traditional public forums to spread their views without the need for a permit.[1] However public officials may impose reasonable regulations of time, place, and manner on such activity when such regulations are needed. For example, an individual standing on a busy street corner making a political or religious statement is a common sight in the downtown areas of many large cities. These speakers are usually left alone by police so long as their speechmaking occurs without the assistance of sound equipment. If a crowd begins to form, police have a responsibility to regulate the crowd before asking the speaker to cease. In addition, if sound equipment is used, a permit may be required. If a crowd begins to form and movement of sidewalk or street traffic is impeded, the speaker may be asked by police to move on or face arrest for disorderly conduct.[2]

Can an individual go door-to-door to solicit donations for his or her cause?

Yes. Door-to-door fundraising for political, religious, or public-issue reasons is protected by the First Amendment. Thus, individuals may go door-to-door for such purposes.[3] However, such solicitations are subject to reasonable regulations of time, place, and manner. One of the most common regulations is a notice posted by the occupant of the dwelling stating that

solicitors are not welcome. While the courts have not definitively held that ignoring such a notice is tantamount to tres-
passing, the judiciary's sympathy towards the privacy of the
home suggests that a solicitor ignores such a sign at his or her
own risk.[4] In addition, some statements by the Supreme Court
suggest that municipal authorities may be able to require solicitors to give advance notice to the police department as a means
of protecting against crime and undue annoyance.[5] At least one
court has approved such a requirement; therefore care should
be taken in each jurisdiction to find out whether such a requirement exists.[6] On the other hand, if a local ordinance prohibits
door-to-door fundraising or proselytizing during early evening
hours, it may be invalid.[7]

LEAFLETTING

What is "leafletting"?

Leafletting is one of the most traditional means of communicating political and religious viewpoints. Typically, leafletting
is the handing out of pamphlets, leaflets, and other similar
printed materials to willing recipients in places open to the
public. It is protected by the First Amendment because it is
an inexpensive, nondisruptive means of communication that
can be utilized by anyone who feels a need to communicate his
or her views to an immediate audience. "[P]amphlets ha[ve]
become historic weapons in defense of liberty."[8]

Reasonable Regulation of the Time of Leafletting

Can public officials regulate the time of leafletting on a traditional public forum?

Probably not. A leafletter is free to pass out his or her leaflets
on a traditional public forum like a street, sidewalk, or park at
any time the forum is open to the public. Leafletting is a
sufficiently nondisruptive activity that can usually go on without
disturbing other activities at the same time and place. On the
other hand, if a public forum like a park is routinely closed at
night, a leafletter must abide by the closing rule just like anyone
else or be subject to arrest.[9]

Can public officials regulate the time of leafletting on locations open to the public that are not traditional public forums like streets, sidewalks, and parks?

Yes. Leafletting at locations other than traditional public forums is open to a greater degree of regulation than would be the case for streets, sidewalks, and parks. Officials can impose reasonable time regulations at such sites that are consistent with needs arising from the primary use of the site. For example, if public officials voluntarily open the lobby of a public office building to leafletting, they may be free to set limits on the times leafletting can occur in order to avoid undue interference with the ingress and egress of the building's occupants at times when there is likely to be serious congestion.[10]

Reasonable Regulation of the Place of Leafletting

Can public officials ban leafletting on streets, sidewalks, and parks?

No. The Supreme Court has held that because leafletting is one of the most fundamental ways people with limited funds can reach an audience, public streets, sidewalks, and parks cannot be closed to it. In *Schneider v. State*,[11] the Supreme Court ruled that the attempt of municipal officials to impose a citywide ban on leafletting because it causes littering violated the First Amendment. The Supreme Court explained:

> We are of the opinion that the purpose to keep the streets clean and of good appearance is insufficient to justify an ordinance which prohibits a person rightfully on a public street from handing literature to one willing to receive it. Any burden imposed upon the city authorities in cleaning and caring for the streets as an indirect consequence of such distribution results from the constitutional protection of freedom of speech and press.[12]

Can leafletters place their leaflets in letter boxes and mail slots used for the delivery of U.S. mail?

No. The only items that can be placed in U.S. mailboxes and mail slots are letters and boxes with stamps on which postage has been paid. Title 18 U.S.C. § 1725 makes it a criminal offense to deposit "mailable matter . . . on which no postage has been paid" in mail slots and letter boxes used for mail delivery. In a challenge by door-to-door leafletters who sought to use mailboxes, the Supreme Court upheld this law on grounds that mailboxes are an integral part of the United States mail delivery system and are subject to the complete control of the Congress and the United States Postal Service.[13] Therefore, if a leafletter wishes to distribute leaflets to homes and other places where letter boxes or letter slots are present, the leaflets should be placed under the doors or attached to door knobs in order to avoid violating § 1725.

Can leafletting be restricted or prohibited on public property that is not open to the public or that is open to the public only on a limited basis?

The courts have been much less sympathetic to leafletting on public property that is not regarded as a traditional public forum than it has been to leafletting on streets, sidewalks, and parks. Therefore, leafletting on public property that is not open to the public or is open on a limited basis can probably be restricted or prohibited as long as there is no official discrimination or censorship. For example, in *Heffron v. International Society of Krishna Consciousness*,[14] the Supreme Court sustained a ban on leafletting at a state fair by adherents of the Hari Krishna religion because fair officials believed that the movement of pedestrians on a crowded state fairway would be impeded. Leafletters were required to distribute their message from rented booths on the same basis as other fair exhibitors. On the other hand, the courts have found leafletting to be constitutionally protected in places like bus stations and airports.[15]

Can leaflets be distributed to persons in vehicles stopped at intersections?

Not usually. Officials have the authority to prohibit it to assure that traffic moves through the intersection safely and efficiently, if they choose. Thus, in *United States Labor Party v. Oremus*,[16] a statute stating that "no person shall stand on a highway for the purpose of soliciting employment, business, or contributions from the occupant of any vehicle" was found to be a valid prohibition against sales of political newspapers in the intersection of a street. The court explained that people engaged in First Amendment activities are required to obey traffic laws on the same basis as anyone else. The court pointed to an established constitutional rule that "[w]here a restriction of the use of highways . . . is designed to promote the public convenience in the interest of all, it cannot be disregarded by the attempted exercise of some civil right which in other circumstances would be entitled to protection."[17]

Is there a right to go door-to-door and ring doorbells in order to hand leaflets to the occupants of private residences?

Usually. The right to distribute leaflets has been interpreted to encompass approaching private homes, ringing doorbells, and distributing the leaflets to the occupants.[18] However, it should also be noted that many residences display signs indicating that door-to-door solicitations of any kind are not welcome. Although the power of the state to impose criminal sanctions on a political protestor for failure to obey the sign has never been ruled on by the Supreme Court, it is generally a wise idea to obey the sign. Failure to obey the sign may result in charges for criminal trespass or the like. The courts are quite sympathetic to homeowners' interests in being left alone.[19]

Reasonable Regulation of the Manner of Leafletting

Is it necessary to obtain a permit before handing out leaflets and pamphlets on a traditional public forum?

Probably not. Although the Supreme Court has never directly addressed this question, spontaneous leafletting on traditional public forums is so well established it is unlikely a permit requirement would be upheld in court. The law enforcement problems associated with regulating the potentially large numbers of people present at parades and demonstrations are not presented by individual leafletters circulating among pedestrians and handing leaflets to willing recipients.

Can a permit be required if there is a charge for the leaflet or fundraising is done at the time a leaflet or other printed material is handed out in order to support the leafletter's views?

This question has not been definitively settled by the courts. It is not usually a problem when the fundraising is done on traditional public forums. Nonetheless, because the exchange of a leaflet for money or a solicitation of money at the time that the leaflet is given away has some of the qualities of a commercial transaction, many government officials believe they can regulate political fundraising transactions.[20] They contend that, to the extent that permits for the sale of goods on the streets may be required, a similar permit can be required for the sale of leaflets to raise money to support the positions advocated by the leafletter.

Most jurisdictions do not enforce laws requiring notice to police or permits for the occasional fundraising often done in conjunction with the distribution of leaflets, but it is important to check with local authorities to be sure of the requirements in each place. This is particularly true if the fundraising effort is to be extensive and continue over a long period of time.

Does a leaflet have to identify the person or group responsible for its message?

Not usually. The Supreme Court has held that the distribution of anonymous political leaflets is a constitutionally protected activity because "[a]nonymous pamphlets, leaflets, brochures and even books have played an important role in the progress of mankind. Persecuted groups and sects from time to time throughout history have been able to criticize oppressive practices and laws either anonymously or not at all."[21] However a few lower courts have upheld restrictions on anonymous leaflets that are part of an election campaign in order to prevent "dirty tricks."[22]

PICKETING

What is picketing?

In the context of political protest, the term picketing usually refers to a single person or line of people standing or walking near a specific location as a means of communicating a particular viewpoint on a public issue. It also refers to the posting of persons near a specific location for the purpose of persuading others not to enter or transact business there. The term picketing covers both public-issue picketing and labor picketing. However, because this book is about the rights of protestors addressing public issues, the information that follows is directed at public-issue picketing, not labor picketing. This distinction should be kept in mind because the legal doctrines applicable to public issue picketing are different than those applicable to labor picketing.[23]

Is picketing about public issues protected by the First Amendment?

Yes. Picketing that seeks to convey a message on a public issue enjoys broad constitutional protection. However, the protection is subject to reasonable regulations of time, place, and manner. The courts have defined the scope of constitutional protection given to picketing in the following terms: "[P]eaceful public issue picketing is protected under the First Amendment as 'symbolic speech' so long as it is in a location generally open to the public. However, this protection will shield one from arrest only if his picketing does not interfere with legitimate State interests such as the regulation of traffic on public streets and sidewalks."[24] To the extent that there are limits on the constitutional protection given to picketing, it is because picketing is simultaneously comprised of a "speech" element and a "conduct" element. The speech element derives from the viewpoint that the picketing is intended to communicate. The conduct element derives from the fact that a picket line has the capacity to obstruct the movement of nonpicketers and may, in some instances, be physically intimidating. The conduct element of speech is subject to content-neutral regulations designed to minimize disruptions of competing activities.

On what locations does picketing receive the broadest First Amendment protection?

Picketing on traditional public forums receives broad constitutional protection because traditional public forums are owned by the government and are open to the public. Picketers are as much a part of the public as any other users of a public forum and, in addition, are engaged in activities the First Amendment treats as particularly important. Also, as a practical matter, when picketing occurs on traditional public forums, pedestrians and others who wish to avoid the picketing usually have ample opportunity to do so. When picketing occurs at less traditional public locations, constitutional protections are substantially diminished.

Is it legal to picket a private residence?

It depends on the circumstances. If the purpose of the picketing is to target a private home in order to say something to or about its occupants, the picketing may be prohibited by a statute or ordinance. According to the Supreme Court decision in *Frisby v. Schultz*,[25] "focused picketing taking place solely in front of [and directed towards] a particular residence" can be prohibited by state and local laws. The Court distinguished focused residential picketing from marching or walking past private residences while moving through a neighborhood. It ruled that the latter was constitutionally protected. The courts have not yet determined whether picketing that is focused on a large apartment building can be prohibited in the same fashion as the picketing of a single family dwelling. If, however, a residence is occupied by a public official, the picketing might retain some First Amendment protection. The Supreme Court has yet to address this situation.

Can limitations be imposed on the number of people who participate in picketing at any one time?

Yes, if the limitations are reasonable. An across-the-board limitation on the number of picketers that is imposed by statute or ordinance is probably unconstitutional because it is not tailored to individual situations. Numerical limits can be imposed on picketing without violating the Constitution only if they address specific regulatory problems and are not imposed because of the content of the picketers' message.[26] Thus, a numerical limitation designed to prevent picketers from cordoning off an entrance to a public or private building is permissible.[27] However, an across-the-board limit that is not tailored to individual situations is unconstitutional because it imposes limitations on situations in which no limitations are needed.[28]

Can picketers be required to remain a specified distance from a site they want to picket?

Sometimes. If the site being picketed is also being used for an activity with which picketing is interfering, then reasonable regulations of the time, place, and manner can be imposed. Thus, a distance restriction on picketing that requires picketers to remain a specified number of feet from a public school when school is in session is probably constitutional as long as there is evidence that it is needed and is not excessive.[29] Distance restrictions on picketing have sometimes been imposed by court order after picketers have been asked to leave a site and have refused to do so. The operators of such sites have filed suit for injunctive relief and have obtained court orders setting restrictions on distance or on the numbers of picketers after having proved that the picketing was so disruptive that distance restrictions were necessary.[30]

DISPLAY OF SIGNS AND POSTERS

Is the display of signs and posters protected by the First Amendment?

Yes. The display of signs and posters is a traditional means of communication that receives broad First Amendment protection. The broadest protection exists when the sign or poster is displayed by a person who is carrying it. However, the protections diminish when the sign or poster is placed at a fixed location and remains there after its owner has gone.[31] Like other speech activities, legitimate regulation of the display of signs and posters is based on time, place, and manner considerations. These regulations may usually be found in statutes, ordinances, and in some cases, local zoning codes. If a speaker wishes to place a sign at a site for an extended period of time, it is wise to consult with appropriate public officials to find out if such a display is permitted and if a permit is required.

Can a permit be required to display hand-held signs or posters?

Not on a traditional public forum. The right to be present on a traditional public forum includes the right to display handheld signs or posters. Therefore if a permit is required to hold an assembly or parade, the issuance of the permit automatically covers the signs or posters. On the other hand, if the poster is to be left at the site after the protestor leaves or if it is to be displayed at a nontraditional forum, a permit may be necessary, or there may be laws or regulations prohibiting unattended signs and posters.[32]

Can officials require that signs displayed on public forums be hand-held?

Yes. One court has sustained the requirement that a political poster displayed during parades, assemblies, and picketing near the White House must be in physical contact with its possessor to protect against its being used as a weapon.[33] Such a requirement might also be imposed for aesthetic reasons. It ensures that signs are not propped against walls, fences, or trees and left there indefinitely creating long term litter or visual clutter. However, the validity of such a requirement is related to governmental interests based on the particular place and circumstance where the sign is displayed. In addition, if the requirement is not imposed uniformly, it may be invalid. Finally, if demonstrators wish to leave signs at a location after they have left, they may have to comply with local permit restrictions governing the display of signs.

Can officials regulate the materials and construction of handcarried signs displayed on public forums?

Yes. If the materials and construction of hand-carried signs are reasonably regulated for safety and traffic control reasons, the regulations are permitted by the time, place, and manner doctrine. Such regulations include size limitations, requirements that signs be made of flexible materials, and requirements that signs not be attached to sticks large enough to become weapons. Thus, in *White House Vigil v. Clark*,[34] prohibitions against rigid signs and restrictions on sign supports were sustained so that the signs could not be used as weapons or thrown in the event of conflict with police.

Is there a constitutional right to attach signs to public property such as trees, poles, or buildings?

No. In *Los Angeles City Council v. Taxpayers for Vincent*,[35] the Court upheld an ordinance prohibiting the posting of signs on public property as a means to avoid visual clutter. "[The] problem addressed by this ordinance—the visual assault of the citizens of Los Angeles presented by an accumulation of signs posted on public property—constitutes a significant substantive evil within the City's power to prohibit."[36] The Court approved the restriction, in part, because it believed that there were adequate alternative ways for a communicator to reach his or her audience.

Is there a constitutional right to display signs and posters in the front window or on the lawn of your own home?

Probably. The lower courts have repeatedly invalidated ordinances and zoning restrictions that ban the outdoor display of traditional political signs on private property in residential areas. The Supreme Court has not addressed the question. The basis for the lower court rulings is that other kinds of signs such as "for sale" signs have been permitted and the ban of political signs is discriminatory.[37] In addition, the courts have suggested that the banning of all political signs unduly interferes with an individual's use of his or her private property.[38] However, to the extent that political signs can be displayed, they are still subject to reasonable time, place, and manner restrictions. Thus, reasonable restrictions can be imposed on the time of display, construction standards, and size.

NOTES

1. *See Heffron v. International Society of Krishna Consciousness*, 452 U.S. 640 (1981).
2. It is not clear that such a charge would lead to a conviction, but there are circumstances in which it might. *Meyer v. City of Chicago*, 44 Ill. 2d 1 (1969), *cert. denied*, 397 U.S. 1024 (1970).
3. *Village of Schaumberg v. Citizens for a Better Environment*, 444 U.S. 620 (1980).
4. *Martin v. Struthers*, 319 U.S. 141 (1943).
5. *Hynes v. Mayor*, 425 U.S. 610 (1976).
6. *National Foundation v. City of Fort Worth*, 415 F.2d 41 (5th Cir. 1969), *cert. denied*, 396 U.S. 1040 (1970).
7. *Watseka v. Illinois Public Action Counsel*, 796 F.2d 1547 (7th Cir. 1986), *aff'd*, 479 U.S. 1048 (1987).
8. *Schneider v. State*, 308 U.S. 147, 160 (1939).
9. *Id.*
10. *Perry Education Association v. Perry Local Educators' Association*, 460 U.S. 37 (1983).
11. 308 U.S. 147 (1939).
12. 308 U.S. at 162.

13. *United States Postal Service v. Greenburgh Civic Associations*, 453 U.S. 114 (1981).
14. 452 U.S. 640 (1981).
15. *Wolin v. Port of New York Authority*, 392 F.2d 83 (1969); *Jamison v. City of St. Louis*, 828 F.2d 1280 (8th Cir. 1987).
16. 619 F.2d 683 (7th Cir. 1980).
17. *Cox v. New Hampshire*, 312 U.S. 569, 574 (1941).
18. *Martin v. Struthers*, 319 U.S. 141 (1943).
19. *See Frisby v. Schultz*, 108 S. Ct. 2895 (1988).
20. *Murdock v. Pennsylvania*, 319 U.S. 105, 114–16 (1943).
21. *Talley v. California*, 362 U.S. 60, 64 (1960); *see also Wilson v. Stocker*, 819 F.2d 943 (10th Cir. 1987).
22. *Morefield v. Moore*, 540 S.W.2d 873 (Ky. 1976); *but see People v. White*, 116 Ill. 2d 171, 506 N.E.2d 1284 (1987).
23. For a discussion of labor picketing, see the ACLU handbook, *The Rights of Employees and Union Members* (forthcoming 1992).
24. *Medrano v. Allee*, 347 F. Supp. 605, 623 (S.D. Tex. 1972) *vacated and remanded on other grounds sub nom. Allee v. Medrano*, 416 U.S. 802 (1974). *See also Carey v. Brown*, 447 U.S. 455, 466–67 (1980).
25. 105 S. Ct. 2895 (1989).
26. *Police Department of Chicago v. Mosley*, 408 U.S. 92 (1972).
27. *Davis v. Francois*, 395 F.2d 730, 734 (5th Cir., 1968).
28. *LeFlore v. Robinson*, 434 F.2d 993 (5th Cir. 1970) *vacated on other grounds*, 446 F.2d 715 (5th Cir. 1971).
29. *See Mosley v. Chicago Police Department and Grayned v. Rockford*, 408 U.S. 104 (1972).
30. *Concerned Jewish Youth v. McGuire*, 621 F.2d 471 (2d Cir. 1989); *Bering v. Share*, 106 Wash. 2d 212, 721 P.2d 918 (Wash. 1986).
31. *White House Vigil for ERA Committee v. Clark*, 746 F.2d 1518 (D.C. Cir. 1984).
32. *See Los Angeles City Council v. Taxpayers for Vincent*, 466 U.S. 789 (1984) and *White House Vigil for ERA Committee v. Clark*, *supra* note 31.
33. *White House Vigil for ERA Committee v. Clark*, 746 F.2d at 1534.
34. 746 F.2d 1518 (D.C. Cir. 1984).
35. 466 U.S. 789 (1984).
36. *Los Angeles City Council v. Taxpayers for Vincent*, 466 U.S. 789, 807 (1984).
37. *Linmark Associates, Inc. v. Willingboro*, 431 U.S. 85 (1977).
38. *Mathews v. Town of Needham*, 596 F. Supp. 932 (D. Mass. 1984); *Meros v. City of Euclid, Ohio*, 594 F. Supp. 259 (N.D. Ohio 1984).

XI

Nontraditional Forums for
Speech Activities

**Are there places in addition to streets, sidewalks, and
parks where speech activities are protected by the First
Amendment?**

Yes. Speech activities are protected by the First Amendment
to one degree or another in a variety of locations on public
property. However, in contrast to the broad constitutional protections for speech activities on traditional forums like streets,
sidewalks, and parks, the constitutional protections given to
speech activities on nontraditional forums are subject to much
broader restrictions. In fact, the Supreme Court has divided
public forums into three categories: (1) traditional public forums, (2) designated forums, and (3) nonpublic forums.

Traditional public forums can always be used for speech
activities subject to reasonable restrictions of time, place, and
manner. Designated forums are government owned sites that
officials have voluntarily opened to speech activities even
though they are not obliged by the Constitution to do so. Once
opened, these sites are subject to reasonable regulations of
time, place, and manner including those that reflect the primary purpose for which the site is used. Finally, nonpublic
forums are government owned sites that, because of their special characteristics, do not have to be made available for speech
activities, even if some speech activities have been previously
allowed on an ad hoc basis. The Supreme Court has summarized this framework in the following terms:

> In places which by long tradition or by government fiat
> have been devoted to assembly and debate, the rights of
> the State to limit expressive activity are sharply circum-
> scribed. . . . A second category consists of public property
> which the State has opened for use by the public as a place
> for expressive activity. The Constitution forbids a state to
> enforce certain exclusions from a forum generally open to
> the public even if it was not required to create the forum
> in the first place. Although a State is not required to

indefinitely retain the open character of the facility, as long as it does so it is bound by the same standards as apply in a traditional public forum. . . . Public property which is not by tradition or designation a forum for public communication is governed by different standards. We have recognized that the "First Amendment does not guarantee access to property simply because it is owned or controlled by the government."[1]

If public officials voluntarily create a public forum, do they have to open it to everyone on a nondiscriminatory basis?

As a general rule, when public officials voluntarily designate a site as a public forum, they must open it on a nondiscriminatory basis.[2] This means they cannot choose among speakers based on the content of each speaker's communication. However, notwithstanding the obligation to act nondiscriminatorily, officials still have discretion to allow public property serving a specialized function to be used by some outsiders without opening the property to everyone. For example, the decision of high school officials to allow school grounds to be used for a charity marathon does not create an obligation for them to allow the same grounds to be used for political protest activities.[3] The scope of official power to choose among users of specialized government property is still being defined by the courts.

Once a nonpublic forum has been officially designated to be a public forum, can officials ever turn it back into a nonpublic forum?

Yes. The government is free to change its mind about designating a nontraditional site as a public forum. However, the basis for deciding to prohibit speech activities previously allowed must be unrelated to the content of the communications affected by the newly enforced prohibition. Thus, in *Knolls Action Project v. Knolls Atomic Power Laboratory*,[4] an appeals court upheld the decision of administrators of a nuclear research facility to prohibit leafletting on facility property that had previously been allowed. The court explained that the ban on leafletting was legitimate because prior leafletting had created traffic congestion and safety problems. The ban was therefore not an effort to censor the message of particular leafletters.

STATE CAPITOL BUILDINGS

Can the grounds surrounding a state capitol building be used for speech activities?

Yes, if the grounds are open to the public. In *Edwards v. South Carolina*,[5] the Supreme Court stated that a peaceful demonstration on state capital grounds was "an exercise of . . . basic constitutional rights in their most pristine and classic form."[6] This language suggests that the capitol grounds, including sidewalks to and from the building, are indistinguishable from a traditional public forum. However, a note of caution should be added. Since deciding the *Edwards* case, the Supreme Court has repeatedly confined its description of traditional public forums to streets, sidewalks, and parks. This leaves open the possibility that there are circumstances in which the lawns adjacent to state capitol buildings might not be open to speech. If there is doubt about a particular location, it is wise to inquire of appropriate public officials.

Is there a constitutional right to engage in protest activities in the lobbies, halls, and other open areas of a state capitol building?

Because the inside areas of any government building are not traditional public forums, public officials may have the power to require that all protest activities take place on public sidewalks and other locations outside.[7] The scope of this governmental power varies from situation to situation. Typically, however, legislators and other public officials voluntarily allow nondisruptive protest activities in areas of capitol buildings that are open to the public. As a result, if there is an effort to declare the inside of a capitol building out-of-bounds to a particular group of protestors, it may be possible to challenge the exclusion on grounds that it is a form of content discrimination.

On the other hand, even if protest activities have been allowed in the past, the exclusion of protest activities from the inside areas of a capitol building may be enforceable in some circumstances. The most obvious would include protests that interfere with the transaction of the public's business or complicate building security problems. The best way to deal with potential restrictions is by learning of them in advance and, assuming no content discrimination is involved, trying to work out satisfactory accommodations with appropriate officials where possible.

COURTHOUSES

Are protest activities outside a public courthouse protected by the First Amendment?

It depends. The Supreme Court has ruled that statutes prohibiting picketing or demonstrating outside a courthouse where trials take place are valid. Thus, in *Cox v. Louisiana*,[8] it upheld a state statute banning picketing or parades in or near a state courthouse "with the intent of interfering with [the] administration of justice or [of] influencing any judge, juror, witness or court officer."[9] In upholding the statute, the Court suggested that it was valid even though it was being used by state officials to ban all protests near state courthouses. The statute in *Cox* treated all court-related protest activities as if they automatically threatened interference with judicial proceedings. The Court explained that "[a] State may protect against the possibility of a conclusion by the public . . . that the judge's action was in part a product of intimidation and did not flow only from the fair and orderly working of the judicial process."[10]

On the other hand, if there is no statute, ordinance, or court order prohibiting peaceful protest activities near court buildings, they are lawful. Moreover, if the court building that is the site of the protest activities houses an appellate court rather than a trial court, peaceable protest activities on nearby sidewalks are constitutionally protected. Thus, in *United States v. Grace*,[11] the Supreme Court held that picketing on sidewalks adjacent to the Supreme Court's own building in Washington was constitutionally protected because sidewalks were traditional public forums.

Are protest activities inside court buildings ever legal?

No. There is no reported case that holds that protest activities inside of court building are constitutionally protected. Courts are generally fearful of the potential that such activities have for disturbing judicial proceedings. The only possible exception might be a protest in a public building that contains offices or facilities for government operations unrelated to the judiciary.

For example, in many communities public buildings contain both a mayor's office and courtrooms. In such cases it is possible—not certain—that nondisruptive protest activities in lobby areas that are directed at the mayor and not at judicial proceedings in the building are constitutionally protected.[12]

PUBLIC AUDITORIUMS, LOBBIES, AND FAIRS

Is there a constitutional right to rent public auditoriums for use as sites for political meetings, concerts, and controversial plays?

Yes. While publicly owned or operated auditoriums are not traditional public forums, they are usually operated as sites for musical performances, plays, and other activities that large numbers of people attend. As a result, they have to be made available on a nondiscriminatory basis. This means that if an auditorium is rented to some users, it must be available for other users who are willing to pay the rent and whose activities suggest no likelihood of damage or physical abuse of the facility. This principle was established in *Southeastern Promotions, Ltd. v. Conrad* where the Supreme Court overturned the refusal of a municipality to rent out a city-operated auditorium to a group performing the hit musical *Hair* because of objections to the controversial contents of the production.[13]

Is there a constitutional right to engage in speech activities in the lobbies or waiting rooms of public buildings?

Under some circumstances. It is obvious that lobbies of public buildings are not streets, sidewalks, or parks and therefore are not traditional public forums, automatically open to speech activities. However, public officials often make the lobbies of buildings available for political campaigning, art displays, musical performances, and other activities. Once that occurs, public officials are required by the Constitution to make the same place available for comparable speech activities on a nondiscriminatory basis.[14]

In addition, where protestors sought to engage in nondisruptive leafletting in the waiting room of a welfare office, one court ruled that even though a welfare office waiting room is not a traditional public forum, leafletting there is still constitutionally protected. This conclusion was reached because the waiting room was a proper site for private conversation with those waiting to be served and the quiet distribution of leaflets by a few leafletters was regarded as indistinguishable from private conversation.[15] On the other hand, another court ruled that a community organization has no constitutionally protected right to enter a crowded public hospital lobby to read a statement and distribute leaflets criticizing the hospital's administration. The court concluded in this case that the speech activities interfere with hospital functions.[16]

To what extent can public officials regulate speech activities on the fairgrounds of a state or county fair?

The Supreme Court has ruled that a publicly owned fairground is not a traditional public forum.[17] As a result, fair officials have broad discretion to regulate speech activities on fairgrounds during a fair in order to facilitate crowd control. This discretion extends to prohibiting leafletting or sale of religious literature at any location other than at a booth rented to exhibitors by fair officials. The applicability of this ruling to welfare waiting rooms and hospital lobbies has not been considered by the Supreme Court.

SCHOOLS AND UNIVERSITIES

Are protest activities by nonstudents on the sidewalks, streets, or other places near public schools while school is in session protected by the First Amendment?

The extent of power of public officials to regulate speech activities near public schools is determined by whether those activities will interfere with school activities. If prosecutions are initiated by school officials or police trying to restrict speech activities near public schools in order to prevent interference with educational activities, the prosecutions are likely to be successful. On the other hand, if school officials try to restrict speech activities near public schools because they disapprove of the content of a protestor's message, they are engaging in unlawful censorship. For example, in *Grayned v. City of Rockford*,[18] the Supreme Court upheld an ordinance prohibiting any "person, while on public or private grounds adjacent to any building in which a school or any class thereof is in session, [from willfully making] any noise or diversion which disturbs or tends to disturb the peace or good order of such school session."[19] In the Court's view, the ordinance protected the state interest "in having an undisrupted school session conducive to the students' learning."[20] By way of contrast, however, in *Police Department of Chicago v. Mosley*,[21] the Court invalidated a ban on all picketing within 150 feet of a school because the ban contained an exception for labor picketing. According to the *Mosley* Court, "government may not grant the use of a forum to people whose views it finds acceptable, by denying use to those wishing to express less favored or more controversial views."[22]

Are speech activities inside of a public school protected by the First Amendment?

A school building is not a traditional public forum so persons other than students and staff do not have an automatic legal or constitutional right to engage in speech activities there. The only time such a right comes into existence is when school officials have previously allowed outsiders to use school property for speech activities. Thus, where a school has allowed military recruiters to recruit on school premises, it has been required to permit a peace group to use the same premises to articulate its views.[23]

On the other hand, students and staff have First Amendment rights on school premises that outsiders do not have. Students are entitled to engage in on-premises speech activities that are not sponsored by the school administration unless the activities materially and substantially interfere with schoolwork or school discipline.[24] Thus, the wearing of antiwar armbands and of some political buttons have been held to be constitutionally protected where there was no showing that they interfered with schoolwork or discipline. There are, however, some political buttons and symbols containing derogatory messages capable of provoking student reactions that interfere with schoolwork or discipline. If the interference can be established, the buttons and symbols are subject to regulation.[25]

The scope of First Amendment protection for on-premises speech activities by school staff members depends on the nature and the context of the communication. School administrators have broad discretion to regulate speech that occurs as part of the actual teaching process.[26] However, where a teacher wears an armband or a button to communicate political views on matters unrelated to the curriculum, he or she may not be disciplined unless the communication "reasonably [leads] school officials to forecast substantial disruption of or material interference with school activities."[27]

Do nonstudents have a right to use public school auditoriums for their speech activities?

Even though school premises are not traditional public forums, school officials often make school auditoriums available to outsiders for use when school is not in session and when there are no school activities scheduled there. Once school officials have decided to make an auditorium available to outsiders, they must do so on a nondiscriminatory basis. Thus, courts have required a school board to rent its school auditorium to a racially discriminatory organization because the auditorium was available for use by other private organizations.[28]

Is there a right to use elementary and secondary school classrooms and related areas for speech activities during non-school hours?

As a general rule, classrooms, halls, and cafeterias are not public forums and are therefore not open to the public for speech activities. Thus, a court has upheld the refusal of school officials to make school facilities available to a nonschool sponsored student group seeking to use school facilities for a peace exposition that was to be open to the general public. It did so on grounds that the facilities had not been opened to political speech activities in the past and therefore did not constitute a public forum.[29] On the other hand, when it can be shown that classrooms and other school facilities have been made available for some nonschool related speech activities in the past, courts have held that the same locations must be made available to all similar activities on a nondiscriminatory basis.[30] Finally, the Supreme Court has upheld a federal statute prohibiting public secondary schools receiving federal aid from barring student religious group meetings on school premises, during noninstructional time.[31]

Is there a right to engage in speech activities on the sidewalks and other outside areas of a state university campus?

Yes. The courts have held that speech activities on state college campuses are entitled to broader First Amendment protection than has been applied to speech activities near public schools. This has occurred because students on those campuses are young adults who are attending school voluntarily. The speech activities are an important part of normal university life and, absent unusual circumstances or overtly disruptive conduct, are therefore unlikely to interfere with the education process. Thus, walkways and other open areas between university buildings that are open to the public have been held to be public forums that can be used by nonstudent speakers for peaceable speech activities.[32]

Can public university administrators regulate campaign practices for student government elections?

According to at least one court, university administrators can impose broader regulations of campaigning in student government elections than can be imposed on political communications unrelated to school-sponsored elections. Thus, *Alabama Student Party v. Student Government Association*[33] upheld student government campaign regulations that restricted distribution of campus literature to three days prior to the election, prohibited distribution of campus literature on election day, and limited election debates to the week of the election. This was justified on the ground that the university has broad control over the school-related activities of its students. However, the Supreme Court has never ruled on the validity of such broad restrictions on university student speech activities.

Is there a right to engage in sales and distribution of political or religious literature in the public areas of a student union located on a state university campus?

Typically, student unions are buildings that contain public areas suitable for student distribution of political literature and large enough to allow students to engage in nondisruptive political discourse with one another. As a result, at least one court has held that nonstudents can sell or distribute political literature in the public areas of the union because it is the rough equivalent of a public forum, which must be made available to speakers on a nondiscriminatory basis.[34]

Does a state university have to make classrooms available for speech activities when they are not being used for classes?
The same general rule is applicable to classrooms as is applicable to other school facilities that are not open to the general public. Classrooms are not public forums and therefore need not be opened to speech activities. However, once they are opened to some speech activities, they must be made available to others on a nondiscriminatory basis. Thus, in *Widmar v. Vincent*,[35] the Supreme Court required the University of Missouri to make a classroom available to a university student group for religious worship and discussion because other student groups were allowed to use the classrooms for student meetings. The scope of the general rule is not entirely clear, however. A university's obligation to make classrooms available to student groups on a nondiscriminatory basis may not extend to nonstudent groups. In order for a nonstudent group to claim a right to use of a university's classroom, it probably will have to show that classrooms have been made available to other nonstudent groups.

JAILS

Is there a First Amendment right of protestors to engage in speech activities on grounds surrounding a jail facility?
Not usually. The Supreme Court has held that the lawns, sidewalks, driveways, and other areas of jail property that comprise the outside portions of a jail facility are not public forums for speech activities even though the public has easy access to them.[36] According to the Court, jail officials can forbid such activities because they require extremely broad discretion to control jail property effectively. Thus, it has stated that "[t]he State, no less than a private owner of property has power to preserve the property under its control for the use to which it is lawfully dedicated."[37]
On the other hand, if jail officials allow some speech activities on the grounds outside jail facilities, they must allow others on an equal basis.[38] Moreover, the courts have never addressed

the question of whether jail officials can forbid speech activities on traditional forums like public streets and sidewalks that are adjacent to jail property. It is likely that the courts will conclude that traditional public forums near jails can only be regulated consistently with the time, place, and manner doctrine and cannot be treated by officials as if they were private property.[39]

Is there a constitutional right to distribute leaflets or to engage in protest activities inside of a jail?

No. The scope of First Amendment protections for protest activities in a jail is quite restricted. The only protest activity ever sustained by the Supreme Court is the right to write letters complaining about jail conditions to outsiders.[40] The courts have been reluctant to hold that controversial speech activity among inmates inside of an institution is constitutionally protected.[41]

MUNICIPAL TRANSPORTATION FACILITIES

Is there a constitutional right to distribute leaflets, solicit donations, or purchase space for political ads in the common areas of a municipal airport or bus station?

Yes. The common areas of municipal airports and bus stations have features that make them much like traditional public forums.[42] In particular, they are owned by the government and they are open to any pedestrian who wishes to use them. As a result many courts have ruled that for purposes of distributing leaflets and newspapers and for the purpose of soliciting donations, the common areas of municipal airports and bus stations are the equivalent of public forums. "The Terminal building is an appropriate place for expressing one's views precisely because the primary activity for which it is designed is attended with noisy crowds and vehicles, some unrest and less than perfect order."[43] In addition, at least one court has ruled that there is a right to purchase advertising space for political ads in such areas on a nondiscriminatory basis.[44]

However, not all areas of an airport or bus terminal are public forums. "[T]hose parts of the terminal restricted to [transportation] personnel are private, absent unusual circumstances. Likewise, the arrival and departure gates, where only ticketed passengers may go, are not public forums."[45] The right to set up card tables and to use picket signs is more problematical. Officials may argue that large objects like signs and tables can present safety or crowd congestion problems. The success of such an argument turns on the actual physical size of the area and the number of pedestrians moving through it at a given time.

Is there a right to engage in leafletting or other nondisruptive speech activities on transit vehicles?

Probably not. The interior of a transit vehicle usually is quite confined. As a result people using the vehicle for transportation purposes are not able to avoid the leafletter or speaker even if they wish to do so. They therefore become a captive audience. The courts have ruled that the government may protect captive audiences on transit vehicles from unwanted intrusions if it chooses to.[46]

Is there a right to purchase advertising space to display political advertising on public buses and rapid transit vehicles?

It depends. The Supreme Court has ruled that there is no First Amendment right to purchase space for political ads even though the same space is made available to commercial advertisers.[47] The Court has taken the position that transportation officials can bar all political advertising as a means of protecting riders from being forced to view ads that might be disturbing or might confuse riders into thinking that the officials agree with the content of the political ad. On the other hand, officials cannot refuse a particular political advertisement while allowing others. If they do so, they become censors who are violating the First Amendment by discriminating against disfavored speakers.[48]

MILITARY BASES AND INSTALLATIONS

Does the First Amendment protect peaceful protest activities on military bases or installations?

No. The Supreme Court has ruled that military bases and installations are not public forums because they serve specialized functions that are inconsistent with political activities.[49]

Thus, military base commanders can enforce regulations prohibiting "demonstrations, picketing, sit-ins, protest marches, political speeches and similar activities."[50] In fact as far as the courts are concerned, military bases are such unique institutions that partisan political speech activities can be excluded even though other speech activities such as a rock musical or religious services conducted by a visiting preacher have been allowed. In the view of the Supreme Court, the exclusion of political activities is a legitimate way to insulate the military from involvement in civilian politics.

Do military authorities have to permit speech activities on portions of bases and installations that have been opened to the public for other purposes?

It depends. If a portion of a military base or installation has been permanently opened to the public, speech activities must be permitted in a way that is consistent with the general use of the site. For instance, in *Flower v. United States*,[51] a street that ran through a military base was opened to the public for unrestrained use and was being heavily used in a manner that made it a integral part of the local road system. As a result, the Supreme Court ruled that leafletting on the portion of the street running through the base was constitutionally protected because the street was a traditional public forum just like any other public street. On the other hand, the holding of an open house on a military base that was attended by five thousand members of the general public does not automatically turn any portion of the base into a public forum during the open house.[52]

POST OFFICE SIDEWALKS

Is there a right to distribute political literature and solicit political donations on post office sidewalks?

In *United States v. Kokinda*,[53] the Supreme Court ruled that the United States Postal Service can prohibit the solicitation of political contributions and sale of books on post office sidewalks. It views such activities as "inherently disruptive of the postal service's business."[54] Therefore anyone who engages in soliciting donations or selling literature on post office sidewalks is subject to arrest.

On the other hand, in the course of arguing the *Kokinda* case, the postal service informed the Supreme Court that it permits individuals "to engage in political speech on topics of their choice and to distribute literature soliciting support, including money contributions, provided there is no in-person solicitation for payments on the premises."[55] As long as the postal service adheres to this policy, protestors remain free to leaflet and speak on post office sidewalks, so long as they do not take the additional step of personally soliciting money or selling goods.

INTERNAL MAIL SYSTEMS AND CHARITY PAYROLL PROGRAMS

Can protestors seeking to communicate with government employees be prohibited from using a government agency's internal mail system?

Usually. In the Supreme Court's view, a government agency's internal mail system is not a public forum and is therefore subject to the discretionary control of the agency. For example, in *Perry Education Association v. Perry Local Educator's Association*,[56] the Supreme Court ruled that a school district could deny an uncertified teachers' union access to the district's internal mail system, even though the competing union (which was certified), the Boy Scouts, and others were permitted to use it. The Court concluded that the school district's interest in maintaining peaceful labor relations justified an agreement with the certified union that excluded the uncertified union from using school mail facilities. The Court's reasoning did not preclude the possibility that in situations unrelated to labor relations, if some outsiders were given access to the school mail boxes, the exclusion of others based on the content of their views might violate the First Amendment.

If a government agency implements a salary check-off program that allows employees to have a portion of their paychecks paid directly to one or more not-for-profit charities providing direct services to the needy, does the agency have to include political or civil rights groups as well?

No. The Supreme Court has ruled that a salary check-off

program for charitable purposes is not the equivalent of a public forum.[57] In the Court's view, the across-the-board exclusion of legal defense and political advocacy groups avoids "the reality and the appearance of government favoritism or entanglement with particular viewpoints."[58] On the other hand, if the exclusion from the program is based on official distaste for the viewpoint of the would-be participant, then the exclusion is unlawful.

NOTES

1. *Perry Education Association v. Perry Local Educators' Association*, 460 U.S. 37, 45–46 (1983).
2. *Widmar v. Vincent*, 454 U.S. 263 (1981).
3. *Student Coalition for Peace v. Lower Merion School District*, 596 F. Supp. 169 (E.D. Pa. 1984).
4. 771 F.2d 46 (2d Cir. 1985).
5. 372 U.S. 229 (1963).
6. 372 U.S. at 235.
7. *Dallas Association of Community Organizations for Reform Now v. Dallas County Hospital District*, 656 F.2d 1175 (5th Cir. 1981).
8. 379 U.S. 559 (1965).
9. *Id.* at 560.
10. *Id* at 565.
11. 461 U.S. 171 (1983).
12. *See Sefick v. City of Chicago*, 485 F. Supp. 644 (N.D. Ill. 1979) (Finds speech activities in the lobby of a public building containing administrative offices and courtrooms are constitutionally protected.)
13. 420 U.S. 546 (1975); *see also Concerned Women for American Education and Legal Defense Foundation v. Lafayette County*, 883 F.2d 32 (5th Cir. 1989).
14. *Sefick v. City of Chicago*, 485 F. Supp. 644 (N.D. Ill. 1979).
15. *Albany Welfare Rights Organization v. Wyman*, 493 F.2d 1319 (2d Cir. 1774) *cert. denied*, 419 U.S. 838 (1974).; *see also Unemployed Workers Union v. Hackett*, 332 F. Supp. 1372 (D.R.I. 1971); *New York City Unemployed and Welfare Council v. Brezenoff*, 742 F.2d 718 (2d Cir. 1984).
16. *Dallas Association of Community Organizations for Reform Now v. Dallas County Hospital District*, 656 F.2d 1175 (5th Cir. 1981).
17. *Heffron v. International Society of Krishna Consciousness*, 452 U.S. 640 (1981).

18. 408 U.S. 104 (1972).
19. *Id.* at 107.
20. *Id.* at 119.
21. *Id.* at 92.
22. *Id.* at 96.
23. *Searcey v. Crim,* 815 F.2d 1389 (11th Cir. 1987); *Clergy and Laity Concerned v. Chicago Board of Education,* 586 F. Supp. 1408 (N.D. Ill. 1984).
24. *Tinker v. Des Moines Independent School District,* 393 U.S. 503 (1969).
25. *Blackwell v. Issaquena County Board of Education,* 363 F.2d 749 (5th Cir. 1966).
26. *Fowler v. Board of Education,* 819 F.2d 657 (6th Cir. 1987).
27. *James v. Board of Education,* 461 F.2d 566, 572 (2d Cir. 1972).
28. *National Socialist White People's Party v. Ringer,* 473 F.2d 652 (4th Cir. 1973); *Knights of the KKK v. East Baton Rouge Parish School Board,* 578 F.2d 1122 (5th Cir. 1978).
29. *Student Coalition for Peace v. Lower Merion School District,* 596 F. Supp. 169 (E.D. Pa. 1984).
30. *Country Hills Christian Church v. Unified School District No. 512,* 560 F. Supp. 1207 (D. Kan. 1983).
31. *Board of Education of Westside Community Schools v. Mergens,* 110 S. Ct. 2356 (1990).
32. *Spartacus Youth League v. Board of Trustees of the Illinois Industrial University,* 502 F. Supp. 789 (N.D. Ill. 1980).
33. 867 F.2d 1344 (11th Cir. 1989).
34. *Spartacus Youth League v. Board of Trustees of the Illinois Industrial University, supra* note 32.
35. 454 U.S. 263 (1981); *see also Board of Trustees v. Fox,* 109 S. Ct. 3028 (1989).
36. *Adderly v. Florida,* 385 U.S. 39 (1989).
37. *Id.* at 47.
38. *Mosely v. Chicago Police Department,* 408 U.S. 92 (1972).
39. *See Grace v. United States,* 461 U.S. 171 (1983).
40. *Procunier v. Martinez,* 416 U.S. 396 (1974).
41. *See Jones v. North Carolina Prisoners Union,* 433 U.S. 119 (1977).
42. *Jamison v. City of St. Louis,* 828 F.2d 1280 (8th Cir. 1987).
43. *Wolin v. Port of New York Authority,* 392 F.2d 83, 90 (2d Cir. 1968).
44. *U.S. Southwest Africa/Namibia Trade and Cultural Council v. United States,* 708 F.2d 760 (D.C. Cir. 1983).
45. *Fernandes v. Limmer,* 663 F.2d 619, 627 (5th Cir. 1982).
46. *Lehman v. Shaker Heights,* 418 U.S. 298 (1974).
47. *Id.*

48. *Planned Parenthood Association/Chicago Area v. Chicago Transit Authority,* 767 F.2d 1225 (7th Cir. 1985); *Lebron v. Washington Metropolitan Area Transit Authority,* 749 F.2d 893 (D.C. Cir. 1984).
49. *Greer v. Spock,* 424 U.S. 828 (1974).
50. 424 U.S. at 831.
51. 407 U.S. 197 (1972).
52. *See United States v. Albertini,* 472 U.S. 675 (1985). *But see Brown v. Palmer,* 689 F. Supp. 1045 (D. Colo. 1988).
53. 110 S. Ct. 3115 (1990).
54. *Id.* at 3123.
55. *Id.* at 3121.
56. 460 U.S. 37 (1983).
57. *Cornelius v. NAACP Legal Defense and Education Fund,* 473 U.S. 788 (1985).
58. 473 U.S. at 807.

XII

Special Problems of Speakers in Public Places: Private Property and Injunctions

SPEECH ACTIVITIES ON PRIVATE PROPERTY

Does the owner of private property have a legal obligation to allow unwanted speech activities on his or her property?

Not as a general rule. The purpose of the First Amendment is to prevent government officials from censoring the speech of private individuals and groups. Except in special cases, the First Amendment places no restriction on the discretion of a private property owner to determine who can use his or her property. This discretion extends to determining whether and when private property may be used as a site for speech activities. Therefore, even if the private property is an ideal site for a certain speech activity and there is no available alternative site, the owner may still refuse to allow the activity. This is true even if the owner has previously allowed other speakers with whom he is more sympathetic to use his property for substantially identical activities. If protestors attempt to use the property over the owner's objection, they are subject to arrest and prosecution for trespass or disorderly conduct.

Is there a right to engage in speech activities on the premises of a privately owned shopping center?

Not usually. The Supreme Court has ruled that privately owned shopping centers are indistinguishable from other private property even though shopping centers are open to the public.[1] Therefore, in most states, shopping center owners can allow or exclude speech activities as they see fit. The only exception to the power of shopping center owners to exclude speech activities occurs in a few states that have state constitutions with provisions protecting some kinds of speech activities on private property that the owner has opened to the public.[2]

Is there a right to engage in speech activities at migrant labor camps and other property owned by corporations where employees live, work, and purchase daily necessities?

There is probably no First Amendment right to engage in speech activities on private property where migrant workers live and are employed.[3] However, at least one lower court decision concluded that there might be a First Amendment right to engage in some speech activities at such sites.[4] Moreover, some courts have taken the position that state law allows migrant worker residents of such camps to invite speakers into the camps without obstruction by the camp owners.[5]

INJUNCTIONS AGAINST SPEECH

Do injunctions that prohibit or restrict speech activities violate the First Amendment?

Usually. Injunctions against speech activities that are based on the content of the speaker's message are rarely granted by the courts. The courts commonly refer to such injunctions as "prior restraints" of speech and treat them as presumptively invalid. This means as a practical matter that in order for a public official to obtain an injunction against speech, he or she must be able to show that the law authorizes such an injunction and that the evidence supporting the necessity of the injunction is overwhelming. There are few cases in which these prerequisites can be met.[6]

One of the few areas of the law in which the courts have indicated a degree of willingness to approve injunctions against speech activities has been the wrongful use of public forums for picketing, parading, or demonstrating. In this area, the courts have suggested that if a permit is denied for use of a traditional public forum, public officials may have a responsibility to enforce that denial by going to court and obtaining an injunction against the activity.[7] Similarly, some courts have shown a willingness to enjoin sidewalk picketing at abortion clinics when the picketing was conducted in such a way that it harassed or interfered with the patients and with clinic activities.[8] An explanation for the limited tolerance of injunctions against some speech activities on public forums is that some injunctions are an effort to enforce regulations of the time, place, and manner of speech and are not an effort to censor the speaker's ideas.

In the event that an injunction is issued against speech activities, the speaker has a First Amendment right to a stay of the injunction or immediate review.[9]

Can an injunction against speech activities be obtained without giving the speakers notice of the proceedings in which the injunction is being requested and an opportunity to oppose the request?

Not as a general rule. The Supreme Court has stated that injunctions against speech activities are not to be issued unless the speakers to whom the injunction will apply have had notice and an opportunity to participate in the injunction proceedings.[10] This is to assure that censorship is not imposed by a judge who is relying on a biased or incomplete presentation of the facts and law by a single party to a controversy. For example, if a government official or private party seeks an injunction against a public demonstration on the ground that it will block access to a building, and the demonstrators are not present at the injunction hearing, there is a risk that the judge will issue an injunction based on a misunderstanding of what the demonstrators are actually planning.

In unusual circumstances, judges will issue an injunction against speech activities when the targets of the injunction have not had notice of court proceedings and are not present in court. These circumstances usually arise where the party seeking the injunction has been able to persuade the court that every reasonable effort has been made to notify the speakers of the proceedings but was unsuccessful, or the speakers were notified but failed to appear at the hearing. However, if such an injunction is issued, the judge has the duty to make sure it is entered only for a period long enough to enable the defendants to be given notice and an opportunity to be heard in defense.

If a judge arbitrarily enjoins legitimate speech activities, can the speakers ignore the injunction and engage in the activity anyway?

No. The courts are intolerant of parties who ignore court orders, even if the orders have been entered erroneously.[11] Thus, persons who are subject to injunctions are required to obey them until they have been set aside, modified, or overturned. The Supreme Court has suggested that there might be an exception to this general rule if the injunction is "transparently invalid or ha[s] only a frivolous pretense to validity."[12] Moreover, it may be that in some cases the courts will tolerate the violation of an invalid injunction if the injunction is issued under circumstances that preclude the parties named in the injunction from having a genuine opportunity to challenge it.[13] Nonetheless, because the courts so often impose penalties for ignoring injunctions, it is unwise to violate such an order without first seeking to have it overturned.

NOTES

1. *Hudgens v. NLRB*, 424 U.S. 507 (1976).
2. *Pruneyard Shopping Center v. Robins*, 447 U.S. 74 (1980). *See also Southcenter Joint Venture v. National Democratic Policy Committee*, 113 Wash. 2d 413, 780 P.2d 1282 (1989), *Alderwood Associations v. Washington Environmental Council*, 635 P.2d 108 (Wash. 1981).
3. *Illinois Migrant Council v. Campbell Soup Co.*, 574 F.2d 374 (7th Cir. 1978).
4. *Petersen v. Talisman Sugar Corp.*, 478 F.2d 73 (5th Cir. 1973).
5. *Franceschina v. Morgan*, 356 F. Supp. 883 (S.D. Ind. 1972).
6. *New York Times Co. v. United States*, 403 U.S. 713 (1971), *Nebraska Press Association v. Stewart*, 427 U.S. 539 (1976); *United States V. Progressive Magazine*, 467 F. Supp. 990, *on motion for reconsideration*, 486 F. Supp. 5 (W.D. Wis.), *appeal dismissed*, 610 F.2d 819 (7th Cir. 1979).
7. *Collin v. Chicago Park District*, 460 F.2d 746 756–57 (7th Cir. 1972).
8. *Portland Feminist Women's Health Center v. Advocates of Life, Inc.*, 859 F.2d 681 (9th Cir. 1988).
9. *National Socialist Party of America v. Skokie*, 432 U.S. 43 (1977).
10. *Carroll v. President and Commissioners of Princess Anne*, 393 U.S. 175 (1968).
11. *Walker v. Birmingham*, 388 U.S. 307 (1967).
12. 388 U.S. at 315.
13. *National Socialist Party of America v. Skokie*, 432 U.S. 43 (1977).

PART 3
Government Investigation and Surveillance

XIII

Investigations of Political Activists

To what extent has the government investigated lawful political activity?

Until 1976 the FBI, as well as the CIA and the army, routinely investigated Americans who were believed to pose a threat, whether based on domestic or national security, to the United States because of their political beliefs and activities, even though there was no indication that those persons were engaging in any illegal activity: suspected socialists and anarchists in the 1920s, labor activists in the 1930s, communists in the 1940s and 50s, civil rights activists, black nationalists, antiwar activists, women's liberationists, and the New Left in the 1960s and 70s, not to mention the Ku Klux Klan and other right wing hate groups throughout this whole period.[1]

Many such investigations were justified in the name of protecting national security from hostile foreign intervention: President Lyndon Johnson ordered the investigation of the anti-Vietnam War movement because he believed it was influenced by foreign powers; President Kennedy authorized the investigation of Martin Luther King, Jr., because of allegations that King was being influenced by Communists and therefore controlled by the Soviet Union.

The most notorious FBI operations were known as COINTELPRO, for "counterintelligence program," and were designed to actively disrupt targeted groups through illegal and covert means. The FBI maintained several such programs throughout the 1960s (they were "officially" terminated in 1971) targeted at the Communist party, the Socialist Workers party, white hate groups, black nationalists, the New Left, among others. In 1986 the Socialist Workers party won $264,000 in damages for the FBI's illegal activities.[2] In 1989 the government settled two lawsuits brought against it for illegal COINTELPRO activities. In one, it paid $170,000 to the wife and estate of a U.S. Communist party leader for a "snitch-jacket" operation in which it planted a forged letter to make it appear that he was an FBI informant.[3] In the other, the government admitted it had investigated the National Lawyers Guild and engaged in counterintelligence programs even though it had no reason to believe that the NLG was engaged in criminal activities, and it agreed not to conduct any such investigation of the NLG in the future.[4]

Does the government still investigate persons engaged in lawful political activity?

Yes. Government investigative agencies, principally the FBI, still investigate persons engaged in political activity, although not nearly on the same scale as was done prior to the mid 1970s. However, in the 1980s the FBI launched a massive investigation of the Committee in Solidarity with the People of El Salvador (CISPES) because the bureau believed that CISPES was engaged in international terrorism on behalf of the Farabindo Marti National Liberation Front (known by its spanish acronym FMLN) in El Salvador. While there is little legal basis for the FBI to engage in this kind of investigation, there are few limitations on its doing so.

How has the FBI's policy changed?

In 1976, following the disclosures in the mid 1970s of the FBI's illegal and unconstitutional investigative practices and the recommendations of the most thorough congressional investigation of the FBI's (and other intelligence agencies') political surveillance record,[5] the Ford administration for the first time issued an executive order[6] and formal attorney general guidelines[7] that spell out the procedures that must be followed for conducting FBI investigations and explicitly take into account the protection of First Amendment rights.

The guidelines and the executive order, however, are subject to unilateral revision by the president and were in fact changed by both Presidents Carter and Reagan. President Reagan revised the guidelines in 1983 with two sets (domestic and national security), both of which were updated and amended in 1989. In accordance with the domestic guidelines, the FBI may now initiate a full investigation only when it believes there is a reasonable indication that a federal crime has been, is being, or will be committed. This limit does not apply to national security investigations under the national security guidelines, an exception that gives the FBI significant leeway to investigate the political activities of Americans.

The guidelines governing domestic investigations also counsel the FBI to give particular consideration to the protection of constitutional rights. They state that the FBI's duty to protect the public safety "must be performed with care to protect individual rights and to insure that investigations are confined to matters of legitimate law enforcement interests."[8]

As drafted, the guidelines were intended to "give the public a firm assurance that the FBI is acting properly under the law."[9] Furthermore, the guidelines assert as a "General Principle" that "[i]t is important that such investigations not be based solely on activities protected by the First Amendment or on the lawful exercise of any other rights secured by the Constitution or laws of the United States."[10] But a federal appeals court has ruled that the guidelines allow the FBI to investigate groups that merely engage in the advocacy of illegal activities, even if there is no indication that they will commit such acts.[11] While recognizing that the Constitution protects such advocacy from criminal prosecution,[12] the court ruled that the Constitution allows investigation of such advocacy in order to protect society from the danger of the advocated violence.[13]

The guidelines also recognize the special problems that can arise when dealing with politically motivated crimes. The section in the domestic guidelines on criminal intelligence investigations advises that "special care must be exercised in sorting out protected activities from those which may lead to violence or serious disruption of society. As a consequence, the guidelines establish safeguards for group investigations of special sensitivity, including tighter management controls and higher levels of review."[14]

However, the threshold for opening investigations under these guidelines is quite low—the mere potential for criminal activities can suffice—leaving the door open for broad investigations of political groups. Furthermore, the guidelines specifically state that the government may collect information about public demonstrations of groups under surveillance. Thus, as the record of the CISPES case suggests, the government continues to investigate the activities of U.S. political activists.[15]

How do FBI investigations violate the rights of political activists?

The First Amendment guarantees "freedom of speech" and

"the right of the people peaceably to assemble" and proscribes any laws infringing those rights. Accordingly, the Supreme Court has emphatically upheld the "freedom to engage in association for the advancement of beliefs and ideas," regardless of whether such association is for "political, economic, religious or cultural matters."[16]

Even action by the government that indirectly limits First Amendment rights is forbidden. As the Supreme Court stated in 1965, "Inhibition as well as prohibition against the exercise of First Amendment Rights is a power denied to government."[17] This is what is known as a "chilling effect." For example, the very fact that the FBI may be investigating a person or group could inhibit those and other persons from engaging in activities protected by the First Amendment for fear of what the government may do to them.

However, the Supreme Court has ruled that "a constitutionally impermissible chilling effect upon the exercise of . . . First Amendment rights" can *only* apply to people with "a claim of *specific present objective* harm or a threat of specific future harm."[18] Thus, the Supreme Court held that persons cannot sue the government on the claim that they were chilled from expressing their First Amendment rights by the mere existence of an army data-gathering system, even though the system had previously been used to collect intelligence files on nonmilitary persons engaged in domestic political activity. The Court dismissed the case on the grounds that the claim was only a "subjective chill" and there was no indication that any of the plaintiffs themselves had been subject to surveillance or in any other way harmed.[19]

Furthermore, just because someone might actually be chilled from engaging in a certain activity because of governmental action does not necessarily mean that that person's constitutional rights have been violated. The government can legally take certain action that might have a chilling effect where it has a compelling interest substantially related to the conduct being chilled. Thus, if the government can show that it has a compelling interest in continuing the surveillance that outweighs the chill upon the participants, the government conduct may continue, at least to a limited extent.

For example, in a suit brought by the Socialist Workers party against the FBI, the court of appeals found that the government had a compelling interest to continue using informants (in order not to compromise the identities of the FBI's informants), pending final outcome of the lawsuit, even though persons wanting to attend meetings might be chilled from coming for fear that their attendance would be reported back to the FBI. The court did, however, order the FBI to cease passing the information to other government agencies.[20] Subsequently the court ruled that the use of informants in this case was illegal and awarded the Socialist Workers party $264,000 in damages for the FBI's activities, which also included harassment and illegal break-ins.[21]

While the courts have declined to hold that investigations of political activity are unconstitutional per se, the use of certain intrusive investigative techniques—wiretaps, electronic eavesdropping, break-ins, and mail openings—may violate political activists' privacy rights and their Fourth Amendment right against unwarranted search and seizure and generally can be used only upon issuance of a court order based on probable cause. The government has employed numerous investigative techniques that are harmful and, in some circumstances, did so to harass and disrupt persons or groups with whom it disagreed.

Not only can the surveillance itself violate the rights of protesters, but the information collected and kept on file at the FBI can also be used against people when disseminated to or accessed by other federal, state, or private agencies; such information could be used for other investigations, as well as in consideration of a government job or a security clearance. Similarly, an FBI interview with someone at the place of employment or with a private employer could affect that person's employment standing, if the employer took adverse action based on the fact that the employee was being investigated by the FBI.

Which government agencies are most likely to investigate persons engaged in political activity?

The FBI is the principal law enforcement and domestic intelligence agency of the federal government, the one with which political activists are most likely to have dealings. Other investigative agencies include the Central Intelligence Agency (CIA), the National Security Agency (NSA), the Internal Revenue Service (IRS), the Secret Service, the Defense Intelligence

Agency (DIA), the intelligence departments of the army, navy, and air force, and state and local police agencies. Most of the information presented in this section concerns the FBI. Activities and capabilities of the other agencies are considered separately in chapters 15 and 16.

NOTES

1. For fuller descriptions of FBI political surveillance, *see generally Intelligence Activities and the Rights of Americans, Book 2, Final Report of the Select Committee to Study Governmental Operations with Respect to Intelligence Activities*, S. Rep. No. 755, 94th Cong., 2d Sess. (1976) (hereinafter "Church Committee Book 2"); *Supplementary Detailed Staff Reports on Intelligence Activities and the Rights of Americans, Book 3, Final Report of the Select Committee to Study Governmental Operations with Respect to Intelligence Activities*, S. Rep. No. 755, 94th Cong., 2d Sess. (1976) (hereinafter "Church Committee Book 3"); M. Halperin, J. Berman, R. Borosage, C. Marwick, *The Lawless State: The Crimes of the U.S. Intelligence Agencies* (1976); F. Donner, *The Age of Surveillance: The Aims and Methods of America's Political Intelligence System* (1981); F. Donner, *Protectors of Privilege: Red Squads and Police Repression in Urban America* (1990); A. Theoharis, *The Aims and Methods of America's Political Intelligence System* (1980); N. Blackstock, *COINTELPRO: The FBI's Secret War on Political Freedom* (1976); B. Glick, *War at Home: Covert Action against U.S. Activists and What We Can Do about It* (1989); T. Branch, *Parting the Waters: America in the King Years* (1988). Also, approximately fifty thousand pages of publicly released FBI COINTELPRO documents are available in the reading room at FBI headquarters in Washington, DC.
2. *Socialist Workers Party v. Attorney General*, 642 F. Supp. 1357 (S.D.N.Y. 1986).
3. *Albertson v. United States*, No. 84–2034 (D.D.C. 1989) (settlement agreement dated September 28, 1989).
4. *National Lawyers Guild v. Attorney General*, No. 77–999 (S.D.N.Y. October 12, 1989) (stipulation and order of settlement and dismissal).
5. Church Committee Book 2, *supra* note 1.
6. Exec. Order No. 11905, 41 Fed. Reg. 7703 (1976) (Issued by President Ford). President Carter revised the executive order on intelligence activities in 1978, Exec. Order No. 12036, 43 Fed. Reg. 3674 (1978), and President Reagan revised it again in 1981, Exec. Order No. 12333, 46 Fed. Reg. 59941 (1981).

7. *Attorney General's Guidelines on Domestic Security Investigations* (March 10, 1976) (issued by Attorney General Edward Levi; revised in 1983 by Attorney General William French Smith, and updated in 1989; these guidelines are commonly known as the Smith Guidelines but will be referred to in this book as the "domestic guidelines"). *See also* discussion on attorney general's guidelines in chapter 14.

8. Domestic guidelines, *supra* note 7.

9. *Id.* at 1.

10. *Id.* at § I (General Principles).

11. *Alliance to End Repression v. Chicago*, 742 F.2d 1007 (1984) (reversing lower court injunction of guidelines for violating consent decree that prohibited such FBI investigations).

12. *Brandenburg v. Ohio*, 395 U.S. 444 (1969).

13. *Alliance to End Repression v. Chicago, supra* note 11, at 1015–16 (the "cost to the values protected by the First Amendment . . . would be outweighed by the benefits in preventing crimes of violence, provided that the FBI did not prolong its investigation after it became clear that the only menace of a group under investigation was rhetorical and ideological").

14. Domestic guidelines, § III.

15. *See, e.g.*, Glick, *War at Home, supra* note 1, at 19–38. Covert Action Information Bulletin (1989).

16. *NAACP v. Alabama*, 357 U.S. 449, 460 (1958).

17. *Lamont v. Postmaster General*, 381 U.S. 301, 309 (1965) (Brennan, J., concurring).

18. *Laird v. Tatum*, 408 U.S. 1, 13–14, *reh'g denied*, 409 U.S. 901 (1972) (emphasis added).

19. *Id.*

20. *Socialist Workers Party v. Attorney General*, 387 F. Supp. 747 (S.D.N.Y.), *vacated in part*, 510 F.2d 253 (2d Cir.), *appl. for stay denied*, 419 U.S. 1314 (1974).

21. *Socialist Workers Party v. Attorney General*, 642 F. Supp. 1357 (S.D.N.Y. 1986).

XIV

FBI Investigations

What kinds of investigations does the FBI conduct?

The FBI has two major functions: domestic law enforcement (which includes combatting terrorism in the United States and against U.S. persons abroad) and counterintelligence (which includes such national security functions as preventing foreign spies from collecting U.S. intelligence information, uncovering Americans who are spying on behalf of foreign powers, collecting information from Americans on events abroad, and combatting international terrorism in the United States).

LEGAL AUTHORITY

What is the FBI's legal basis for investigating political activists?

The FBI's legal authority for investigating Americans is quite diffuse. It has authority to investigate criminal activities in order to prevent and solve federal crimes. But the FBI also has an ill-defined national security function of protecting the country from hostile foreign interference, such as espionage and international terrorism. On its own initiative and pursuant to presidential delegation, the FBI has claimed the authority to investigate any person or group perceived to be a threat to U.S. national security, even if no criminal activity is suspected.[1]

The FBI has no explicit legal authority to conduct counterintelligence and other national security investigations that do not involve violations of U.S. law. Congress created the FBI as a law enforcement bureau of the Justice Department to detect and investigate crimes and to conduct such other investigations regarding official matters under the control of the Department of Justice and Department of State.[2] However, because counterintelligence investigations do not necessarily involve violations of U.S. law, it is not clear that the FBI's statutory authority extends to counterintelligence. But presidents since Franklin Delano Roosevelt have asserted an inherent constitutional power of the executive branch to protect the national security and have unilaterally assigned the FBI to perform that function. There is no comprehensive FBI charter that spells out the legal authority of the FBI, including its authority to conduct counterintelligence, but that also ensures the bureau does not violate the strict bounds of the Constitution that protect our political rights.

Are there rules or restrictions on government investigations?

The First Amendment in and of itself does not bar intelligence investigations aimed at combatting terrorism or other violations of federal law.[3] The Supreme Court has put some limitations on the investigation of political activities—e.g., control of wiretaps[4] and infringement on political association[5]—but many of the other issues involving political investigations either have not come before the Court or have been dismissed on other grounds. Nor has Congress passed any laws expressly prohibiting political investigations. An attempt in the late 1970s to pass a comprehensive FBI statutory charter, which would have defined the limits of the FBI's investigative authority, failed. The Privacy Act of 1974 prohibits the government from maintaining files on persons of activities protected by the First Amendment.[6]

Thus, most of the rules governing FBI surveillance emanate from executive branch directives—executive orders, attorney general guidelines, internal FBI instructions—and are subject to such limits as the Constitution imposes. Unlike statutes or the Constitution, however, these rules can be changed at any time without congressional or public review. Indeed, the controlling executive orders and guidelines were changed by Presidents Ford, Carter, and Reagan upon taking office. The lack of a statutory foundation for the FBI makes it harder both to hold government officials legally accountable for their actions and to ensure that they adhere to procedures designed to protect constitutional rights.

Furthermore, the rules and guidelines governing the FBI do not apply to other federal agencies, nor to state and local police agencies. Only a handful of states and localities have rules and guidelines for police investigatory procedures, most of which are the result of agreements settled on in court.[7] In Chicago, there is a court approved consent decree that applies to FBI investigations as well.[8]

GUIDELINES

Are there different guidelines for different types of FBI investigations?

Yes. Investigations involving criminal activities—e.g., general crimes, organized crime, domestic terrorism—are controlled by the "Attorney General's Guidelines on General Crimes, Racketeering Enterprise and Domestic Security/Terrorism Investigations" (hereafter referred to as the "domestic guidelines").[9]

Investigations involving national security—e.g., espionage, international terrorism—fall under the "Attorney General's Guidelines for FBI Foreign Intelligence Collection and Foreign Counterintelligence Investigations" (hereafter referred to as the "national security guidelines").[10] The national security guidelines also control investigations involving international terrorism, which are deemed distinct from law enforcement and often involve political activities.

Terrorism, whether international or domestic, has emerged as the principle basis for many investigations of political activity now undertaken. While terrorism basically involves the same law enforcement problems as any other criminal action—murder, kidnapping, arson, robbery, or whatever—it is treated as a special phenomenon. According to the statute that authorizes electronic surveillance in national security cases, terrorism is defined as activities that "involve violent acts or acts dangerous to human life that are a violation of the criminal laws of the United States or of any State . . . [and that] appear to be intended to intimidate or coerce a civilian population; to influence the policy of a government by intimidation or coercion; or to affect the conduct of a government by assassination or kidnapping."[11] Under the domestic guidelines, terrorists are defined as those "whose goals are to achieve political or social change through activities that involve force or violence."[12] Once a group has been deemed a terrorist organization, certain rules and procedures apply that may afford less civil liberties protection than otherwise would be the case.

How well have the guidelines worked in protecting First Amendment rights?

The establishment of FBI guidelines that include language concerning the protection of First Amendment rights was an important first step in eliminating the practice of political investigations. The domestic guidelines state explicitly that "[i]t is important that such investigations not be based solely on activities protected by the First Amendment or on the lawful exercise of any other rights secured by the Constitution or laws of the United States."[13] The guidelines have thus at least brought the First Amendment into the vocabulary of the FBI. The simple fact that the agents conducting and managing domestic investigations must now think about the First Amendment and the rights of those people under investigation serves at least as a minimal check upon the FBI's conduct.

In addition to requiring greater awareness on how to conduct investigations involving political activities, the guidelines also impose certain procedures and restrictions for using intrusive surveillance techniques. The requirements vary depending on the type of technique employed, from a judicial warrant for a phone tap to the agent's exercise of discretion for examination of public records or for the physical or photographic surveillance of any person.[14] The specific procedures and uses of investigative techniques are discussed below in chapter 17.

But the guidelines are limited in their effectiveness. There is still no guarantee they will prevent the violation of civil liberties. Even though, for example, instructions for domestic security investigations now contain warnings that the investigation should not infringe on First Amendment rights, such language has become so routine and standardized that it can lose its meaning. Agents in the field offices who conduct the investigation, as well as those at FBI headquarters in Washington who supervise and oversee the investigation, can easily ignore the warnings found in the instructions as well as in the guidelines. Thus, the real question becomes how well the agents follow procedures and how well FBI headquarters supervises the investigation.

Furthermore, the guidelines are not civilly enforceable and cannot be enforced upon the FBI by outside parties. Thus, persons subject to an investigation that violated the guidelines cannot sue the FBI for such violations. They can only sue if there was a violation of a statute or of the Constitution.

The President's Executive Order on United States Intelligence Activities, which spells out the responsibilities and functions of all of the intelligence agencies, also governs only FBI national security investigations.[15] Executive Order 12333 notes, like the guidelines, that the procedures it authorizes "shall protect constitutional and other legal rights and limit use of such information to lawful governmental purposes." But it expressly permits the use of highly intrusive techniques (such as break-ins) in certain national security cases without obtaining a warrant.

What is the difference between domestic and international terrorism?

Distinguishing between domestic and international terrorism is important because of the differences in the two sets of guidelines for handling such investigations. The guidelines governing international terrorism investigations give the bureau greater leeway and discretion and afford the subject less protection of First Amendment rights.

The difference between domestic and international terrorism can be quite hazy, due largely to a broad use of the word "international." According to the FBI, domestic terrorism must "involve groups or individuals whose terrorist activites are directed at elements of our government or population without foreign direction."[16] International terrorism, on the other hand, "involves terrorist activity committed by groups or individuals who are foreign based and/or directed by countries or groups outside the United States or whose activities transcend national boundaries."[17] From this definition, the FBI can designate an organization as "international" for purposes of the guidelines even though it is composed primarily of Americans, it operates in the United States, and it seeks to influence U.S. policy. Thus, a U.S. political group operating in the United States and concerned with U.S. policy can be targeted under the international terrorism guidelines if it has any contact or dealings with foreign elements.

While the FBI has stated that it "does not construe the lawful exercise of First Amendment rights as preparation for or aiding and abetting acts of international terrorism,"[18] actual practice does not bear this out. When the FBI investigated the Committee in Solidarity with the People of El Salvador (CISPES) beginning in 1983, it interpreted CISPES's political and humanitarian support of the FMLN—activities clearly protected by the First Amendment—as aiding and abetting international terrorism.[19] The FBI can also investigate such groups as the U.S. Communist party under the national security guidelines if the bureau suspects it of receiving money from foreign sources.

Domestic Guidelines

Do the domestic guidelines take into account the constitutional rights of political organizations?

Yes. The domestic guidelines require that the FBI take special factors into account before proceeding with a domestic security investigation. In particular, the bureau must consider "(1) the magnitude of the threatened harm; (2) the likelihood it will occur; (3) the immediacy of the threat; and (4) the danger to privacy and free expression posed by an investigation."[20]

In this way, the FBI is supposed to balance its law enforcement interests against the political and civil rights of the targets, and proceed only when the first clearly outweighs the second. Such consideration is supposed to take place at the highest levels of the FBI and the Justice Department and be reviewed every 180 days by the FBI and once a year by the Justice Department. (In the Justice Department, the Office of Intelligence Policy and Review [OIPR] performs this function.)

In addition, the security section of the domestic guidelines notes that "*mere speculation* that force or violence might occur during the course of an otherwise peaceable demonstration *is not sufficient* grounds for initiation of an investigation under this section."[21] This "mere speculation" test reiterates the general policy of the guidelines that there must be "an objective, factual basis for initiating the investigation."[22]

However, domestic security investigations, like organized crime investigations, allow the FBI to maintain ongoing investigations of organizations that they suspect are continuously engaged in criminal conduct but whose individual membership may fluctuate. These investigations are known as "criminal intelligence" investigations and do not end upon any one decision to prosecute or not but continue as long as the organization meets the standard for such investigations.

When can the FBI initiate an investigation on an individual under the domestic guidelines?

The procedures for criminal intelligence investigations, whether for domestic security/terrorism or for racketeering enterprises, apply only to two or more persons—i.e., groups or organizations—and not to individuals. Investigations of individuals or of groups not engaged in organized crime or domestic security threats, are governed by the "general crimes" section of the domestic guidelines.

These guidelines authorize the FBI to open an investigation "when facts or circumstances reasonably indicate that a federal crime has been, is being, or will be committed."[23] This is known as the "reasonable indication" standard. It means that the person in charge of the investigation must consider whether the facts and circumstances show a fair likelihood of past, present, or pending criminal action. While this standard allows for subjective application, the guidelines do stress that "[t]here must be an objective, factual basis for initiating the investigation; a mere hunch is not enough."[24]

The reasonable indication standard is substantially lower than what is needed to establish "probable cause." Probable cause is the standard stated in the Fourth Amendment of the U.S. Constitution for issuing search warrants and is the basis for making arrests. It requires a direct factual link between the particular suspects and the alleged crime.

The FBI needs far less specificity to open an investigation than to make an arrest. An investigation opened under the reasonable indication standard allows the FBI an opportunity to establish probable cause in order to make an arrest. Where no probable cause is found, the investigation must be closed. While no specific timetable is outlined, the guidelines state that investigations "shall be terminated when all logical leads have been exhausted and no legitimate law enforcement interest justifies their continuance."[25]

In a normal general crimes investigation, the guidelines allow for a "preliminary inquiry" based on a standard even lower than reasonable indication. Preliminary inquiries may proceed upon "information or an allegation not warranting a full investigation," such as an anonymous tip. This step "allows the government to respond in a measured way to ambiguous or incomplete information and to do so with as little intrusion as the needs of the situation permit."[26] Preliminary inquiries are intended to be short, and must be completed within ninety days (although thirty-day extensions are allowed), at which time a full investigation is opened or the matter is closed. Preliminary inquiries are not used for criminal intelligence investigations.

When can the FBI investigate U.S. organizations engaged in First Amendment activities?

The FBI's authority to investigate political organizations or groups in the United States suspected of domestic criminal activities (including terrorism) falls under the domestic security section of the domestic guidelines. This section of the guidelines applies to any organization or group of two or more persons; it does not apply to investigations of a lone individual, even if that person engages in domestic security or terrorist-type criminal activities. However, individuals who belong to such groups can be investigated and indexed in the FBI's files under these guidelines. Nor does the domestic security section apply to cases under the national security guidelines, which leave the FBI broader authority to investigate domestic groups.

What is the standard for opening a domestic security investigation?

The domestic security section of the guidelines relies on the same "reasonable indication" standard used for general crimes investigations. But the "indication" is of a different sort than for general crimes. Domestic security investigations focus on "enterprises, other than those involved in international terrorism, whose goals are to achieve political or social change through activities that involve force or violence."[27] This "enterprise standard" limits the FBI to conducting investigations only where it has a reasonable indication that two or more people are part of a group, or "enterprise," that seeks to advance "political or social goals *wholly or in part* through activities that involve force or violence and a violation of the criminal laws of the United States."[28]

What effect does the "enterprise standard" have on investigations of political organizations?

The enterprise standard means that investigations are focused on entire enterprises in order to determine "the structure and scope of the enterprise as well as the relationship of the members." This standard was designed originally to deal with organized crime groups, whose primary, if not sole, purpose is crime and where all, or almost all, of the members of the groups are suspected of illegal activity.

But the government also employs the enterprise standard for domestic security investigations. While it may be effective for small cell-groups where all or most of their members are suspected of criminal conduct, it is more difficult to apply to political groups engaged in legitimate political activity in addition to alleged criminal activity. In such cases, the "enterprise" should be only those persons who are actually suspected of illegal conduct, and the FBI should be limited to investigating only those persons in the illegal enterprise, not the whole organization.

However, because the enterprise standard is not well defined, it appears that the enterprise is often viewed by the FBI as the entire political group, not the criminal faction (if it exists). Certainly that is what happened in the CISPES case. Indeed, there the enterprise was not only CISPES and its chapters, but any affiliated group.[29]

National Security Guidelines

Do national security investigations differ from domestic security investigations?

Yes. However, it is impossible to make a full comparison because significant parts of the national security guidelines are for the most part classified. The national security guidelines were designed primarily for counterintelligence purposes rather than for law enforcement. Accordingly, the FBI is given more leeway in espionage investigations because they concern national security and because they are perceived to have less of an impact on the rights of Americans.

But it is clear that the standards for national security investigations under the national security guidelines are less restrictive than for domestic security investigation. (Note, however, that these standards were tightened in 1989 in response to the CISPES investigation.) Furthermore, because these guidelines control international terrorism investigations targeted at Americans engaged in political activities, it is very difficult to know whether and to what degree the FBI investigates Americans and whether such investigations comply with the FBI's own standards. In addition, these guidelines control other national security investigations that affect political rights, such as the investigation of the U.S. Communist party (CPUSA) (this is a national security investigation because the CPUSA is an alleged agent of the Soviet Union and other "foreign powers").

How do the standards between domestic security and national security investigations differ?

The primary difference is that the national security guidelines authorize the FBI to conduct investigations without indication that criminal conduct is involved (i.e., without a criminal predicate). International terrorism investigations rely on the same standard used in the Foreign Intelligence Surveillance Act (FISA), which has a quasi-criminal predicate (the FISA standard includes support for international terrorism without requiring that the support be criminal).[30] Also, the national security guidelines pay less heed to the impact such investigations could have on the exercise of First Amendment rights than do the domestic security guidelines.

Do the national security guidelines use the enterprise standard?

While the standards in the national security guidelines are classified, it does appear that they employ the enterprise standard used for domestic security investigations. But enterprise seems to have been defined much more broadly, thus allowing the FBI to investigate whole political organizations even when it knows that many, if not most, members are not suspected of being involved in international terrorism. This is exactly what happened when the FBI opened an international terrorism investigation on CISPES: the whole organization came under surveillance even though the FBI suspected only a small group was engaging in criminal activities, which itself proved completely unfounded. The domestic security guidelines do not give quite so much leeway.

The attorney general revised the national security guidelines in 1989 in an attempt to rectify this problem after the FBI director conceded that the national security guidelines "do not contain sufficient guidance and sufficient specificity regarding international terrorism investigations of groups that are primarily composed of persons in the United States."[31]

Does the government apply different standards for domestic and foreign-based groups for national security investigations?

Yes. For example, Executive Order 12333 authorizes all of the intelligence agencies to infiltrate organizations in the United States for the purpose of influencing the activities of the organization or its members only where "the organization concerned is composed primarily of individuals who are not United States persons and is reasonably believed to be acting on behalf of a foreign power."[32] The Foreign Intelligence Surveillance Act also gives greater protection to organizations composed primarily of U.S. persons (a "U.S. person" is a U.S. citizen or a permanent resident alien).[33]

Similarly the national security guidelines define an international terrorist as "an individual or group that knowingly engages in international terrorism or activities in preparation therefor, or knowingly aids or abets any person engaged in such activities."[34] Under this definition, only the nature of the activities matters, not the composition of the group. Prior to the 1989 revision of the national security guidelines, a group composed wholly or primarily of U.S. persons could be deemed an international terrorist organization if at least some portion of its activities occur outside of the United States, if it engages in the "preparation" of international terrorism (such as providing personnel or training),[35] or if it is believed to be an "agent" of a foreign power.[36]

Thus, the FBI found authority to engage in an international terrorism investigation of CISPES on the grounds that it "supported" and provided funds to an organization engaged in international terrorism, even though the FBI claims that First Amendment activities cannot be construed as aiding and abetting international terrorism.[37]

Do the national security guidelines apply to U.S. persons "supporting" groups that may be planning criminal activities abroad, even though such support does not violate U.S. law?

Yes. Under the guidelines, the FBI can investigate persons or groups who engage in "foreign intelligence support activities" or who "aid and abet" foreign agents or international terrorists.[38] Yet the FBI has interpreted such "support" in a way that does not necessarily involve criminal activity. Political, economic, or humanitarian support could be, and has been, interpreted to fall within the scope of the guidelines.

Does the use of investigative techniques in national security investigations differ from domestic security investigations?

The techniques used for national security and domestic security investigations are virtually the same, but the authority to use them differs. The national security guidelines allow the FBI to employ more intrusive techniques with less high-level or judicial authorization. Physical searches, which would require a judicial warrant for a domestic security investigation, only require the approval of the attorney general for a national security investigation.[39] Thus the executive continues to engage in warrantless searches, "black bag jobs," in national security cases. Similarly, the frequency and level of review within the FBI is less for national security than for domestic security investigations. While the approval of the attorney general is required in place of the warrant, even that can be waived in "exigent circumstances."[40] (See also the chapter 17 on investigative techniques.)

In addition, Congress has given the FBI certain "national security" exemptions from the standard requirement of a court order for obtaining financial or electronic communications information on Americans. For example, the Right to Financial Privacy Act and the Electronic Communications Privacy Act (ECPA), which prevent access to financial records or records of telephone calls or of electronic communications without a warrant, give the FBI authority to obtain such records simply by making a written request to a bank or communications common carrier for such information. This so-called national security letter must be signed by the director of the FBI or his designee and must certify that "(1) the information sought is relevant to an authorized foreign counterintelligence investigation; and (2) there are specific and articulable facts giving reason to believe that the person or entity to whom the information pertains is a foreign power or an agent of a foreign power."[41]

EFFECT OF GUIDELINES

Does the FBI collect information on protected political activity in the course of a legitimate criminal investigation?

Yes. The First Amendment does not immunize individuals or organizations from legitimate criminal investigation. If the government has the requisite indication that individuals or groups are engaging in criminal activity, it can investigate them even if they are also engaged in First Amendment activities. Furthermore, the FBI continues to assert its right and need to monitor public events and collect public information—e.g., demonstrations,[42] newspaper articles, open meetings—in the course of an ongoing investigation. The domestic guidelines state that "[n]othing in these guidelines is intended to prohibit the FBI from collecting and maintaining publicly available information consistent with the Privacy Act."[43] (The Privacy Act prohibits the government from maintaining files on persons engaged in activities protected by the First Amendment.[44]) Such surveillance is supposed to be limited to information connected to and in furtherance of the investigation of criminal wrongdoing.

How would the guidelines apply to an organization such as the Ku Klux Klan?

The Ku Klux Klan engages in all sorts of protected First Amendment activity—demonstrations, marches, leaflets, publications—but it also has a long record of violent criminal conduct. In all likelihood, only a small number of members or supporters of any given local Klan chapter actually take part in the crimes. So, can the FBI conduct a domestic security investigation of the whole Ku Klux Klan, or must it only investigate the enterprise composed primarily of persons engaged in criminal activity? This question comes into sharper focus when a new chapter of the Klan is opened. Assume that the FBI has a "reasonable indication" that some members of this new chapter are involved in a criminal network with members of other chapters; can the bureau then open an investigation of the whole new chapter, or must it refrain from investigating anyone except those people it suspects of possible criminal conduct?

The answer to the first part of the question is yes. The FBI says it cannot know which members are the criminal suspects unless it looks into all of them, if only to distinguish the innocent from the guilty. But the enterprise standard could allow the FBI to investigate every chapter of a nationwide organization even when the FBI is targeting only a small number of members and knows that most members are not criminally suspect. This is what happened in the Committee in Solidarity with the People of El Salvador (CISPES) case and probably happens with the Ku Klux Klan as well. A narrower reading of the enterprise standard (as well as its application to international terrorism investigations) would preclude the FBI from conducting a CISPES-type investigation. In September 1988 the FBI acknowledged that it was wrong to expand that investigation nationwide and that it will keep such investigations more narrowly focused in the future.[45] This would be more consistent with a narrow reading of the enterprise standard. Whether this extends to KKK investigations is unclear.

Have there been any improper investigations since the implementation of the guidelines?

Yes. The most well known instance is the FBI's investigation of CISPES; it is not known how many other such investigations have taken place.

What is known is that between 1983 and 1985, the FBI conducted an international terrorism investigation of CISPES that involved all 59 FBI field offices and led to 178 spin-off investigations, resulting in files being collected on 2375 individuals and 1330 groups.[46] Among other things, the FBI infiltrated and surveilled numerous political organizations and church groups and engaged in photographic and visual surveillance of meetings, demonstrations, rallies, and university activities.

Not only did the FBI guidelines fail to prevent this unlawful investigation from taking off in the first place, but the FBI failed to follow the procedures already present in the guidelines for conducting and supervising the investigation. In the CISPES case, FBI headquarters often sent out contradictory instructions. While they contained warnings against violating First Amendment rights, the same documents also instructed field agents to monitor and collect information on purely political activity. On occasion, when field agents would ask for clearer instructions as to how to proceed without violating First Amendment rights, headquarters failed to give clearer guidance; instead it urged the field agents to pry more deeply into the political activities of CISPES and its members.[47]

The FBI has since admitted that the CISPES investigation should not have happened. The director of the FBI testified to Congress in September 1988 that the investigation failed to meet the test required for initiating it.[48] He also admitted that, once initiated, it should not have proceeded and expanded the way it did. The FBI insists, however, that the CISPES investigation was an aberration and was not politically motivated. An investigation of the CISPES investigation by the Senate Select Committee on Intelligence reached similar conclusions.[49]

There is a concern that the FBI has continued to engage in politically motivated investigation and harassment even after the CISPES investigation.[50] For example, there have been well over one hundred incidents of break-ins from 1982 through 1989 of church and activist groups opposing U.S. policy in Central America in which no valuables were taken, but files were stolen and offices overturned.[51] An inquiry into these incidents by a House Judiciary Subcommittee in 1987 produced no evidence that the FBI was directly involved in those break-ins.[52]

In 1990 allegations have been made that the FBI engaged in political surveillance and harassment of Earth First!, an environmental organization. The House Judiciary Subcommittee on Civil and Constitutional rights is looking into the matter.[53]

AUTHORIZATION AND REVIEW

Who authorizes FBI investigations?
Domestic security investigations may be authorized by either the director of the FBI or a designated assistant director upon a written recommendation that the appropriate enterprise stan-

dard has been met. The authorization lasts only for 180 days, and must be reauthorized by the director or assistant director every 180 days thereafter. Notice of all domestic security investigations must be given to the Office of Intelligence Policy and Review (OIPR) in the Department of Justice within 180 days and to the attorney general upon his request.[54]

The procedures for authorizing national security investigations are classified.

Who conducts FBI investigations?

FBI investigations are actually conducted by the FBI field offices, located in major cities throughout the country, including Puerto Rico.[55] Field offices are run by the Special Agent in Charge (SAC), who oversees the FBI agents' handling of the various ongoing investigations. Many investigations are run out of numerous field offices, although most are coordinated by the field office where the investigation originated (known as the office of origin, or "OO").

In the CISPES case, for example, the international terrorism investigation originated in the Dallas field office in March 1983, which coordinated the investigation for two years until it recommended that the Washington, D.C. field office be named the office of origin in order to take over coordinating responsibilities.[56] While only eleven field offices were authorized by headquarters to investigate CISPES at the beginning, after approximately six months the investigation was expanded to all fifty-nine field offices.

What is the process of review and supervision for FBI investigations?

The guidelines require that the FBI director or a designated senior headquarters official must review a domestic security investigation every 180 days prior to reauthorizing it.[57] The guidelines also require that "[e]ach investigation should be reviewed at least annually to insure that the threshold standard is satisfied and that continued allocation of investigative resources is warranted."[58] However, investigations can stay open even if the threshold standard is not met if the subject is "temporarily inactive in the sense that it has not engaged in recent acts of violence, nor is there any immediate threat of harm—yet the composition, goals and prior history of the group suggests the need for continuing federal interest."[59]

Within FBI headquarters alone there are approximately seven levels in the chain of command between the director and the case supervisor (who directly oversees the investigation being conducted out of the field offices).[60] Due to the large number of cases handled by the FBI and the way in which headquarters' management is structured, details about particular cases rarely come before the director after the initial sign-off, if the director himself even reviewed the case at the beginning. The CISPES investigation demonstrated the extent to which "critical decisions . . . were made at the lowest supervisory level at FBI headquarters."[61]

Following CISPES, FBI Director Sessions instituted new procedures requiring higher level review and oversight within headquarters. The Senate CISPES Report recommended that "an investigation having First Amendment implications comparable to the CISPES case should have the Director's personal review."[62]

The FBI has a Legal Counsel Division that is supposed to advise the FBI of the legal implications of investigations and investigative techniques and an Inspection Division that is supposed to "report on the effectiveness and propriety of the work of every field office and FBI Headquarters division in meeting the objectives set by Bureau leadership."[63]

The Justice Department's Office of Intelligence Policy and Review (OIPR) must also review all such investigations once a year. These investigations may also be subject to congressional oversight, although there is no formal procedure in place to review all investigations involving First Amendment activities.

How effectively does such supervision and review protect First Amendment rights of persons and groups under investigation?

The CISPES investigation demonstrated that the system of authorization, supervision, and review was wholly inadequate to protect against undue investigation of First Amendment activities. The FBI itself admitted in hindsight that there was no credible evidence for suspecting that CISPES was engaged in any criminal activities, let alone international terrorism, and thus that it had no valid basis for opening the investigation.

After a two-and-one-half year investigation, the Justice Department's Office of Intelligence Policy and Review concluded that CISPES was "involved in political activities, involving First Amendment rights, and not international terrorism."[64] Consequently, the FBI revised its written policies and its training and internal inspection procedures in order to prevent a repeat of the CISPES investigation, by requiring higher level review of investigations involving First Amendment rights and by better training of FBI agents on how to deal with activities protected by the First Amendment.[65]

The Senate CISPES Report found no "significant FBI political or ideological bias" in the CISPES investigation. But it did find that the FBI placed a "conscious emphasis" on investigating organizations that support "terrorist groups" opposed to countries allied with the U.S. government.[66] While it is true that the FBI has also investigated groups that support right-wing "terrorists," those investigations were narrow criminal investigations of only the particular individuals suspected of criminal conduct, rather than broadbased intelligence investigations of a whole political movement.

When are investigations closed?

Investigations should be closed any time they fail to substantiate the allegations upon which they were based. This decision is usually made by a high-level headquarters official upon periodic review (i.e., every 180 days or every year). Field offices can recommend to headquarters that an investigation be closed if it can find no substantiating information.[67]

The Office of Intelligence Policy and Review can also recommend that investigations be closed upon its annual review of ongoing FBI investigations. It was OIPR that finally recommended the CISPES investigation be closed in June 1985 when it reported that "[t]he information provided does not appear to meet the standards of the Attorney General's guidelines. It appears that this organization is involved in political activities, involving First Amendment rights, and not international terrorism."[68]

However, OIPR has stated that it does not substitute its own judgment for the FBI's: "In terrorism cases, in particular, because of the nature of the threat, if at the outset there are allegations and there are activities that may be at the time ambiguous, could be either First Amendment or terrorist related, . . . we tend to give the benefit of the doubt to the Bureau to those allegations. . . . [I]f, after two years pass, nothing has gone on to substantiate the allegations, we will take a hard second look and may very well close it down."[69] A former counsel to the OIPR in the Carter administration testified that from his "general experience, . . . the investigations that are shut down tend to be shut down one to two years after—in hindsight—they should have been."[70]

Can an investigation be reopened?

Yes. Investigations can be reopened if new information meets the same standards as required for opening a new investigation. The guidelines state, "An investigation which has been terminated may be reopened upon a showing of the same standard and pursuant to the same procedures as required for initiation of an investigation."[71]

What happens with files when an FBI investigation is closed?

In general, all of the offices (either the field office or headquarters) maintain whatever files they have collected in the course of a particular investigation. Such files are indexed according to name, subject matter, and type of investigation. All indexed information can be accessed upon request in the course of subsequent investigations. However, not all names in a file are necessarily indexed. If someone's name appears in a file, e.g., on a list of persons who attended a meeting or rally, the FBI has no systematic way of looking up that person if that name is not indexed (unless an agent remembers reference to that person can be found in a particular file or someone finds it by reading through the file).

The FBI can destroy files only in accordance with procedures established by the National Archives and Records Administration pursuant to the Federal Records Act.[72] Files on international terrorism investigations, as well as on any investigation considered "exceptional," such as one that has been the subject of testimony before a committee of Congress, must be preserved.[73] (But under the Privacy Act, the government cannot maintain files on activities protected by the First Amendment.) Many of the files on the FBI COINTELPRO operations, for example, are maintained by and publicly available from the FBI. Files can also be removed from the FBI and preserved by the National Archives.[74]

NOTES

1. *See* S. Ungar, *FBI* 131–34 (1976).
2. The Federal Bureau of Investigation was created by the Act of March 22, 1935, ch. 39, tit. II, 49 Stat. 77 (now codified in 28 U.S.C. § 531 *et seq.* [1988]).
3. *See, e.g., Alliance to End Repression v. Chicago*, 742 F.2d 1007, 1015 (7th Cir. 1984) (The FBI " 'has a right, indeed a duty, to keep itself informed with respect to the possible commission of crimes; it is not obliged to wear blinders until it may be too late for prevention.' *Socialist Workers Party v. Attorney General*, 510 F.2d 253, 256 [2d Cir. 1974] [per curiam].").
4. *See, e.g., Katz v. United States*, 389 U.S. 347 (1967) (warrant required for electronic surveillance); *United States v. United States District Court*, 407 U.S. 297 (1972) (commonly known as the "Keith" case) (warrant required for domestic security electronic surveillance).
5. *NAACP v. Alabama*, 357 U.S. 449 (1958); *Lamont v. Postmaster General*, 381 U.S. 301 (1965); *Buckley v. Valeo*, 424 U.S. 1 (1976). *But see Laird v. Tatum*, 408 U.S. 1, *reh'g denied*, 409 U.S. 901 (1972).
6. 5 U.S.C. § 552a(e)(7) (1988). *See generally* the ACLU handbook, E. Hendrick, T. Hayden, and J. Novick, *Your Rights to Privacy* (2d ed. 1990).
7. For example, Chicago, *Alliance to End Repression v. Chicago*, 561 F. Supp. 537 (N.D. Ill. 1982); Los Angeles, *Coalition against Police Abuse v. Board of Police Commissioners*, No. C243458 (Super. Ct. of Cal., order entered February 22, 1984); New York City, *Handschu v. Special Services Division*, 605 F. Supp. 1384 (S.D.N.Y. 1985); Memphis, *Kendrick v. Chandler*, No. 76–449, (W.D. Tenn. September 14, 1976); state of Michigan, *Benkert v. Michigan State Police*, No. 74–023–934-AZ (Wayne Co. Cir. Ct., Mich., order entered orally May 2, 1975). Seattle, Washington, is the only jurisdiction with comprehensive statutory guidelines regulating police investigations of First Amendment activities. Seattle, Wash. Mun. Code ch. 14.12 (1980) (Seattle, Wash., Police Intelligence Ordinance 108333 [1979]) (amended by Seattle, Wash. ordinance 109237 [1980]).
8. *Alliance to End Repression v. Chicago*, 91 F.R.D. 182 (N.D. Ill. 1981).
9. *Attorney General's Guidelines on General Crimes, Racketeering En-*

terprise and Domestic Security/Terrorism Investigations (March 7, 1983), revised effective April 22, 1989 to incorporate several changes in the law governing use of electronic surveillance in the Electronic Communications Privacy Act of 1986 (these guidelines are commonly known as the Smith Guidelines, after Attorney General William French Smith, but will be referred to in this book as the "domestic guidelines").

10. *Attorney General's Guidelines for FBI Foreign Intelligence Collection and Foreign Counterintelligence Investigations* (April 18, 1983), amended on September 4, 1989 (in response to the CISPES investigation) to include additional procedures and guidance relating to counterterrorism investigations of large groups, some or most of whose members are engaged in apparently lawful political activities (these guidelines are commonly known as the FCI Guidelines but will be referred to in this book as the "national security guidelines").

11. 50 U.S.C. § 1801(c) (1982) (Foreign Intelligence Surveillance Act of 1978, Pub. L. No. 95–511, 92 Stat. 1783).

12. Domestic guidelines, *supra* note 9, § III.B.

13. *Id.* § I.

14. *Id.* II.B(6).

15. Exec. Order No. 12333, 46 Fed. Reg. 59941 (1981) (this order replaced President Carter's Exec. Order No. 12036).

16. *Terrorism in the United States: 1988,* Terrorist Research and Analytical Center, Counterterrorism Section, Criminal Investigative Division, Federal Bureau of Investigation (December 31, 1988), at 34.

17. *Id.*

18. *Alliance to End Repression v. Chicago,* No. 74-C–3268, joint motion and stipulation (dated November 3, 1980), *approved in* 91 F.R.D. 182 (N.D. Ill. 1981).

19. *See* Stern, *The FBI's Misguided Probe of CISPES, Center for National Security Studies Report No. III,* June 1988 (hereinafter *Misguided Probe*).

20. Domestic guidelines, *supra* note 9, § III.B.1.a.

21. *Id.* (emphasis added).

22. *Id.* § II.C.1.

23. *Id.*

24. *Id.*

25. *Id.* § I (General Principles).

26. *Id.* § II.B.1.

27. *Id.* § III.B.

28. *Id.* (emphasis added).

29. *See The FBI and CISPES: Report of the Select Committee on Intelli-*

gence, United States Senate, Together with Additional Views (July 14, 1989) (hereinafter "Senate CISPES Report").

30. *Compare* national security guidelines § II.N. *with* Foreign Intelligence Surveillance Act of 1978, § 101(b)(2), 50 U.S.C. § 1801(b)(2) (1982) (definition of international terrorism).

31. *See* Senate CISPES Report, *supra* note 29, at 130–31.

32. Exec. Order No. 12333 § 2.9(a)–(b).

33. 50 U.S.C. § 1801(i) (1982) (defining such groups as U.S. persons).

34. National security guidelines, *supra* note 10, § II.O.

35. *See* Senate CISPES Report, *supra* note 29, at 131, nn. 88–89 (relying on Foreign Intelligence Surveillance Act definitions and legislative history).

36. The revised guidelines now give groups or organizations "substantially composed of U.S. persons" stronger protection. National security guidelines, *supra* note 10, § II.W.

37. In 1989 a bill, H.R. 50, was introduced in Congress by Congressmen Don Edwards (D-Cal.) and John Conyers (D-Mich.) that would restrict the FBI from initiating or conducting any investigation that may involve the collection of information about the exercise of First Amendment rights by a United States person or by any organization (whether composed primarily of U.S. persons or not) engaged in First Amendment activities to situations where "specific and articulable facts reasonably indicate that the subject of the investigation has engaged, is engaging, or is about to engage in a Federal criminal offense."

38. National security guidelines, *supra* note 10, §§ I, II.O.

39. National security guidelines, *supra* note 10, § VI.E.; *see also* Exec. Order No. 12333 § 2.4(b); *but see* Foreign Intelligence Surveillance Act, 50 U.S.C. § 1802(a) (requiring judicial warrant for electronic surveillance in national security cases, except when directed only against a foreign power "with no substantial likelihood" of hearing U.S. persons).

40. National security guidelines, *supra* note 10, § VI.E (Emergency Procedures).

41. 18 U.S.C. 2709(b) (1988). The extent to which the national security letter has been used has not yet been documented. However, the technique was used quite regularly in the CISPES investigation to obtain telephone call records on people under surveillance even before it was authorized by statute. *See* Senate CISPES Report, *supra* note 29, at 106.

42. Surveillance of these activities are controlled in part by the FBI guidelines for reporting on civil disorders and demonstrations. *Re-*

porting on Civil Disorders and Demonstrations Involving a Federal Interest. See generally part 2 of this book.

43. Domestic guidelines, *supra* note 9, § I (General Principles).

44. 5 U.S.C. § 552a(e)(7) (1988).

45. Testimony of FBI Director William S. Sessions before the Senate Select Committee on Intelligence, September 14, 1988; the House Judiciary Subcommittee on Civil and Constitutional Rights, September 16, 1988; and the House Permanent Select Committee on Intelligence, September 29, 1988.

46. In 1981 and 1982 the FBI conducted a domestic criminal investigation of CISPES to see if it had violated the Foreign Agents Registration Act (FARA).

47. For further elaboration on the FBI's handling of the CISPES investigation, see Senate CISPES Report, *supra* note 29; Stern, *Misguided Probe, supra* note 19.

48. Testimony of FBI Director William S. Sessions before the House Judiciary Subcommittee on Civil and Constitutional Rights, September 16, 1988, in *Hearings before the Subcommittee on Civil and Constitutional Rights of the Committee on the Judiciary, House of Representatives,* 100th Cong., 2d Sess. (June 13 & September 16, 1988, Serial No. 122), at 134–35 (hereinafter "CISPES Hearings") ("Absent the information provided by Frank Varelli, there would not have been sufficient predication for an international terrorism investigation of CISPES"; "Varelli's information was unreliable").

49. Senate CISPES Report, *supra* note 29. In September 1990, the GAO issued a report showing that the FBI monitored First Amendment activities in 11% of the 19,000 international terrorism investigations it conducted from 1982 to 1988. GAO, "International Terrorism: FBI Investigates Domestic Activities to Identify Terrorists" (September 1990).

50. *See generally* B. Glick, *War at Home: Covert Action Against U.S. Activists and What We Can Do about It* (1989).

51. *See* statistics compiled by the Movement Support Network, an Anti-repression project of the Center for Constitutional Rights in cooperation with the National Lawyers Guild (666 Broadway, 7th Floor, New York, NY 10012), cited in *Break-ins at Sanctuary Churches and Organizations Opposed to Administration Policy in Central America: Hearings before the Subcommittee on Civil and Constitutional Rights of the Committee on the Judiciary, House of Representatives,* 100th Cong. 1st Sess., (February 19 & 20, 1987, Serial No. 42), at 231–68.

52. *See Id.*

53. *See* Bari, *For FBI, Back to Political Sabotage*, New York Times, August 23, 1990, at A23.

54. Domestic guidelines, *supra* note 9, § III.B.4 (authorization and renewal).

55. The number of FBI field offices was reduced by one to fifty-eight in 1989 when the Butte, Montana, field office was turned into a regional office; the number may be reduced again when the Alexandria, Virginia, field office is merged with the Washington, D.C., field office.

56. *See* the Senate CISPES Report, *supra* note 29, at 21–61; *see also* Stern, *Misguided Probe*, *supra* note 19.

57. Domestic guidelines, *supra* note 9, § III.B.4.f.

58. *Id.* § III.B.4.d.

59. *Id.*

60. In descending order: director, executive assistant director, assistant director (for the various divisions: e.g., criminal, intelligence), deputy assistant director, section chief (e.g., terrorism, organized crime), unit chief, and case supervisor. *See* Senate CISPES Report, *supra* note 29, at 119.

61. Senate CISPES Report, *supra* note 29, at 134. Six FBI agents were disciplined for their negligent management of the CISPES investigation, including a section chief and a unit chief at FBI headquarters along with several agents at the Dallas field office.

62. *Id.; see also* Additional Views of Senator Arlen Specter, in *id.* at 141–42 ("Where First Amendment rights are involved . . . any FBI investigation should have been subject to the personal oversight of the Director himself.").

63. *Id.* at 137.

64. *Id.* at 61.

65. *Id.* at 134–37.

66. *Id.* at 102.

67. In the CISPES investigation, for example, the Phoenix field office recommended that it close its investigation after concluding that the local target organization, the Tucson Committee for Human Rights in Latin American (TCHR), was not engaged in any criminal activity. CISPES Document No. HQ-199-8848-128X (November 9, 1983), at 3, cited in Stern, *Misguided Probe*, *supra* note 19, at 23. Ironically, FBI headquarters instructed Phoenix to keep the investigation open in case the TCHR was a "front organization for CISPES." CISPES Document No. HQ-199-8848-150 (January 6, 1984), cited in Stern, *Misguided Probe*, at 23.

68. Quoted in Senate CISPES Report, *supra* note 29, at 61.

69. Testimony of Deputy Counsel of OIPR, quoted in Senate CISPES

Report, *supra* note 29, at 122–23 (testimony from Senate Select Committee on Intelligence hearings, April 13, 1988).

70. Testimony of Kenneth C. Bass in "CISPES and FBI Counter-Terrorism Investigations," in CISPES Hearings, *supra* note 48, at 110.

71. Domestic guidelines, *supra* note 9, § III.B.4.d.

72. 44 U.S.C. § 3301 *et seq.* (1982); *see also American Friends Service Committee v. Webster*, 720 F.2d 29 (D.C. Cir. 1983).

73. *See* Senate CISPES Report, *supra* note 29, at 139.

74. *See, e.g., Wilkinson v. FBI*, No. CV 80–1048-AWT(Tx), para. 5 (Cen. Dist. CA., March 19, 1987) (stipulation and order). In the CISPES case, the Senate Intelligence Committee recommended that the files be removed from FBI custody and transferred to the Archives. Senate CISPES Report, *supra* note 29, at 140. In 1988 CISPES itself sued the government to have the files removed from the FBI. In October 1989 the FBI agreed that it would transfer the CISPES files to the National Archives. *See* Letter from FBI Director Sessions to Congressman Don Edwards (October 27, 1989).

XV

Other Agencies Responsible for Conducting Investigations Within the United States

Do other agencies investigate the activities of persons and organizations within the United States?

There are numerous other federal agencies that conduct investigations within the United States. The most important from a First Amendment perspective are: the Central Intelligence Agency (CIA), the National Security Agency (NSA), the Defense Intelligence Agency (DIA), the intelligence components of the army, navy, air force and marine corps, the Secret Service, and the Internal Revenue Service (IRS). Although there are other agencies that conduct investigations, e.g., the Drug Enforcement Agency and the Bureau of Alcohol, Tobacco, and Firearms, no evidence suggests they have systematically collected large amounts of information about First Amendment activities.

CENTRAL INTELLIGENCE AGENCY (CIA)

Are there restrictions on CIA activities in the United States?

Yes. When Congress created the CIA in 1947, it expressly prohibited the agency from undertaking any "police, subpoena, law-enforcement powers, or internal-security functions" within the United States.[1] However, in 1967 at the behest of President Johnson, the CIA initiated an extensive domestic surveillance program against American political dissenters (e.g., civil rights, antiwar, women's movement, New Left) under such operations as CHAOS, MERRIMAC, and RESISTANCE.[2] As a result, the special Senate committee that investigated such activities (known as the Church Committee) recommended that the CIA, and all of the other foreign and military intelligence agencies, be prohibited by statute from engaging in domestic security functions.[3]

Greater statutory restrictions on the CIA were never enacted in part because many of the recommendations made in 1976 had already been incorporated into the president's executive order on intelligence activities.[4] However, executive orders, unlike statutes, are subject to unilateral revision by the president. In 1981 the Reagan administration issued a new executive order on intelligence activities easing some of the restrictions that had been placed upon the CIA.[5] While the language in the new executive order opens the door for CIA domestic surveillance, the available evidence gives no indication that the CIA has again investigated Americans engaged in political activities in the United States. (Of course the covert nature of such surveillance makes it exceedingly difficult to know whether it has occurred.)

Can the CIA investigate persons within the United States?
Yes, in limited circumstances. Executive Order Number 12333 authorizes the CIA to operate in the United States, "in coordination with the FBI," for purposes of counterintelligence[6] and foreign intelligence collection.[7] The CIA is also authorized to act in the United States to investigate its own employees for security purposes (security clearances, etc.). In those instances, the CIA is authorized to engage in physical surveillance, undisclosed participation in U.S. organizations, and even in electronic surveillance with a court order under the Foreign Intelligence Surveillance Act (FISA).[8] However, the CIA is barred from conducting unconsented physical searches within the United States [9] and from opening mail in U.S. postal channels.[10] The CIA guidelines governing such activities generally employ the same procedures and exceptions that apply to FBI national security investigations.[11]

Who authorizes CIA investigations?
The CIA guidelines require the director of central intelligence (DCI) to authorize investigation of U.S. persons but allow the DCI to group related cases together and authorize them by a single recommendation.[12] Each recommendation, whether individual or group, must contain a statement of the facts and circumstances relied upon to support a determination by the DCI that undisclosed participation is essential to achieve one of the noted lawful purposes.[13] Authorizations may be oral

or written, but oral authorizations must be promptly confirmed in writing.

Can the CIA provide assistance to other federal and state law enforcement agencies?

Yes.[14] For other federal agencies, the CIA may provide assistance if the DCI makes a report describing the nature of the assistance to be provided (including its duration) and explaining the basis for the conclusion that the CIA can provide the desired, and otherwise unavailable, help. Before the CIA may assist a state law enforcement agency, the DCI must—in addition to the two conditions just mentioned—find that human life is in jeopardy.[15] In either case, the attorney general must approve it.[16]

NATIONAL SECURITY AGENCY (NSA)

What is the National Security Agency?

The National Security Agency is a component of the Defense Department and has two primary missions: (1) to intercept, decode, and analyze electronic signals transmitted anywhere in the world and report its findings to executive branch officials and (2) to encode and transmit sensitive information from the U.S. government to American embassies, foreign governments, military commands, and any other sensitive locale.[17]

Has the NSA collected information about the First Amendment activities of U.S. persons?

Yes. In the 1960s the NSA began to collect information on suspect names, words, and phrases by processing "watch lists" at the request of other agencies, such as the FBI, CIA, and Department of Defense (DOD). Between 1967 and 1973 NSA collected information on about twelve hundred American citizens whose names appeared on the watch lists.[18] In 1969 NSA launched project MINARET to intercept information about the activities of American citizens or groups that "m[ight] result in civil disturbances or otherwise subvert the national security."[19] In the fall of 1973 questions about the propriety and legality of MINARET were raised, and NSA terminated the project.

The NSA also conducted Operation SHAMROCK, "a special program in which the NSA received copies of most international telegrams leaving the United States between August 1945 and May 1975."[20] The Church Committee stated that SHAMROCK was the "largest governmental interception program affecting Americans ever undertaken" and concluded that it directly violated the Fourth Amendment privacy rights of the targets.[21]

When is information considered "collected" by the NSA?

NSA collects and stores virtually every electronic signal that it intercepts, but it does not analyze them all. Rather, certain messages are drawn from the entire pool according to their likelihood of providing important intelligence information. "Data acquired by electronic means is 'collected' only when it has been processed into [an] intelligible form."[22]

MILITARY INTELLIGENCE

Have the intelligence agencies of the military services investigated First Amendment activities of civilians?

Yes. The Church Committee concluded that in the late 1960s intelligence units of the military services (army, navy, air force) collected information on the political activities of private citizens, monitored domestic radio transmissions, and assisted other law enforcement agencies engaged in political spying.[23] The army in particular engaged in an intensive surveillance campaign, beginning in 1967, against groups opposed to the Vietnam War and other domestic political opposition groups; the army claims to have significantly scaled back the program in 1970 and 1971 after its activities were publicly disclosed.[24] The Supreme Court ruled that "the mere existence, without more, of a governmental investigative and data-gathering activity"[25] does not violate the First Amendment, where the persons bringing the lawsuit "freely admit that they complain of no specific action of the Army against them . . . [and t]here is no evidence of illegal or unlawful surveillance activities."[26]

Similarly, documents released in the fall of 1989 show that since February 1989 the State Department has been collecting information and distributing reports, within the agency as well as to local police and foreign embassies, on a wide range of political demonstrations and activities.[27] While the State Department probably does have authority to collect such information on activities at foreign missions, it has no such authority or reason to keep files on political activities occurring at other locations.

Are there restrictions on intelligence gathering by the NSA and the other military intelligence agencies?

Yes. The DOD components are subject to all of the laws and executive orders that apply to the FBI and other intelligence agencies. They are also subject to Defense Department guidelines, similar to the FBI and CIA guidelines.[28] The NSA, for example, must follow the procedures in the Foreign Intelligence Surveillance Act (FISA) in order to collect electronic information on Americans. (Note, however, that the DOD guidelines deem the NSA only to have "collected" information that it actually processes; information received is not "collected" until it has been "processed into [an] intelligible form."[29])

SECRET SERVICE

Does the Secret Service conduct investigations on Americans?

The Secret Service is a branch of the Treasury Department that is, among other things, charged with guarding the president, former presidents, presidential candidates, visiting dignitaries, and other persons designated as "protectees" by the secretary of treasury or the president. To ensure the security of its protectees, the Secret Service may perform investigations similar to those conducted by the FBI, in order to prevent the possibility of an attack. Unlike the FBI, the Secret Service has a very limited jurisdiction and may investigate only persons or organizations that are a threat to its protectees. Such prevention investigations, however, can result in investigations of groups engaged in legitimate dissent.

INTERNAL REVENUE SERVICE (IRS)

Can the Internal Revenue Service audit persons or organizations for expressing ideas which are unpopular or contrary to government policy?

Federal law prohibits the Internal Revenue Service from initiating investigations of anyone unless there is reason to suspect that person has violated, or intends to violate, U.S. tax law.[30] Nevertheless, during the 1960s and early 1970s the IRS did investigate persons and groups (of both the right and left) solely because of their political activity.[31] The IRS also gave the FBI tax returns of people and groups suspected of nothing but engaging in unpopular, though protected, First Amendment expression. Subsequent to these abuses, reforms were adopted to prevent the IRS from conducting politically based tax investigations and from disseminating confidential tax return information.[32] Despite these changes, in the 1980s a number of persons opposed to the government's Central American policy claimed they were audited by the IRS shortly after they returned from trips to Nicaragua.[33]

NOTES

1. 50 U.S.C. § 403(d)(3) (1988) (National Security Act of 1947).

2. These activities were terminated in 1973 and 1974. *See generally* "CIA Intelligence Collection About Americans: CHAOS and the Office of Security," at 679–732, in *Supplementary Detailed Staff Reports on Intelligence Activities and the Rights of Americans, Book 3, Final Report of the Select Committee to Study Governmental Operations with Respect to Intelligence Activities*, S. Rep. No. 755, 94th Cong., 2d Sess. (1976) (hereafter "Church Committee Book 3").

3. *Intelligence Activities and the Rights of Americans, Book 2, Final Report of the Select Committee to Study Governmental Operations with Respect to Intelligence Activities*, S. Rep. No. 755, 94th Cong., 2d Sess. (1976), at 297–304 (recommendations) (hereafter "Church Committee Book 2").

4. Exec. Order No. 11905, 41 Fed. Reg. 7703 (1976) (Issued by President Ford).

5. Exec. Order No. 12333, 46 Fed. Reg. 59941 (1981).

6. "Counterintelligence" means information gathered and activities conducted to protect against espionage and other clandestine intelligence activities, sabotage, international terrorist activities or assassinations conducted for or on behalf of foreign powers, organizations, or persons but not including personnel, physical, document, or communications security programs.

7. "Foreign Intelligence" means information relating to the capabilities, intentions, and activities of foreign powers, organizations, or persons but not including counterintelligence except for information on international terrorist activities.

8. *See* discussion on FISA in chapter 17 on surveillance techniques.

9. *See* CIA Regulation: Procedures Relating to Certain Unconsented Physical Searches and Mail Opening and Mail Surveillance Activities Directed against U.S. Persons, dated July 28, 1979, at 1, §§ 1, 9.

10. *Id.* at § 21(h)–(i)(1); *see also Birnbaum v. U.S.*, 588 F.2d 319 (2d Cir. 1978) (U.S. ordered to pay $1000 in damages to three persons whose mail was opened by the CIA).

11. *See generally* CIA Regulation: Procedures Relating to Physical Surveillance of U.S. Persons, dated July 28, 1979; CIA Regulation: Procedures Relating to Undisclosed Participation in Domestic Organizations, dated April 24, 1981; CIA Regulation: Procedures Relating to Certain Surreptitious and Continuous Electronic or Mechanical Monitoring, dated July 28, 1979.

12. *Id.*

13. *Id.*

14. *See* CIA Regulation: Procedures Relating to the Provision of Expert CIA Personnel to Law Enforcement Authorities, dated July 18, 1979, §§ 1–7.

15. *Id.* at § 7.

16. *Id.* §§ 6–7.

17. *See generally* J. Bamford, *The Puzzle Palace* (1982).

18. *See* "National Security Agency Surveillance Affecting Americans," in Church Committee Book 3, *supra* note 2, at 743–52.

19. *Id.* at 749 & n. 50.

20. *Id.* at 765 ("in the last two or three years of SHAMROCK's existence, about 150,000 telegrams per month were received by NSA analysts"); *see also* Bamford, *supra* note 17.

21. Church Committee Book 3, at 765; *see also Halkin v. Helms*, 598 F.2d 1, *reh'g en banc denied*, 598 F.2d 11 (D.C. Cir. 1978), *appeal after remand*, 690 F.2d 977 (D.C. Cir. 1982) (damage claims against NSA dismissed because the necessary evidence to prove unlawful surveillance was withheld under the state secrets privilege); *Jabara v. Kelley*, 476 F. Supp. 561 (E.D. Mich. 1979), *vac. sub nom. Jabara v. Webster*, 691 F.2d 272 (6th Cir. 1982), *cert. denied*, 464 U.S. 863 (1983) (NSA transmission of summaries of warrantless surveillance of electronic communication to the FBI did not violate Fourth Amendment).

22. Department of Defense Directive 5240.1-R, at 2-1.

23. *See* "Improper Surveillance of Private Citizens by the Military," in Church Committee Book 3, *supra* note 2, at 785–834.

24. *See Laird v. Tatum*, 408 U.S. 1 (1972); *see also* C. Pyle, *CONUS Intelligence: The Army Watches Civilian Politics*, Washington Monthly (January 1970).

25. *Laird v. Tatum*, 408 U.S., at 10.

26. *Id.* at 9 (quoting the court of appeals ruling, *Tatum v. Laird*, 444 F.2d 947, 953 (D.C. Cir. 1971)).

27. U.S. Department of State, Domestic Intelligence Update/Domestic Activities Update.

28. Department of Defense Directive 5240.1-R.

29. *Id.* at 2-1.

30. 26 U.S.C. § 6103(i)(1) (1986).

31. Church Committee Book 2, *supra* note 3 at 53 n. 183, *citing*, Memorandum, Attorney Assistant to Commission to Director, IRS Audit Division, April 2, 1962; *see also* D. Burnham, *A Law unto Itself: Power, Politics and the IRS* (1990).

32. *See, e.g.*, 26 U.S.C. § 6103(i)(1) (1986) (tax return information available only upon court order that it will be used for investigation or prosecution of criminal violations) and § 6103 generally.

33. *See* Nadine Epstein, *U.S. Border Agents Charged with Rights Abuse*, Christian Science Monitor, April 13, 1988; D. Burnham, *Foes of Reagan Latin Policies Fear They're under Surveillance*, New York Times, April 19, 1985, at B20.

XVI

State and Local Police Surveillance of Protected Political Expression

Do state and local law enforcement agencies investigate persons engaged in First Amendment activities?

Yes. Like the FBI, many state and local police departments have investigated persons and organizations engaged in First Amendment activities since the turn of the century.[1] Police intelligence gathering units were formed to monitor and in some cases to disrupt the activities of newly emerging labor groups.[2] But following World War II, intelligence units shifted their primary focus from the labor movement to perceived threats from "foreign totalitarian powers."[3] Consequently, such persons, who were generally left-wing political activists, were regularly targeted by local and state police intelligence units. These intelligence units, commonly known as "red squads," also investigated right-wing groups that engaged in unprotected, violent, political expression, such as the Ku Klux Klan and Nazi parties.

What has been the scope and breadth of this surveillance?

In several places, city and state police have conducted surveillance operations that rival those performed by the FBI. Between 1930 and 1970, state and local red squads collected information on several million individuals and organizations. For instance, the New York City Police maintained dossiers on at least 250,000 people which totaled 300,000 pages.[4] The Michigan State Police kept files on over 38,000 residents which totaled over 500,000 pages, while Detroit amassed files on 100,000 persons and groups.[5] Likewise, Chicago kept records on 100,000 organizations, including 1 million names, in its intelligence files.[6] And the Los Angeles Police Department was required to purge files collected on 50,000 people.[7] Still other police departments, large and small, have wrongfully gathered or maintained information about activities protected by the First Amendment.[8]

Do local intelligence units investigate different targets than the FBI?

For the most part, state and local police intelligence units have targeted the same types of groups and individuals as the FBI: communists, socialists, labor and left-wing political groups, and a few right-wing hate groups.[9] However, local police are also known to have investigated local political adversaries of incumbent politicians or the police departments. Police surveillance teams have been used by sitting mayors in Chicago and Seattle to monitor the lawful activities of their political opponents.[10] In 1983 it was discovered that the Los Angeles Police Department had kept files on its mayor, three members of the police commission and several judges and state legislators.[11] Surveillance crews were used in San Diego to monitor police officers engaged in organizing a police labor union, while other jurisdictions have spied upon officers who were critical of their department's promotion policies.[12] In 1989 it was reported that city and telephone company officials in Cincinnati, Ohio, engaged in illegal electronic surveillance of political activists as well as local and national government officials from 1972 to 1984.[13]

STATUTORY CONTROLS

Are there limits on state and local investigation of First Amendment activities?

Yes. Certain limits are imposed upon police investigations by the federal and state constitutions, federal and state statutes, and state and local guidelines and regulations. The First Amendment applies equally to the states, protecting political speech and association.[14] Similarly, the federal law on wiretapping places limits on the use of electronic surveillance during state or local police investigations.[15] The FBI guidelines and the executive order on intelligence, however, do not apply to state and local activities.

Although states are free to enact statutes or adopt regulations that are more protective of First Amendment rights than federal law, few have done so. Currently only Seattle, Washington, has passed legislation directed specifically towards regulating police political surveillance operations. In fact, most state law enforcement agencies operate with fewer restrictions on political surveillance than does the FBI (except for cities that have agreed to court approved guidelines based on the FBI model—e.g., Chicago, Los Angeles, and New York. See below.)

The Seattle ordinance is specifically designed to regulate the conduct of police intelligence units in order to protect First Amendment rights.[16] This ordinance has several important features. First, it prohibits the police from collecting information about the lawful political, religious, or sexual activities of targets unless a senior police officer (lieutenant or higher) authorizes an investigation in writing.[17] Such investigations may be authorized only where there is reason to believe the target has committed or is about to commit a crime.[18]

Second, the ordinance strictly regulates the type of surveillance techniques the department may use. Two such techniques, agent provocateurs and harassment, are flatly banned, while the use of informants and infiltrators is significantly restricted.[19] Third, oversight procedures are established which require the mayor to appoint an auditor to conduct random inspections of all relevant investigations to ensure their compliance with the ordinance. The auditor must (1) issue an annual report detailing the department's record of compliance and (2) notify all persons and organizations that are investigated without proper authorization.[20]

Lastly, the law permits those improperly investigated to sue the city for damages and prescribes administrative punishment for police officers who violate it.[21] The Seattle ordinance is a model by which the needs of the law enforcement community can be accommodated without jeopardizing First Amendment rights.

Do states regulate electronic surveillance of protected expression by law enforcement agencies or private persons?

Most states have laws regulating public and private use of electronic surveillance. While the states can be more stringent than the federal law, they cannot be less protective.[22] A slight majority of states have laws that generally parallel the federal law.[23] In these states a private person or police department may record the phone conversation of another without a court order, provided one of the parties to the conversation has consented to the electronic monitoring.[24] This rule, known as "one-party consent," means that law enforcement officers may record a conversation where at least one party to the conversation consents to monitoring the conversation, regardless of whether any of the other parties to the same call are aware that the conversation is being monitored.

But states are free to enact legislation that provides greater protection of all parties to a conversation. Numerous states have adopted an "all-party consent" rule which bars the police (without a warrant) or private persons from recording a conversation without the consent of all parties to that conversation.[25] Nevertheless, growing fear about the illegal drug trade has prompted some states to modify the all-party consent rule. Illinois, for instance, amended its law so that it maintains the all-party requirement for private parties but allows the police to monitor conversations with the consent of one party and a judicial warrant.[26]

COURT ORDERS

Are there court-imposed regulations on investigating First Amendment activities?

A few cities and states now have court orders that restrict their police departments from investigating lawful political activities.[27] These orders are similar to the Seattle ordinance in that they set forth special criteria for initiating, overseeing, and terminating investigations of First Amendment activities.

How do the court orders differ from the Seattle ordinance?

While the court order and guidelines under which the Los Angeles Police Department (LAPD) now operates has many of the features present in the Seattle ordinance, there are also some differences.[28] First, it bars the LAPD from conducting a full investigation about a target's First Amendment activities unless the department can articulate a "factually demonstrable connection between the subject of the investigation and reasonably foreseeable criminal activity."[29] The order makes clear that "somewhat stronger" factual linkage is required by California law than would be necessary at the federal level.[30] Where the police department reasonably suspects criminal activity but cannot satisfy the above standard, it may conduct a "preliminary investigation" limited solely to "corroborating or refuting" any allegations of criminal activity.[31] Requiring the department to find evidence of criminal behavior prior to initiating a full investigation reduces the likelihood that targets will be investigated for engaging in lawful political activity.

Next, the order contains procedural safeguards designed to ensure that it is obeyed. One major check is the requirement that all preliminary investigations be authorized by the commanding officer of the Anti-Terrorist Division (ATD).[32] Moreover, officers are barred from conducting electronic and undercover surveillance during preliminary investigations.[33] Instead, they must limit their investigations to inspections of public and police department records and interviews with persons "connected with" the target.[34] With few exceptions, preliminary investigations must be terminated after six months unless they result in the initiation of a full investigation.[35]

Full investigations have similar requirements with one notable difference. Undercover investigators and electronic surveillance may be used but cannot commence without the express approval of the chief of police and an undercover investigation committee composed of civilians.[36]

Finally, the Los Angeles order establishes an audit/oversight committee to review the adequacy of the guidelines and all information collected for intelligence purposes and to prepare a report annually detailing the committee's findings, including a general description of all violations of the guidelines.[37]

However, unlike the Seattle ordinance, the Los Angeles court order provides no civil remedy for those who are improperly investigated. Nor do the guidelines include administrative sanctions for officers who violate them.

Two other cities, New York[38] and Chicago,[39] are bound by similar orders. These orders contain many of the requirements and safeguards found in the Los Angeles order. For instance, both orders contain a criminal predicate[40] and bar the police from initiating an investigation without written authorization.[41] Both also contain automatic termination provisions that end investigations at the expiration of one or two months unless sufficient evidence is found to continue.[42] And both orders provide for routine audit/oversight reports that detail compliance and violations of the respective order.[43]

But, unlike the Los Angeles and Chicago orders, the New

York decree fails to set forth specific guidelines to govern the use of intrusive investigative techniques. Moreover, the order has no training requirement to ensure that police officers understand and obey it. Finally, the New York order has no preliminary investigatory stage to limit the potential for abusing people's First Amendment rights.[44] The Chicago order, on the other hand, limits preliminary investigation to no more than seventy-two hours.[45]

The Chicago and Los Angeles orders are quite similar, with one notable difference remaining. The Chicago order sets forth narrowly tailored procedures for conducting surveillance at public gatherings.[46] In addition to the requirements described earlier, the police may only conduct surveillance at public gatherings designed to "prevent substantial interference with traffic in the [area], ensure adequate public services, and protect public health and safety."[47] Information collected at these gatherings may not be merged with information collected pursuant to other investigations.[48] The Chicago order also requires that First Amendment information be "purged" from investigative files and kept under seal and inaccessible to future police investigations.[49]

How effective have these restrictions been in preventing the collection of information protected by the First Amendment?

While it appears that open-ended red squad investigations have pretty much ceased in cities without ordinances or orders as well as those with, there have been numerous reports of police departments engaging in improper political surveillance.[50] Police departments in New York, Georgia, and California have acknowledged they conducted some investigations improperly and still more complaints have been filed in these and other states.[51] The New York City Police Department admitted as recently as 1985 it had monitored conversations broadcast on a radio station known to have a predominately black audience.[52] The department has since agreed to stop monitoring radio call-in programs. Disclosures in 1989 indicate that Cincinnati officials engaged for over fifteen years in illegal wiretaps of political activists and local political opponents.[53]

Yet there is evidence that suggests some departments have stopped collecting vast amounts of information about protected expressive activity. Auditors of the Los Angeles Anti-Terrorist

Division (ATD) have concluded the department is complying with its stringent surveillance guidelines.[54]

FEDERAL/STATE COOPERATION

To what extent do federal, state, and local police departments cooperate with one another on political surveillance operations?

The federal government supports state intelligence organizations in several ways. Under the attorney general guidelines for domestic investigations, the FBI may directly furnish information it has gathered to state or local police agencies under certain circumstances.[55] State and local agencies, in turn, provide a great deal of information to the federal agencies. This trading of information and files among law enforcement agencies occurs both formally and outside of legal channels. Indeed, one of the first undertakings of an FBI agent when beginning an investigation is to inquire as to what information the local police have on the subject. In its investigation of the Committee in Solidarity with the People of El Salvador (CISPES) from 1983 through 1985, the FBI in a number of cities relied heavily on information provided by local police, suggesting that the local police had been investigating CISPES even before the FBI.

The government has also created numerous entities to facilitate training and information sharing between it and state and local police agencies. For example, the Law Enforcement Assistance Administration (LEAA), which operated in the 1970s, spent several million dollars to help create a national training academy for police intelligence officers from throughout the United States.[56]

The LEAA also helped establish the Regional Information Sharing System (RISS), which is a federal partnership with state and local law enforcement agencies. RISS is comprised of seven regional projects, and its objective is to assist state and local agencies in targetting "criminal conspiracies and activities spanning jurisdictional boundaries."[57] There are over twenty-four hundred member agencies in the RISS. The programs provide to state and locals agencies information sharing, data analysis, telecommunications, investigative support, equipment sharing, training, and technical assistance.[58] The RISS allows the FBI and other federal agencies to participate in state and local law enforcement activities without necessarily being bound by their respective federal agency guidelines.

RISS is part of a growing national and state-operated intelligence gathering network, which also includes the National Crime Information Center (NCIC). The network also includes some quasi-governmental organizations. For example, the Law Enforcement Intelligence Unit (LEIU) was formed to collect and supplement the FBI's national crime information index.

LEIU is a national association of over 235 police departments located throughout the U.S. and Canada. Although LEIU commonly employs police officers and routinely acquires information from them, runs primarily on public money, and is now administered by the California Department of Justice, LEIU maintains it is a private organization.[59] Accordingly, restrictions designed to prevent abuses of the First Amendment by the police do not apply to LEIU.[60] Furthermore, because LEIU is considered a private organization, the public has no right of access to the information it collects.

PRIVATE ACTIVITIES

What role do private organizations play in supporting police surveillance operations?

Many police departments utilize information gathered by private organizations.[61] As is also true for the FBI, these agencies welcome information volunteered by persons and groups that may be useful for law enforcement purposes. A majority of such sources are publicly available. For example, police departments throughout the nation subscribe to such watchdog reports as *Klanwatch*,[62] numerous Anti-Defamation League (ADL) reports, and *Information Digest*.[63]

All of these journals provide details on such matters as organizational meetings, perceived strategies and objectives, and the names and beliefs of group leaders.[64] Because this information is publicly available, police officials are free to read it. In short, they view these periodicals as a public effort to make everyone, including the police, aware of potentially dangerous persons and organizations operating within the community. However, there is evidence of greater cooperation between police agencies, such as the FBI, and private groups that supply information about political activities.[65]

Private groups can also engage in intrusive surveillance activities. Much of the technology utilized by the police for investigative purposes (e.g., for electronic surveillance equipment such as microphones, telephone tap and trace devices, cameras, etc.) is readily available to private persons. While private use of such equipment without the consent of the targets could violate applicable criminal law, such use is very difficult to control.[66]

Does this cooperation threaten First Amendment rights?

It is possible that private organizations are being used to skirt restrictions imposed upon intelligence gathering. A Heritage Foundation report issued in 1980 recommended using "private corporations that have specialized in providing information on terrorist movements as a way of overcoming federal intelligence curbs."[67] The tendency of law enforcement officers to treat "terrorist" and "subversive" or "radical" as synonyms heightens worries that protected expressive activity will be monitored.[68]

An indication of possible illegal activities by private or foreign intelligence operatives comes from the break-ins that have occurred at over one hundred sanctuary churches and organizations opposed to the Reagan administration's Central American policy.[69] Over the course of several years, organizational files, membership lists, financial records, mail, and phone answering machines have been tampered with or stolen from these groups while money and articles of value remained undisturbed.[70] A congressional investigation could find no evidence that the FBI was responsible.[71] Although there is no direct evidence of who was responsible for the break-ins, the nature of the information sought suggests that the perpetrators had political motives and were employed either privately or by a foreign intelligence agency operating in the United States if not by the FBI.

A similar incident occurred in California, only this time a private group was directly linked to the theft. An officer of the Los Angeles Police Department, Anti-Terrorist Division, admitted he had helped a right-wing group, Western Goals Foundation, computerize references (totaling one hundred boxes) to files on "subversives" that he had taken from the

LAPD intelligence unit.[72] Individual officers may break the law because they think their supervisors expect it of them (even if never stated explicitly, in order to preserve plausible deniability of their superiors)[73] or because they believe that extralegal actions are justified to defend U.S. national security.

Although no connection was made between any law enforcement agency and the illegal conduct in either of these cases, the need to fill a perceived intelligence void has sparked some private groups to collect and disseminate information previously collected by red squads. The absence of laws governing cooperation between police departments and private intelligence organizations increases the potential for abuse of First Amendment rights.

NOTES

1. *See generally* F. Donner, *Protectors of Privilege: Red Squads and Police Repression in Urban America* (1990); F. Donner, *The Age of Surveillance: The Aims and Methods of America's Political Intelligence System* (1980); *Intelligence Activities and the Rights of Americans, Book 2, Final Report of the Select Committee to Study Intelligence Activities*, S. Rep. No. 755, 94th Cong., 2d Sess. (1976) (hereinafter "Church Committee Book 2").

2. Donner, *Age of Surveillance, supra*, at 30–32.

3. *See* Church Committee Book 2, *supra* note 1, at 21.

4. A. Adler & J. Peterzell, *Courts Curtail Some Actions of Police Intelligence Units*, In These Times, vol. 5, no. 9, (1981).

5. *Id.*

6. D. Burnham, *Police Intelligence Records Here Are Purged of a Million Names*, New York Times, February 9, 1973, at A1.

7. R. Lindsey, *Los Angeles Police Subject of Inquiry*, New York Times, January 17, 1983, at A9.

8. Police departments in Seattle, Wash., Memphis, Tenn., Detroit, Mich., Milledgeville, Ga., and New York City have agreed or been forced to stop collecting information protected by the First Amendment. Regarding Georgia, see E. McConville, *Town Officials Admit Illegal Spying to Thwart Union Organizers*, Washington Post, August 8, 1979, at A1. Regarding Seattle, see D. Young, *Long-secret Police Spy File Revealed*, Seattle Post Intelligencer, April 10, 1978, at A1. Regarding Memphis, see Adler & Peterzell, *supra* note 4, at A1.

9. For a thorough treatment of police surveillance see collection of articles in 55 U. Det. J. Urb. Law 853–1107 (1978).

10. New York Times, July 26, 1984, at A14; Kevin Krajick, *Policing Dissent: The New Limits on Surveillance,* Police Magazine, September 1981, at 8.

11. Ramona Ripston, *L. A. Thought Police Knuckle Under,* Rights, February–April 1985, at 9.

12. Krajick, *supra* note 10, at 9.

13. *See* Chavez, *Report That Cincinnati Was Webbed in Illegal Wiretaps Sets City on Edge,* New York Times, July 27, 1989. The local telephone company denied any knowledge of such wiretaps and successfully sued the two former employees who implicated it for defamation. *See Two Ex-Phone Workers Guilty in Ohio Wiretap Trial,* New York Times, January 24, 1990, at A19; *$210,000 Assessed in Punitive Damages in Wiretapping Case,* New York Times, February 14, 1990, at A23.

14. *See, e.g., Fiske v. Kansas,* 274 U.S. 380 (1927); *Near v. Minnesota,* 283 U.S. 697 (1931); *DeJonge v. Oregon,* 299 U.S. 353 (1937); *Hague v. CIO,* 307 U.S. 496 (1939); *Brandenburg v. Ohio,* 395 U.S. 444 (1969); *NAACP v. Alabama,* 357 U.S. 449 (1958).

15. 18 U.S.C. §§ 2510–20 (1988), Title III of the Omnibus Crime Control and Safe Streets Act of 1968, Pub. L. No. 90-351 (June 19, 1968), as amended.

16. Seattle, Wash. Mun. Code, ch. 14.12 (1980) (Seattle, Wash., Police Intelligence Ordinance 108333 [1979]) (amended by Seattle, Wash. ordinance 109237 [1980]).

17. *Id.* at chs. 11, 13, 14.

18. *Id.* at ch. 13(d).

19. *Id.* at chs. 23, 24, 26.

20. *Id.* at ch. 31.

21. *Id.* at chs. 33, 34, 38.

22. *See, e.g., U.S. v. McKinnon,* 721 F.2d 19 (1st Cir. 1983).

23. *See* W. Caming, *When Tape-Recording a Phone Call Is Permissible,* Privacy Journal (October 1988) (noting that approximately thirty states fall into this category).

24. *See, e.g.,* N.Y. Penal Law § 250.00 (McKinney 1980) (New York); N.J. Stat. Ann. § 2A:156A-4(d) (West 1985) (New Jersey); Ohio Rev. Code Ann. § 2933.52(B)(4) (Anderson 1987) (Ohio); Conn. Gen. Stat. Ann. §§ 53a–187 (West 1985 & Supp. 1988) (Connecticut).

25. *See, e.g.,* Mass. Gen. Laws Ann. ch. 272, § 99 (West 1970 & Supp. 1989) (Massachusetts); Mich. Comp. Laws Ann. § 750.539(c) (West 1968 & Supp. 1988) (Michigan); Md. Cts. and Jud. Pro. Code Ann. § 10–402 (1988) (Maryland); Cal. Penal Code § 631 (West 1988 &

Supp. 1989) (California); Wash. Rev. Code Ann. § 9.73.030(1)(a) (1988) (Washington); 18 Pa. Cons. Stat. Ann. § 5704(4) (Purdon 1988 & Supp. 1989) (Pennsylvania).

26. Ill. Rev. Stat. ch. 38, paras. 14-2, 14-3 (1979 & Supp. 1989).
27. *See generally Alliance to End Repression v. Chicago*, 561 F. Supp. 537 (N.D. Ill. 1982); *Coalition against Police Abuse v. Board of Police Commissioners*, No. C243458 (Super. Ct. of Cal., order entered February 22, 1984); *Handschu v. Special Services Division*, 605 F. Supp. 1384 (S.D.N.Y. 1985); *Kendrick v. Chandler*, No. 76-449, (W.D. Tenn. September 14, 1976); *Benkert v. Michigan State Police*, No. 74-023-934-AZ (Wayne Co. Cir. Ct., Mich., order entered orally May 2, 1975).
28. *See* Standards and Procedures for the Anti-Terrorist Division, Los Angeles Police Department, January 31, 1984, promulgated pursuant to court order in *Coalition against Police Abuse, supra* note 27.
29. *Id.* at 7–10.
30. *Id.*
31. *Id.*
32. *Id.* at 7–9.
33. *Id.* at 18.
34. *Id.* at 8.
35. *Id.*
36. *Id.* at 8, 18.
37. *Id.* at 30.
38. *Handschu v. Special Services Division*, 605 F. Supp. 1384 (S.D.N.Y. 1985).
39. *Alliance to End Repression v. Chicago*, 561 F. Supp. 537 (N.D. Ill. 1982).
40. *Alliance*, 561 F. Supp., at 564; *Handschu*, 605 F. Supp., at 1421.
41. *Alliance*, 561 F. Supp., at 563; *Handschu*, 605 F. Supp., at 1421.
42. *Alliance*, 561 F. Supp., at 567; *Handschu*, 605 F. Supp., at 1421.
43. *Alliance*, 561 F. Supp., at 568–69; *Handschu*, 605 F. Supp., at 1423–24.
44. *Alliance*, 561 F. Supp., at 565.
45. *Id.* at 564–65.
46. *Id.* at 565–66.
47. *Id.* at 566.
48. *Id.*
49. *Id.* at 564.
50. *See generally* G. T. Marx, *Undercover: Police Surveillance in America* (1988); B. Glick, *War at Home: Covert Action against U.S. Activists and What We Can Do about It* (1989); F. Donner, *supra* note 1.
51. *See generally* S. Burkholder, *Red Squads on the Prowl*, The Progres-

sive, (October 1988). Actions have been filed on several occasions in both Chicago and Los Angeles alleging violations and seeking enforcement of their respective court orders. *See, e.g., Coalition against Police Abuse v. Board of Police Commissioners: In re Libros Revolucion Bookstore,* before the Los Angeles Board of Police Commissioners and chief of police (August 1, 1989) (Complaint re possible violations of *CAPA* Consent Decree and Judgment); *Rubin v. City of Los Angeles,* 190 Cal. App. 3d 560, 569, 235 Cal. Rptr. 516 (1987).

52. F. Beal, *N.Y.C. Police "Black Desk": COINTELPRO Revisited,* Frontline, August 3, 1987, at 4, col. 1.

53. *See* Chavez, *supra* note 13.

54. D. Freed, *Audit Finds Police Intelligence Unit Complying,* Los Angeles Times, April 2, 1986, at 2. On August 1, 1989 a complaint was filed with the Los Angeles police chief notifying that violations of the consent decree may have occured and requesting the department to look into it. This is the first step in the enforcement procedures outlined in the Los Angeles decree.

55. *See, e.g., Attorney General's Guidelines on General Crimes, Racketeering Enterprise and Domestic Security/Terrorism Investigations* (March 7, 1983), revised effective April 22, 1989) (hereinafter "domestic guidelines"), at 18 ("Dissemination of Information").

56. Kotkin & Wallace, *Police Given "Spy" Classes at Institute,* Washington Post, May 14, 1978, at A1. The academy, designated the Western Regional Organized Crime Training Institute (WROCTI), trains police officers on how to conduct electronic and photographic surveillance, infiltrate organizations, and utilize informants and undercover officers. In its first three years of operation, WROCTI trained 3,295 officers, 499 of whom came from thirty states. Wallace, *California's Own Political Police,* Inquiry, February 6, 1978, at 20.

57. *See The RISS Law Enforcement Program: A Federal Partnership with State and Local Law Enforcement,* Office of Justice Programs, U.S. Department of Justice, at 1 (undated); *see also Bureau of Justice Assistance: RISS Program, Analysis of Date Relating to Membership and Service Activities of the Regional Information Sharing Systems Projects and the Leviticus Project, 1985–1987,* Institute for Intergovernmental Research (October 1988) (study supported by award from the Office of Justice Programs, U.S. Department of Justice).

58. *The RISS Law Enforcement Program, supra* note 57, at 4–5.

59. Kotkin & Wallace, *supra* note 56, at 19; Krajick, *supra* note 10, at 14. *See also* Linda Valentino, *The LEIU: Part of the Political Intelligence Network,* First Principles, (January 1979).

60. LEIU collected information protected by the First Amendment but claims it stopped doing so in 1976. Krajick, *supra* note 10, at 14.

Nevertheless, fearing that LEIU was still collecting protected information, the Michigan legislature barred its police departments from participating in the organization. Krajick, *supra* note 10, at 14.

61. *See generally* Haddad & Burton, Confidential Memorandum re Sources of State Police Information, Office of Legislative Oversight and Analysis, The Assembly, State of New York, February 20, 1976; State Police Surveillance: Report of the New York State Assembly Special Task Force on State Police Non-criminal Files, Mark Alan Siegel, Chair, September 1977.

62. Klanwatch is published by the Southern Poverty Law Center.

63. Information Digest is edited by John and Louise Rees. *See* Haddad & Burton, *supra* note 61.

64. Klanwatch and the ADL monitor many racial hate groups such as the KKK, skinhead, and neo-Nazi organizations. Information Digest tracks numerous left-wing political groups as well as the KKK and Nazi parties. *See also* C. Berlet, *The Hunt for the Red Menace: The FBI, Right-Wing Paranoid Theories, and McCarthy's Shadows*, at 27–32 (Political Research Associates, Cambridge, Mass., April 10, 1989) (lists fourteen current and inactive organizations that publish newsletters on political activities).

65. *See, e.g.*, Berlet, *Hunt for the Red Menace, supra* note 64.

66. *See A Corporate Story*, New England Business, 23ff. (May 1989) (U.S. Surgical Corp. use of informants to infiltrate animal rights group).

67. Krajick, *supra* note 10, at 23.

68. *See* Glick, *War at Home, supra* note 50.

69. *See Break-ins at Sanctuary Churches and Organizations Opposed to Administration Policy in Central America: Hearings before the Subcommittee on Civil and Constitutional Rights of the Committee on the Judiciary, House of Representatives*, 100 Cong., 1st Sess. (February 19 & 20, 1987, Serial No. 42).

70. *Id.* at 59.

71. A House Judiciary Subcommittee investigation was not able to find evidence that the FBI was involved in any of these incidents, nor were investigators able to ascribe these break-ins to anyone else. *Id. See also The FBI and CISPES: Report of the Select Committee on Intelligence, United States Senate, Together with Additional Views* (July 14, 1989), at 108 ("found no evidence that the FBI was involved in any burglaries or break-ins").

72. A California police officer admitted that he took one hundred cartons of computerized files held by the LAPD intelligence unit and delivered them to a private data bank operated by a right-wing political organization, Western Goals. *See* Washington Times, May 25, 1983,

at 12A. *See also* Blake & Sappell, *Gates Informed PDID Files Were Hidden, Ex-Aide Says,* Los Angeles Times, April 26, 1984, at 1A.

73. Oliver North and John Poindexter claimed such higher authorization in defense of criminal charges relating to the Iran-Contra affair. President Reagan denied having given such authorization.

XVII
Surveillance Techniques

What kind of surveillance techniques does the government employ?

When the government conducts an investigation, it uses numerous surveillance techniques that vary in their degree of intrusiveness. The least intrusive techniques, according to the attorney general's FBI guidelines—such as the examination of internal files and of public records, personal interviews, and physical and photographic surveillance—can be used at the discretion of the local agent without supervisory approval at any stage of an investigation. The most intrusive—physical and electronic searches (such as phone taps and room bugs) and mail openings—require a judicial warrant; the use of pen registers and trap-and-trace devices (which record phone numbers dialed to and from a given phone) also now requires a judicial warrant. Techniques that the government views as intermediate—mail covers (recording the information on the outside of envelopes without opening them), requests for bank records and telephone toll records, and the use of various kinds of informants, infiltrators, and undercover agents—are subject to department regulation or attorney general guidelines.[1] These standards do not necessarily apply to investigations pursuant to the "Guidelines for FBI Foreign Intelligence Collection and Foreign Counterintelligence Investigations" ("national security guidelines").[2]

Can the FBI go beyond collecting information and disrupt the activities of organizations that it is investigating?

Yes, but only in some circumstances. The practice of disrupting organizations under investigation was a part of COIN-TELPRO (for "counterintelligence program"), the FBI's domestic covert action program used from 1956 to 1971 in order "to 'disrupt' and 'neutralize' target groups and individuals."[3] Not only did the FBI act directly to disrupt such groups; it also trained and directed informants to engage in activities intended to disrupt the organizations they had infiltrated. The FBI deployed such techniques as illegal break-ins, sending anonymous letters, creating internal dissension, encouraging gang warfare, and falsely labeling members of groups as police informers. Following the issuance of the attorney general guidelines in 1976, these practices were supposed to have been brought to a halt. Nothing that has been released on the public record as of 1990 indicates that the FBI has resumed COINTELPRO-type disruptive activities and harassment of Americans (although the FBI clearly has engaged in unlawful investigations).

Have limits been put on disruption and harassment activities?

The attempts that were made in the late 1970s and the 1980s to pass legislation to prohibit the FBI from engaging in such activities were not successful. Indeed, Executive Order 12333, which was signed by President Reagan in 1981 and governs all of the intelligence agencies including the FBI, allows the FBI to engage in "undisclosed participation in organizations in the United States" in accordance with procedures approved by the attorney general and also permits "influencing the activity of the organization or its members" when done as part of a lawful FBI investigation or if the organization "is composed primarily of individuals who are not United States persons and is reasonably believed to be acting on behalf of a foreign power."[4]

The FBI is also restricted by court rulings. For example, in 1986 a federal court ruled that the Socialist Workers party was entitled to $264,000 in damages from the United States government for the illegal investigative activities of the FBI, which involved a massive surveillance campaign over a period of almost forty years and included disruption activities, break-ins, and the use of informants.[5] Also in 1986 four FBI agents were ordered to pay five antiwar and civil rights activists $30,000 each for damages suffered as a result of the FBI's COINTELPRO operations.[6] In its 1989 settlement with the National Lawyers Guild, the FBI agreed not to use any of the information it had collected on the NLG over a forty year period; the FBI admitted that it had no legal basis for conducting the investigation and that neither the organization nor its members had been suspected of criminal activity.[7]

LESS INTRUSIVE TECHNIQUES

File and Index Search

What is a file and index search?

The first thing that the FBI or any investigative agency does when starting an investigation is look through its own files to see if they contain any information relevant to the investigation. This is considered a preliminary step and does not require the approval of any supervisory agent. The agency looks for things like previous arrest or conviction records or an indication that the person's name has come up in an earlier investigation.

At its headquarters in Washington and at all of its field offices the FBI maintains an extensive file system of information collected pursuant to its investigative activities. But it can only retrieve information that is indexed by the name of an individual or organization. The FBI will do an "indices check" of files at headquarters and any and all field offices it deems appropriate to the investigation. It can make a successful search only if the name of the person or group is already on the index. Not all names that come up in an investigation are indexed. Thus, even if someone's name appears in an FBI file, it does not necessarily mean the FBI will be able to associate that file with that person at a later date.[8]

In the fall of 1989 the FBI admitted that it does a routine "name check" on anyone who writes a letter to the FBI director or other high level official. The FBI stated that the "review does not include searches for criminal convictions or other illegal activity, but does include a check to determine whether a person is the subject of a Federal investigation."[9] The FBI did similar checks on at least 266 persons who were involved in opposing the FBI's use of librarians to monitor high tech spying activity (known as the Library Awareness Program) to see if they were part of a Soviet plot to undermine the FBI.[10] Records of these checks are then indexed to the person's name. The ACLU believes the FBI's practice of inquiring about and keeping records on persons who write letters or criticize FBI policy violates section (e)(7) of the Privacy Act and the First Amendment.

Privacy Act Exception
Are there restrictions on the kind of information the FBI can keep in its files?
Yes. Section (e)(7) of the Privacy Act states explicitly that no agency of the federal government can keep any "record describing how any individual exercises rights guaranteed by the First Amendment unless expressly authorized by statute or by the individual about whom the record is maintained or unless pertinent to and within the scope of an authorized law enforcement activity."[11] This law embodies the principle that the government may not investigate or keep records on political activity for its own sake.

Are there exceptions to section (e)(7)?
Yes. The exception in section (e)(7) for "an authorized law enforcement activity" allows the FBI to maintain files on persons and groups involved in First Amendment activities, so long as the information pertains to some legitimate law enforcement purpose. "Law enforcement activity" can be broadly interpreted to allow for the collection and maintenance of information on seemingly protected political activities.

For example, as a way of preventing crime before it happens, police agencies keep files on groups and individuals whom they feel might pose a threat based on the political activities of those groups, to which they can refer when a potentially threatening occasion arises. A situation like this occurred in connection with the Democratic National Convention in San Francisco in 1984, when a working group of federal, state, and local police agencies kept files on at least ninety-five political groups as a security precaution against possible violent activity, including such groups as the KKK, CISPES, the Catholic Charities of Oakland, and the American Civil Liberties Union. While this activity may have occurred for purposes of crowd control rather than criminal investigation, it demonstrates the extent to which the government can monitor political activity. Furthermore, counterintelligence or international terrorism investigations carried out under the national security guidelines need not be based on criminal activity; under these guidelines the FBI can investigate and maintain files on persons or groups if they are suspected of being agents of foreign governments or organizations.

Has section (e)(7) of the Privacy Act ever been enforced in court?

Yes. The courts have held that "an order for the expungement of records is, in proper circumstances, a permissible remedy for an agency's violation of the Privacy Act."[12] The FBI has never been formally ordered to do so however, because whenever someone brings forth a convincing case requiring it to remove or destroy records it has offered to do so out of court,[13] thus negating the necessity for the courts to enforce such destruction under section (e)(7).

However, in 1987 the FBI did agree to a legal stipulation (which does not have the same force as a final court order) requiring that it transfer from the FBI to the National Archives and place under a five-year seal the complete files and records pertaining to a group who brought a case under the Privacy Act.[14] As this case indicates, the existence of the (e)(7) provision probably does have an effect on FBI procedures and how they collect and maintain such information.

In May of 1988, Todd Patterson, a New Jersey high school student, filed suit against the FBI for illegally maintaining files on him in violation of section (e)(7).[15] The FBI began to investigate Mr. Patterson in 1983, when he was twelve years old, because he was receiving mail from the Soviet Union and other eastern bloc countries; he had requested information from countries around the world as part of a seventh grade project to compile an encyclopedia of the world. The FBI routinely keeps track of mail going to and from various foreign countries. The bureau claims that once it found out in 1983 that the recipient of the mail was a student, it closed the investigation. However, when Patterson requested his FBI file under the Freedom of Information Act, he found entries dating from 1985 (the FBI would not release the documents themselves).

In February 1989 a federal district court ruled, after reviewing the whole contents of Patterson's file in secret, that the FBI acted lawfully and that its actions would not harm Patterson in any way.[16] While not ordering it to do so, the court encouraged the FBI to expunge Patterson's file as it had previously offered to do.[17] After the ruling came down, new documents showed that the FBI continued to keep a file on Patterson through at least 1988. Accordingly, in April 1989, Patterson asked the court to consider the new evidence and vacate its earlier ruling.[18] This request was denied, and the ruling was upheld on appeal.[19]

In similar litigation, the Committee in Solidarity with the People of El Salvador (CISPES) has sued the FBI to remove the files collected during the FBI's 1983–1985 national security investigation,[20] which the FBI has admitted should never have taken place.[21] In October 1989 the FBI voluntarily agreed to remove the CISPES files and place them in the National Archives.

Public Records Search

What is a public records search?

The FBI will search public records in much the same fashion as it does its own records. Public records include newspapers, books, print and electronic media, phone directories, title registries, and the like. To the extent that any person is allowed to look at these records, the FBI is no less entitled. The only issue, then, is not whether the FBI can look at them, but for what purpose it is looking at them. Under section (e)(7) of the Privacy Act, the FBI could not keep public records in its files solely for the purpose of monitoring the exercise of "rights guaranteed by the First Amendment."

Does the FBI search federal, state, and local government records?

The FBI will also request any records that other federal agencies, as well as state and local governments, may have on the subject. Dissemination of records among such agencies may be subject to certain restrictions. For example, voluntary employment information may not be transferable. Access to tax and social security information is also restricted.[22] Similarly, school records cannot be released or disseminated outside of the education system without the consent of the student or student's parent.[23]

Personal Interview

When does the FBI conduct personal interviews?
FBI agents conduct various kinds of personal interviews without prior authorization from a supervisory agent. This includes interviewing the person who brought in the complaint (if there is such a person) and previously established informants and confidential sources (which must comply with the attorney general's Guidelines on the Use of Informants and Confidential Sources).[24] The FBI may also interview the potential subject of the investigation.[25]

Finally, agents can interview "persons who should readily be able to corroborate or deny the truth of the allegation, except this does not include pretext interviews or interviews of a potential subject's employer or coworkers unless the interviewee was the complainant."[26] Pretext interviews are interviews where the agent does not reveal his or her identity as an FBI agent. Interviews with employers or coworkers are supposed to be given special attention because of the potential for employment discrimination that could come to a person who is suspected of being under investigation by the FBI. Both of these types of interviews are still allowed, but they require higher level approval.

Voluntary Cooperation

Must one cooperate when questioned by the FBI?
No. People are entitled to refuse to provide information to the police.[27] The police can compel someone to respond only with a court ordered subpoena. Otherwise, cooperation is purely voluntary. Thus, an interviewee can simply refuse to answer any questions at all.

How should someone respond when being questioned by the FBI?
Whether or not someone intends to cooperate, the most effective response is to insist that all questions be asked and answered in writing and that the FBI state in writing the legal authority under which it is conducting the interview. Faced with this situation, the FBI will often back off and stop its questioning rather than put the questions in writing. One can also simply decline to answer any questions.

If the questioning does proceed, it is important to do so in writing. Otherwise the agents who conduct the interview will write a report based on their recollection of the subject's answers. That report then becomes the official record of the conversation and may not accurately reflect the conversation that took place. The report and any other information provided at a personal interview can be used as evidence at legal proceedings and will be compared with any subsequent testimony the subject gives.

Persons being questioned can also request the presence of a lawyer, who may advise against answering certain questions. Again, requesting an attorney may itself dissuade the FBI from continuing its inquiry.[28]

What could happen if a person chooses not to cooperate with the FBI?
Refusal to cooperate with a voluntary inquiry is absolutely permissible and should not bear any recrimination upon the interviewee. In general, the FBI will not press the matter further when someone does not cooperate voluntarily. However, it is possible that refusal to answer questions could result in the continuation of an investigation that might otherwise have stopped based on that cooperation. The government can also issue a subpoena requiring a person to testify before a grand jury. Furthermore, giving false statements to the FBI, or any other federal investigative body, even when not under oath, is a criminal offense.[29]

Is a person under investigation when being questioned as a witness (i.e., will the FBI open a file on that person for refusing to cooperate)?
No. But the FBI will most likely keep a seperate record of that witness's refusal to cooperate, which could be retrieved for subsequent reference. A witness is a person of "investigative interest" and not the subject of an investigation.

Physical and Photographic Surveillance

When is physical and photographic surveillance authorized?
The attorney general's guidelines allow FBI agents to conduct physical and photographic surveillance of any person with-

out supervisory approval. Thus, in the course of an investigation, an agent can follow someone, stake out his or her home or workplace, and write down or photograph anything in sight such as license plate numbers, physical locales, and persons entering or leaving. However, the guidelines do place greater restrictions on photographing public demonstrations: "The FBI shall not undertake to photograph any demonstration or the preparation therefor in carrying out its responsibilities."[30]

There is very little to prevent a police agency from conducting such physical and photographic surveillance of public activities. The government claims that it is just as entitled as any private person or journalist to watch or photograph any person, place, or thing in a public setting. The courts have upheld the right of the police to observe activities from public places,[31] so long as such surveillance does not violate the First Amendment.[32]

MORE INTRUSIVE TECHNIQUES

Mail Cover

What is a mail cover?

A mail cover is the recording of information appearing on the outside cover of any mail, without actually opening the mail. The courts have ruled that this type of procedure is not considered a Fourth Amendment search or seizure,[33] nor a violation of the postal laws that protect against obstruction of the mails,[34] and therefore a warrant is not required. (Note, however, that in the case of mail opening a warrant is required only for the opening of first-class mail;[35] thus, even the contents of non-first-class mail can be checked as part of a mail cover.[36])

Mail covers are governed by a federal regulation that gives three grounds for their use: protecting the national security, locating a fugitive, and obtaining evidence of the commission of a crime.[37] For national security mail covers, the head of the requesting law enforcement agency must request a mail cover from the chief postal inspector. It cannot last for more than one hundred-twenty days without being renewed. Criminal and fugitive mail covers can be approved by a regional postal inspector but must be renewed every thirty days. In general, incoming mail is afforded less protection than outgoing.

Are there any restrictions on the use of mail covers?

Yes. The First Amendment protects persons against mail covers that infringe upon the rights of free speech and political association. In 1978 a federal court invalidated the federal regulation on national security based mail covers because it failed to define the term and thus left the government too much room for abuse.[38] The court ruled that "National security as a basis for the mail cover is unconstitutionally vague and overbroad. Without any qualification or explanation of what is meant by national security an investigation can be initiated on the assertions of an overzealous public official who disagrees with the unorthodox, yet constitutionally protected views of a group or person."[39]

The decision in no way affected mail covers based on "good faith" criminal or fugitive investigations.[40] The government subsequently issued new regulations that defined "national security" with greater specificity.[41] In a subsequent legal challenge, the court upheld the new mail cover regulations.[42]

In the 1978 case discussed above, a high school student sent a letter as part of a class assignment to the Socialist Labor party, but accidentally addressed it to the Socialist Workers party (SWP). The FBI had had a mail cover on the SWP since 1973 for "national security" purposes. As a result of the correspondence, the FBI proceeded to investigate the student; it closed the case when it learned the nature of her inquiry, but it maintained a file on her under the category of "subversive" matter. (The FBI subsequently agreed to destroy the file.)[43]

In 1988 a similar case arose when Todd Patterson, a high school student, was investigated by the FBI because of his correspondence with the Soviet Union. The federal courts, without specifying that a mail cover was used, upheld the FBI's investigative conduct as pursuant to an "authorized law enforcement activity."[44]

Pen Register and Trap-and-Trace Device

What is a pen register and a trap-and-trace device?

A pen register records the phone numbers dialed from a particular telephone number; a trap-and-trace device records numbers dialed to the phone. They are the telephone equivalent of a mail cover. But unlike mail covers, a judicial warrant is now required by law to obtain either a pen register or a trap-and-trace.[45] (While the courts have ruled that warrants for pen registers are not mandated under the Fourth Amendment, as they are for phone taps, Congress chose in this case to provide greater protection of individual rights than that afforded by the Constitution.) Even without the law, the domestic guidelines require the FBI to obtain a federal court order that must be extended every thirty days in order to use a pen register.[46]

However, a warrant is not necessarily required for pen registers and trap-and-trace devices in foreign counterintelligence and international terrorism investigations. Federal law has created certain national security exceptions from the standard warrant requirement when investigating financial or electronic storage information of Americans; these also require the attorney general's approval. For example, the Right to Financial Privacy Act (RFPA) and the Electronic Communications Privacy Act (ECPA), which prevent access to financial records or interception of electronic communications without a warrant, give the FBI a blanket exception to the warrant requirement for such information in national security cases.

Does the government need a warrant to get access to private records stored at third-party locations, such as at banks or telephone companies?

Yes, except in national security cases. In 1976 the Supreme Court ruled that the government did not need a warrant to obtain the financial records—e.g., cancelled checks—of persons or organizations that are held by a financial institution.[47] In response, Congress passed the Right to Financial Privacy Act (RFPA) in 1978 to prohibit the government from accessing financial records without a court order.[48] In 1986 Congress passed the Electronic Communications Privacy Act (ECPA) to provide similar warrant protection to other transactional records and to stored wire and electronic communications.[49] However, both the RFPA and the ECPA contain exemptions from some of the warrant requirements for foreign counterintelligence and international terrorism investigations.[50] The exemption in the ECPA pertains only to telephone toll and other electronic communication transactional records, but does not include unlisted numbers.[51] Efforts by the FBI to get Congress to extend the ECPA "national security letter" have failed as of 1990.

While designed "to protect against unauthorized interception of electronic communications," the ECPA gave the FBI mandatory authority in cases of national security to request telephone subscriber information, toll billing records, and other electronically communicated transactional records. This means that the director of the FBI can order whomever holds the records to turn them over without a court order simply by making a written request for such information. This so-called national security letter must certify that "the information sought is relevant to an authorized foreign counterintelligence investigation; and (2) there are specific and articulable facts giving reason to believe that the person or entity to whom the information pertains is a foreign power or an agent of a foreign power."[52]

Library and Video Store Borrowing Records

Can the government search library records without a warrant?

Yes, except where there is a state statute prohibiting such searches without a warrant.[53] The FBI requests the library borrowing and use records of persons whom it suspects may be engaged in espionage. The FBI also asks librarians to report on any person whom they think is suspicious. Some of these activities are performed under what the FBI calls its "Library Awareness Program." The program is ostensibly used for counterintelligence purposes to monitor foreign spies who may utilize libraries to research U.S. technology and recruit U.S. persons to assist them.[54]

The Library Awareness Program not only infringes on the First Amendment and privacy rights of library users, all of whom should be afforded unfettered access to unclassified material regardless of their nationality, it also imposes undue burdens on librarians who may feel compelled to report on "suspicious" behavior about which they are unable or unwilling to make judgments.[55]

The FBI says that this program is used only in the New York

City area and only at scientific and technical libraries where espionage activities are most prevalent. However, librarians have reported that the FBI has conducted activities that greatly resemble the Library Awareness Program in libraries across the country.[56] In November 1988 the FBI announced that it was narrowing the scope of the Library Awareness Program, but that it retained the right to make such requests in order to keep track of hostile intelligence service activities.[57] In the fall of 1989 the FBI released approximately twelve-hundred pages of its three-thousand-page file on the Library Awareness Program under a Freedom of Information Act suit brought by the National Security Archive.[58] These documents revealed that the FBI engaged in background checks on at least 266 persons who "were connected in any way" with the program "to determine whether a Soviet active measures campaign had been initiated to discredit the LIBRARY AWARENESS PROGRAM."[59]

Can the government search borrowing records of video stores without a warrant?

No. In 1988 Congress passed a law prohibiting the disclosure of video rental and retail records without a warrant.[60] This bill was developed in response to the disclosure of the video rental records of Judge Robert Bork during his confirmation process as a Supreme Court justice. Prior to that time, there was no statutory protection against such disclosure.

Informants

Is there a right of privacy or confidentiality with respect to informants?

In general, no. There is nothing to stop anyone with whom a person talks from revealing the conversation to anyone else, including the police.[61] The courts have refused to apply the Fourth Amendment warrant protection against unreasonable searches and seizures to the use of informants. While the government cannot tap a phone or bug a room without a warrant, they can send in a person to listen to and report back all that he or she has heard.

Are informants allowed to make concealed recordings of conversations without a warrant?

Yes, except in some states. There are no federal legal restrictions on informants' use of concealed recording devices to record conversations at which they are present.[62] Because there is no legal restriction against informing, there is also no restriction on the way in which the informant records the conversation. The restrictions on the use of other electronic intercepts, such as phone taps and bugs (see below), simply do not apply to electronic recordings made of personal conversations between people who are in the presence of one another.

However, a number of states do require prior judicial authorization in order for informants or undercover agents to use concealed recording devices. This requirement goes beyond what federal law provides, and applies only to state law enforcement agencies.[63]

What kinds of informants does the government use?

An informant is any person who provides information to a law enforcement agency who does not formally work for the agency. An agency employee who engages in informant activities is considered an undercover agent. Another source of human intelligence is the "confidential source." These are persons who provide the FBI with information available to them through their professional position, such as bankers, telephone employees, and landlords.[64]

Informants range from the casual, voluntary walk-in, to the person who is paid and directed. Some informants are recruited—prompted by money, disillusionment, or vengeance—to provide information on groups to which they already belong. Others are hired in advance and then infiltrated into the target organization. This section deals primarily with the use of informants in intelligence investigations, which are more likely to affect political activists, rather than criminal investigations.

What are the rules on the use of informants?

The rules governing the use of informants emanate from Executive Order Number 12333,[65] which prohibits intelligence agencies (including the FBI) from undisclosed participation in any "United States" organization except in accordance with procedures approved by the attorney general.[66] The executive order also prohibits such agencies from "influencing the activity of the organization or its members" except when done as part of a lawful FBI investigation or if the organization "is composed primarily of individuals who are not United States persons and is reasonably believed to be acting on behalf of a foreign power."[67]

Informants are allowed to influence the activities of the organizations they infiltrate for two purposes only: to maintain cover and to prevent violence. The informant guidelines explicitly instruct informants "to try to discourage violence" whenever they learn that persons under investigation may try to commit a violent crime.[68]

The attorney general procedures governing informants are principally found in the FBI's Guidelines on the Use of Informants ("informant guidelines"),[69] which state that informants may only be used in the course of an authorized investigation.[70] The guidelines state explicitly that because the use of informants "may involve an element of deception and intrusion into the privacy of individuals or may require government cooperation with persons whose reliability and motivation may be open to question . . . it is imperative that special care be taken not only to minimize their use but also to ensure that individual rights are not infringed and that the government itself does not become a violator of the law."[71]

The informant guidelines prohibit informants from participating in acts of violence, using unlawful techniques to collect information, and from initiating or participating in criminal activity.[72] These restrictions were put in place because FBI informants used to engage in such activities at the behest of the FBI under COINTELPRO.

For example, Gary Rowe, an FBI informant who infiltrated the Ku Klux Klan from 1959 to 1965, participated in many acts of violence in order to maintain his cover in a KKK "Action Group" that beat up African-Americans and other civil rights workers. Rowe was one of the participants of a group that murdered civil rights worker Viola Liuzzo in 1965; his testimony was instrumental in obtaining the conviction of the Klansmen responsible for the killing.[73]

Are there different rules for informants and undercover agents?

Undercover agents are employees of the FBI (or other law enforcement agency); informants are not. The standards on the use of informants cannot exceed those for undercover agents—"informants may [not] be used for acts or encouraged to commit acts which the FBI could not authorize for its undercover Agents."[74]

But the standards for employing undercover agents differ from the informant standards: while the FBI can use informants only after it has opened a full investigation, it can use undercover agents at the preliminary inquiry stage, except in domestic security investigations.[75]

In the CISPES case, however, the FBI directed an informant, Frank Varelli, to infiltrate CISPES's Dallas chapter in June 1981 even though the FBI did not even officially begin to investigate CISPES until September 1981.[76] The bureau claims it can use informants on groups it is not investigating if such groups are sufficiently connected to other ongoing investigations. The FBI has not publicly asserted that CISPES was connected to any other ongoing investigation in this way.

The informant continued to infiltrate CISPES after the FBI closed that initial investigation in February 1982 and was the principal source of information for reopening the counterintelligence investigation in March 1983. A subsequent investigation by the FBI concluded that Varelli had provided false and misleading information and that the investigation should never have been opened and would not have been without that information.[77]

MOST INTRUSIVE TECHNIQUES

The most intrusive techniques are those that constitute a search under the Fourth Amendment and thus require a judicial warrant based on probable cause. The Fourth Amendment states, "The right of the people to be secure in their persons, houses, papers, and effects, against unreasonable searches and seizures, shall not be violated, and no warrants shall issue, but upon probable cause, supported by oath or affirmation, and particularly describing the place to be searched, and persons or things to be seized." These techniques include electronic surveillance—e.g., wiretaps and bugs—mail opening, and physical searches of homes, offices, and (under some circumstances) vehicles and packages.

Electronic Surveillance

What is electronic surveillance?

Electronic surveillance is the undisclosed monitoring of oral or electronic communications through and by electronic means.[78] The two most common techniques are tapping telephones and bugging rooms. But technology has opened the way for new surveillance techniques of such things as computer information (electronic mail), cellular phones, satellite transmissions, and paging devices. Indeed, Congress had to pass a new law in order to make these technologies subject to warrant procedures already required for taps, bugs, and physical searches.[79]

Domestic Electronic Surveillance

Does the government need a warrant for unconsented electronic surveillance?

Yes, except in very rare circumstances, the government must get a judicial warrant based on probable cause that a crime has been, is being, or is about to be committed in order to tap a telephone, bug a premises, or obtain other electronic information without the consent of at least one of the parties to the communication. In 1967 the Supreme Court ruled that Fourth Amendment protection against unreasonable searches and seizures applied to wiretaps and buggings just as it did to physical searches.[80] The following year Congress passed a domestic wiretap law specifying the procedures for intercepting "wire or oral communications."[81]

Wiretaps have been challenged as unconstitutional because they constitute a "general search" in violation of the Fourth Amendment requirement that the warrant "particularly describ[e] the place to be searched, and the persons and things to be seized." The Supreme Court rejected that argument and ruled that the "particularity" requirement is adequately satisfied by identifying the telephone line and the type of communications to be seized, even though some conversations will be overheard that have no criminal connection.[82]

Are there exceptions to the warrant requirement?

Yes. There are several exceptions to the warrant requirement under the domestic wiretap law. Federal law now allows for the use of wiretaps without a warrant (1) when one party consents to it,[83] (2) in emergency situations, so long as an application for a warrant is made within forty-eight hours,[84] and (3) by the Federal Communications Commission and other telephone operators when done as part of standard business operations.[85] Furthermore, the domestic wiretap law also does not cover national security cases; these are covered by the Foreign Intelligence Surveillance Act (FISA).[86]

Can someone volunteer to have his or her phone tapped without a warrant and without informing other callers?

Yes. The federal statute employs what is known as the "one-party consent" rule: as long as one party to a conversation consents to the surveillance, no warrant is required.[87] The same standard applies here as applies to the use of informants with concealed recording devices (the informant, as a party to the conversation, has given consent). (See questions on informants above.)

Some states have an "all-party consent" rule, which requires that all parties to the conversation must give their consent before the conversation can be recorded. This means that anyone, including the police, who wants to record a phone conversation without a warrant must inform all of the other parties and obtain their consent before recording the conversation.[88] Many all-party consent states have exceptions for the police. Illinois, for instance, maintains the two-party requirement for private parties but allows the police to monitor conversations with the consent of one party and a judicial warrant.[89] (Note that these same procedures also apply to concealed recordings by informants.)

Can private individuals record their own conversations?

Yes, except in some states. The federal law allows for one-party consent for recording private conversations. But in those states that require all-party consent, it is a crime to record one's own telephone conversation without the consent of all the other parties. This rule generally applies to any call taking place in that state, even if the call originates in another state that does not have the all-party consent rule.[90]

Does the federal electronic surveillance statute apply to the states?

Yes. The federal wiretap law applies equally to all states.[91] Many states have enacted laws based on the federal model. However, the states are free to enact more restrictive measures to give greater protection to individual privacy, which many states have done.[92]

What are the procedures for obtaining a warrant for domestic electronic surveillance?

Any law enforcement agency—whether it be the FBI or any other federal, state, or local agency—that applies for a wiretap warrant must give a detailed statement under oath and in writing describing the reasons for the tap, the violations of law that are under investigation, the identities (if known) of the persons and phones to be tapped, the type of communication used, and any previous applications for warrants by the agency.[93] The warrants can be issued for no longer than thirty days, with an option to extend for thirty-day periods based upon the same criteria as the original application.[94]

Does the government have to specify the identity of every person and the place it is tapping?

No. The government can get a warrant for a wiretap even if it does not know the identity of the person or persons it is probing or the specific phone that will be used. The warrant application can list named persons and persons "as yet unknown." The courts have been very lenient in not requiring the government to list the names of persons whose conversations are overheard, so long as the other elements of probable cause have been satisfied.[95] The only persons who are allowed to be named are those for whom there is probable cause of criminal activity, although failure to name them will not necessarily invalidate the tap.[96] Persons for whom there is no probable cause cannot be named in the warrant order; but information produced during the tap can be used for their arrest and indictment,[97] unless the order specifically limits the tap to the persons named (which is seldom done).[98]

In 1986 the wiretap law was amended in part to loosen the rule requiring the government to specify the exact phone to be tapped.[99] The purpose was to give the government flexibility in dealing with targets who deliberately change phones to thwart interception.[100] In cases where the phone is not specified, the law still requires that the warrant must specify the person under surveillance. The 1986 amendments also made it a crime to warn someone without authorization that he or she is the subject of a wiretap.[101]

Does the government have to notify persons that they were the subject of electronic surveillance?

Yes, in most circumstances. The Fourth Amendment implicitly requires that the police notify all persons subject to a search of their intent and purpose.[102] In a traditional physical search of a premises, the person is necessarily notified of the search by the presence of the police and the showing of the warrant or the leaving behind of the warrant and an inventory of seized items. The same, however, is not true for phone taps or for mail openings, where such notice does not necessarily occur.

Because contemporaneous notification of a phone tap would defeat its very purpose, the wiretap law requires that all persons who are named in the warrant, and anyone else whom the judge decides, must be notified that they were tapped within ninety days after the termination of the surveillance; they must also be notified ninety days after an application for a warrant has been rejected, even if no surveillance occurred.[103] Also, anyone who is going to be indicted must be given copies of the warrant at least ten days prior to any court proceeding (assuming the ninety-day requirement has not already been invoked); this requirement can be waived by the judge if notice was not possible and no prejudice to the defendant will result.[104] There is, however, no notice requirement for unindicted persons in national security wiretaps authorized under the Foreign Intelligence Surveillance Act (FISA).

But the law does not require that notice be given to everyone who was overheard on the wiretap. Persons not named in the warrant are entitled only to notice at the "discretion" of the judge who issued the order.[105] At least one court has ruled that it was okay for the government not to notify several defendants who were not named in the wiretap order if the government could not get their addresses, so long as one other defendant was notified.[106] But a person on at least one end of the conversation is supposed to receive notice.

The federal courts have generally been lenient in enforcing the ninety-day notice deadline, so long as no prejudice resulted against the defendant in preparing a defense.[107] However, at least one state court has required that the ninety-day notice be strictly enforced, with failure to comply resulting in the loss of the use of the wiretap information.[108]

Can the government enter a private premises to install a listening device?

Yes, but only with a court order. The electronic surveillance law does not give the government the authority, as a matter of right, to use any means to install a tap or a bug.[109] However, the law does confer upon the courts the power to authorize surreptitious entries where necessary in order to install the surveillance device.[110] The judge does not need to issue a separate order for the installation.[111] However, Executive Order Number 12333 authorizes the FBI to engage in unconsented physical searches without a warrant if the target is deemed an "agent of a foreign power." The executive branch claims it has inherent authority to engage in such break-ins without a warrant, and the courts have never ruled whether or not such practice is constitutional.[112] Note that new technology makes it possible to tap phone lines without having actually to enter the premises.

Does the government need a warrant to plant a listening device in a public place?

It depends on whether there is a reasonable expectation of privacy. A person giving a public speech has no expectation of privacy, and therefore no warrant would be required. However, a warrant would be required to monitor a private conversation between two persons on a park bench.[113] In situations where a person either has been informed that the conversation may be monitored or voices an assumption that the conversation is being monitored, there is no expectation of privacy; in those circumstances, no warrant is required.[114]

Are there limitations on the type of information that can be monitored through electronic surveillance?

Yes. The statute requires that the government minimize the monitoring of any conversations that are not specified in the warrant.[115] This minimization requirement was designed to prevent a general search of all communications; only conversations pertinent to the activity under investigation can be monitored. "Pertinent," however, is open to broad interpretation—e.g., "any and all information directly or indirectly helpful to the investigation."[116]

The persons who are monitoring the conversations do have an obligation to turn off the recording devices during personal calls. But they will still have to listen to some extent in order to determine whether or not it actually is a personal call. The longer the surveillance continues, the easier it is to distinguish personal from pertinent. The mere identity of certain individuals could be an adequate signal that the call is personal and therefore cannot be recorded or otherwise monitored. But often, pertinent and nonpertinent information occur in the same call. Targets also can mask pertinent information in nonpertinent language, using code words, etc.

The courts have given broad leeway to minimization procedures, such that "the cases show a strong inclination to find pertinent any conversation that has any conceivable connection to the investigation, no matter how remote."[117] Furthermore, when the government fails to minimize, the usual result is the removal from use of only the nonpertinent conversations.[118]

Can the government use information from a wiretap about criminal activities not contemplated in the warrant?

Yes. The statue allows the government to use such windfall evidence, so long as it informs the judge and amends the order as soon as possible.[119] Again, however, the courts have been lenient in holding this requirement to a strict standard.[120]

National Security Electronic Surveillance

Are there different standards governing national security electronic surveillance?

Yes. In 1972 the Supreme Court ruled that the Fourth Amendment requires warrants for national security electronic surveillance in the United States, but held that different procedures may be appropriate in such cases.[121] Accordingly, Congress passed the Foreign Intelligence Surveillance Act of 1978 (FISA) to establish procedures for national security wiretaps.[122]

The FISA can be used only for foreign intelligence collection purposes and such electronic surveillance can target only "foreign powers" and "agents of foreign powers" (as defined in the statute). Foreign intelligence includes international terrorism, foreign powers include international terrorist organizations, and agents of foreign powers include anyone, including U.S. persons, who engages in "international terrorism" or knowingly "aids or abets" an international terrorist.[123]

Does the FISA distinguish between U.S. persons and non U.S. persons?

Yes. The criminal standard for the warrant and the protection of First Amendment rights only apply to U.S. persons.[124] Thus, foreigners and nonresident aliens (including illegal and undocumented aliens) can be subject to FISA surveillance without being suspected of criminal activity or for engaging in First Amendment activities, but only if they are officers or employees of a foreign power or are acting on behalf of a foreign power engaged in clandestine intelligence activities (e.g., espionage and intelligence collection) in the United States.[125]

What is a "U.S. person"?

The FISA defines a U.S. person as a U.S. citizen, a permanent resident alien, a U.S. corporation, or an unincorporated association composed primarily of U.S. citizens or permanent resident aliens.[126] Under U.S. law in general, a "person" can also be a group, entity, association, corporation, or foreign power.[127]

What is a "foreign power"?

The FISA provides the only statutory definition of "foreign power," although the national security guidelines use the exact same definition: "(1) a foreign government or any component thereof, whether or not recognized by the United States; (2) a faction of a foreign nation or nations, not substantially composed of United States persons; (3) an entity that is openly acknowledged by a foreign government or governments to be directed and controlled by such foreign government or governments; (4)

a foreign-based political organization, not substantially composed of United States persons; or (6) an entity that is directed and controlled by a foreign government or governments."[128]

What is an "agent of a foreign power"?

The FISA also provides the only statutory definition of "agent of a foreign power." The definition in the national security guidelines is classified, but it is believed to be similar to the one in the FISA.[129] However, it is not clear whether the national security guidelines require that U.S. persons be or "may be" involved in criminal activities, as does the FISA.

The FISA states that an agent of a foreign power is (1) any non-U.S. person who "acts in the United States as an officer or employee of a foreign power [as defined in the statute], or as a member of a foreign power" or who "acts for or on behalf of a foreign power which engages in clandestine intelligence activities in the United States contrary to the interests of the United States, when the circumstances of such person's presence in the United States indicate that such person may engage in such activities in the United States, or when such person knowingly aids or abets any person in the conduct of such activities or knowingly conspires with any person to engage in such activities"; or (2) any person, including U.S. persons, who "knowingly engages in clandestine intelligence gathering for or on behalf of a foreign power," "knowingly engages in any other clandestine intelligence activities for or on behalf of a foreign power [under the direction of a foreign intelligence service]," "knowingly engages in sabotage or international terrorism, or activities that are in preparation therefor, for or on behalf of a foreign power," or knowingly "aids or abets" or "conspires with" any person in the conduct of any of the above activities.[130]

What is "international terrorism"?

The FISA, as well as the national security guidelines, defines international terrorism as "activities that involve violent acts or acts dangerous to human life that are a violation of the criminal laws of the United States or of any State, or that would be a criminal violation if committed within the jurisdiction of the United States or any State; [and that] appear to be intended to intimidate or coerce a civilian population; to influence the policy of a government by intimidation or coercion; or to affect the conduct of a government by assassination or kidnapping."[131]

Does national security electronic surveillance require a different showing of probable cause for a warrant than domestic surveillance?

Yes. The government need only show probable cause that the person "may be" involved in criminal activity, rather than that the person "is" involved, in order to get a court order for a national security electronic surveillance.[132] For non-U.S. persons (i.e., persons who are neither U.S. citizens nor U.S. permanent resident aliens), there is no criminal standard, although the government does have to demonstrate that the person is an officer or employee of a foreign power or is acting on behalf of a foreign power engaged in clandestine intelligence activities (espionage) in the United States.[133] The courts have rejected every legal challenge that the FISA violates the Fourth Amendment for not having an absolute criminal standard on the grounds that the FISA adequately balances the Fourth Amendment interests of the targets with the national security responsibilities of the government.[134]

Furthermore, criminal defendants who are targets of a FISA wiretap are not entitled to review the warrant to make sure the wiretap was properly authorized, as they would be able to in the case of a domestic wiretap. The FISA allows the judge to review the legality of the surveillance in secret if the government asserts that public disclosure would harm the national security,[135] which the government almost always does.

Must the government notify persons subject to national security electronic surveillance who are not indicted, as required for domestic taps?

No. The government does not have to notify persons that they were subject to national security electronic surveillance if those persons are not subject to court proceedings. The domestic law requires that such persons be notified within ninety days after the surveillance ceases or ten days before any court proceeding. The FISA requires notice only when the government intends to use evidence derived from a FISA surveillance against a person in court.[136]

In emergency circumstances, the government can begin

FISA surveillance without a court order, so long as an application for a court order is made within twenty-four hours.[137] In those instances where a court rejects the government's application, immediate notice is also required, although it can be postponed for ninety days or permanently suspended upon a "showing of good cause" by the government.[138] The law also requires that any information obtained from a warrantless surveillance on communications for which a warrant was required "shall be destroyed upon recognition, unless the attorney general determines that the contents indicate a threat of death or serious bodily harm to any person."[139]

Can the government engage in electronic surveillance without a warrant in national security cases?

Yes. In extremely rare circumstances, the FISA allows the attorney general to authorize electronic surveillance without a court order for up to one year for surveillance that is solely directed at communications used exclusively between or among foreign powers where there is "no substantial likelihood that the surveillance will acquire the contents of any communication to which a United States person is a party."[140] This section of the FISA allowing for warrantless surveillance is used primarily for leased lines connecting embassies with their home government. It does not apply to reqular embassy lines, where there is a great likelihood that U.S. persons will use them.

Is there a special FISA court that considers applications for warrants for national security electronic surveillance?

Yes. The FISA created a special court, known as the Foreign Intelligence Surveillance Court (FISC), to issue and hear appeals for such warrants in a secure setting so as to minimize the risk of disclosing classified information. In over four thousand cases from the court's inception in 1979 through 1987, the FISC has approved every government application for a warrant and for an extension of a warrant.[141]

Mail Opening

Can first-class mail be opened without a warrant?

No. The opening and reading of first-class, domestic mail is considered a search under the Fourth Amendment and thus requires a judicial warrant for authorization under the same probable cause standard that applies for searching a home or tapping a phone.[142] As with phone taps, however, the standard of contemporaneous notice requirement does not apply to mail openings. Also, the executive branch asserts that it needs no warrant for mail opening in national security cases.[143]

Can non-first-class mail be opened without a warrant?

Yes. The Constitution and the law only protect first-class mail from warrantless searches. All non-first-class mail—including sealed packages, newspapers, magazines, pamphlets, and other printed material—may be opened without a warrant. The postal regulations state explicitly that the use of non-first-class mail is deemed as consent by the sender to postal inspection of the contents.[144]

Can international mail be opened without a warrant?

Yes. The customs service is given specific authority to search envelopes from abroad at the border without a warrant; but they must have "reasonable cause to suspect there is merchandise which was imported contrary to law."[145] The Supreme Court has ruled that this authority includes letter-class international mail as well as packages.[146] The Court reasoned that because border searches are in general permissible without a warrant, a warrant should not be required for material sent through the mail. However, border searches of mail are still held to a higher standard than are border searches of persons or automobiles: mail search must be based on a "reasonable cause to suspect" (other standard searches do not require individualized suspicion).[147]

Can international mail be read without a warrant?

No. The law distinguishes between opening mail to search the contents for illegal material and actually reading the mail. Thus, to read international mail there must be specific authorization to do so by a search warrant.[148] When the Supreme Court authorized non-warrant searches of international mail, it specifically limited its ruling to the search of things "other than correspondence, while the reading of any correspondence inside the envelopes is forbidden."[149]

Physical Searches

Can the government enter a private premises to search and seize material without a warrant?

No, except in certain circumstances. The Fourth Amendment requires that all physical searches be done with a warrant based on probable cause and that the target be given notice of the search. There are, however, a number of exceptions to the warrant requirement that apply to normal law enforcement activities—such as "incident to a lawful arrest" (allows search of person for weapons and other illegal things following arrest),[150] "plain view" (allows, for example, search of car if illegal material is within plain view and car was stopped for a valid law enforcement purpose),[151] "hot pursuit" (allows for entrance and search of a premises when in hot pursuit of a person subject to arrest who runs into the premises).[152]

Does the government engage in physical searches for national security purposes without a warrant?

Yes. The executive branch claims that it has the inherent authority to engage in physical searches for national security purposes without a warrant.[153] The executive orders on intelligence activities issued by Presidents Ford, Carter, and Reagan authorize the FBI to engage in "unconsented physical searches" without a warrant upon a showing that the target is a "foreign power" or an "agent of a foreign power" under the national security guidelines (the Carter executive order required that the president approve such searches; the Ford and Reagan orders require only attorney general approval; all of them state that such searches must not violate constitutional and other legal rights).[154]

These executive orders followed upon the revelation that from the end of World War II until the mid 1970s, the FBI and the CIA conducted a large number of illegal break-ins (known as "black bag jobs") against American citizens. While some of these break-ins were done for espionage purposes, many were used against "subversive elements" (i.e., political organizations not engaged in criminal activity) in order to obtain information, such as membership and mailing lists, to plant listening devices, and to disrupt their activities.[155]

The Carter administration on three occasions in 1980 sought

and received judicial warrants from the Foreign Intelligence Surveillance Court (FISC) under FISA procedures for electronic surveillance.[156] But like FISA surveillance, and unlike most Fourth Amendment physical searches, the government was not required to give notice to the targets that the premises had been searched. In 1981 the FISC ruled, upon the recommendation of the Reagan administration, that it had no legal authority under the FISA to authorize national security-related physical searches because the FISA only authorizes the court to deal with electronic surveillance. In 1990 Congress contemplated extending the FISA procedures to physical searches, but no law was passed.[157]

Does the government need a warrant to "search" places or activity from the air?

No. The courts have ruled that aerial surveillance does not require a search warrant.[158] Things that can be seen from an airplane are deemed to be in public view and thus not given Fourth Amendment protection. Modern technology allows for extremely accurate aerial surveillance by plane, helicopter, or satellite. Such monitoring of particular events or activities in the United States is still governed by the relevant regulations and guidelines that apply to the human surveillance of such public activities. In a 1989 case the Supreme Court upheld a warrantless aerial surveillance by a helicopter but indicated that it would not be constitutional in situations where the surveillance techniques are not available to the general public and are sufficiently rare to give rise to a reasonable expectation of privacy.[159]

NOTES

1. *See Attorney General's Guidelines on General Crimes, Racketeering Enterprise and Domestic Security/Terrorism Investigations* (March 7, 1983) (also known as the Smith Guidelines) (hereafter "domestic guidelines").
2. *Attorney General Guidelines for FBI Foreign Intelligence Collection and Foreign Counterintelligence Investigations* (April 18, 1983) (also known as the FCI Guidelines) (hereafter "national security guidelines").

3. "COINTELPRO: The FBI's Covert Action Programs against American Citizens" (hereafter "COINTELPRO"), at 3, in *Supplementary Detailed Staff Reports on Intelligence Activities and the Rights of Americans, Book 3, Final Report of the Select Committee to Study Governmental Operations with Respect to Intelligence Activities*, S. Rep. No. 755, 94th Cong., 2d Sess. (1976) (hereafter "Church Committee Book 3").

4. Exec. Order No. 12333, 46 Fed. Reg. 59941 (1981), § 2.9.

5. *Socialist Workers Party v. Attorney General*, 642 F. Supp. 1357 (S.D.N.Y. 1986).

6. *Hobson v. Wilson*, 556 F. Supp. 1157 (D.D.C. 1982), *aff'd in part, rev'd in part*, 737 F.2d 1 (D.C. Cir. 1984), *cert. denied, sub nom. Brennan v. Hobson*, 470 U.S. 1084 (1985), *on remand sub nom. Hobson v. Brennan*, 646 F. Supp. 884 (1986).

7. *National Lawyers Guild v. Attorney General*, No. 77-999 (S.D.N.Y. October 12, 1989) (stipulation and order of settlement and dismissal).

8. However, as the FBI progresses with the computerization of the full text of its files, it will be able to search for any name appearing in any file, even if the name is not specifically indexed.

Recently, the FBI created an internal database known as the Terrorist Information System (TIS). The system stores not only such information as the subjects, victims, witnesses, and close relatives and associates relevant to terrorism investigations, but also the names of groups and members suspected of both domestic and international terrorism. As of July 1, 1987 there were 101,705 individuals and 468 organizations or enterprises entered in the system. Letter dated August 24, 1987, from Acting FBI Director John E. Otis to Congressman Don Edwards, Chair, Subcommittee on Civil and Constitutional Rights.

9. M. Wines, *FBI Chief Defends Acts on Librarians*, New York Times, November 8, 1989, at A21.

10. D. Johnston, *Documents Disclose FBI Investigations of Some Librarians*, New York Times, November 7, 1989, at A1.

11. 5 U.S.C. § 552a(e)(7) (1988).

12. *Hobson v. Wilson*, 737 F.2d 1, 64 (D.C. Cir. 1984), *cert. denied*, 470 U.S. 1084 (1985), *citing Clarkson v. I.R.S.*, 678 F.2d 1368, 1376–77 (11th Cir. 1982), *appeal after remand* 811 F.2d 1368, *cert. denied*, 481 U.S. 1031 (1987); and *Albright v. United States*, 631 F.2d 915, 921 (D.C. Cir. 1980); *see also Reuber v. United States*, 750 F.2d 1039, 1068 (D.C. Cir. 1984).

13. *See, e.g., Patterson v. FBI*, 705 F. Supp. 1033, 1047 (D.N.J. 1989), *aff'd*, 893 F.2d 595, *reh'g en banc denied*, 893 F.2d 595 (3d Cir. 1990) ("[T]he FBI offered to expunge the name of Todd Patterson from its

records" even though the court ruled that "it would be inappropriate for this Court to now order the FBI to expunge plaintiff's name from its files.").

14. *Wilkinson v. F.B.I.*, No. CV 80-1048-AWT (Tx), para. 5 (Cent. Dist. CA., March 19, 1987) (stipulation and order).

15. *Patterson v. FBI, supra* note 13.

16. *Id.* "[T]he *in camera* inspection also allows this Court to assure plaintiff that any records maintained by the FBI on him do not reflect negatively on his character or conduct. Accordingly, the Court can assure plaintiff that the law enforcement activity conducted by the FBI in this case should not in any way inhibit him from pursuing any legitimate exercise of his First Amendment rights, including writing letters to countries throughout the world. Furthermore, plaintiff's fear of an aborted or limited public service career arising out of these events is misplaced." 705 F. Supp. at 1044–45.

17. *Id.* at 1047.

18. *Patterson v. FBI*, C.A. 88-2319, motion to vacate the judgment or in the alternative to supplement the record (D.N.J. April 6, 1989).

19. *Patterson v. FBI*, 893 F.2d 595, *reh'g en banc denied*, 893 F.2d 595 (3d Cir. 1990).

20. *CISPES v. Sessions*, No. 88-3430 (D.D.C. 1988).

21. Testimony of FBI Director William S. Sessions before the Senate Select Committee on Intelligence, September 14, 1988; the House Judiciary Subcommittee on Civil and Constitutional Rights, September 16, 1988; and the House Permanent Select Committee on Intelligence, September 29, 1988.

22. 26 U.S.C. § 6103 (1988) (tax code).

23. 20 U.S.C. § 1232g(b) (1988).

24. Domestic guidelines, *supra* note 1, § II.B.6.d.

25. *Id.* § II.B.6.e.

26. *Id.* § II.B.6.f.

27. *See, e.g., Moya v. U.S.*, 761 F.2d 322, 325, n. 2 (7th Cir. 1984) ("We do not condone dishonesty with police officers. We note, however, that people are entitled to refuse to provide information to the police. [Citations omitted.] Nevertheless, many people have difficulty forthrightly refusing to give police officers requested information."); *U.S. v. Woods*, 720 F.2d 1022 (9th Cir. 1983); *U.S. v. Giuliani*, 581 F. Supp. 212 (N.D. Ill. 1984).

28. For information on what to do if the FBI calls, contact your local ACLU office or call the Rights Watch Hotline, 312-427-4559.

29. For example, many of the persons indicted in the Iran-Contra affair— e.g., Oliver North, John Poindexter, Joseph Fernandez—were charged with making unsworn false statements to the various investi-

gative bodies, such as the Tower Commission and congressional committees.

30. FBI guidelines for *Reporting on Civil Disorders and Demonstrations Involving a Federal Interest,* § V.E.

31. *See, e.g., California v. Ciraolo,* 476 U.S. 207 (1986).

32. *Founding Church of Scientology v. FBI,* 459 F. Supp. 748 (D.D.C. 1978); *Dunlap v. City of Chicago,* 435 F. Supp. 1295 (N.D. Ill. 1977).

33. *See, e.g., U.S. v. Choate,* 576 F.2d 165 (9th Cir.), *cert. denied,* 439 U.S. 953 (1978); *U.S. v. Bianco,* 534 F.2d 1076, 1086–87 (2d Cir. 1976).

34. *Cohen v. U.S.,* 378 F.2d 751 (9th Cir. 1967), *cert. denied,* 389 U.S. 897 (1967) (mail cover does not violate 18 U.S.C. §§ 1702–3 of the postal service laws).

35. 39 U.S.C. § 3623(d) (1982).

36. 39 C.F.R. § 233.3(c)(1) (revised July 1, 1987).

37. 39 C.F.R. § 233.3 (revised July 1, 1987).

38. *Paton v. La Prade,* 469 F. Supp. 773 (D.N.J. 1978).

39. *Id.* at 782.

40. *Id.*

41. " 'To protect the national security' means to protect the United States from any of the following actual or potential threats to its security by a foreign power or its agents: (i) An attack or other grave hostile act; (ii) sabotage, or international terrorism; or, (iii) clandestine intelligence activities." 39 C.F.R. § 233.3(c)(5).

42. The court's opinion was unpublished; *but see Socialist Workers Party v. Attorney General,* 642 F. Supp. 1357, 1426 (S.D.N.Y. 1986).

43. *Paton v. La Prade,* 469 F. Supp. at 776, n.4.

44. *Patterson v. FBI,* 705 F. Supp. 1033 (D.N.J. 1989). The court recommended that the FBI volunteer to destroy the file. *Id.* at 1047. The court of appeals upheld the ruling. 893 F.2d 595, *reh'g en banc denied,* 893 F.2d 595 (3d Cir. 1990).

45. 18 U.S.C. § 3121 *et seq.* (1988) ("no person may install or use a pen register or trap and trace device without first obtaining a court order").

46. Domestic guidelines, *supra* note 1, § IV.B.5 ("Pen registers must be authorized pursuant to Department policy. This requires an order from a federal district court and an extension every 30 days, under the December 18, 1979, memorandum from the Assistant Attorney General in charge of the Criminal Division to all United States Attorneys.").

47. *U.S. v. Miller,* 425 U.S. 435 (1976) (no constitutional right to the privacy of financial records).

48. Right to Financial Privacy Act of 1978, Pub. L. No. 95-630, Tit. XI, 92 Stat. 3641; 12 U.S.C. § 3401 *et seq.* (1988).

49. The Electronic Communication Privacy Act of 1986 (ECPA), Pub. L. No. 99-508, 100 Stat. 1848, 18 U.S.C. § 2701 *et seq.*

50. 12 U.S.C. § 3414(a)(5)(A) (1988) (RFPA); 18 U.S.C. § 2709(b) (1988) (ECPA).

51. 18 U.S.C. § 2709(b) (1988).

52. *Id.*

53. As of March 1989, thirty-seven states and the District of Columbia have statutes protecting the confidentiality of library borrowing records. The American Library Association is encouraging the remaining states to pass laws protecting library records.

    An effort in 1988 to pass a federal law protecting such records nationwide was unsuccessful due to the FBI's efforts to exempt itself from the restrictions of the bill in national security cases. The bureau sought a national security letter exemption to any warrant requirement in the context of the same bill.

54. The Library Awareness Program was first made known by reports in The Nation (April 9, 1988) and The New Yorker (May 30, 1988).

55. *See* testimony of ACLU and American Library Association in *FBI Counterintelligence Visits to Libraries, Hearings before the House Committee on the Judiciary, Subcommittee on Civil and Constitutional Rights,* 100th Cong., 2d Sess., June 20 and July 23, 1988 (Serial No. 123).

56. *See id.; see also* Libraries Visited by the FBI, in Stipulation, *National Security Archive v. FBI,* C.A. No. 88-1507 (D.D.C. May 1, 1989), at 10–11 (listing twenty library visits).

57. *See* B. McAllister, *FBI to Limit Probes of Library Users,* Washington Post, November 11, 1988, at A3.

58. Stipulation, *National Security Archive v. FBI,* C.A. No. 88-1507 (D.D.C. May 1, 1989).

59. FBI Document: *Airtel,* TO: Director, FBI; FR: ADIC, New York (No. 081138, February 6, 1989), quoted in, D. Johnston, *Documents Disclose FBI Investigations of Some Librarians,* New York Times, November 7, 1989, at A1.

60. 18 U.S.C. § 2710 (1988).

61. *United States v. White,* 401 U.S. 745, 749, *reh'g denied,* 402 U.S. 990 (1971) (a person has no "justifiable or constitutionally protected expectation that a person with whom he is conversing will not then or later reveal the conversation to the police"). This case involved a concealed recording by an informant.

62. *Id.*

63. As of 1990 approximately six states require judicial warrant for wiring police agents. Michigan, Washington, and Alaska require it by statute.

Mich. Comp. Laws Ann. § 750.539(c)–(d) (West 1968 & Supp. 1988) (Michigan); Wash. Rev. Code Ann. § 9.73.030(1)(a) (1988) (Washington); Alaska Stat. § 42.20.300 (1983), *see also Ruberts v. State,* Sup. Ct. Op. No. 550 (file No. 934); 453 P.2d 898 (1969), *cert. denied,* 396 U.S. 1022, *reh'g denied,* 397 U.S. 1059 (1970); Ill. Rev. Stat. ch. 38 paras. 14-2, 14-3 (1979 & Supp. 1989) (Illinois); 18 Pa. Cons. Stat. Ann. § 5704(4) (Purdon 1988 & Supp. 1989) (Pennsylvania). Montana requires it by state court ruling. *State v. Solis,* 693 P.2d 518 (Mont. 1984).

64. *See generally* "The Use of Informants in FBI Domestic Intelligence Investigations" (hereinafter "Use of Informants"), at 225–70 in Church Committee Book 3, *supra* note 3.

65. Exec. Order No. 12333, § 2.9, 46 Fed. Reg. 59941 (1981).

66. *See, e.g.,* domestic guidelines & national security guidelines, *supra* notes 1 & 2; *Attorney General Guidelines on the FBI's Use of Informants in Domestic Security, Organized Crime, and Other Criminal Investigations* (December 15, 1976) (hereinafter "informant guidelines").

67. Exec. Order No. 12333; *see also* national security guidelines, *supra* note 2.

68. Informant guidelines, *supra* note 66, at 3.

69. *See* informant guidelines, *supra* note 66 (these guidelines may not be wholly inclusive of all the rules on the use of informants, which stem also from individual instructions and recognized practice).

70. *Id.* at 1–2.

71. *Id.* at 1.

72. *Id.* at 3.

73. *See* "Use of Informants," *supra* note 64 in, Church Committee Book 3, at 239–44.

74. Informant guidelines, *supra* note 66, at 2.

75. *Attorney General's Guidelines on Undercover Operations, General Authority (2),* at 2 (January 1980); *see also* J. Berman, "The Lessons of ABSCAM: A Public Policy Report of the American Civil Liberties Union," at 39 (October 10, 1982).

76. *The FBI and CISPES: Report of the Select Committee on Intelligence, United States Senate, Together with Additional Views,* 101st Cong., 1st Sess. (July 14, 1989), at 66–70, 129 (hereinafter "Senate CISPES Report").

77. *See supra* note 21.

78. *See generally* J. C. Carr, *The Law of Electronic Surveillance* 258 (1977) and supplements.

79. The Electronic Communications Privacy Act of 1986 (ECPA), 18 U.S.C. § 2701 *et seq.*

80. *Katz v. United States,* 389 U.S. 347 (1967); *Berger v. New York,* 388 U.S. 41 (1967).

81. 18 U.S.C. §§ 2510–20 (1988), Title III of the Omnibus Crime Control and Safe Streets Act of 1968, Pub. L. No. 90-351 (June 19, 1968), as amended. This law was amended under the Electronic Communications Privacy Act of 1986, *supra* note 79, to include "electronic communications" in order to bring the law up to date with new technologies.

82. *U.S. v. Donovan,* 429 U.S. 413 (1977).

83. 18 U.S.C. § 2511(2) (1988).

84. 18 U.S.C. § 2518(7) (1988).

85. 18 U.S.C. § 2511(2) (1988).

86. 50 U.S.C. §§ 1801, *et seq.* (1982 & 1986 Supp.), Pub. L. No. 95-511, 92 Stat. 1783.

87. 18 U.S.C. § 2511(2)(c),(d) (1988) ("It shall not be unlawful under this chapter for a person acting under color of law to intercept a wire, oral, or electronic communication, where such person is a party to the communication or one of the parties to the communication has given consent to such interception.").

88. *See, e.g.,* Mass. Gen. Laws Ann. ch. 272, § 99 (West 1970 & Supp. 1989) (Massachussets); Mich. Comp. Laws Ann. 750.539(c) (West 1968 & Supp. 1988) (Michigan); Md. Cts. and Jud. Proc. Code Ann. §§ 10–402 (1988) (Maryland); Cal. Penal Code § 631 (West 1988 & Supp. 1989) (California); Wash. Rev. Code Ann. § 9.73.030(1)(a) (1988) (Washington).

89. Ill. Rev. Stat. ch. 38, paras. 14-2, 14-3 (1979 & Supp. 1989); *see also* 18 Pa. Cons. Stat. Ann. § 5704(4) (Purdon 1988 & Supp. 1989) (Pennsylvania).

90. *See, e.g.,* Wash. Rev. Code Ann. § 9.73.030(1)(a) (1988).

91. *See, e.g., U.S. v. McKinnon,* 721 F.2d 19 (1st Cir. 1983).

92. *See* Carr, *supra* note 78, at § 2.03–4.

93. 18 U.S.C. § 2518 (1988).

94. *Id.*

95. *U.S. v. Donovan,* 429 U.S. 413 (1977); *U.S. v. Kahn,* 415 U.S. 143 (1974); *U.S. v. Figueroa,* 757 F.2d 466 (2d Cir.), *cert. denied,* 474 U.S. 840 (1977).

96. *U.S. v. Donovan, supra* note 95.

97. *U.S. v Kahn, supra* note 95.

98. *U.S. v. George,* 465 F.2d 772, 773–74 (6th Cir. 1972).

99. 18 U.S.C. § 2518(11) (1988).

100. *See Report of the Senate Judiciary Committee on S. 2575, the Electronic Communications Privacy Act of 1986* (hereinafter "ECPA Re-

port"), S. Rep. No. 99-541, at 5, 31–33, reprinted in 1986 U.S. Code Cong. & Admin. News 3559, 3585–87.

101. 18 U.S.C. § 2232(c) (1988).

102. *See, e.g., Ker v. California,* 374 U.S. 23 (1963); *U.S. ex rel. Richards v. Rundel,* 285 F. Supp. 407 (E.D. Pa. 1968).

103. 18 U.S.C. § 2518(8)(d) (1988).

104. 18 U.S.C. § 2518(9) (1988).

105. *See, e.g., U.S. v. Fury,* 554 F.2d 522 (2d Cir.), *cert. denied sub nom. Quinn v. U.S.,* 433 U.S. 910 (1977), *cert. denied,* 436 U.S. 931 (1978); *U.S. v. Iannelli,* 339 F. Supp. 171 (D. Pa.), *aff'd,* 477 F.2d 999 (3d Cir.) & *aff'd,* 480 F.2d 918 (3d Cir. 1973), *aff'd,* 420 U.S. 770 (1977); *U.S. v. John,* 508 F.2d 1134 (2d Cir.), *cert. denied,* 421 U.S. 962 (1975) (notice must be given by judge who issued the order).

106. *U.S. v. Buschman,* 386 F. Supp. 822 (E.D. Wis. 1975).

107. *See, e.g., U.S. v. Rizzo,* 492 F.2d 443 (2d Cir.), *cert. denied,* 417 U.S. 944 (1974) (one month delay deemed not prejudicial); *U.S. v. Manfredi,* 488 F.2d 588 (2d Cir. 1973), *cert. denied,* 417 U.S. 936 (1974).

108. *See Washburn v. State,* 19 Md. App. 187, 310 A.2d 176 (1973); *but see Poore v. State,* 39 Md. App. 44, 384 A.2d 103 (1978) (failure to file a proper timely inventory should not result in suppression of the evidence unless prejudice was demonstrated).

109. *See, e.g., Application of U.S.,* 563 F.2d 637 (4th Cir. 1977).

110. *Dalia v. U.S.,* 441 U.S. 238 (1979).

111. *U.S. v. Scafidi,* 564 F.2d 633 (2d Cir. 1977), *cert. denied,* 436 U.S. 903, 912, *reh'g denied,* 439 U.S. 960 (1978).

112. *See* Testimony of Mary C. Lawton, Counsel for Intelligence Policy, Department of Justice, before the Subcommittee on Legislation, House Permanent Select Committee on Intelligence, U.S. House of Representatives, on Physical Searches for Foreign Intelligence, 101st Cong., 2d Sess., May 24, 1990; Cinquegrana, *Warrantless Physical Searches for Foreign Intelligence Purposes: Executive Order 12333 and the Fourth Amendment,* 35 Cath. U. L. Rev. 97 (1985).

113. *See* 18 U.S.C. § 2510(2) (1988) (" 'oral communication' means any oral communication uttered by a person exhibiting an expectation that such communication is not subject to interception under circumstances justifying such expectation").

114. *See, e.g., People v. Califano,* 5 Cal. App. 3d 476, 482, 85 Cal. Rptr. 292, 296 (1970); *People v. Canard,* 257 Cal. App. 2d 444, 463–64, 65 Cal. Rptr. 15, 28–29, *cert. denied,* 393 U.S. 912 (1968).

115. 18 U.S.C. § 2518(5) (1988).

116. Carr, *supra* note 78, at 258.

117. Note, *Post Authorization Problems in the Use of Wiretaps: Minimization, Amendment, Sealing and Inventories,* 61 Cornell L. Rev. 92, 108–9 (1975). *See* cases cited in Carr, *supra* note 78, at 226, n. 277.
118. *See* Carr, *supra* note 78, at 266 & 1985 Supp.
119. 18 U.S.C. § 2517(5) (1988). *See also* Carr, *supra* note 78, at § 5.09.
120. *See, e.g., U.S. v. DePalma,* 461 F. Supp. 800 (S.D.N.Y. 1978).
121. *United States v. United States District Court,* 407 U.S. 297 (1972) (commonly known as the Keith case). The court stated: "Moreover, we do not hold that the same type of standards and procedures prescribed by Title III [domestic wiretap law] are necessarily applicable to this case. . . . Congress may wish to consider protective standards for the latter which differ from those already prescribed for specified crimes in Title III." *Id.* at 322.
122. Foreign Intelligence Surveillance Act of 1978 (Pub. L. No. 95-511, 92 Stat. 1783), codified at 50 U.S.C. §§ 1801–11 (1982 & 1986 Supp.).
123. *Id.* at § 1801 (1982).
124. A U.S. person is a U.S. citizen, a permanent resident alien, a U.S. corporation, or an unincorporated association composed primarily of U.S. citizens or permanent resident aliens. 50 U.S.C. § 1801(i) (1982).
125. *Id.* § 1801(a) (1982).
126. *Id.* § 1801(i) (1982).
127. *See, e.g., id.* § 1801(m) (1982).
128. *Id.* § 1801(a) (1982); national security guidelines, *supra* note 2, § II.J.
129. The national security guidelines define "for or on behalf of a foreign power" as: "the determination that activities are for or on behalf of a foreign power must be based on consideration of the extent to which the foreign power is involved in: 1. control, leadership or policy direction; 2. financial or material support; or 3. leadership, assignments, or discipline." National security guidelines, *supra* note 2, § II.L.
130. 50 U.S.C. § 1801(b) (1982); *see also* definitions in CIA Regulation: Procedures Relating to Undisclosed Participation in Domestic Organizations, at 50 (April 24, 1981).
131. 50 U.S.C. § 1801(c) (1982); national security guidelines, *supra* note 2, § II.N.
132. 50 U.S.C. § 1801(b)(2) (1982) (U.S. persons cannot be considered agents of a foreign power unless they are suspected of engaging in some kind of criminal conduct).
133. 50 U.S.C. § 1801(b)(1) (1982).
134. *See, e.g., United States v. Duggan,* 743 F.2d 59 (2d Cir. 1984); *see also* Cinquegrana, *The Walls (and Wires) Have Ears: The Back-*

ground and First Ten Years of the Foreign Intelligence Surveillance Act of 1978, 137 U. Penn. L. Rev. 793, 816–20 (1989), for a fuller description of the constitutional issues and p. 817, n. 126 for a listing of all the cases involving public review of FISA surveillance through January 1989. Note that the Supreme Court has yet to rule on the FISA as of 1990.

135. 50 U.S.C. § 1806(f) (1982) (*in camera, ex parte* review).
136. 50 U.S.C. § 1806(d) (1982).
137. 50 U.S.C. § 1805(e) (1982).
138. 50 U.S.C. § 1806(j) (1982).
139. 50 U.S.C. § 1806(i) (1982).
140. 50 U.S.C § 1802(a)(1) (1982).
141. *See* Cinquegrana, *supra* note 134, at 814–15.
142. *In the Matter of Jackson*, 96 U.S. 727, 24 L. Ed. 2d 877 (1877). Opening first-class mail is also proscribed by statute. 39 U.S.C. § 3623(d) (1982).
143. *See supra* note 112.
144. 39 C.F.R. § 135.7; *see also U.S. v. Riley*, 554 F.2d 1282 (4th Cir. 1977); *Santana v. U.S.*, 329 F.2d 854 (1st Cir.), *cert. denied*, 377 U.S. 990 (1964).
145. 19 U.S.C. § 482 (1988).
146. *U.S. v. Ramsey*, 431 U.S. 606 (1977).
147. *See, e.g., U.S. v. Sandoval Vargas*, 854 F.2d 1132, 1136–37 (9th Cir. 1988) ("statutory standards for mail searches and traditional border searches are different").
148. *See, e.g.,* 19 C.F.R. § 145.3 (1987) (custom officer cannot read mail unless search warrant specifically authorizes it).
149. *U.S. v. Ramsey*, 431 U.S., at 624.
150. *Jones v. U.S.*, 357 U.S. 493 (1958); *Harris v. U.S*, 331 U.S. 145, *reh'g denied*, 331 U.S. 867 (1947).
151. *Texas v. Brown*, 460 U.S. 730 (1983).
152. *See, e.g., Thompson v. McManus*, 512 F.2d 769 (8th Cir.), *cert. denied*, 421 U.S. 1014 (1975).
153. *See supra* note 112.
154. *See* Exec. Order No. 11905, § 5(b)(iii)(3), 41 Fed. Reg. 7703 (1987) (Ford); Exec. Order No. 12036, §§ 2–204, 43 Fed. Reg. 3674 (1978) (Carter); Exec. Order No. 12333, § 2.4(b) (Reagan).
155. *See* Church Committee Book 2 at 61–62.
156. *See* Cinquegrana, *supra* note 134, at 821–23.
157. *See* S. 2726 (the Counterintelligence Improvements Act of 1990), § 14 ("To provide for a court order process for physical searches similar to that for electronic searches"); *Hearings before the Subcommittee*

on Legislation, House Permanent Select Committee on Intelligence,
U.S. House of Representatives, on Physical Searches for Foreign
Intelligence,* 101st Cong., 2d Sess., May 24, 1990.

158. *See, e.g., Washington v. State,* 462 So. 2d 763 (Alabama, 1984), *cert.
denied,* 471 U.S. 1101 (1985).

159. *Florida v. Riley,* 488 U.S.———, 102 L. Ed. 2d 835, 109 S. Ct. 693,
reh'g denied, 104 L. Ed. 2d 172 (1989); *see also* N. C. McCabe,
*From Open Fields to Open Skies: The Constitutionality of Aerial
Surveillance,* in 16 Search and Seizure Law Report No. 9 (October
1989).

XVIII

Recourse for Persons and Organizations Subject to Unlawful Surveillance of Political Activities

FREEDOM OF INFORMATION ACT AND PRIVACY ACT[1]

How can an individual or organization determine whether it has been the target of political surveillance?

Short of catching the government in the act, the only way to learn of government surveillance is to obtain direct evidence—documents or official testimony—of the government's activities. The usual ways to obtain documents of federal activities, such as those of the FBI, are through the Freedom of Information Act (FOIA) and the Privacy Act.[2] These laws require all agencies of the government to provide information they have pertaining to the request (except for information that can be withheld under any of the nine exemptions[3]). Almost all states have similar FOIA type statutes allowing access to state government information.[4]

For example, the FBI's unwarranted investigations of the Committee in Solidarity with the People of El Salvador (CISPES) from 1981 to 1985 were formally exposed through the FOIA after an FBI informant disclosed that he had infiltrated and surveilled CISPES from 1981 until 1985. The files released under the FOIA revealed that the FBI conducted nationwide investigations of CISPES over a period of five years.[5]

CISPES made the initial request for its files in May 1986. Not until eighteen months later, after CISPES filed suit in federal court, did the FBI release the 1300 pages of the approximately 3700 pages on file in FBI headquarters. Subsequently, the FBI also released files from some of the field offices that participated in the investigation. As of 1990, CISPES was still awaiting the release of additional files from the FBI field offices.

Will a new file be started on someone requesting a file, even if no file previously existed?

A file will be kept regarding the request. But this file is not an investigatory file and is not supposed to be accessed for investigative purposes. FOIA and Privacy Act requests are usually handled by separate offices within the agency set up specifically to deal with such requests. The FBI, for example, has a Freedom of Information-Privacy Acts section that handles all such requests. A FOIA correspondence to the FBI should not be disseminated to the FBI investigation sections, and FBI investigations should not have access to FOIA requests.

Who can make a request for files?

Any "person" can request their own files from any executive branch "agency." "Person" under the FOIA includes U.S. citizens, permanent resident aliens, foreign nationals, as well as corporations, unincorporated associations, universities, and even state and local governments and members of Congress.[6] The Privacy Act applies only to individuals who are U.S. persons.[7] "Agency" includes federal agencies, offices, and departments, as well as independent federal regulatory agencies (such as the Federal Trade Commission or the Environmental Protection Agency), and federal government controlled corporations (such as the U.S. Postal Service or the Tennessee Valley Authority).[8] The FOIA does not apply to Congress,[9] the federal courts,[10] or the president's personal staff and units of the executive office of the president whose sole function is to advise and assist the president.[11]

Can the government withhold certain information from release under the FOIA and the Privacy Act?

Yes. The FOIA contains nine exemptions for information the government does not have to release.[12] The major exemptions are for national security information (which is anything that is properly classified),[13] information used for law enforcement purposes—the release of which would cause various specified forms of harm,[14] information that would violate the privacy of other persons,[15] information specifically exempted by other statutes,[16] and information concerning internal personnel rules and practices of an agency.[17] The other exemptions concern trade secrets,[18] inter- and intra-agency memoranda,[19] reports of agencies responsible for regulating financial institutions,[20] and geological data concerning wells.[21]

How does one request his or her files?

All one has to do is write a letter to the government agency requesting whatever information is wanted. Many agencies require that requests for personal files include a notarized signature of the requester in order to protect against privacy violations. The FBI requires, in addition, that the requester provide his or her complete name, date, and place of birth.

The agency is then required to search for and provide all information that it possesses responsive to the request, subject to whatever exemptions that apply (see above for list and reference to the nine exemptions). While the law requires a response within ten working days, the actual time can take much longer, depending on how many requests come before the agency. Most agencies respond to requests on a first-come-first-served basis. For example, because of the large volume of requests it gets, the FBI can take many months if not years to respond.[22]

If the agency withholds all or part of the request, the requester can appeal within the agency (the agency normally supplies information on when and where to appeal). If the administrative appeal fails, the requester can sue the agency in federal court.

LITIGATION

What can an individual or organization do once it learns it has been the subject of unlawful investigation?

The easiest and perhaps most important action is to expose publically the misconduct of the investigating agency through the news media. The major legal remedies available are to sue in court to get an injunction either to stop the investigation, if it is still ongoing, or to restrict the government from reopening an investigation at a future time. One can also sue to have inaccurate files corrected, to have files expunged or archived, and for money damages for statutory or constitutional violations. Government officials can also be held criminally liable for violating certain statutes. One can also seek protection by legislation, either through general statutes to restrict the government from engaging in unwarranted investigations and from employing certain investigative techniques, or through private bills and other specific legislation to require the destruction or protection of files.

How easy is it to sue the government successfully for an unlawful investigation?

Not very. For a long list of reasons, the government is rarely found liable for violating the constitutional or statutory rights of Americans engaged in political activity. The government generally defends these cases as justified in order to protect national or internal security. And the courts tend to be very deferential to the government's claims.

Most cases brought against the government never even make it to trial. Many are thrown out of court because the plaintiffs are unable to obtain from the government the necessary information to prove their cases. The government is allowed to withhold information when it might disclose official state secrets or the identity of an informant, even if it results in dismissal of the plaintiff's suit against the government.[23]

Furthermore, the law on what kinds of investigations the government can and cannot engage in is unsettled. The First and Fourth Amendments to the Constitution afford general, but by no means absolute protection from government investigation. There are very few statutes prohibiting government investigatory conduct (and most of these statutes were not in place when the governmental conduct at issue in the existing lawsuits took place).

INJUNCTIONS

Is it possible to get a court order to stop an ongoing investigation?

Technically yes, but practically it is very difficult. Efforts to enjoin the government from engaging in investigative practices that violate First Amendment rights generally fail because in most such cases the practice has stopped by the time the issue comes to the courts.[24] The courts will intervene only to stop or enjoin an undue government investigation where the investigation is either taking place or imminent.

Thus, unless you know and have firm evidence that an investigation is taking place or is about to take place, it is virtually impossible to convince a court that there is a danger, let alone that the court should stop it. Furthermore, the courts will generally not grant an injunction to prevent a future investigation of a particular group, even where there was a significant past practice, unless there is evidence of a real and immediate threat that the injury will be continued or repeated. Nor will they rule on speculative or hypothetical threats.[25]

Can government investigations be restricted by the courts?
Yes. In a number of instances, the courts have approved settlement agreements imposing guidelines to restrict local and federal police investigations from impinging on First Amendment activities. These agreements generally resulted from suits by persons and groups who sued the government seeking an injunction and damages for past and alleged continuing unlawful investigation of First Amendment activity. Such settlements have been reached in Chicago,[26] New York,[27] and Los Angeles[28] and apply to the local police departments. These class action suits were brought because of the practices of the local departments' so-called red squad sections, which routinely investigated and harassed individuals and groups engaged in political activities. (See below for more information on state and local departments.) Plaintiffs agreed to the settlements in large part because of the difficulty of winning the case at trial.[29]

Separate settlement agreements applying to the activities of the FBI and the CIA were also reached in the Chicago red squad case.[30] One agreement imposed guidelines on the FBI based on four major principles: (1) no political spying—FBI investigations must be based on a criminal predicate and cannot be based solely on First Amendment activities; (2) no disruption or harassment of political activities—prohibits the FBI from engaging in any kind of COINTELPRO-type activities to impair the exercise of First Amendment rights; (3) minimal intrusion— FBI must use the least instrusive means possible when conducting any investigation; (4) minimization on the collection and retention of First Amendment information—prohibits the FBI from keeping any information on political activities that is not necessary for an ongoing investigation.

These principles were based upon the FBI charter legislation considered in the 1970s and upon internal FBI directives and policy and were meant to go further than the Levi Guidelines (predecessor to the Smith Guidelines [i.e. domestic guidelines] that control FBI domestic investigations) that were in place at the time by more explicitly defining what can and cannot be investigated and what techniques can be used.[31]

How does the Chicago FBI settlement agreement affect the application of subsequent FBI guidelines?

The four principles of the Chicago FBI settlement agreement are supposed to supercede the attorney general's guidelines and any revision thereof as they are applied in Chicago. In 1984 the court of appeals held that the Reagan administration's domestic guidelines of 1983[32] did not violate the consent decree.[33]

Is it possible to have inaccurate government files corrected?

Yes. The Privacy Act explicitly provides individuals the right to request amendment of a record on the ground that the record is "not accurate, relevant, timely, or complete."[34] This right applies not only to factual information, but also opinions and judgments.[35] The Privacy Act applies only to individuals and not organizations.

EXPUNGEMENT OR REMOVAL OF FILES

Is it possible to have files expunged?

Yes. The Privacy Act also prohibits the government from maintaining any "record describing how any individual exercises rights guaranteed by the First Amendment unless expressly authorized by statute or by the individual about whom the record is maintained or unless pertinent to and within the scope of an authorized law enforcement activity."[36]

The courts have held that "an order for the expungement of records is, in proper circumstances, a permissible remedy for an agency's violation of the Privacy Act."[37] The FBI has never been required to do so by court order because whenever someone brings forth a convincing case requiring it to remove or destroy records, it has offered to do so out of court, thus denying the opportunity for the courts to set a precedent requiring such destruction under section (e)(7).[38]

Is it possible to remove files from a government agency and place them in the National Archives (or some other neutral location)?

Yes. The National Archives has the general responsibility of preserving government records it deems to be of historical significance.[39] Such documents can be put under seal for a certain period of time during which no one can have access and after which access is open to all interested parties, private or public.[40]

For example, in 1989 the government settled a lawsuit brought by the National Lawyers Guild (NLG) for illegal FBI investigations and agreed to put all "FBI files on the Guild" under seal until the year 2025, at which time the files would be transferred to the National Archives.[41] Also in 1989, the FBI agreed to transfer all files on its investigation of the Committee in Solidarity with the People of El Salvador (CISPES) from 1983 through 1985 to the National Archives after CISPES brought suit against the FBI demanding such action.[42]

In 1987 the FBI agreed to a legal stipulation (which does not have the same force as a final court order) requiring that it transfer from the FBI to the National Archives and place under a five-year seal the complete files and records pertaining to the group who brought the case under the Privacy Act.[43] In 1976 the Department of Justice voluntarily transferred to the National Archives an investigative database known as the Interdivisional Information System that included illegal investigation files of the FBI, the Department of Justice (DOJ), and other government agencies in liaison with the DOJ. (The outgoing administration had wanted to destroy the system because it revealed government abuses.)

Is it better to have files expunged or preserved?

There is no easy choice between the competing choices of expungement or preservation. While expungement protects the privacy interests of the individual, preservation ensures a historical record of government misconduct. The primary concern in either case is to prevent further government access to the information by removing the files from the agency. An unlawful investigation means that the files should not have been compiled in the first place and that the government should not be able to make use of them. But even if the government

336 Government Investigation and Surveillance

is denied access to the files for internal purposes, a person's privacy can be violated by the mere public disclosure of his or her political activity that would result if the documents were preserved and made publicly available.

One solution would be to allow all individuals a choice depending on whether or not they want their own names and/or files expunged. But similar problems could arise under this scenario because to give people this choice requires that all persons named in the files be notified. Such an effort would require not only notifying some persons who were previously unaware that they are named in a government investigation, but would also require a new investigative effort to locate them so that they could be notified.

On the other hand, it is extremely important that as complete an account as possible of all government misconduct be preserved for the historical record. The lessons learned from an analysis of such records helps to keep the government accountable and to keep it from repeating the same mistakes (not that there is any guarantee). However, it is often the case that much of what can be released publicly will have come out through litigation—the rest being indefinitely withheld for national security reasons under FOIA exemptions. Where there is no possibility of obtaining the release of the remaining documents, it may be preferable simply to have the remaining documents expunged.

DAMAGES

Is it possible to sue the government or particular government officials for an improper investigation?

Yes. A number of statutes allow persons who have been injured to sue the government or government officials. Some statutes apply only to government officials, and some apply to both the government itself and to government officials. It is also possible to sue government officials for direct violations of constitutional rights.[44] For a claim to succeed, however, there generally has to be evidence that the government committed real injury to a person or organization; the fact of mere surveillance is usually not enough to win a case.

Most damage claims against the government are made under the Federal Tort Claims Act (FTCA), which allows actions against the government "for money damages . . . for injury or loss of property, or personal injury or death caused by the negligent or wrongful act or omission of any employee of the Government while acting within the scope of his office or employment, under circumstances where the United States, if a private person, would be liable to the claimant in accordance with the law of the place where the act or omission occurred."[45] Persons must file such claims within two years after the action occurred or after the parties learned or should have learned about it,[46] and must first make the claim with the government agency before going to court.[47] Furthermore, the claim must be based on the law of the state where the act took place. If that state has no applicable state law, then no action can be brought.

The Socialist Workers party, for example, sued the government under the FTCA and was awarded $264,000 in damages for various illegal investigative activities by the FBI, such as disruption activities (COINTELPRO), illegal break-ins, and illegal use of informants.[48] Lillie Albertson received $170,000 from the government in a settlement of a suit she brought for the FBI's COINTELPRO harassment of her deceased husband, who was a leader in the U.S. Communist party; the FBI successfully planted a forged letter in his coat pocket to make it appear that he was an FBI informant in order to discredit him within the party.[49]

Other statutes allow injured persons to recover damages for government actions that violate the terms of the statute. The Privacy Act allows persons to recover from the U.S. government when the government intentionally or wilfully fails to maintain properly an individual's record which has an adverse effect on that individual.[50]

The domestic wiretap law allows any person to recover damages from any person, whether government official or private person, "who intercepts, discloses, or uses, or procures any other person to intercept, disclose, or use such communications" in violation of this law.[51]

The Foreign Intelligence Surveillance Act (FISA) provides damages for persons who have been "subject to an electronic surveillance or about whom information obtained by electronic surveillance of such person has been disclosed or used in violation of" the statute.[52] Foreign powers and agents of foreign powers who are not U.S. persons cannot make such a claim.[53]

What is the likelihood for success in recovering damages under federal law?

Winning civil damages under any of these statutes is exceedingly rare, both because of the difficulty in obtaining the necessary evidence from the government to prove that the agency or the official acted wilfully or intentionally and because of the difficulty in actually proving the claim. In national security cases especially, the courts have afforded the government wide discretion to withhold evidence that would be necessary for the case in order to protect the confidentiality of sources and methods (e.g., the names of informants) or to protect "state secrets" even if it results in the dismissal of the claim.[54]

The major problem with the FTCA is that it is wholly dependant on the law of the state where the injury occurred. The FTCA does not apply to violations of the federal Constitution. For example, in the *Socialist Workers Party* case, the plaintiffs had to prove that the federal government violated the law of New York, New Jersey, California, and the District of Columbia. While the court found that the FBI did violate those laws in that case, it can be difficult to find a state law that adequately covers the violation of someone's First or Fourth Amendment rights.

As of 1989 there is no record of a successful case for damages under the Foreign Intelligence Surveillance Act (FISA). However, there is one case where persons have won damages against the government under the domestic electronic surveillance statute for politically motivated wiretaps.[55]

Additionally, the courts have ruled that damage claims under the Privacy Act must show that the government agency acted either "without grounds for believing it to be lawful, or must flagrantly disregard the individual's rights under the [Privacy] Act."[56] There is no record of successful claims under the Privacy Act in cases involving political activities or any other First Amendment rights as of 1989.

Is it possible to sue the government directly under the Constitution for violations of constitutional rights?

Yes. The Supreme Court has ruled that the Constitution

does allow persons to recover damages for direct violations of constitutional rights. In 1971 in *Bivens v. Six Unknown Named Agents of the Federal Bureau of Narcotics*,[57] the Supreme Court ruled for the first time that a person can sue for civil damages directly under the Constitution. In that case, the government agents had illegally searched the plaintiff in violation of the Fourth Amendment. The Supreme Court has since extended the *Bivens* doctrine (as it is known) to cover constitutional violations of the Fifth and Eighth Amendments[58] and has suggested that it would also apply to the First Amendment.[59] However, *Bivens* is not applicable in all situations involving constitutional rights.

Can government officials be held criminally liable for engaging in illegal investigative activities?

Yes. It is a crime to burglarize,[60] open mail,[61] or tap phones (with certain exceptions under the FISA) without a warrant.[62] The Privacy Act also makes it a crime for unlawfully maintaining or disclosing an individual's file.[63] As of 1989 there have been no convictions of government officials for violations of the Privacy Act, the FISA, or the domestic wiretap law in cases involving political activities.[64]

There has been only one criminal conviction of government officials for engaging in illegal intelligence activities against Americans. In 1980 two high-level FBI agents, W. Mark Felt and Edward S. Miller, were convicted of violating the civil rights of persons against whom they had authorized illegal break-ins in the search for suspects in the Weathermen bombings. Although sentenced to prison, both men were pardoned in 1981 by President Reagan before serving any time on the grounds that they acted without criminal intent.[65]

NOTES

1. For more information on how to use the FOIA and the Privacy Act, see the ACLU handbook on *Your Right to Government Information*, by C. Marwick; *see also* the ACLU handbook, E. Hendrick, T. Hayden & J. Novick, *Your Rights to Privacy* (2d ed. 1990). The ACLU also publishes a sixteen-page pamphlet on "Using the Freedom of Information Act: A Step by Step Guide," by A. Adler and annual

editions of *Litigation under the Federal Freedom of Information Act and Privacy Act,* a litigation manual. These publications are available from the ACLU Washington Office, 122 Maryland Avenue, NE, Washington, D.C. 20002, phone: (202) 544-1681.

2. 5 U.S.C. §§ 552 & 552a (1988), as amended in 1974 and 1986, respectively.

3. 5 U.S.C. § 552(b) lists nine exemptions by which documents requested under the FOIA and the Privacy Act can be withheld.

4. *See, e.g., Freedom of Information: A Compilation of State Laws,* compiled by the Subcommittee on Administrative Practice and Procedure of the Committee on the Judiciary, United States Senate, 95th Cong., 2d Sess. (1978).

5. For more information on the CISPES investigation, see chapter 14 on FBI investigations.

6. 5 U.S.C. § 551(2) (1988); *see also Stone v. Export-Import Bank of the United States,* 552 F.2d 132 (5th Cir. 1977), *cert. denied,* 434 U.S. 1012 (1978) ("person" means foreign citizens, corporations, and governments).

7. 5 U.S.C. § 552a(2) (1988) (individual defined as U.S. citizen or permanent resident alien).

8. 5 U.S.C. § 552(f) (1988).

9. 5 U.S.C. § 551(1)(A) (1988).

10. 5 U.S.C. § 551(1)(B) (1988).

11. H. Rep. No. 1380, 93d Cong. 2d Sess. 15 (1974) (legislative history of FOIA), cited in A. Adler, ed., *Litigation under the Federal Freedom of Information Act and Privacy Act,* 169 (1990); *see also Soucie v. David,* 448 F.2d 1067 (D.C. Cir. 1971).

12. 5 U.S.C. § 552(b) lists nine exemptions by which documents requested under the FOIA and the Privacy Act can be withheld.

13. 5 U.S.C. § 552(b)(1) (1988) (matters that are "(A) specifically authorized under criteria established by an Executive order to be kept secret in the interest of national defense or foreign policy and (B) are in fact properly classified pursuant to such Executive order").

14. 5 U.S.C. § 552(b)(7) (1988) (matters that are "records or information compiled for law enforcement purposes, but only to the extent that the production of such law enforcement records or information (A) could reasonably be expected to interfere with enforcement proceedings, (B) would deprive a person of a right to a fair trial or an impartial adjudication, (C) could reasonably be expected to constitute an unwarranted invasion of personal privacy, (D) could reasonably be expected to disclose the identity of a confidential source, including a state, local, or foreign agency or authority or any private institution which furnished information on a confidential basis, and in the case of a

record or information compiled by criminal law enforcement authority in the course of a criminal investigation or by an agency conducting a lawful national security intelligence investigation, information furnished by a confidential source, (E) would disclose techniques and procedures for law enforcement investigations or prosecutions, or would disclose guidelines for law enforcement investigations or prosecutions if such disclosure could reasonably be expected to risk circumvention of the law, or (F) could reasonably be expected to endanger the life or physical safety of any individual").

15. 5 U.S.C. § 552(b)(6) (1988) (matters that are "personnel and medical files and similar files the disclosure of which would constitute a clearly unwarranted invasion of personal privacy").

16. 5 U.S.C. § 552(b)(3) (1988) (matters that are "specifically exempted from disclosure by statute . . . provided that such statute (A) requires that the matters be withheld from the public in such a manner as to leave no discretion on the issue, or (B) establishes particular criteria for withholding or refers to particular types of matters to be withheld").

17. 5 U.S.C. § 552(b)(2) (1988) (matters that are "related solely to the internal personnel rules and practices of an agency").

18. 5 U.S.C. § 552(b)(4) (1988) (matters that are "trade secrets and commercial or financial information obtained from a person and privileged confidential information").

19. 5 U.S.C. § 552(b)(5) (1988) (matters that are "inter-agency and intra-agency memorandums or letters which would not be available by law to a party other than an agency in litigation with the agency").

20. 5 U.S.C. § 552(b)(8) (1988) (matters that are "contained in or related to examination, operating, or condition reports prepared by, on behalf of, or for the use of an agency responsible for the regulation or supervision of financial institutions").

21. 5 U.S.C. § 552(b)(9) (1988) (matters that are "geological or geophysical information and data, including maps, concerning wells").

22. The State Department says that it has about a nine-month waiting period for FOIA and Privacy Act requests; the CIA takes even longer.

23. *See, e.g., Halkin v. Helms,* 598 F.2d 1 (D.C. Cir. 1978) (state secrets privilege); *In re United States,* 565 F.2d 19 (2d Cir. 1977), *cert. denied,* 436 U.S. 962 (1978) (informant's privilege).

24. *See Alliance to End Repression v. Chicago,* 91 F.R.D. 182, 198 (N.D. Ill. 1981) ("Indeed, this court is aware of no judicial declaration or injunction ever entered against CIA or FBI domestic intelligence activities, even on behalf of a single litigant, much less in a class action"—prior to this court's action.).

25. *See generally Socialist Workers Party v. Attorney General,* 642 F.

Supp. 1357, 1425–32 (S.D.N.Y. 1986); *see also Halkin v. Helms*, 690 F.2d 977 (D.C. Cir. 1982); *Laird v. Tatum*, 408 U.S. 1, *reh'g denied*, 409 U.S. 901 (1972).

26. *Alliance to End Repression v. Chicago*, 561 F. Supp. 537 (N.D. Ill. 1982).

27. *Handschu v. Special Services Division*, 605 F. Supp. 1384 (S.D.N.Y. 1985).

28. *Coalition against Police Abuse v. Board of Police Commissioners*, No. C243458 (Sup. Ct. of Cal., order entered February 22, 1984).

29. *See, e.g., Alliance to End Repression v. Chicago*, 91 F.R.D. 182, 197–98 (N.D. Ill. 1981) (substantive law on whether such government investigative activity is illegal is unsettled; procedural problems such as state secrets and informants' privileges, mootness, and possibility of less than satisfactory relief).

30. *Id.* at 198.

31. *Id.* at 205 (pertinent provisions of the FBI settlement agreement).

32. *The Attorney General's Guidelines on General Crimes, Racketeering Enterprise and Domestic Security/Terrorism Investigations* (March 7, 1983) (hereafter "domestic guidelines").

33. *Alliance to End Repression v. Chicago*, 561 F. Supp. 575 (N.D. Ill. 1983), *aff'd*, 733 F.2d 1187, *rev'd*, 742 F.2d 1007 (7th Cir. 1984) (en banc).

34. 5 U.S.C. § 552(d)(2) (1988).

35. *See, e.g., R.R. v. Department of the Army*, 482 F. Supp. 770, 773–74 (D.D.C. 1980); *Turner v. Department of the Army*, 447 F. Supp. 1207, 1213 (D.D.C. 1978), *aff'd*, 593 F.2d 1372 (D.C. Cir. 1979). *But see Blevins v. Plummer*, 613 F.2d 767, 768, n.3 (9th Cir. 1980); *Bernson v. ICC*, 625 F. Supp. 10, 13 (D. Mass. 1984).

36. 5 U.S.C. § 552(e)(7) (1988). *See also* chapter 17 at text accompanying notes 11–21.

37. *Hobson v. Wilson*, 737 F.2d 1, 64 (D.C. Cir. 1984), *cert. denied*, 470 U.S. 1084 (1985), *citing Clarkson v. IRS*, 678 F.2d 1368, 1376–77 (11th Cir. 1982), *appeal after remand*, 811 F.2d 1396 (11th Cir.), *cert. denied*, 481 U.S. 1031 (1987) *and Albright v. United States*, 631 F.2d 915, 921 (D.C. Cir. 1980), *remanded*, 558 F. Supp. 260 (D.D.C. 1982), *aff'd*, 732 F.2d 181 (D.C. Cir. 1984); *see also Reuber v. United States*, 750 F.2d 1039, 1068 (D.C. Cir. 1984), *aff'd after remand*, 787 F.2d 599 (D.C. Cir. 1986).

38. *See, e.g., Patterson v. FBI*, 705 F. Supp. 1033, 1047 (D.N.J. 1989) *aff'd*, 893 F.2d 595 (3d Cir. 1990) ("[T]he FBI offered to expunge the name of Todd Patterson from its records" even though the court ruled that "it would be inappropriate for this Court to now order the FBI to expunge plaintiff's name from its files.").

The Senate Select Committee on Intelligence recommended that the FBI remove from its custody all of the files on the CISPES investigation either by expunging or transferring them to the National Archives. *The FBI and CISPES: Report of the Select Committee on Intelligence, United States Senate, Together with Additional Views* (July 14, 1989), at 140 (hereinafter "Senate CISPES Report"). In October 1989, the FBI agreed to do so. *See* below note 42.

39. *See American Friends Service Committee v. Webster*, 720 F.2d 29 (D.C. Cir. 1983) (government agencies cannot destroy documents without appropriate archivist review).

40. *See also* recommendation of the Senate Intelligence Committee, in Senate CISPES Report, *supra* note 38, at 140.

41. *National Lawyers Guild v. Attorney General*, No. 77–999 (S.D.N.Y. October 12, 1989) (stipulation and order of settlement and dismissal).

42. *See* Letter from FBI Director William Sessions to Congressman Don Edwards, Chair, Subcommittee on Civil and Constitutional Rights, House Committee on the Judiciary, dated October 27, 1989.

43. *Wilkinson v. F.B.I.*, No. CV 80–1048-AWT (Tx), para. 5 (Cen. Dist. CA., March 19, 1987) (stipulation and order).

44. *See Bivens v. Six Unknown Named Agents of the Federal Bureau of Narcotics*, 403 U.S. 388 (1971) and its progeny.

45. 28 U.S.C. § 1346(b) (1988).

46. 28 U.S.C. § 2401(b) (1988) (two year statute of limitations on tort claims against the United States); *see also Socialist Workers Party v. Attorney General*, 642 F. Supp. 1357, 1402 (S.D.N.Y. 1986).

47. 28 U.S.C. §§ 2672 & 2675 (1988).

48. *Socialist Workers Party v. Attorney General*, 642 F. Supp. 1357, 1364, 1417–22 (S.D.N.Y. 1986) ($42,500 for disruption activities, $96,500 for surreptitious entries (black-bag jobs), and $125,000 for use of informants); *see also Blair v. Baumgardner*, No. 77-C–390, stipulated order of dismissal (E.D. Wisc. May 16, 1979) (settlement agreement awarding $48,000 to plaintiff for FBI COINTELPRO harassment; claim filed under the FTCA and was the first successful claim against the FBI for COINTELPRO activities); *National Lawyers Guild v. Attorney General*, No. 77–999 (S.D.N.Y. October 12, 1989) (stipulation and order of settlement and dismissal) (no money damages, but FBI admits past actions against NLG, is enjoined from future surveillance and harassment, and sealed files are transferred to the National Archives).

49. *Albertson v. United States*, No. 84–2034 (D.D.C. September 28, 1989) (settlement agreement).

50. 5 U.S.C. § 552a(g) (1988).

51. 18 U.S.C. § 2520 (1988).

52. 50 U.S.C. § 1810 (1988).

53. *Id.*

54. *See, e.g., Ellsberg v. Mitchell*, 709 F.2d 51, 57 (D.C. Cir. 1983), *cert. denied sub nom. Russo v. Mitchell*, 465 U.S. 1038 (1984), *appeal after remand*, 807 F.2d 204 (D.C. Cir. 1986); *Halkin v. Helms (Halkin II)*, 690 F.2d 977, 990 (D.C. Cir. 1982).

55. *Halperin v. Kissinger*, 606 F.2d 1192 (D.C. Cir. 1979), *aff'd in part, cert. denied in part*, 452 U.S. 713, *reh'g denied*, 453 U.S. 928 (1981). *But see Chagnon v. Bell*, 468 F. Supp. 927 (D.D.C. 1979), *aff'd*, 642 F.2d 1248 (D.C. Cir. 1980), *cert. denied*, 453 U.S. 911 (1981) (dismissal of suit based on qualified immunity).

56. *Sullivan v. Veterans Administration*, 617 F. Supp. 258, 261–62, (D.D.C. 1985), *citing, Albright v. United States*, 732 F.2d 181, 189 (D.C. Cir. 1984).

57. 403 U.S. 388 (1971).

58. *Davis v. Passman*, 442 U.S. 228 (1979) (Fifth Amendment); *Carlson v. Green*, 446 U.S. 14 (1980) (Eighth Amendment).

59. *Bush v. Lucas*, 462 U.S. 367 (1983) (court made clear that individuals are entitled to a remedy for violation of their First Amendment rights). Virtually all of the circuit courts have explicitly recognized a First Amendment *Bivens* cause of action. *See, e.g., White v. Boyle*, 538 F.2d 1077 (4th Cir. 1976).

60. 18 U.S.C. § 2236 (1988).

61. 18 U.S.C. §§ 1701–2 (1988).

62. The domestic wiretap law and the FISA both have criminal provisions for violations of the statutes. 18 U.S.C. § 2511 (1988) (domestic wiretap law); 50 U.S.C. § 1809 (1988) (FISA). In August 1990, a U.S. federal judge was convicted under 18 U.S.C. § 2511 for illegally notifying someone that he was the target of a wiretap. *See Judge Found Guilty in Obstruction of Justice*, New York Times, August 24, 1990, at A18.

63. 5 U.S.C. § 552a(i) (1988).

64. Note that the domestic wiretap law applies to private persons as well as government officials; private persons can thus be prosecuted for violating this law.

65. In 1977 former FBI agent John J. Kearney was indicted on five counts of conspiracy, mail opening, and illegal wiretapping, but he was never brought to trial.